Nettie Palmer

UQP AUSTRALIAN AUTHORS

General Editor: L.T. Hergenhan
Reader in Australian Literature
University of Queensland

Also in this series:

Marcus Clarke edited by Michael Wilding
Henry Lawson edited by Brian Kiernan
Five Plays for Stage, Radio and Television edited by Alrene Sykes
The 1890s: Stories, Verse and Essays edited by Leon Cantrell
Rolf Boldrewood edited by Alan Brissenden
The Jindyworobaks edited by Brian Elliott
Hal Porter edited by Mary Lord
Barbara Baynton edited by Sally Krimmer and Alan Lawson
Henry Kingsley edited by J.S.D. Mellick
Joseph Furphy edited by John Barnes
New Guinea Images in Australian Literature edited by Nigel Krauth
Australian Science Fiction edited by Van Ikin
The Australian Short Story: An Anthology from the 1890s to the 1980s edited by Laurie Hergenhan
R.D. FitzGerald edited by Julian Croft
Catherine Helen Spence edited by Helen Thomson
James McAuley edited by Leonie Kramer

In preparation:

Randolph Stow edited by A.J. Hassall
John Shaw Neilson edited by Clifford Hanna
Nineteenth Century Prose edited by Elizabeth Webby

Nettie Palmer

Her private journal *Fourteen Years*,
poems, reviews and literary essays

EDITED BY VIVIAN SMITH

University of Queensland Press
ST LUCIA • LONDON • NEW YORK

First published 1988 by University of Queensland Press
Box 42, St Lucia, Queensland, Australia

Typeset by University of Queensland Press
Printed in Australia by The Book Printer, Melbourne

Distributed in the UK and Europe by University of Queensland Press
Dunhams Lane, Letchworth, Herts. SG6 1LF England

Distributed in the USA and Canada by the University of Queensland Press,
250 Commercial Street, Manchester, NH 03101 USA

Cataloguing in Publication Data

National Library of Australia
Palmer, Nettie, 1885-1964.
Nettie Palmer.
I. Palmer, Nettie, 1885-1964. I. Smith, Vivian, 1933- . II. Title (Series: UQP Australian authors).

A828'.208

British Library (data available)

Library of Congress
Palmer, Nettie. 1885-1964.
[Selections. 1988]
Nettie Palmer / edited with an introduction by Vivian Smith.
p. cm. -- (UQP Australian authors)
Bibliography: p.
Includes index.
I. Smith, Vivian Brian. II. Title. III. Series.
PR9619.3.P27A6 1988
828--dc19 88-17606

ISBN 0 7022 2130 9

Contents

CONTENTS

Acknowledgments

I should like to thank Laurie Hergenhan for help and advice in the preparation of this volume and Clare Hoey who compiled the index to *Fourteen Years*. I am grateful to the late Helen Palmer for the support she gave to my work, and regret that she did not live to see this collection in print.

Acknowledgments are due to the Equity Trustees, Melbourne, for granting permission to use material from the Estate of E.V. and J.G. Palmer; to Clem Christesen, the founding editor of *Meanjin*, whose Meanjin Press Books published the first edition of *Fourteen Years*; to Verdon Morcom, who has generously permitted the reprinting of the pen drawings (not wood engravings as designated in the facsimile) that accompanied it; and to Margaret O'Hagan of Fryer Library, University of Queensland, who kindly made available the edition of *Fourteen Years*.

Introduction

Nettie Palmer is an important figure in Australian writing, with a major place in its development and reception in the 1920s and 1930s, when the bulk of her work was written and the foundations of her future volumes laid. But even during her lifetime the full range of her literary work was not widely known. A great deal of her writing has gone uncollected. Her books, which usually appeared in limited editions at unpropitious times in the history of Australian publishing, have long been out of print.

Janet Gertrude (Nettie) Palmer was born at Bendigo (then called Sandhurst) on 18 August 1885 to Katie and John Higgins. She grew up in Melbourne, where her father was an accountant. He was not an intellectual like his brother Henry Bournes Higgins, the judge, and he was in worldly terms the least successful member of his family. But Nettie's parents set a high priority on intellectual achievement. Nettie was educated at the Presbyterian Ladies' College, and enrolled at the University of Melbourne in 1905, where she graduated in 1909 as a Bachelor of Arts, with a Diploma of Education. In 1910, with the financial help of Henry Bournes Higgins, she travelled to London to further her studies in French and German, and to Berlin and Paris to prepare for the International Diploma of Phonetics, which she was awarded early in 1911. She returned to Melbourne and received her Master's degree in Arts from that university in 1912. In 1914 she returned to London to marry Vance Palmer on 23 May.

The couple had first met in Australia before Vance Palmer's second trip to England in 1910, and had kept up a long, detailed correspondence since the end of 1908. Their early letters were extremely revealing, both of their feelings for each other and of their temperamental differences and ways of life. Vance headed his letters 'Back of Beyond' or 'West of Sunset'. His life was one of isolated teaching, recording his first contacts with blacks and half-castes and hermits. Nettie wrote from gregarious Melbourne of her university studies in English and Greek, her involvement with the socialist movement, her enthusiasm for the work of Bernard O'Dowd as well as for the most cosmopolitan of French and German writers, and of her plans to write a study of Tolstoy and the Symbolists. So began what was often referred to as one of Australia's most important literary partnerships.

The purpose of this volume is to focus on Nettie Palmer's individual achievement as a writer and a critic. Some aspects of her work cannot be fully evaluated in complete isolation from the work of Vance Palmer. It has often been suggested that her literary career was overshadowed by his and that she may have sacrificed much of her own creativity for her family. The extent to which this is true, and the complexities of their marriage, remain in the realm of conjecture, and for every piece of evidence supporting one view, a contrasting one can be selected. I have chosen to emphasise the sense of partnership which characterised their relationship as being conducive to a proper perception of Nettie Palmer's unique achievement. Nettie certainly helped Vance as a critic; it was she who was largely responsible for the abridgment of *Such is Life* published in London in 1937; she helped him with much of the research and the fact-finding that went into *National Portraits* and the A.G. Stephens collection. On the other hand, Vance helped her with the preparation of the manuscripts of her early volumes of poetry, *Fourteen Years* and *Henry Handel Richardson*, and he gave her some assistance with her early survey of modern Australian writing. They even published a few articles under joint names. Letters and diaries suggest that throughout their marriage they sustained an atmosphere of collaboration, discussion and mutual stimulus. Their common interest in writing (Australian and European) and the development of a national Australian culture was one of the preoccupations that first drew them together and it remained undiminished throughout their lives. Both were determined from an early age to make their way as writers and their lives have a special significance for us because they were among the few Australians of the time who tried to make writing their way of life. I shall therefore occasionally speak of them jointly where this seems to be the only adequate way of accounting for a whole area or topic which they shared without demarcation lines of individual contribution.

When World War I started, the Palmers were at Trégastel in Brittany. Nettie Palmer was writing verse, which she had first started to do as a schoolgirl, while Vance was writing for serious journals as well as producing commercial pulp serials. In early September 1914 they returned to London. Their plans for the immediate future had been centred on Europe, but the possibilities for that new kind of career were suddenly closed. Palmer's position as a freelance writer, and the difficulties of newspapers in wartime, made their position extremely insecure. By September 1915 they were back in Australia. Nettie published two books of poetry in England before her return. She knew that overseas publication, especially in London, could help to strengthen her literary reputation, and she was determined to establish a writing career. In 1915 a daughter Aileen was born; a second daughter, Helen, was born in 1917.

On their return to Australia the Palmers lost no time in making contact with congenial writers and in trying to establish themselves as journalists and critics so as to be part of the Australian literary scene. Both had been impressed overseas by the Irish literary revival and the Abbey Theatre experiment and they hoped to establish its equivalent in Australia. They wanted to build up some sense of a literary community in the Australia of their time and to contribute to the growth of a modern Australian literary consciousness. It is of special, almost symbolic significance that both were involved in the re-issuing of *Such is Life*, being convinced that the full recognition of this book would mark a new stage in Australian literary development. They became members of the Australian Author's and Writer's Guild and helped to form the Melbourne Literary Club in 1917. Nettie Palmer began the round of talks and papers, with occasional coaching and teaching, that was a feature of her literary career. Until the birth of Helen she wrote a column for the Melbourne *Argus* as well as articles for *Fellowship* and *The Socialist*. From 1918 to 1920 Vance Palmer was with the AIF overseas. After his return, when they were living at Emerald, Victoria, Nettie's writing became an important source of their income and in certain senses a full time career.

Nettie Palmer was always prepared to give talks and lectures to interested clubs and societies, but it was the written word that carried her ideas most widely in the twenties and thirties. Literary journalism and good reviewing were seen as ways of contributing to the development and advancement of Australian literary culture. By the early thirties, when the economic situation was closing various outlets, a considerable body of work had been built up.

Nettie's journalism is voluminous. Her output contains a deal of ephemera – short book notes and composite reviews limited by space and the demands imposed by editors or the newspaper format, with some overlap and repetition. Some of it suffers from obvious historical limitations and many of the issues (such as the appropriate subject matter for Australian writers) have inevitably receded into the past, but most of it is still lively and interesting and the best of it has retained its validity and acuteness. It presents us with a body of work that greatly enriches our sense of Australia's cultural awareness in the twenties and thirties. It belongs, with A. G. Stephens's work, to the best criticism of its time, remarkable for its combination of originality with fundamental soundness of values.

Basically Nettie was concerned with breaking down colonial

attitudes and the particular form of provincialism, or philistinism or insularity that refused to consider local writing on its own merits. She was particularly anxious to encourage an intelligent, critical attitude towards Australian writing and to increase the Australian writer's sense of an audience. She was convinced of and unembarrassed by the fact that some kinds of writing were better and more worthwhile than others. She wrote not only about writing, but also about publishing, bookselling and censorship. Her interests were not exclusively literary. She wrote on the Australian accent, the Australian ugliness, Australian suburbs, Australian English, on surfing in Australia, Italian immigrants, the necessity for preserving pioneer records, and even on Australian wooden houses. She wrote nature notes and discussed questions of ecology. She wrote about the multicultural Australia of her day. She wrote on women's issues and focused on women who had played a creative role in Australian life. She wrote general essays (the mode has since gone out of fashion) on buses, conversation, bird song, old Melbourne, and questions of style. She was concerned with stimulating an interest in the general attitudes of Australians towards their heritage and in enhancing the quality of Australian cultural life.

Nettie Palmer was always aware that the writing of good and original criticism was a difficult art in itself and that it was particularly arduous to give a just assessment of the work of contemporaries. She believed that a responsive public could nourish the writer who usually had to work alone, by giving some sense of belonging to a community: ('it takes readers as well as writers to make a literature'). She was convinced that Australian writing was important for Australians, apart from any universal standards, and that competent, lively and engaged criticism was needed in the Australia of her day. It was a need that she was determined to fill.

Nettie Palmer had been writing since she was a schoolgirl and by the early twenties had already established her reputation. Her two books of poems, *The South Wind* (1914) and *Shadowy Paths* (1915), had no sequels. Both books show competent craftsmanship and a sense of surface style that derives from the early Yeats, Symons, and Verlaine, and the poets of the nineties. There are echoes of Kendall, Brennan and O'Dowd. The poems range from her feelings about Melbourne in 1908 through images of Stromboli, Berlin, Brittany, and the outbreak of war, to delicate pieces about motherhood and her young child. They are written in the slightest lyric forms and measures, with a sensitive period frailty. The interestingly titled 'The Bush, Our Mother' begins characteristically:

> He that knows his land,
> He that knows and loves her,
> Half may understand
> What a passion moves her,
> She thereafter ever guides his hand.

'The Escape' begins:

> Her life is all a burden like the ticking of a clock,
> Her feet must move in city streets, her days are counted all,
> To beat against her life would be to strike on living rock,
> Alas, she owns no heavenly powers to bring the waterfall.

It is accomplished verse in a minor key and it has much biographical and historical interest. Nettie Palmer moves easily between Europe and Australia and some of the poems where she reflects on the Bush may be read in part as a kind of dialogue (for example, 'The Flute') with the spirit of Bernard O'Dowd, who had considerable influence on her early thought and writing, though more from the point of view of ideas than style. She is at her best, I think, in poems like 'Wattle Grove' and 'The Barrack Yard' where an objective central image gives a certain sharpness of edge to her wistful melancholy.

Nettie Palmer did not develop further as a poet.[1] It was in her literary journalism and commentary that a sustained development took place. Her active interest in what was happening in literature overseas continued, and gave breadth and sureness to her perceptions of local literature. She knew French and German, had studied Greek and later took up Spanish in order to study South American colonial literature. This wider awareness gave a distinctive tone to her commitment to the cause of Australian letters and the growth of an indigenous culture.

Her first substantial critical work, apart from newspaper journalism and her association as editor with the magazine *Birth*, was *Modern Australian Literature 1900-1923* (Melbourne 1924), a succinct account of Australian writing which won the Lothian prize for an essay on Australian literature written since 1900. Zora Cross's *Introduction to the Study of Australian Literature* had appeared in 1922, but Nettie Palmer's essay was the first systematic, modern *critical* study to be produced. It was a pioneer work that greatly facilitated the task of the critics who followed. It was superseded by H. M. Green's *An Outline of Australian Literature* (1930) which was more wide-ranging in reference and scope, but it was a remarkably sound and thorough piece of work, and in view of the difficulties facing the systematic student of Australian literature in the 1920s it was strikingly free of errors.[2]

Modern Australian Literature was well received, reviewers agreeing that the book had grip and style and that it filled a gap. Mrs Mary Kernot, an acquaintance of Nettie Palmer and of Henry Handel Richardson, was however surprised that no mention had been made in it of the author of *Maurice Guest* and *The Getting of Wisdom*. Nettie Palmer's diary (31 July 1924) records the fact that Mrs Kernot was lending her these novels. On 11 August she writes: 'Saw Mrs Kernot especially about H.H.R. – photos, letters, details'. Then on 13 August: 'Rereading *Maurice Guest* in the evening and thinking over its author', and 2 September: 'Mrs Kernot wrote, saying H.H.R.'s new part of Richard Mahony will soon be published'. So began, fortuitously, Nettie Palmer's lifelong devotion to the novelist of whose work she was to write the first full-length study.

Very little of Nettie Palmer's criticism was collected in book form. Throughout the twenties she contributed articles to a number of papers, *The Woman's Mirror*, the Brisbane *Courier*, the Brisbane *Sunday Mail*, the Melbourne *Argus*, the Brisbane *Telegraph*, and the Sydney *Bulletin*. Most of this was freelance journalism, introducing contemporary Australian writers and their work to as wide an audience as possible. Articles like those on Katharine Susannah Prichard and on Mary Gilmore in *Woman's Mirror* 1926 were belletristic and, in the best sense of the word, popular. Much of Nettie Palmer's writing was, however, critical and appreciative.

By 1929 Nettie Palmer had started to contribute a personal column which later became 'A Reader's Notebook' to *All About Books*, a semi-popular literary journal, which ran from 14 December 1928 till its demise on 16 March 1938. Nettie Palmer planned to issue a revision of 'A Reader's Notebook' as a volume in the mid-thirties, but the commercial failure of *Talking it Over* put an end to that idea. Nettie Palmer's reviews (she was superseded by F.T. Macartney) were singled out for praise by H.M. Green in his *A History of Australian Literature*, but Green overlooked her much more important and extensive contribution to the *Illustrated Tasmanian Mail*, a paper of whose existence he seems to have been unaware.

When the history of modern Australian newspapers and journals is written, a special place will have to be found for the *Illustrated Tasmanian Mail*.[3] In the 1920s this weekly carried syndicated articles on folk music by Bela Bartok; on the latest developments in French painting by Van Dongen; Karel Capek wrote on the cinema and drama. There were interviews with Epstein; and notices of the music of Ravel, Debussy, Elgar, and Hindemith, as well as articles such as 'The Philosophy of Norman Lindsay' which appeared on 28 May 1930. This is a brief cross-section of some of the items that appeared in this alert and curiously cosmopolitan journal. Nettie Palmer's contributions to it began on 29 July 1927 and became a weekly, then later a fortnightly item until April 1933. Altogether Nettie Palmer published in five-and-a-half years 212 articles of an average of fifteen hundred words each in the *Illustrated Tasmanian Mail*, and this was only part of her total output in those years which also included the writing of *Henry Bournes Higgins: A Memoir* and the editing of the influential *An Australian Story Book* (1928) as well as many journalistic items elsewhere.[4]

The series, headed *Readers and Writers, A New Literary*

Causerie (the initial subtitle *with especial reference to Australian Writers* was omitted after 7 September 1927), began as a form of high literary gossip, aimed at stimulating the circulation of opinion. There are notes on Katharine Susannah Prichard, G.B. Shaw, George Gordon McCrae, the award of the Nobel Prize to Pirandello; Ring Lardner and Chester Cobb are discussed together; there is a plea for the preservation of letters 'not only Wentworth's, Higinbotham's, Kendall's, but the correspondence of interesting, unknown people that might have helped to fill in the background of an earlier day'. The comments, while generally conversational and informative, manage to link criticism with interpretations, as when Nettie Palmer says Theodore Dreiser 'is never a master of actual words', or in commenting on Trollope's assessment of the Australian character: '[Trollope] . . . leaves out the most important of all, which is a slow delicacy in perception and response, and seems the peculiar possession of those bred in the bush' – a point she neatly illustrates by reference to Lawson's 'Telling Mrs Baker'.

By November 1927, when Nettie Palmer has already written something of interest about a number of Australian writers from Barbara Baynton to Henry Handel Richardson, from Furphy to Lawson, the nature of the causerie is changing; article-length appreciations begin to appear. The first, on Peacock, is followed by 'The Reputation of John Shaw Neilson', and this conscious but flexible and unstrained merging of overseas and Australian writers characterises the series as a whole and Nettie Palmer's literary discussion at its best. She brings the same quality of attention to bear on R.D. FitzGerald's *To Meet the Sun*, or the poems of Henry Tate, as on Thomas Mann's *The Magic Mountain*, or Osbert Sitwell's *England Reclaimed*.

It is hardly an exaggeration to say that no important English or American writer and certainly no significant Australian writer between 1927 and 1933 failed to get a mention in her columns. It is her achievement that within the limits of weekly and fortnightly literary journalism, and working largely within what is now called the belletristic tradition, she was able to produce much relevant criticism and lively, alert comment, the best of which retains permanent value.

She dealt with a wide range of authors, from established writers like Spenser, Goethe, Dickens, Ibsen, and Strindberg, to modern classics, many authors of which were living at the time she wrote: Yeats, Hardy, D. H. Lawrence, Sigrid Undset, W. H. Davies, as well as Henry James, Conrad, Proust, Joyce, Pound, O'Neill, and Thomas Mann. She included authors such as Martin Andersen Nexo and Johan Bojer who were less well known outside their own countries, and she was particularly responsive to developments in American writing. She was as quick to welcome the work of new critics like Edmund Wilson and F. R. Leavis as to comment on the developing colonial literatures of Canada and South Africa or 'Modern Negroid Literature'. She had a special interest in New Zealand writers. She wrote general literary articles, such as those on 'Book Collecting' and 'Best Sellers', as well as more detailed and specific studies of individual works.

Her articles fall into four broad groups: the classics, modern books and writers, general discussions, and Australian writers and writing. Of these the articles on modern literature and Australian writers have retained most interest, intrinsically and historically.

When occasion demanded, Nettie Palmer could give sharp particular judgments. She wrote two articles in the *Illustrated Tasmanian Mail* on Galsworthy. The first is a competent account of *The Forsyte Saga* with some history of its publication; the second, 'John Galsworthy: From Artist to Purveyor', traces the decline in Galsworthy's artistic integrity that began with *The White Monkey*: she shows symbol in Galsworthy's work degenerating into pun and illustrates the point well from a slapstick scene in *The Pigeon* and another from the second act of *Old English* where 'everything turns on the *enfant terrible* who has brought in a dead rat and the lawyer who, in a professional way, begins to "smell a rat"'. It is interesting to note that by such limited and economical means Nettie Palmer arrives at a judgment of Galsworthy not unlike that made by D. H. Lawrence in his 1928 Galsworthy scrutiny. I make this point, not unduly to elevate the status of her criticism, but as a way of suggesting that her views were generally those of the most discerning opinion of her time.

Her opinions of overseas writers could be trenchantly independent. Writing of Aldous Huxley in April 1929, she 'places' his erudition; judges *Point Counter Point* to be glittering journalism; claims that Huxley is a writer of ingenuity rather than imagination and from the point of view of values finds in him a sceptical materialism showing him to be on the side of and in the service of the Philistines.

One of her most impressive and characteristic pieces of early criticism concerns Osbert Sitwell's *England Reclaimed*. 'The book is not even a part of England Reclaimed. One might perhaps call it "A Corner of England Re-decorated".' An equally independent view emerges in her account of *The London Mercury* and the kind of literary values represented by J.C. Squire and his associates; and she is trenchant in her discussions of Arnold Bennett's commercialism.

For all her valid criticisms, Nettie Palmer's articles appear in the main based on appreciative discrimination. She writes of Thomas Hardy's *Winter Words* that all Hardy's faults and qualities arise from the same source: 'his constant endeavour to make poetry out of the intractable'. She admires Alice Meynell, with whom she seems to have some affinity, for her personal qualities as much as for her writing, and into 'Mr Bennett and Mrs Woolf' – a most intelligent discussion of the issues raised by Virginia Woolf's revolutionary essay 'Mr Bennett and Mrs Brown' – she manages to squeeze an explication of Joyce's line 'He put on his impermeable, took up his impregnable and walked out of his immobile' that had recently appeared in *Transition*. Yeats's *The Tower* is capably accounted for soon after its appearance (20 June 1928), as are the English translations of Thomas Mann's *The Magic Mountain* and Feuchtwanger's once famous Munich novel, *Success*. 'The Philosophy of Ezra Pound' is a responsible assessment of Pound's critical attitudes with a sensitive feeling for some of the early poems. These articles suggest some of the cultural possibilities available in the period, and show how little time lag there was in the availability of such works in Australia.

While retaining her interest in the European tradition, Nettie Palmer took every opportunity to discuss the work of Australian writers and their peculiar situation. She was anxious to air their views and win them an audience, and nearly two-thirds of the total number of articles she wrote were devoted exclusively to Australian writers or writing, without counting direct or indirect allusions and references in others.

Nettie Palmer was a skilful and deliberate promoter of contemporary Australian literature. She critically publicised Australian books and pursued the cause of a national literature. Henry Handel Richardson was the subject of five articles and was mentioned in others, and other women writers, especially Miles Franklin ('Brent of Bin Bin') and Katharine Susannah Prichard, also received detailed and sympathetic attention in articles on individual works as they appeared. Other studies were devoted to Paul Wenz, Tom Collins, Price Warung, Barbara Baynton, Shaw Neilson, Furnley Maurice, R.D. FitzGerald, Dowell O'Reilly, Bernard O'Dowd, Henry Tate, Hugh McCrae, Henry Lawson, Barnard Eldershaw, Mary Gilmore, Martin Mills (Martin Boyd), and Frank Dalby Davison. Many of them received their first detailed scrutiny in the pages of the *Illustrated Tasmanian Mail* or the Brisbane *Courier* and several were to receive no other until the development of Australian literary studies after World War II. Nettie Palmer was also among the first to draw attention to certain books such as *Tom Petrie's Reminiscences* (for which she wrote a long introductory preface when she had it re-published in 1932) and M.M. Bennett's *Christison of Lammermoor*, which had fallen into neglect.

Nettie Palmer tried to give the same quality of critical attention to Australian books that she gave to those of overseas writers. However, one imagines that she was sometimes forced to write with one eye on the text, the other on the audience she had to attract, to concentrate on qualities and not to emphasise limitations. She was much sharper on overseas than on Australian writers, being aware of the difficulties Australian writers had to face at the time and the lack of appreciation or recognition they endured in their home country. However critical she was, her articles remained untouched by the notes of resentment and revenge that mar so much reviewing in Australia. The immediate value of the Australian writers she discussed was of more concern to Nettie Palmer than their survival value and she knew that good criticism could be written about minor authors and simple writing. Nettie Palmer's evaluations were largely right and just in their time and place, and many of them retain a permanent relevance. Above all she was not an uncritical admirer of the merely Australian. She praised contemporary writers like Barnard Eldershaw and Katharine Susannah Prichard for their seriousness of intention, their sincerity and freshness of outlook, and their adequate powers of expression, making no bigger claims. This attitude is well expressed by her friend and contemporary F.T. Macartney in his *Australian Literature* (1956): 'What the circumstances rather call for, in a country obliged to build up its own literary life no less than its separate economic and political welfare, is a judicious appreciation of the local impact as being important on its own account, leaving the matter of larger or permanent merit to be determined in the only possible way.'

Nettie Palmer's concern with the advancement of Australian literary and cultural life is expressed most openly in some of her articles – a few are almost manifestos – such as 'The Australian Novel' (15 August 1928), 'The Need for Australian Literature' (17 April 1929), 'The Arts in Australia' (11 September 1929), 'The Truth About Australian Poetry' (16 October 1929), 'Building Jerusalem' (14 May 1930), 'Colonial Wares' (30 July 1930), 'Creative Writing in Australia' (13 May 1931), and 'Ten Years Ago: *Dark Ages* in Australian Writing' (13 January 1932). These titles indicate how consistent was Nettie Palmer's attack on colonial-provincial attitudes (the epithet is her own) and how insistently she felt their pressure.

'The Need for Australian Literature' is an essential document of the twenties. It introduces very intelligently the concept of double standards that was to cause so much discussion in the literary journalism of the fifties. Nettie Palmer puts the case thus:

> We want literature that is 'best' in two senses. Literature being an interpretation of life, we cannot do without it. Milton calls to his muse: 'That which is dark, illume'. And we see light dawn on chaos. Bunyan reveals the city of Mansoul. Conrad in our own day has made us 'perceive men's drives in their natural relation to the seen universe around them'. Such are some of the achievements of great literature, literature whose value is absolute, equal for all readers, whatever their own environment or way of life. All great literature has this absolute value, whether it has what I would call a relative value or not.
>
> And what is this relative value? By relative value I would mean the sheer usefulness of a literary work in interpreting a given environment to the people in it and to its observers. A region or a way of life does not begin to exist until it has been interpreted by one artist after another . . . . To illuminate whole tracts of life, that is then the relative achievement of the artist, the absolute achievement being the illumination of life as a whole . . . . Without this illumination . . . the human nature in Australia must 'appear to the imagination absolutely uncanny and ghost-like', or merely uninteresting, unfit for literature unless or until the artists make it into something understandable . . . . Only the artists . . . can show us the features and meaning of what we are perhaps beginning to love.

This credo strikes a note that is repeated throughout Australian critical comment, most perceptively, for instance, in Judith Wright's introduction to *Preoccupations in Australian Poetry* (1965) – 'the true function of an art and a culture is to interpret us to ourselves, and to relate us to the country and the society in which we live'. In various pieces of her literary journalism Nettie Palmer asserts that writers must interpret and humanise their country, and give the lie to D. H. Lawrence's statement that Australia is 'a country with no word written across it yet'. Elsewhere she is even more insistent in her demands that Australian writers should write as *Australians*, not as colonials. In the course of an attack on the trivial and trivialising imitation-English verse found in too many local anthologies, she writes:

> I look forward to an Australian anthology that will really find what power there was, here and there, in our careless balladists, and will put their work side by side with lyrics from Chris Brennan and Shaw

> Neilson . . . . *To have made agreeable verse . . . is no particular achievement for an Australian unless, perhaps, as an exercise* [my italics]. To have struck an authentic note, one not merely derivative but expressive of new life, is to contribute something to the world's store of thought and beauty. Such poems in recent times are, in Russia, those of Alexander Blok . . . in Ireland . . . those of Yeats.

It was perhaps to ask too much. Elsewhere, her generalisations need special scrutiny when they lead her to write:

> The point is . . . that the life and problems of various parts of Australia show immense contrasts, from pearling at Broome to legislating at Canberra. Our writers have the task of gradually revealing it all to us.

Nettie and Vance Palmer were both inclined to see the writer's task as 'naming the country', and given the time at which they were writing their instinct may have been right. (Miles Franklin wrote in her unpublished Notebook [c. 1953] 'simpler writings prepare the tilth for genius not born to every generation'.) But Nettie Palmer's formulation is misleading: it diminishes the novelist's task and relegates it to the sphere of sociology ('pearling at Broome, legislating at Canberra'). It explains why she welcomed and even sometimes praised books for dealing with life in Perth or in the forests of Tasmania; and it helps to explain, speaking broadly, the aesthetic limitations of much Australian fiction of the time where the material was merely transcribed and not transformed.

Nettie Palmer is on surest ground when she writes of the literary situation in Australia in the twenties and early thirties. She points to the absence of sound publishing houses and to the poor publishing conditions, the lack of weekly and monthly reviews which are indispensable to the growth and nourishment of a sound literary culture, the unavailability or inaccessibility of Australian books (she notes that one cannot obtain copies of *Such is Life* or the works of Price Warung), the impossibility of making a living by writing alone, and the indifference to local work. She complains in 1930:

> There is no country in the world where so little is known of its own literary work in past and present; no country in which ignorance in such matters is so heartily condoned and even admired!

In the course of writing of Will Dyson's famous lecture, 'The Arts in Australia', Nettie Palmer supports his judgment that Australia is intellectually suburban, derivative and unresponsive, and she reiterates his point that the old isolation is lessening and that we 'must grow in association with the rest of mankind, and this can only be by creating culture as well as by enjoying it'.

In one of her most impressive articles, 'Colonial Wares', she defines most clearly her central concerns. Of the 'colonial' attitude in political and social life, she says:

> It is marked by a certain rawness of judgment, a timidity of thought, as of people not fully adult or confident of their power and authority to act as complete human beings. Three or four generations have not been enough to allow us to get thoroughly rooted in the soil. Waves of uncertainty sweep over us. Is this continent really our home, or are we just migrants from another civilisation, growing wool and piercing the ground for metals, doomed to be dependent for our intellectual and aesthetic nourishment – our books, interpretations of art, theories of the social order – on what is brought to us by every mail from overseas?

To formulate a question is often to go some way towards answering it, and here Nettie Palmer defines an attitude that her writing helped to change. In articles such as these she does not merely serve Australian literature, she contributes to it.

At the end of her essay *Modern Australian Literature* (1924) Nettie Palmer had complained that isolation, indifference and the inaccessibility of texts made it hopeless to search for signs of specific literary movements and influence in Australia. She commented on the lack of any sense of continuity in literary developments ('promising movements tend to run into the sand') and the way interesting material was scattered and lost ('Numberless short stories of value lie buried in the files of newspapers').

An Australian Story Book (1928) was her answer. It showed the kind of fiction she believed in – fiction which tried to interpret a new environment – and it demonstrated her standards applied to the work that was available. It is historically important for the way it rescued items like Lance Skulthorpe's 'The Champion

Bullock Driver', which it virtually discovered and put into permanent circulation in Australian literature. Its interest now lies in how adequately it reflects the state of the Australian story of its period and in the way it sets a standard against which the writing of the time can be measured.[5]

At the same time Nettie commented on the paucity of biographical studies of significant figures of the Australian past, and again, as if to set an example, in 1931 she produced *Henry Bournes Higgins: A Memoir*, one of the few studies of its kind to appear at that period. *Henry Bournes Higgins*, based on family papers, was inspired by a deep sense of family piety and personal affection for, and gratitude to, her uncle, Justice Higgins, who was largely responsible for the establishment of the Federal Arbitration Court, and whose famous Harvester judgment of 1907 led to the concept of the basic wage. Nettie Palmer's finely written introduction to the study of the great judge, who was also involved in early Australian educational movements, remains a leading work in its field.

Nettie Palmer's newspaper column and broadcasting had impact and influence on the cultural life of the time, and the publication in 1932 of a short collection of some of her best essays, *Talking it Over*, confirmed her position as the most important non-academic critic of her period.

In 1932 she worked on a book entitled *Green Island*. Conceived in the tradition of E.J. Banfield's descriptive books, and reflecting Nettie's lifelong concern with our natural heritage, it mixed some enchanting pages of observations with subjective reflection. It also included some of her ink drawings. Unfortunately it was never finalised for publication, though the manuscript volumes in the National Library show the revision that went into it over the years.

Nettie Palmer was asked by the Women's Centenary Council to edit a Commemorative Gift Book as part of the Centenary Celebration of the state of Victoria and the City of Melbourne; the proceeds from the Gift Book were to be devoted to the Memorial for Pioneer Women. Her diaries record the immense amount of correspondence this honorary editing involved. Apart from an extract from *The Fortunes of Richard Mahony*, a sketch by Katharine Susannah Prichard and an article by Alice Henry, the Gift Book consists largely of journalistic articles on 'Australian Pioneer Women', 'Girls' Education', 'University Women', 'Women and Art', and 'Victorian Women in Music', and it gives a competent account of the wide variety of achievement in these fields. The whole is illustrated by a number of woodcuts and paintings which reflect the taste of the time. Copy no.1 of the Gift Book was presented to Queen Mary.

Nettie and Vance Palmer left for Europe in March 1935. In London they decided to retain the connection with the Australian press which offered them better outlets than any they could find abroad, and they sent articles back to the *Argus* and the *Bulletin* on their experiences. Vance Palmer was invited to represent Australia at the Writers' Congress in Paris, but at the time he was caught up with the idea of writing for films, and Nettie went instead. Some of her experiences of the time – her meetings with Christina Stead, a lecture by André Gide – are recorded in *Fourteen Years*. On her return to London, the pleasant round of meetings continued, with Havelock Ellis, Rebecca West, F.R. and Q.D. Leavis – all finely accounted for in *Fourteen Years*. There were other meetings, not described, with fellow Australian writers like Brian Penton, Jack McLaren, and Leslie and Coralie Rees; and plans to edit an anthology, *The Spirit of Australia*, with Jack Lindsay.

On 17 April 1936 a letter came from Cape, the publisher, asking Vance Palmer to abridge *Such is Life*. Edward Garnett wrote 'Don't think of the author, think of the book'. The request to abridge *Such is Life* was an extraordinary coincidence and seemed to strengthen the Palmers' position. It was one of the books Nettie and Vance most admired and they saw the whole status of Australian writing, as well as the position of the non-expatriate Australian writer, to be intimately involved in its recognition. It was the book they had worked hard for in 1917; re-publication of the book had been discussed with Angus and Robertson on the eve of their departure for London. The Palmers were convinced that the proper appreciation of this book would mark a new stage in Australian literary culture.

On 11 May the Palmers left for Spain. At Mongat Nettie did most of the work on the abridging of *Such is Life*, while Vance continued writing his novel *Legend for Sanderson*. By 3 July the complete abridgment of *Such is Life* was posted off to Cape.

There is a deep Furphian irony in the whole of the Palmers' association with *Such is Life*. No one had done more to help this book. They well knew the problems associated with presenting an abbreviated version of Furphy's work, but they could hardly have foreseen the extraordinary abuse that would greet their version in Australia. Vance Palmer, who referred to *Such is Life* as a 'work of unremitting guile', offended militant nationalists like Miles Franklin and Kate Baker in comparing it with Mark Twain's *Life on the Mississippi* rather than with something 'high prophetic'. Kate Baker especially condemned the removal of the 'encyclopaedic pages' and the attempt to present Furphy exclusively as a novelist. In a sense the abridgment was misguided because impossible. Nevertheless it was this much abused and emasculated version of *Such is Life* that first brought the work into full prominence, and the discussions and publicity it provoked stimulated the serious critical study of Furphy that began in the early forties.[6]

The Palmers' stay in England and Europe was blighted by the fact that they could find very few permanent or satisfactory outlets for their work. They planned to return to Australia in September; Nettie was to return later after attending the Writers' Conference in Madrid. Politicial events decided otherwise. On 19 July revolution broke out in Barcelona and the Palmers returned to Paris. On 4 September Nettie sailed for Australia and arrived in Melbourne on 12 October. From 14 October when she began work on 'Spanish Street' and her speeches, 'Spain in Ferment', Nettie's life was an extremely busy round of talks and lectures. She immediately helped form a Spanish Relief Committee and for the next months all her energy was to go into collecting money for the victims of the Spanish Civil War. Two urgent pamphlets sprang out of these experiences, *Spanish Struggle* (1936) and *Australians in Spain* (1937), as well as a number of newspaper articles and contributions to the New Zealand independent fortnightly *Tomorrow*.

The defeatism of the late 1930s affected the Palmers deeply: the ideal society, the literary revival they had hoped and worked for, started to seem like some remote dream. They themselves were ageing. Nettie found no further forum or platform quite like the one she had had in the *Illustrated Tasmanian Mail* and *All About Books*. Questions of family and health started to dominate her thoughts as Australia moved closer to World War II.

The Palmers had become increasingly concerned at what seemed to them not only a lack of proper respect for but a positive indifference to the achievements of the past. In *Fourteen Years* Nettie Palmer wrote, on 13 November 1937, on returning from a poorly attended unveiling of a statue to Higinbotham:

> The whole affair makes me wonder if there isn't some essential lack in us, something missing that keeps our life from having meaning and depth – interest in our past, reverence for those who have shown outstanding qualities of mind or spirit. When we look back it is on great empty spaces; the significant dead have no memorials; the few statues in our parks are mainly of forgotten grandees and kings. It must be because we have no sense of ourselves as a people, with a yesterday and a tomorrow. I can't help remembering that little fishing-village in Britanny where we lived when we were first married; on some rock rising from a wheatfield a bronze plaque, in memory of a local poet or hero. How these simple memorials added another dimension to the day-to-day life of the village!

The next decade and more became a time to turn back to the past and to take stock. The Palmers had always believed that Australian criticism and creative writing could only fully develop by 'keeping in touch with the larger world', and both had long realised that only the development of flexible inner standards could save Australian literary culture from the twin evils of colonial defeatism on the one hand and provincial or nationalistic self-assertion on the other – the profound inferiority complex that A.A. Phillips was later to call the cultural cringe.

Nettie Palmer had become increasingly convinced that critics and writers would be more fruitfully engaged in a patient attentiveness to the past, in looking at what had been achieved, than restlessly clamouring for the great Australian novel or assertively dismissing what had been done. New movements were trying to develop, new magazines beginning; Nettie was critical of their rootlessness. She felt that what the Australian writer needed was a sense of continuity with his own 'useable past', and that the constant process of having to start all over again from the beginning would, if prolonged, hold back the development of Australian writing indefinitely. A series of local literary movements ending in frustration and defeat, like the Pioneer Players or the Jindyworobak Movement, without the support of substantial individual literary achievement, was unlikely to provide the sense of continuity needed.

While responding to what was worthwhile in the Jindyworobak movement, for instance, Nettie Palmer nevertheless notes laconically in her diary (24 February 1939) 'letter from R. Ingamells . . . using all Vance's old slogans but exaggerated'. To C.B. Christesen in the early stages of *Meanjin*'s development, in letters that balance warmth of response and encouragement with critical astringency and detachment, she complains of 'rootless reviews', excessive enthusiasm and over-praise for minor writers, as well as failures of style, tone and art. In a letter to Rex Ingamells (10 May 1944), she writes 'Sometimes one is shocked by the difficulty in this land of ours, of knowing what has been done and said. It is as if we had no past.' Earlier (10 August 1936), she wrote to Frank Dalby Davison from Paris: 'I've felt constantly the inconsecutive nature of our literary life in Australia.'[7] It is a guiding thread in much of her thinking and writing. She constantly stressed in letters, lectures and broadcasts that there could be no secure development of an Australian literary culture in the future without a mature understanding of the problems, limitations and achievements of the past.

By the 1940s, Nettie and Vance had become established as leading figures in Australian writing, and more and more official tasks as guardians of Australian literary culture fell to them. It became a time of memorials, tributes, sketches and experiments either in newspapers and journals or in radio broadcasts. A chronological list of all the hard and inconspicuous work they were engaged on is hardly necessary. It had become a part of their lives to read the manuscripts submitted to them, to comment on the new works appearing, to act as judges in literary competitions and to take a friendly interest in various cultural activities. They continued to review and to lecture; they regularly broadcast, and in fact the radio became their most important general outlet at this time. It is always hard to assess accurately the influence and impact of work of this kind, but not difficult to recognise its importance and value in the day-to-day life of letters and the way it contributes a particular stimulus to the cultural atmosphere.

Nettie Palmer's interest in Australian literature and life cannot be separated from her continued interest in the foreign contribution to it. She was active on several committees for refugees in the late thirties and the early war years. Her translation of Irma Schnierer's *Liesel Fragt Warum (Liesel Asks Why)* was published in 1940, and she started to translate some of Esther Landolt's work, such as *Ewige Herde*, but only half finished the translation (and all trace of it seems to have been lost). As well as keeping up with the work of newcomers and pressing forward with her study of Latin American literature – she saw important similarities between the Australian and the Uruguayan situation in particular [8] – Nettie Palmer was turning back to the figures who had most impressed her in the past, and doing what she could to 'establish memorials to the significant dead'. Some aspects of this work need detailed attention.

As early as May 1921, when she was associated as editor with the poetry magazine *Birth*, Nettie Palmer had been impressed by the poems of Lesbia Harford. Her diary for 24 May 1921 reads:

> The May number of *Birth* came, filled with poems by L.V.H. It's Lesbia Verner (Keogh) Harford, and the poems are astonishing.

And in an almost unknown article 'Notes for an anthology' (1940) [9] Nettie wrote:

> The faults Australian poetry in general had round 1920 were not those of what Mr Max Harris lately called the bush-blurb or the ballad boys (he was alluding to modern nostalgic imitations). On the contrary its weaker and larger side was then full of accepted and outworn poeticalities: 'pilgrims grey' were relieved by 'wine ruby red' or by 'loaves of laughter' – all in the tradition of Daley's 'Sunset Fantasy'. What virtues our poetry then possessed were indicated for those who could read, in a few gleamings from *Birth* or the *Bookfellow* (which of course was Stephen's Red Page intermittently facing the world alone), and in a few small volumes that appeared in a blaze of obscurity and were not linked, in people's minds, either with one another or with our growing stream of consciousness to which they essentially belonged.[10]

Lesbia Harford's poems *were* astonishing for their time in Australia, astonishing also for the strange unconventional life of the author that they reveal. Lesbia Harford (1891–1927) was a Melbourne graduate in law and philosophy who gave up legal work to experience at first hand the life of a factory girl and to devote herself to the cause of women workers. Always in poor health, she died at the age of thirty-six, leaving behind her a group of verses which Nettie Palmer edited and introduced in 1940 (published 1941). One can understand the impression of novelty these poems must have made in their place and time, with their subjects of menstruation, sexual fears and ambivalent feelings about factory girls, as well as their awareness of industrialism.

Of wider national interest was Alice Henry, whose *Memoirs* Nettie Palmer compiled and edited in 1943. Difficulties of publication in wartime resulted in the *Memoirs* being multigraphed in an edition of 100 copies which was distributed to some Australian and American libraries in 1944. Nettie's *Postscript* is itself a memoir of the author and there is a chronological resumé of Alice Henry's life, with a bibliography.

Alice Henry (1857–1943) was clearly a remarkable woman. An Australian journalist and a staunch advocate of women's rights, she returned to Australia in 1933 for the last years of her life; Nettie Palmer had made her acquaintance when she returned for a brief visit in 1925. Nettie Palmer's diary and agenda do not list her personal impressions of Alice Henry, but she was clearly a figure she admired, and she never missed an occasion to visit her. It was

Miles Franklin, at one time closely associated with Alice Henry, who suggested writing the memoirs. They consisted of thirty-one chapters of varying length covering the whole range of her life. The bulk is devoted to important meetings: George Bernard Shaw and Mrs Pankhurst are given separate chapters, but most space is devoted to figures like Margaret Dreier Robins, the first president of the National Trade Union League, Mary Anderson, Director of the Women's Bureau, US Department of Labour, Elizabeth Christman, Secretary-Treasurer of the National Woman's Trade Union League, Agnes Weston and Stella Miles Franklin; and to projects like the Hull-House Players and the establishment of Bryn Mawr Summer School for working women, which later became the Hudson Shore Labour School.

Alice Henry's memoirs were dictated when she was in her eighties. They make little attempt to portray the people she met or was involved with and many of the chapters are hardly more than personal tributes or acknowledgments. They do not avoid the dead tones of the factual report; but Nettie Palmer saw the value of preserving such historical documents until the time came for the right interpreter to use them.

The death of Henry Handel Richardson on 20 March 1946 made Nettie Palmer determined to complete her long projected study of the novelist whose work she had been familiar with for over twenty years. On 2 August 1946, she and Vance left Melbourne for Queensland to spend their winter working there. In Brisbane, Nettie helped Vance with the research for the background of *Golconda*, transcribing reports of trade union secretaries and general news of Mt Isa (Diary 22 August). Among other literary tasks she drafted a foreword, which Vance revised and which appeared under his name, for Herz Bergner's *Between Sky and Sea*. From 5 to 14 November Nettie returned to Sydney to study the Henry Handel Richardson papers in the possession of Mary Kernot. She was unable to work with full concentration on this project. Her health had been failing for some years and new demands continually intervened. There were plans for a newer, fuller edition of Lesbia Harford's poems, which involved much searching for manuscripts; and there were inquiries about republishing *Henry Bournes Higgins*. Years of accumulated papers, notebooks and diaries were sorted. At some point the idea of publishing extracts from her private journal seemed to impose itself of its own accord. *Fourteen Years* was taking shape.

Nettie Palmer's diary of 2 September 1947 reads:

> Decided time now come to sort [Notes] out into 8 period-places – Caloundra, Kalorama, Barcelona, Melbourne etc.

In assembling *Fourteen Years*, Nettie Palmer decided to begin at 1925 with the move to Caloundra. The Palmers had moved away from Melbourne somewhat disappointed in the failure of the Pioneer Players experiment and of the city to provide anything like a focal point for a national literary movement. They wanted some sense of change and mobility in their lives and they found they could live more cheaply as writers first at Caloundra and later at Green Island. They had established newspaper contacts; all they needed were the mail services, and these were reliable.

The year 1925 had been a significant one in the Palmers' career since it marked the beginning of their most mature literary work. The decade from 1925 to 1935 was the most copiously productive period in Nettie's life, seeing the publication of over five hundred pieces of literary journalism of quality, as well as a number of books. But 1925 was also an important date in the development of Australian literature between the wars. Henry Handel Richardson was emerging as a major figure, Katharine Susannah Prichard was starting to write her strongest work, and during the following decade a whole new generation of writers like Frank Dalby Davison, Barnard Eldershaw, Leonard Mann, Eleanor Dark and Alan Marshall started to write and publish some of their best work. One can discern in the Palmers' writing, at least until 1935, a nostalgia for the slow, good feeling of the old Australia of Lawson and Furphy. Nettie and Vance belonged to a generation that did not achieve the same firm sense of identity as Lawson and Furphy or, in spite of the fact that they produced some remarkable work, the same height of creative achievement. Their generation belonged to a more genteel, lettered, transitional phase. Their problems were accentuated by the exceptional difficulties of the society and culture in which they found themselves. In Barnard Eldershaw's *The Glasshouse* (1936), Stirling Armstrong, a well-known Australian author who has become something of an exile, states '*There isn't an idiom yet*' — a complaint which seems to voice the uncertainties of a whole literary generation.

Fourteen Years in its unassuming way throws an exceptionally clear light on this whole phase in Australian writing, but by virtue of its style and its sense of personality, it transcends any ascription as an historical document. It is unique in Australian letters as a record of reminiscence, portraits and impressions and in its sense of intimacy with times and places that no later reconstructions can replace. It is unique too in its point of view. Nettie Palmer was clearly aware of the problems which faced the writers of her time, but she was free of the peculiar tensions of the creative writer committed to pioneering a difficult field and running all the risks of artistic failure. She could sympathise and observe, reflect, criticise and record. This gives her work a particular purity and it frees her critical comments and asides from any invidious comparisons with her own creative output. One does not usually adduce a critic's creative work in this way, but with the Australian writers of this generation one often feels that their understanding and experience of their situation and their problems exceeded their creative potential for coping with them. They are sometimes more interesting to read about than to read.

Fourteen Years is a remarkably flexible and wide ranging account of literary and personal encounters in Australia and Europe. Its portraits of, for instance, figures like Havelock Ellis, F. R. Leavis, André Gide, Christina Stead, H. B. Higgins, Basil Burdett, Randolph Bedford, Katharine Susannah Prichard, Miles Franklin, Shaw Neilson, Leon Feuchtwanger and Henry Handel Richardson are impressive for their sympathetic detachment, their assured objectivity of response, their concreteness and immediacy, their sudden shrewdness. Each entry in *Fourteen*

Years has its own value and charm. It moves with remarkable ease and assurance between Australia and Europe, registering life at, say, Green Island with the same economy and fineness as in Barcelona or Paris. A very literary book, it is not all a record of literary meetings. There is the lively account of being caught over-riding in a Spanish train, and the encounter with the hat-maker who paid her fare; descriptions of coral, stone-fish and birds. What particularly strikes one in this book is Nettie Palmer's sure grasp of the concrete, her clear perceptions of personalities, places and things. She hardly ever generalises; encounters and incidents with people or books are allowed to speak for themselves. And she never tries to set herself up as the conscience of the country. She writes with the sureness and poise of a highly individual sense of style. One can point to the beautiful arrangement of balanced sentences with a pungent incisiveness of comment, and the almost colloquial lilt – a combination that seems to guarantee its survival.

Fourteen Years received no wider circulation than that of an edition limited to five hundred copies. It was published in 1948 and has never been reprinted, but it is likely to prove Nettie Palmer's most important contribution to Australian literature. Two other books also have permanent historical interest, and a third completes the list of her published work.

No detailed diary survives for 1948, the year during which Nettie Palmer seems to have worked most concertedly on her monograph *Henry Handel Richardson*, but we know that the study was completed and typed by 19 February 1949.

Like so much of Nettie Palmer's output *Henry Handel Richardson* was a pioneer work, the first full-length study of Richardson to be published. Ever since she had omitted her from *Modern Australian Literature* in 1924, Nettie Palmer had striven to make amends by writing of and referring to her as frequently as possible. In broadcasts, reviews, in lectures and talks, as well as in her efforts to have the Nobel Prize for literature awarded to her in the early thirties, Nettie Palmer had done all she could to bring the name and work of Henry Handel Richardson before the public.

She had for some time planned a full-length study, and behind her monograph lay years of close familiarity with Richardson's work, records of personal meetings and correspondence, some of the most interesting sections of which were included in a nineteen-page appendix. Nettie Palmer's monograph, apart from a reticent biographical chapter, is essentially a series of sensitive interpretative readings and a history of the writing of all Richardson's works from *Maurice Guest* and *The Getting of Wisdom* to *The Young Cosima*. Like much of her criticism it is now dated by the critical modes of the time in which it was written, and while the readings were perceptive and original then, they do not escape the limitations of the conventional character study of novels. Since Nettie Palmer wrote her monograph, much more material has become available to scholars and critics, and modern critical methods have opened up a whole new range of approaches to Richardson's texts and contexts. But the achievement of Nettie Palmer's book as a pioneer study cannot be overstated. Within its limitations it is a forceful and cogent account of Richardson's life and work.

Nettie Palmer planned two other works to follow her monograph on Richardson: a continuation of *Fourteen Years* and the publication of her 1932 Notebooks, *Green Island*. Neither of these eventuated, but in 1952 *The Dandenongs* appeared, a slim volume of local history based on an earlier series of newspaper articles which traces the development of this area from the beginnings of the settlement of Melbourne to the present suburban sprawl.

The point of departure is her idea that

> we are always being told we don't know our country well enough, and this usually means that we have not let our minds wander over the endless spaces enclosed by its outline. But there are other points of view. There is a good deal to be said for letting the mind rest in one spot, small enough to hold the affections and, perhaps, to be understood.

In these chapters, which mingle personal and literary reminiscence with history, Nettie Palmer follows the formation of the Dandenong settlements, and the different families associated with its progress. She writes of the Nobelius nursery, the berry-growers and the timber-getters; of Mooroolbark, Monbulk, Ferntree Gully; of the 'pastoral aspect of the Dandenongs and the wild, natural one'. She sees how the development of any area must be one of continual change and adjustment as well as of repetition. Her book in its unemphatic way contains a plea to preserve the Dandenongs from urban encroachment.

In 1952 Victor Kennedy died and the task of completing the biography of Bernard O'Dowd which he had begun fell to Nettie Palmer. Kennedy had left behind a manuscript containing a large body of material which she completely reshaped to her own design. Though the published work bears their joint signature, the study is unmistakably Nettie's own, and bears the imprint of her personal style. *Bernard O'Dowd* is not in any sense a complete, formal biography. It was conceived as a tribute to an unusual character: a poet and prophet, a lawyer and a man of affairs, and to the influence he exerted on a whole generation of Australian intellectuals.

Of all the writers Nettie Palmer had known, Bernard O'Dowd was the one most inextricably bound up in her own intellectual life and development. He was the first Australian literary figure she wrote of when, writing under the pen-name Owen Roe O'Neill, she complained that O'Dowd was 'the only Irish poet . . . who writes pure thought' [11]. Nettie Palmer constantly mentioned and discussed O'Dowd in her early letters to Vance and advised her younger brother Esmonde Higgins in a letter 10 March 1915 'To read *The Bush* a good deal . . . I mean the last half chiefly. Some of the stanzas are pure poetry . . . though one certainly has to expurgate in reading.' It was to O'Dowd that Nettie devoted the first important critical article she wrote on her return to Australia in 1915, and his name and aptly chosen quotations from his poetry appeared throughout her critical writings. Nettie Palmer believed O'Dowd's *The Bush* (1912) to be the most important poem of its time. In *Modern Australian Literature* (1924) she wrote ' "The Bush" is his most important contribution to Australian literature itself. It is the book a young nation needs, a meditation, a prophetic book, and a seed bed of poetry.' To Nettie Palmer and her generation O'Dowd was a major figure, voicing the nationalist aspirations of the Australia of his time, and proclaiming in his verse the mystique of the bush that was of paramount importance to the writers of the era.

Nettie Palmer devoted all of the first half of 1953 to writing her study. Her diary records visits and interviews with him, scrupulous research into background information and into the tangled thickets and undergrowths of his curious encyclopaedic learning. Her Greek studies were especially valuable when it came to commenting on *Dominions of the Boundary*, while her knowledge of French and English literature brings a breadth and range to the whole that saves it from becoming claustrophobic. Two entries in her diary are revealing of the problems involved:

> *21 July*: N. to pub. lib. to get date right about the C19th transit of Venus, espec. the second one that B.O'D. watched as a little boy. Got evidence in about 2 books. The date is 1874 – as we thought. Bernard would have been about eight. To B. by 3.30 . . . He has been thru' part of the mss and makes some factual suggestions. Also says that some passages need to be developed – but I don't see how this can be done. It isn't as if he had read the whole ms. and got things into proportion. Difficult to please him securely. Asked him about photos of his parents.

> *26 July*: to see O'Dowd again . . . I feel he's hurt by my accidental criticism e.g. of his prosody of Alma Venus ('I consider it contains most of my best work!' So do I, but –). He is obviously used to disciples on the one hand and enemies on the other – not to friends.

As an account of O'Dowd's life and work written by someone who had known him quite closely Nettie Palmer's study is unlikely to be superseded.[12] Its picture of his childhood in a Victorian country town in the 1870s, his Irish Catholic upbringing, his career as librarian and lawyer and the development of his intellectual interests is done with a fine economy, suggesting something of the texture of the times and places in which O'Dowd lived and wrote. While her book is all the better for being written from the point of view of a sympathetic admirer, Nettie Palmer is never uncritical. She makes no extravagant claims for O'Dowd's poetry; she is aware of the waste and dispersal of emotion in much of his writing, the heaviness of some of its assertions and dogmatisms. But she is sensitive to its lighter moments of grace and vision and to the conviction of its affirmations. Her study is most rewarding for its detailed explications, and its reading of *The Bush*; but it is valuable – almost unwittingly – in another way as well. It shows the extraordinary moral isolation of the writer in Australia from other Australian writers of his time, and its attendant dangers of eccentricity, failure of communication and finally sterility.

Nettie Palmer's study was finished by late August and was to be presented to O'Dowd as a tribute, in lieu, so to speak, of the major official honours he had refused throughout his life. It was Nettie Palmer's last major work, and her last memorial to the significant figures of the past. Bernard O'Dowd died on 1 September.

These last two full-length books of Nettie Palmer's confer a curious symmetry on her life's work and interests: the one a study devoted to an Australian expatriate author, involved in the European tradition of art and letters; the other to a nationalistic and encyclopaedic writer who never left home and whose work, although he corresponded with Walt Whitman, is limited to the history of his own country. Both books were born of Nettie Palmer's continual concern for Australian writing and both indicate the ways in which she saw it best able to develop: by constant accessibility to the enriching influences from without and by attention to its own inner problems and resources – by recognition of its own past and a sure grip on the present.

During her lifetime Nettie Palmer built up a reputation for a small but highly individual and distinguished body of work as a poet, biographer, literary journalist and critic, diarist, letter writer, editor and translator, but she never received recognition in the form of academic or other public honours, awards and prizes, so few of which were available to writers of her generation. It would be wrong to make extravagant claims for her output and as unjust to overrate as it would be to underrate her contribution to

Australian writing and its reception. She was not self-seeking, and she cared nothing for undiscriminating praise; she was incapable of flattery or self-promotion. But she liked credit given for work well done and she knew a literature does not consist merely of a few high peaks or isolated masterpieces but is a whole varied landscape in which all kinds of work and achievement have their place, where readers are important as well as writers. Nettie Palmer was an indispensable figure in her time and the history of Australian writing would be the poorer without her achievement. Her life and work are not only individually moving but reflect the aspirations and frustrations of a whole generation of talented writers who were seeking to define their own sense of national character.

Notes

1. Only a few further poems appeared in the twenties. An attempt to write 'kiddies' verses', presumably along lines suggested by Furnley Maurice's *The Bay and Padie Book*, proved unsuccessful.
2. It gets the date of Brennan's *Poems* (1913) wrong, but there is no reason for H. M. Green (*A History of Australian Literature* (1961), vol. 11, p.1,210) to accuse it of omitting William Baylebridge; he is treated under his own name, William Blocksidge. Nettie Palmer had been introduced to his work by Frank Wilmot in October 1923. Present-day readers are more likely to be struck by the omission of William Gosse Hay, five of whose books had appeared, including *The Escape of the Notorious Sir William Heans* (1919).
3. The *Illustrated Tasmanian Mail* began publication as the *Tasmanian Mail* on 7 July 1877. Nettie Palmer's association with the paper ended on 20 April 1933. The paper's final dissolution occurred on 27 June 1935.
4. For a full discussion of Nettie Palmer's contributions to the *Illustrated Tasmanian Mail* see Vivian Smith, 'Vance and Nettie Palmer: The Literary Journalism', *Australian Literary Studies*, vol. 6 no.2, October 1973: 115–27; and in the same issue 'Nettie Palmer: A Checklist of Literary Journalism 1918–1936': 190–96. I have made considerable use of this material in the present edition.
5. George Mackaness's *Australian Short Stories* appeared in the same year and its historical sweep is slightly wider than the Palmer selection, which includes only stories written since 1900, but Nettie Palmer's collection was the most important to appear since A.G. Stephens's *The Bulletin Story Book* (1901).
6. See David Walker, 'The Palmer Abridgment of *Such is Life*', *Australian Literary Studies*, vol. 8, no. 4, October 1978: 494–98.
7. See Vance and Nettie Palmer, *Selected Letters*, ed. Vivian Smith, pp. 178 and 138.

8. Nettie Palmer was very advanced in her sense of the importance of the study of colonial and post-colonial literatures. Her article, 'The Growth of Latin American Literature', *Meanjin*, XIX (1947), suggests several interesting points of comparison between the Australian and Latin American situation and was to form part of a longer investigation. In April 1944 she began to sketch the preface of a work 'tracing the line of our development as a sort of echo of Latin America's' (Journal 1944–45). It was to be called *Literature in Australia: A Brief Survey*. But other tasks intervened and this monograph was abandoned.
9. Palmer Papers, Mitchell Library. Reprinted in J. Ingamells, *Cultural Cross Section* (1941), pp. 19–25.
10. Similar objections had been voiced by Furnley Maurice in his essay 'National Poetry' in *Romance* (1922):

    There is something happening about modern American poetry, but there is no mystery about the poetry that is printed in Australia today. It is the last word in conventional English verse production. It is done to worn-out patterns discarded in the land of their origin. It is more conventional in form and matter than any verse now published in England by English poets.
11. O'Dowd's response appeared in A.G. Stephens's *Australia* 16 May 1907, and is now reproduced in *Fantasies* in the *Collected Poems*; 'A note on O'Dowd', which appeared in *Fellowship* 1918.
12. Hugh Anderson's *The Poet Militant: Bernard O'Dowd* (1969), adds new biographical information about O'Dowd's relationship with Marie E.J. Pitt and takes account of the commentaries and critical articles written since O'Dowd's death, but it could not be said to supersede Nettie Palmer's study.

Note on the Text

Nettie Palmer left an enormous amount of uncollected material, but in making this selection of her work I have decided to collect for the first time principally those texts which either she or Vance Palmer prepared for publication, though much of it was not in book form. A severe self-critic, Nettie Palmer believed that every book, even a miscellaneous collection of essays or an anthology should, so far as possible, be shaped and patterned like a work of art. She shared Kipling's view that nothing was as remediless as bad work once put forward, and she was a conscious stylist, who often advised other writers to take more pains. She also shared the view that there was writing that was good enough to be published in newspapers and reviews where it had its proper home but which did not necessarily have to find a more permanent form between hard covers. The quality of her newspaper articles and reviews was exceptionally high, much higher than most literary journalism today.

The arrangement that follows is, as far as possible, in chronological order of publication, with the exception of *Fourteen Years*, which is placed first in recognition of its importance.

Part I

EDITOR'S NOTE

Fourteen Years: Extracts from a Private Journal 1925–1939, was published by the Meanjin Press, Melbourne, in 1948, in an edition limited to five hundred copies. The text used here is that of number 342, with the date 'January 10th, 1946' changed to 'January 10th, 1936'. Although published in a limited edition, it was a number of years before the volume was sold out, but this was at a time in Australian publishing when serious writers and poets had very small print runs, often from 250 to 500 copies at the most.

There is no other work quite like *Fourteen Years* in Australian writing and it is a text that has gained increasing importance for historians and those interested in the development of Australian culture between the wars. *Fourteen Years* was not written exactly as published. It is in part a reconstruction, and in part a highly selective reassembling of original materials. Some indications of the process involved are shown in the following extracts from Nettie Palmer's pocket diary for 1947:

> *12 June* Sorted *Illustrated Tasmanian* articles, cutting irrelevant paper and discovering a good deal of live wood.
> *8 July* N. wrote, gleaning from ITM articles of 1930 or so.
> *21 July* Still digging out ITM files and linking them with what I've thought of since.
> *2 Sept.* V. let N. read through some *Notes*. Decided time now come to sort them out into 8 period-places (Caloundra, Kalorama, Barcelona, Melbourne, etc.). Need folders for what material I had here by now. Each folder has at least something, some a great deal already in it.
> *3 Sept.* V. looked through N.'s file of rejected printed articles and advised on keeping only a few. Notes already done are enough on general literary subjects: those need interweaving with more personal ones. Drew up a list of names that must be included in some way – practising writers and their purposes. Must get some characteristic phrases and appearances for each from appropriate periods. V. began re-reading old family diaries V. had bought for me, 1934, fitting in with some literary notes on visitors: Pfeffer, Ravitch, Huebner. But need to follow our own writers now – it's just a matter of sorting

more than writing.
4 Sept. N. tinkering with diaries and fitting persons in like mosaic. N.B. must write some of it . . .
8 Sept. Did notes. V. says too warm, too much informed after the event, on Len Mann at Kalorama 1933. Found phrases of his in old diary. Moral: keep good diaries with people's phrases in them.
9 Sept. V. working every day on *Golconda*. . .N. tried to do character reminiscence of AGS. Very slow and stupid [illegible].
10 Sept. Tried AGS yesterday and got nowhere.
11 Sept. I can't write. V. more balanced: going on with *Golconda*. N. got going at end of morning and in afternoon. Did sort of AGS sketch: do for the present. . .
12 Sept. V. said he had done all he hoped on his novel at present and would now help me. Began by suggestions to go into first folder labelled Caloundra.
19 Sept. N. swotting stupidly at note on 'Working Bullocks' when it first appeared. Tried typing it. [This refers to entry 'April 9th, 1927'].
22 Sept. V. composed wonderful note from my articles on Barbara Bayton. . .
27 Sept. N. did note on visit from Paul Wenz in Melbourne. V. said it would do.
28 Sept. N. on evening of Goethe centenary in 1932.
30 Sept. N. did note on Neilson at Hawthorn with Gerald Byrne. [This refers to entry 'December 9th, 1929']. V. has sudden notion that my 'Notebook' should be published privately at 2 guineas (as he should have published his Stephens and Louis Esson letters).
1 Oct. N. did notes on Bertram [Higgins] and O'Dowd. Need revision and quotations from notes at home.
4 Oct. N. finishing note on Masefield in Melbourne; begin one on E.T. Brown . . . . Our worst years were 1937–39, when we were entangled in politics to no avail. We knew what was coming and no one would believe us except some fanatics who believed everything in advance. We knew too many people, for insufficient reasons.
7 Oct. Dolia dead. Worked out note on Barnard Eldershaw in 1933. . .
8 Oct. Did notes on Penton, Huebner always incomplete – needing quotations, cuttings, and Vance's slashing.
9 Oct. Notes on Huebner and Dark.
13 Oct. Grey day. V. planning to begin on London and N. sat down to it after breakfast without doing a stint of housework first, and wrote two London pieces in the morning: on Shelley Wang and Christina Stead (and her husband). Tried to do Ogden too, but got wrecked on his learning.
15 Oct. Dyson and Penton in London. . .Brian Penton in London,

March 1936: his months in Malaga. We were going to Spain next month. And an encounter with Will Dyson in the Chinese Exhibition that February.

16 Oct. N. did note on Philip Henderson in London; revised Hugh McCrae and Georgiana. Evening: first note on Pitter.

20 Oct. N. did Jules Romains finished in evening: this is part of London 1935. Planning Paris 35. V. insists that Paris 1936 can only be taken as supplement to Barcelona. Afraid he's right, as so often.

21 Oct. V. on *Golconda* again. Tackled note on Stewart Macky and Walter Turner, crawling back into November fog 1935 to do it. [See entry for 'December 19th, 1935'.] Another one needed. Stewart in Sussex, in August: but need batch of his letters for that. Trying to get picture of Aurousseau one evening at our flat.

22 Oct. Began note on Kirtly but too sad. That ends London section, except for many notes left in Melbourne (Leavis, Anand, Rebecca West etc.). Looking at Paris 1935. Begin with retrospect as from Medici Fountain, Luxembourg. N. well these times but to get steadiness for any writing I have to take a tablet nearly every day and work while it takes effect. . .

24 Oct. N. slowly pushing into note on remembering in Paris. . .

15 Nov. Began to look at letters. Vast packets of Marjorie Barnard's. . .brilliant letters, sincere and expressive.

16 Nov. Read notes on London encounters (Rebecca West, John Strachey). V. and N. sorted letters at night. Stephens, Stead, Tennant, Serle.

17 Nov. N. working on notes.

19 Nov. N. sorts letters (Eileen Duggan).

24 Nov. V. working on N.'s mss. N. aiming at Jeanne Billard in Paris. Planning Sylvia Beach.

30 Nov. . . V. went through H. McCrae's letters, finding some that might be sprinkled through years of *Diary*. Enjoyed himself.

6 Dec. N. did note on Gide 1935.

18 Dec. N. in Paris June 35.

Fourteen Years is best looked on as an anthology in journal form. It is divided into eight sections which correspond to the main places in which the Palmers lived for varying lengths of time during this period: Caloundra 1925–29; Melbourne 1929–32; Green Island 1932; Kalorama 1932–35; Paris 1935; London 1935–36; Barcelona 1936; and Melbourne 1936–39.

In arranging *Fourteen Years*, notions of symmetry and design were of more importance to Nettie Palmer than an exact pocket diary account of those days. For example, the Kalorama section ends with a description of the MM *Eridan* in Sydney Harbour on 19 March. The Palmers had left for Europe from Melbourne on 16 March 1935. They arrived in Marseilles on 22 April and travelled to Paris where they stayed until they went to London on 30 April. From then to mid-June they stayed in London until Nettie Palmer returned to Paris to attend the International Congress of Writers for the Defence of Culture. Vance was asked to attend as an Australian representative but he was caught up in his own literary plans, with some possibilities of writing for films, so Nettie went instead. No indication of this particular sequence of events can be found in *Fourteen Years* and there is no mention of the six weeks in London that took place during the Paris section. The biographer and historian will in time establish an exact chronology of the Palmers' movements in these years; but in the absence of the original manuscript anomalies or omissions cannot easily be explained.

Most readers of *Fourteen Years* are likely to agree with the Red Page reviewer of the *Bulletin* (presumably Douglas Stewart) who commented on 3 August, 1949: 'There have been few makers of diaries so merciful as Nettie Palmer, for she skips from, say, April 15, 1929, to May 30, 1929, in a single leap; and though one fears she may have omitted some interesting writing, in principle at any rate the publication of only what is really worth preserving is admirable. In effect, she does the reader's skipping for him; and everything that remains is certainly worth publishing.'

Abbreviations used frequently in FOURTEEN YEARS

A. Aileen Palmer, daughter of Nettie and Vance
A.E. George William Russell
A.G.S. A.G. Stephens
H. Helen Palmer, daughter of Nettie and Vance
N. Nettie Palmer
V. Vance Palmer, Nettie's husband

FIVE HUNDRED *copies of this Book have been printed for The Meanjin Press, of which this is Number* 342

Nettie Palmer

Nettie Palmer

FOURTEEN YEARS

Extracts from a Private Journal 1925-1939

1948

The Meanjin Press — Melbourne

Registered in Australia for transmission by post as a book.

Wood-engravings by Verdon Morcom.

MEANJIN PRESS Books are published by C. B. Christesen.
Editorial address: University Extension, The University of Melbourne, Carlton, N.3, Victoria.

Made into a book by
THE NATIONAL PRESS PTY. LTD., 34 Lonsdale St., Melbourne.

THIS book consists of extracts from a journal kept intermittently over the years, the supplement of a day-to-day factual diary. It opens in 1925 and closes just before the Second War—a period chosen arbitrarily, though not without reason. In part the choice, like that of the extracts themselves, was made with an eye on that rather formidable person, the reader. Nothing here was meant for him in the first place; it was a record for myself and, perhaps, some day, one or two friends; but as one grows older the sense of what is personal and intimate becomes relaxed. There is so little to withhold, after all. Yet what is near at hand, with what belonged to remote youth, still puts out claims for privacy.

Many of the people mentioned in these pages are no longer alive, and as I could not ask all for consent to use their words or their letters, I have not asked any. If my friends should think I have taken liberties with them . . . well, I should be sorry. They will believe that nothing here was set down in malice, much in love and gratitude.

N.P.

CALOUNDRA
(1925–1929)

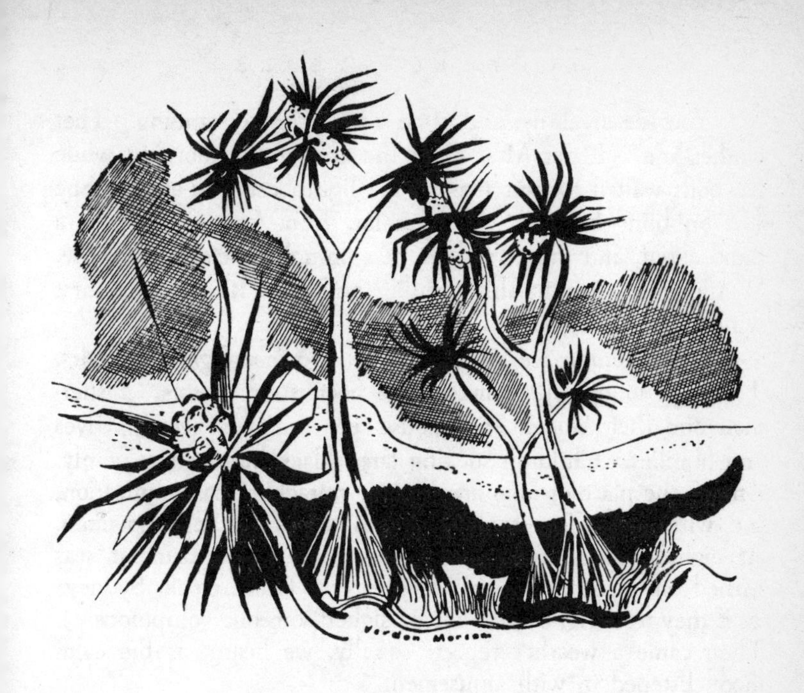

CALOUNDRA

September 20th, 1925

EARLY this morning, we watched a man on a ridge behind Mrs. T.'s house lassooing the branch of a tree with a length of rope. What was he doing? Stretching a clothes-line? But why so high up, and on that slope?

Here in South Queensland, life moves lightly and intimately; you're always looking out of doors at this sunny end of winter. From the narrow shelf of the front veranda, there's the bush sloping towards the ocean in one direction, and towards the Passage with its wide water in another. Along the western skyline stand the unbelievable Glasshouses. Then from the back windows, you look across the open ridges to forest country. You see the casual events of your neighbours' lives, especially when you sit at breakfast in the open sun.

You see dreamily, and often without understanding. That clothes-line? I met Mrs. T. at the end of the morning while we both waited for our mail at the lighthouse post-office. She was bubbling kindly: 'My son-in-law from town's just fixed a radio aerial, and the crystal set he's brought is clear as can be. Would you come in this evening and hear it? It's the first wireless set in Caloundra.'

This evening we went along in the moonlight. In Mrs. T.'s open lounge there must have been sixty visitors. Fishermen and their women; lighthouse-keeper and ex-keeper, wives and families. Children sucking large black humbugs solemnly. And in the place of honour, the new miracle of communication, the wireless. (The son-in-law was a self-effacing showman. At eight o'clock, and before we noticed the instrument was turned on, came heavy strokes—the Post Office clock, Sydney: 'as if they were right in the room,' sighed someone voluptuously). Then came a weather report: squally, we heard, as the calm moon listened in with amusement.

What next? Some 'music' so nondescript that people mostly relapsed into friendly talk while it lasted—as if it were real-life music. So far no statics or interference. The son-in-law muttered technicalities to the few eager youths who could lap up his learning. A speech is announced on the air: 'it's a lecture on Christian Science,' says the son-in-law. For five minutes of it, everyone listens; even the children with their still-revolving jaws. It's so wonderful to have any opinion conveyed whole, like eggs by plane from Sydney. Then people begin asking one another questions. Can everything be caught up by wireless? Could you use it like a listening telescope and direct it to a cathedral service or a trade union meeting? No? Well, who decides what you'll have? It all comes so clear, it might be important some day.

The Sydney clock struck the hour again. The children had sucked away their issue of humbugs. Time to thank Mrs. T. and her son-in-law and go home. We drifted in the moonlight along the strip of rough road. There stood that other aerial mast, the lighthouse, mild winds humming in its flagpole ropes. Its light blinked regularly against the moon, that supreme mistress of communication. Long before wireless, the light was: long before the light, the moon. What was it Andrew Tripcony said yesterday, as patriarchal fisherman in these parts: 'Th' moon's useful; y' always know the tides by her. Quarterflood over the Bar at moonrise. Same at moonset.'

Will the wireless ever catch up with such established guides of mankind?

December 20th, 1925 A YOUNGISH visitor from town had just begun to read Galsworthy and feeling impelled to make literary conversation, said to me yesterday: 'What was the book that came before "The White Monkey"?' I said it was 'To Let,' but she was not satisfied. 'No; it was a much bigger book. One of those sagas . . . I know—"The Forsyte Saga".' So the whole solid structure that Galsworthy built up over the years has been reduced to a sort of porch for one of his fashionable sketchy bungalows.

But perhaps 'The Forsyte Saga' was not such a solid structure, after all. Perhaps one is inclined to credit it with the integrity of its early design. When Galsworthy began it, he was under the influence, the pressure, of men like Conrad and Edward Garnett, who kept him to the austerities of his art as severely as Flaubert kept the young Maupassant. And 'The Man of Property,' that first volume, was something of a masterpiece. What new life it seemed to hold when one read it in those days of youth—in 1906, or thereabouts! It had the form and finish of a French novel, and yet its people were as English as the oaks of Kensington Gardens. There was a compressed richness in every page of it.

In his later books about the Forsytes, Galsworthy never quite reached that level. He seemed to be exploiting people's interest in characters already created, playing with them, adding a white lock here and a wrinkle there. And you noticed he was growing sentimental about some he had originally drawn with a harsh reality. Soames, that tight-lipped, possessive little creature, whose whole mind centred on the idea of property, was becoming a mellow, loveable fellow whose silvering hair you were invited to stroke with sympathy.

And lately Galsworthy has become more flimsy still. Except for the iridescent and unmistakeable surface of his style, there is hardly a trace left of the writer who modelled himself on Turgenev. His latest novels are as full of chic and fashion as an expensive flat, and if you examine the motives of the characters in them you are appalled. Brittle young people who don't seem to have an idea in their heads except to keep jazzing at a post-war pace, and a doting old author with a paternal smile panting to keep up with them.

How calamitous that this trivial world of Monts and Fleurs should have been set up on the base of 'The Man of Property'! Lately Galsworthy has had some straight things to say about the decline in Conrad's books after his rise to popularity, but where Conrad may have lowered his standards an inch or so, Galsworthy seems to have trailed his in the dust.

March 6th, 1926 SURPRISE appearance of four young men, including George Eaton and Dr. Duhig, in a car at sunset. Dinner? They had brought it with them from the hotel and proceeded to lay it out elaborately in the little dining-room. Oysters, chicken and wine. All the materials for a feast, even the trimmings.

Afterwards we sat on the veranda, looking down the Passage, and talking chiefly about the theatre. That was the core of their mission. They were eager to pump fresh life into the Brisbane Repertory movement, and felt this could only be done by the occasional production of original work. For a start, they wanted to put on V's comedy, 'A Happy Family.'

All of them were interested in the ideas and achievements of the Pioneer Players. What had been the quality of their productions? Why had they disbanded? It wasn't easy to find reasons for the comparative failure of that little venture. There were factors of place and time. Melbourne is not an ideal centre for a national movement in any of the arts. It is stiffish, and rather philistine in its genteel, detached way. 'You've got to show me,' is its general attitude toward anything new. Then the time was unpropitious. Since the war young people everywhere seem to have an idea that the cinema is the coming popular art, and that fresh, exciting developments for it lie immediately ahead. To them the theatre appears an outmoded institution, not part of the after-war new world that is coming into being. At any rate, they stayed away enthusiastically from the Pioneer productions. There was Furnley Maurice's retort when Louis Esson asked him had he come to act as our chucker-out:

'Looks as if it isn't a chucker-out you want, but a chucker-in.'

Yet it was inspiriting to hear the way these men talked of creating a theatre here that would reflect our own life. All of them were prepared to put their backs into the effort.

May 3rd, 1926 LIVING in this rather isolated place has made me appreciate the value of local books. Books that may not have much interest for outsiders, but that light up some district for the people who live in it. This district is fortunate; there's Tom Welsby's 'Schnappering,' for instance, which old Tripcony lent me. It was written for fishermen, really, and I know nothing of fishing; but for me it throws a kind of poetry over Moreton Bay—and Caloundra's one of Moreton Bay's widely-separated gateposts—over the quiet anchorages, channels, and tides between the islands, reefs where the schnapper lurk, sailing-boats that were famous in their day, but have long broken up or gone under.

I don't suppose Andrew Tripcony has read half-a-dozen books through in his life, but he clings to this one of Tom Welsby's and gets juice from it. It feeds his own memory, sets him talking as he lies on the cane-lounge of his veranda, his trousers rolled half-way up those brown legs of his that the small boys say are covered with barnacles. For most of his life they've been in the salt water, as he staked the oyster-beds that were his father's before him and, later on, turned to fishing, drawing his nets along the sandbanks. He never seems to feel any drive to get on or make much money. The mullet will come in every May, and there will be always a few visitors wanting to hire punts from him. He grew up on an inlet of the Passage, being one of a numerous brood who lived on whatever the seas sent them, keeping open house for the occasional stockmen, natives and fishermen wandering in. A quiet-voiced, humorous man, with the look of a kindly, experienced walrus.

Experienced—yes; but not through reading or travel. There's no reason to believe he ever left this stretch of half-landlocked water, with its sandbanks and its swans, and he certainly has no impulse to read about foreign places; but books like 'Tom Petrie's Reminiscences' and Welsby's 'Schnappering' enrich the familiar world for him, and perhaps help to make him the decent, essentially-civilized man he is.

September 16th, 1926

FOR the past year I've looked twenty-five miles across at the amazing row of the Glasshouse Mountains, standing along the skyline—pyramid, pillar and dome. It's strange now to find myself lying in a hospital just above the foot of one pyramid, Beerburrum. This little hospital is only 200 feet above the township level, but it's among trees and gets almost a mountain air of its own. A grand place for sky-watching, as you watch skies when you have high fever. You wonder why you have never noticed such marvels at ordinary times, such 'huge cloudy symbols.'

What a time you'll have watching them when you get stronger again! What you have just seen has amazed you—that mediaeval procession with the human tumbler preceding it and twirling like a mace; and then that complex ballet of modern people in a great city. 'There's a cloud like a grand piano,' says a character in Chekhov; but then Chekhov had a chronic fever. There's a cloud like a camel—no, like a whale—Hamlet said; but then he was both fevered and set on teasing old Polonius . . .

And you can't recover that clear, fantastic spectacle when your temperature becomes normal. The clouds drop their insistent patterns and reclaim their literal sober beauty.

But there is a touch of enlightenment about a strenuous fever. To experience a book through the heightened medium—Quixote, for instance! Casting about for something to bring over from Caloundra, V. found a Quixote we had been nibbling at—an old translation, but not unapproachably archaic. When I came here first, he read me chapters of it, day after day. Now I'm normal and able to read for myself, I've read most of the rest of Quixote. But those chapters I've hardly read: I float on them, everything in them is unsteady but glorious—everything from a comical duenna to a fat wineskin or the landscape of La Mancha . . . everything including the strange glory of the idea mankind has known as quixotic.

September 19th, 1926 PROMOTED to the veranda of the hospital and staring all day uphill into the dewy trees, I also prowl into the lounge. There's a small shelf of books. Several have the imprint of the Minister for Home Affairs, who obviously bought them as remainders, and has scattered them through the institutions in his territory. One book is 'Rigby's Romance,' by Tom Collins. The version was published a couple of years ago by De Garis, his editor obviously attempting to come nearer the apparent promise of its title by casting out whole chapters of Rigby's brilliant talk —that talk which so fatally hindered the imminent romance.

Sitting on the veranda, I've been chatting through a french window to a patient inside. A grand little woman with her second baby, she has come down from the strenuous life of a young banana-farm and enjoys (nearly) every moment of the twelve days' freedom. This morning the good-natured youth who does the bedside lamps was speaking to her while he polished. 'That book any good—"Rigby's Romance"?' he asked. ' 'Ow now,' she drawled dreamily, 'veree dr-ry.' The boy gave an extra firm polishing movement. 'Wouldn't think so,' he said, 'to look at the title.'

Poor Tom Collins! After all the trouble he took to be ironic!

November 9th, 1926 A LETTER from Asta Kenney, in London, telling of the work she has been doing lately—translation mostly. How translation into English has improved since the War! Instead of a perfunctory job by a starving hack in Grub Street the Translators' Guild has made it accepted as something between an exact science and a creative art; or at least a labour of love. Edwin and Willa Muir have re-created a series of German novels, and nearly the whole of Proust has been done so well by C. K. Scott-Moncrieff that—well, I for one can hardly remember, except for the feel of the binding, which volumes of Proust I first read in English and which in the original.

Asta tells me she translated, from the Danish, the third volume of Nexo's 'Ditte,' which we were reading lately; but mostly she translates from Norwegian itself. She finds her problems there too:

'Modern Norway—thought and literature—is desperately difficult to understand, even for me. My dear countrymen may know what they mean, but they don't say it in the commonly accepted way; they make up long, weird words that hit you in the emotional centre, and from there the poor translator has to convey them into rational channels.'

Somehow that makes me very happy, in spite of Asta's pangs. To think there exists on earth a language in which people are making up new emotional words as they did in the golden world . . .

December 3rd, 1926 THE most striking piece in Shaw Neilson's 'New Poems' that A.G.S. has just sent me comes at the end—'The Gentle Water Bird'. Striking, partly, because it's a little stricter in rhythm and more directly concerned with ideas than the evocative 'delicate' song we expect from Neilson, but also because of its own quiet strength.

The poem is addressed to Mary Gilmore, who deserved it. I remember how the first letter I had from her, years ago, digressed from everything else to speak of Shaw Neilson and the atrocious life he had to lead—working all day in a gritty quarry and destroying what was left of his already-weak sight. In Melbourne, some time later, did he tell me his eyes were 'sore' sometimes, or did he say 'tired'? ('Let the tired eyes go to the green field' was such a lyrical refrain that a reader might overlook its therapeutic aspect). He was explaining that he hadn't been able to follow what was published; that he could barely read, slowly, Stephens' letters about his work, letters that were urgent for him.

The poem of a water-bird comes obviously from someone who sees things, and even remembers them, without close detail. 'Dim flowers' are generalized by his tired eyes till what he gives is sheer impressionism, as in a landscape painted by Clarice Beckett:

It was a gentle water-bird I knew

. . .

That quiet soldier in his cloak of grey

. . .

the flowers of white and cream

For his purpose, meditative and lyrical, these tone-values are enough, and fitting.

February 9th, 1927 LATELY the idea of editing an 'Australian Storybook' has set me reading the short stories of the 'nineties. Not that I intend to use any of them; the new anthology must begin where A. G. Stephens left off when he made his collection at the end of the century; but I wanted to refresh my memory of what had already been written.

It certainly hasn't been a voyage of exciting discoveries. Who invented the legend that a band of brilliant short-story writers existed in the 'nineties, and that in examining the early files of the *Bulletin* one would stumble upon masterpieces? There wasn't much basis for it. The names are quickening—Alec Montgomery, Louis Becke, Dorrington, Barbara Baynton, Price Warung, Edward Dyson—but the stories above the names are disappointing. Ironic fragments, brisk little dramas separated into scenes by rows of asterisks, sketches of eccentric character, farcical incidents—and that's all. Not much evidence of the subtle, delicate art that can seize upon some episode and give it shape and significance, so that it remains in the mind like a poem.

A page of Lawson's pulls you up with a delicious shock. This is what you've been looking for. Without apparent effort, Lawson takes you straight into his own intimate world and makes you free of it; his easy, colloquial voice has the incantation of rhythm; even his humorous stories stand out from Edward Dyson's in the same way that poetry differs from verse. Until this re-reading, I had accepted Dyson's 'The Golden Shanty' as a sort of classic, but how crude and insensitive it seems beside one of Lawson's comedies! Quite plainly Lawson's short stories have a quality that makes the current grouping of his stories with the others' absurd.

Yet there must have been something about these writers of the 'nineties that gave their readers the sense of a new world being revealed. You can feel it when you place them against the conventional writers of that time—the three-decker novelists and the people who supplied glossy short stories to the American magazines. Whatever else might be said of it, the work of our short-story writers was not marked by a slick emptiness. They were robust; they did not accept circulating-library values; they tried to get near the core of life. This was particularly true of Barbara Baynton and Price Warung. I remember how R. B. Cunninghame Graham, that very eclectic critic, was attracted by Barbara Baynton's writing and compared it with Gorky's—this was somewhere about 1906, when only Gorky's bitter early sketches had come into English. As for Price Warung, he was limited by some conceived necessity to tie his stories to verifiable fact. He could not free himself from the historical convict records. What a masterpiece of pity and terror 'The Secret History of the Ring' might have been if he had been able to lift it from that world into one more definitely his own!

What might have been, though, is not much use to the anthologist. A short story must have its own perfection, or it is nothing. The element of completeness, of art, must enter into it so that it lives as a whole in the mind. Apart from Lawson's work, there is very little use in looking for this kind of perfection in the stories of the 'nineties. If they have left a tradition, it lies in their habit of seeking their subjects directly from life instead of fabricating plots and situations. But there is a greater mastery in Katharine Prichard's story, 'The Cooboo,' published recently in the *Bulletin*, than in the lot of them. What a world of tragedy and strange beauty she has compressed into a couple of thousand words! It is a marvel of economy as well as of feeling—so little stated directly, so much implied. (How is it that in giving the merest necessary background to her story of the remote cattle-country, her phrase 'the tumbled hills' is enough, where it occurs, to make the heart turn over?)

April 9th, 1927

AT last Katharine Prichard's new novel, 'Working Bullocks', is here, and it was worth waiting for. It is as fresh and inspiriting as Louis Esson said it was when he read the manuscript, and it's good to see how he sustains his conviction in a fine Red Page review this week. What strikes me is the confidence Katharine has gained in recent years. She has now set any diffidence aside and writes out of her full self. Confidence is surely one of the main things lacking in our writers up till now, particularly our novelists. They never seemed quite sure of themselves or their public, never were fully convinced of the validity of their own point-of-view, or that there were people to communicate with whose minds were as adult as their own. Katharine's early work was hampered by this. 'The Pioneers' carried a surprising weight of goodness, considering that it had to win the race of an overseas competition; 'Black Opal' had still more. Yet in both books you were only dimly aware of the really original talent hidden behind the conventional cover.

'Working Bullocks' seems to me different not only in quality but in kind. No one else has written with quite that rhythm, or seen the world in quite that way. The creative lyricism of the style impresses me more than either the theme or the characters. From slang, from place-names, from colloquial turns of speech, from descriptions of landscape and people at work, she has woven a texture that covers the whole surface of the book with a shimmer of poetry. As you read, you are filled with excitement by the sheer beauty of the sounds and the images.

And there is the assurance, the confidence, with which it is all done. To gain that is in itself an achievement. It is a break-through that will be as important for other writers as for K.S.P. herself.

August 31st, 1927 A NOTE from S. H. Prior asking me to write an article for the Red Page on the *Bulletin* Novel Competition. Don't bother to pay us compliments, he says in effect, but let us have exactly what you think of the idea's value. This leaves me in rather a quandary. The first thing to say about such a competition is that its value depends entirely on the nature of the selectors and the amount of freedom they are given.

There is no doubt whatever about Prior's good intentions, but the fact that the chosen novels are to be printed as serials makes one a little uneasy. How would 'Jude the Obscure' go as a serial or, to come nearer home, 'The Fortunes of Richard Mahony'? It is not easy to think of either providing curtains for each week's instalment that would whet their readers' appetite for the next act.

Other doubts arise. The plain truth is that our promiscuous reading-public is not used to the deepest kind of reality in books about the background it knows. Since the 'nineties, it has been trained to accept short stories that have a personal view of life—Lawson, Price Warung, Dowell O'Reilly—but as yet it expects our novels to mould themselves on a conventional and accustomed pattern, the pattern of second-rate fiction in all countries—obvious drama and ultimate sunshine. To this public, the man who sets out to be a novelist must be essentially an entertainer, and it does not ask him to be penetrating, or to trouble his head about style, or to have a view of life. It will expect a slick story, using the familiar ingredients expertly in a local setting; and maybe this expectation will put an unconscious compulsion on the judges.

I am tempted to quote, for the benefit of all concerned, part of a letter Conrad wrote to a young Australian author who had sent him a manuscript:

'The principal thing is to write out of the best that is in one. And that one can't do every day. The trouble is not getting paid the uttermost penny; the trouble is in giving good value, in giving stuff with the truth at the back of it; in finding the word, the sentence, the page that satisfies one's conscience, concretes one's vision, expresses the state of one's soul and, at the same time, veils the torment and pain of one's thought.

'If fiction is not approached in a spirit of serious devotion, then the writing of it is a fool's business. There must be purpose in such work. Not in the tale, but in the writing. A "story with a purpose" is, from my point of view, valueless artistically, and therefore it is rubbish. But he who undertakes fiction with no other purpose than earning a living has undertaken a contemptible task. He will never do good work—because he will never think it worth his while to look beneath the surface of things.'

September 25th, 1927 WHAT a strange, attractive character William Baylebridge is—so swiftly generous in his impulses, so shyly elaborate and mannered in his expression of them! A few weeks ago, when I grumbled about the petty journalistic tasks hard-up writers were forced into, and the little time it gave them for their own work, he embarrassed me with an offer that was almost smothered in its cover of apologies and parenthetical clauses:

'. . . And now I come to another matter—the most delicate, the most difficult that ever shook the breast of apprehension—a veritable walking among the eggs (double-yolked, I take it) of friendship. Help me, I beg, with all your patience here, or I shall stumble badly. Keep your pride e'en for larger things, and purge your heart of that commodity in a thing that is nothing. (Here endeth the preamble). If it would be serviceable in any degree, would you allow me to send you ten pounds a month till that competition for the Australian novel closes? Now, away with that raising of the eyebrow, that "God save him" that is about to drop from those doubtful lips. Let us make the business a sweet sin against prejudice, a give and take of no substance either way, a straw not worth waving aside. Write a "yes" into your next letter, and I shall feel I have not been thumped roundly on my pretentious face.'

I had to assure him that he had misunderstood me, that our free-lance work and our small living expenses kept us safe and free; and to-day came another letter full of heavy contrition:

'That "hard-up" you threw on your page was, under the

circumstances as hostile to straight mental walking as the trustless tegument of a banana (let us say) is to physical ambulation; and thereon the feet of my understanding slipped. You use the words fairly enough, of course—'tis the common lot of writers here. But there are degrees in this plight, as in others; and, in any case, enquiry alone could set my mind at ease. My apology, taking heart from your letter, runs to you with both its hands out. And now—a charge we can share gladly—having duly written its hic jacet, let us cast this unhallowed thing from memory.'

November 15th, 1927 AT great old Murrumba this week, I was running my hand along the bookshelves in my room that belonged to a Petrie brother who had left home long ago. Most of the books had been bought by him. I read Boldrewood's 'A Colonial Reformer,' published in 1895 (Macmillan: that smooth, flesh-pink cloth binding; London edition, 3/6).

The book finished with a closely-printed catalogue of Macmillan's books for 1895. (It would have needed Lane's list to give us the Yellow Book and all that it meant. By the way, J. B. Priestley, the essayist, has just compiled an anthology of Lane's poets—it would include the early Yeats, William Watson, Arthur Symons, Lionel Johnson, and a dunamany whatall. Would it have Francis Thompson and John Davidson?

Behold, how on Parnassus' slopes they romp—
The sons of Wat, of David, John and Thomp).

This list of Macmillan's includes twenty-five volumes by Henry James—and he lived and wrote for twenty years more—and six volumes of Kipling, all short stories, except 'The Light that Failed'. The rest of the list says sadly nothing to us now.

And the Boldrewood, 'A Colonial Reformer', plus its 55 pp. catalogue, is a heavy affair—heavy to hold, heavy to read. Good incidental chapters, with natural literary power, but at their close the gentlemanly starch sets in like a killing frost.

To think that this author who had told almost the whole of 'Robbery Under Arms' in the pleasant expressive idiom of Dick Marston, could descend afterwards to this kind of nonsense:

'Here, with the help of a sufficiency of cold water, Mr. Neuchamp (Newchum, of course) restored himself to a condition favourable to the proper appreciation of lunch.'

December 2nd, 1927 SINCE my visit to the Petries' at Murrumba, I have been re-reading 'Tom Petrie's Reminiscences' and making plans to get the book reprinted. In spite of its artless form—the random memories of an old man gathered from him by a devoted daughter as he smoked on the veranda of an evening—it is a valuable source-book. Here is evidence of how the blacks lived and thought from a man who, in a sense, grew up among them. Besides, it has a distinct charm. As you read, the life of that Brisbane settlement of nearly a century ago comes quite near; the windmill that is now the Observatory, the family home at the Bight (Petrie's Bight), the spike of land where the convicts planted maize, since turned into the Botanic Gardens.

Then there are the human figures, white and black, especially Andrew Petrie himself, the Scottish engineer who had come to the settlement in the late 'thirties and made his mark by his energy and public spirit. What a character for Stevenson, or, better still, for the author of 'The House with Green Shutters'! Andrew Petrie had all the virtues except humour, which, at bottom, seems a sense of proportion. For instance, with his Calvinistic morality heavy on him, he could thrash the boy, Tom, for smoking, yet cheerfully let him go off to a bunya-feast in the Blackall Ranges with a mob of wild blacks, many of whom had not met white people before. Isn't this episode typical of the early days! People straining passionately at gnats and swallowing camels without noticing—clinging to a few familiar tabus and conventions in the face of an enormous unknown.

Perhaps it is the way it lights up the old aboriginal folklore that makes the book particularly interesting to me. I had felt instinctively that this district teemed with legend. In the old days it must have had a good food-supply, together with natural features striking enough to release the imagination. There are the grassed banks of oyster-shell, feet deep, you see along the Passage—here the blacks must have come for centuries to eat oysters and fish when they were tired of the bunya-nuts in the ranges. And looking across the plain they would see the strange hieroglyphic mountains strung along the skyline. As Tom Petrie's book shows, they wove their stories about these shining shapes long before Cook was astonished by them and called them the Glasshouses.

February 3rd, 1928 WATCHING sea-eagles on aerial patrol over the miles of unbroken surf-beach to the north, I keep thinking of Robert FitzGerald's poem, published in the *Bulletin* last Christmas. They're impressive creatures, these sea-eagles. Planing, swerving, their serrated dark wings spread, they make an image of implacable power.

FitzGerald's poem is broad as an ode, in seven long varied stanzas; a meditation on the sea-eagles and their country as first perceived by a boy. It begins with a subdued excitement:

Where the land slides into the sea
And is no longer land, but reef and shoal,
A wavering line divides uncertainly
Water from earth; and that's my dangerous goal.

He lets the first vision take possession of his mind, which is clogged by 'the city's dust of noise' (surely the best echo in English of 'fumum et opes strepitumque Romae'). The vision is sustained:

And they have always hung there, always ridden
Upon the liquid sunlight, like great swimmers;
I think they breed there, that their nest is hidden
On a gold cloud-bank where the sunrise glimmers;

Nay, that they never die, but at the last
Sweep flaming through the sunset's carmine portal,
Their wings still motionless and poised and vast,
Royal . . . . immortal.

FitzGerald's a strong enough poet to use hackneyed rhymes like 'portal' and 'immortal,' and make them sound not only fresh but vital and inevitable for his royal theme. He has no strained rhymes in the poem, though he might care to avert some day the rather sickly assonance of that swimmers/hidden quatrain. For all the grandeur, he can write simply, with some of the natural ellipses of conversation: 'and that's my dangerous goal'; but the writing on the two planes is not yet fused into a secure style.

March 3rd, 1928 TO-DAY arrived a letter from Henry Handel Richardson, together with a signed copv of 'The Way Home.' The copy sent by the publishers two years ago is always being lent, and now I needn't be so anxious about losing it.

A re-reading of 'The Way Home' has sent me back to the first volume, and I'm surprised at the way I missed so many of its implications when I came upon it eight years ago. I don't think I was so mistaken about it as Arthur Adams, who passed it by contemptuously as a dull chronicle written by a 'retired grocer', but though I was impressed at the time by the book's reality and depth, I certainly didn't see its significance for this country. It ended so definitely with Mahony shaking the Australian dust from his feet, and Mahony was the core of the book—the other characters, except Mary, were seen from the outside and didn't seem to matter much. My impression at the end of the volume was that Mahony's life on Ballarat would be a mere 'colonial' episode in a long saga.

And then there came Mrs. K.'s quiet protest about my omission of her friend's name from my essay on modern Australian writing. When I went to see her, out came all the books, papers, letters, photographs, from special cupboards. 'Maurice Guest' in English and German; articles on it from Danish and Swiss encyclopaedias; copies of 'The Getting of Wisdom'; even a surviving group-photograph, showing H.H.R. and half-a-dozen other 'young ladies' at the P.L.C., including Mrs. K. So H.H.R. was a woman, and had gone to my own school, where I had never even heard her name . . . I imagine the girls going there now are still in the same state of ignorance –in spite of 'The Getting of Wisdom.'

It's fantastic that with all the newspapers and their gossip-columns you can remain completely uninformed about the people and things that matter. Probably the story of Richard Mahony, if they knew about it, would not be regarded as a good advertisement for the country. It is plain from the second volume that Richard, for all his reactions, is definitely tied to this soil. 'The Way Home' is a bitterly ironic title, surely; where is home to Richard? Not here; not in that England he dreamed about sentimentally in his grocery-store at Ballarat, but hated when he savoured it again. The third volume, due this year, may provide a home for his proud spirit somewhere.

I remember that some time ago, Louis Esson said to me dogmatically, and not troubling about evidence, that the next ten years would see a great development in our writing, especially in the novel. He had no inkling of H.H.R., who was there and fully grown all the time. It seems as if his prophecy may come true.

March 30th, 1928

FROM Hubert Church, in Melbourne, on a point of grammar:

I throw up my hands as regards the use of 'like'. I know nothing of grammar. If ever I learnt any (I can't remember) long since it left me. I know if a sentence is good style or bad style—but could not parse it for Potosi. One must pour out one's ideas from one's own crucible—barring obscurity which besets me at times—and wave them away for good. Once I have launched a poem I never look for it again on any sea.

June 16th, 1928

THIS afternoon, H.B.H., with his associate, John Bourke, left for the sittings of the High Court in Brisbane. The good inside of a week here in Caloundra—an unheard-of spell for him in the middle of the year's work. The break had something to do with a strike of marine cooks that made him come north this year by train instead of steamer; and, as it's nearly half-a-dozen years now since he left the Arbitration Court, strikes don't reflect upon his judgments.

He was in splendid form, erect as I'd ever seen him, and that's saying a good deal—powerful, and yet relaxed as on those summer afternoons at 'Heronswood' when, afternoon-tea over, we used to set off for a sunset walk with the dogs. No signs of fatigue, except that, as always, he reserves the right, if you seem likely to corner him in some discussion, to yawn politely and say, 'I suppose so . . . I suppose so,' closing the argument. He's happy with his associate, this time a man who follows his ideas eagerly. And the weather—so good you could ignore it or lean back against it as you liked. Long afternoons on the sunny, grassed cliffs above the surf-beach, long lunch-times at the hotel, long walks on tracks through the bush.

And talk. Personalities of the High Court, Katharine Prichard's 'Working Bullocks' that I'd sent him last year, accounts of politics in the pre-federation days. We all jogged his memory a good deal, and he went over some old ground, mostly travel. Those days at the outbreak of the War, H.B.H. being in touch with the Webbs, Ramsay MacDonald, and Grey. Remembering how he'd told us about certain things in London soon after, I felt that his present version was not heightened. He has a good deal of quiet humour and a pretty sharp sense of character. Will he ever consider writing his memoirs, or does he feel, as old George Gordon McCrae did, that the people and events of his early manhood are too recent to discuss publicly?

July 1st, 1928 TALKING about the early days of Federation, one afternoon when he was here, H.B.H. fished out some comic verses, celebrating a trip he'd made to Perth in January, 1903, with O'Sullivan, a New South Wales Premier, and Larry Foley. O'Sullivan was an expansive politician, so notorious for his borrowings from overseas that the *Bulletin* always referred to him as Owe'Sullivan. His friend, Larry Foley, a great pugilist in his day, had become a silk-hatted entrepreneur, quite a figure in the social and sporting world.

THE REPENTANT KNIGHT

Don Quixote the modern sets out in the hull of an
Aden-bound boat of the P. & O. line;
He takes on the title of Edward O'Sullivan,
With Larry for Sancho and 'seajoy' for wine.

But what care the waves for the might of Don Foleyo,
For his sinews of steel and his bunches of fives?
You might as well trust to a stick of sapolio
To whiten a nigger or whetten your knives.

Prone, prone in their bunks they awaited the Saracen,
Encircled with belts and with whisky at hand,
For the rolling Britannia their spirits was harassin'
And also the spirits of Jameson's brand.

The whales came along to see the sad spectacle,
And spouted to rival the deeds of the knight,
But Quixote he groaned as he seized the receptacle,
And damned high and low the Australian Bight.

'Say, Foley, to hell with my public works policy,
I'm sick and disgusted with living on loans;
For what we take in, we must give it all out, y' see,
With interest to boot, and expenses and moans.'

Then Sancho he snorted and turned him uneasily:
'Goodbye, Dulcinea del Toboso, now;
Your lover has come to his senses, but queasily,
And no more your beauty supreme will avow.

'In Spain they've an adage that has much publicity:
Consume not the harvest of autumns to come:
Goodbye to your vision of lazy lubricity,
Goodbye to your nostrum for making things hum.'

July 8th, 1928 AT last something is happening in the theatre, according to Louis. He writes about the organization of a new professional company that will make a point of including some original plays in its repertoire, and the first two mentioned are Katharine Prichard's 'Brumby Innes' and Harrison Owen's 'A Happy Husband.'

What a curious pair! Can the choice have been made to confuse those who say that Australian dramatists have a sameness about them? Katherine's Brumby is surely as raw and ravening a figure as has ever been allowed on the boards. And the background of the play—with its corroborees, brutalities, and wild poetry—if its atmosphere can be captured it will certainly send a cold shiver through the stalls.

As for Harrison Owen's play, I don't know anything about it except what I've read in a copy of the *Neue Freie Presse* someone sent me, but it seems the kind of comedy he set out to write when he went to London. There was always a curious modesty about Harrison Owen. He never made any pretensions to creative ability, or even to a knowledge of the life around him. 'I'm just a young man from Geelong,' he used to say. But he had a distinct passion for the theatre, and could spend endless time taking plays by Scribe to pieces to see how they were fitted together. 'A Happy Husband,' his second play, is an international success of an artificial sort. The Viennese critic, after saying that it is a delightful comedy, providing excellent opportunities for fine ensemble work, goes on:

'An English comedy? It is more exactly in the French style of comedy—only with English society figures and a shimmer of Wilde paradox over the whole. It turns on the entrance of a conventional gentleman-burglar (who has studied at Oxford and learnt Latin and a little Greek, and who can smoke or offer a cigarette in the most elegant way) into a conventional triangle scene. The lover, who is where he ought not to be, refuses, for his own sake, to denounce the burglar. The plot gets thicker and thicker, but seems to clear by sheer convolutions and wit in the third act.'

I have been wondering if the new company will have a leading actor capable of playing this elegant gentleman-burglar in one production and Brumby Innes in the next.

October 8th, 1928 THE round, thick, lithe figure of Dick Dalton fascinates me. That easy poise of his, that low, modulated voice, speaking, on the whole, a better English than anyone in the place. When you hear him you forget he's a full-blooded aboriginal, with a clan of piccaninnies and collaterals tucked uncertainly into the scrub on the other side of the saltwater creek.

Last Sunday, when a crowd of country people were down from their orchards in the ranges, he was rowing Dr. Duhig along the channel. The country people were dressed for a holiday occasion—the women in starched frocks, the men in serge suits and stiff collars. Sunday clothes, as decreed by country convention. Few of them could handle oars well. They splashed about and let their dinghies get caught in the current; they flirted water over each other's finery. Dick, moving easily in with his feet braced against the thwarts, watched them with his sad, reflective look. Finally he said:

'You can always tell the bushies; can't you, Doc?'

November 13th, 1928 LUNCH with Randolph Bedford and a party yesterday on the balcony of Parliament House. For years I'd heard people talk of Bedford as a peerless storyteller, one who could hold you breathless in any bar or club, but I've never been satisfied with his published short stories. They have their fine splashes of vitality, humour, imagination; but something—is it in the connective tissue?—makes them emerge as flat and slightly false. There wasn't one of them I could remember except 'Fourteen Fathoms by Quetta Rock.'

But when Bedford tells his stories orally, it's really a different matter, as I'd guessed. They depend on so much more than his words—they're given life by his miming, the turns of his voice, a pause, a gesture, a glance around him. What a raconteur! Yesterday the party consisted mainly of members of his family. He sat at the head of the massive table on this balcony he has made his home and his club, entertaining royally, the light flickering through the jacarandas and playing upon his bald dome as he dressed the salad, mixing oil and vinegar liturgically, pouring out his stories one after another. Stories of mining, of journalism, of the youthful Lionel Lindsay and himself in the Europe of 1905, or thereabouts, when he was pursuing his haughty Explorations in Civilisation. Meanwhile he mixed the salad in its enormous bowl. Come, take, eat this story, he seemed to be saying; hear the green chlorophyll in these leaves dressed with epithets. And an iridescence, more than that twinkling from the salad-spoon, played over his talk. What a pity that all I can remember now of the longest and most dramatic of his stories is that it had to do with a Town Hall and a piece of string on the pavement outside . . .

In a pause I asked him about 'Fourteen Fathoms by Quetta Rock.'

'Ah, that story,' he said, 'I can't get away from it. It's always turning up in magazines and anthologies. And it's true —at least it was founded on fact. Of course, the coincidence of the diver recognizing his wife's body in the cabin underwater by the pendant he had given her, and being overcome by the fact that she was with another man—all that I had to add. But the diver coming upon all those drowned people and being paralyzed by what he saw—that came straight from a Danish steward, talking about his brother in the Flores Sea and why he had given up the diving.'

In a moment he was creating the character of the Danish steward, the atmosphere of a night at Port Said, the foreign voice full of feeling, fumbling brokenly as they leant over the ship's rail:

' . . . Down there he move along slowly, feeling his way t'rough the passages of t' ship. A big shark move along, too, not far ahead of him. He burst open a cabin door and see t' people, all drowned—see t' body of a woman bobbing up against t' wires of a top bunk. He see their faces, how they are frightened. One little boy, he is afraid his father is being taken away; his arms around t' man's knee—his teeth are fastened in t' man's t'igh . . . I tell you, my brudder, he can't bear it. He just signal to be drawn up—quick, quick. A diver have a weak spot—his back. My brudder's back give way. He could be no more a diver. He see too much down there.'

Bedford, as he told the story, was not looking to right or left, nor down the table. His eyes were dazed with horror; he was the Danish steward, the steward's diver brother, the little boy, the father himself—and he couldn't bear what he saw.

A pause, then a click somewhere—two clicks. As if the power were turned off and ordinary light turned on. Bedford was now again the host, with largesse universal as the sun, sending us off with farewells and messages, bestowing patriarchal affection on his progeny, making appointments with one of the secretariat. By next week, with Parliament in recess, he'll be camping on the Diamantina, his gleaming great dome extinguished by his ten-gallon hat, his mind reaching out toward that Life which he always rather crankily asserts is superior to Literature—as if they were separate things.

November 15th, 1928 TURNING up an old letter of Furnley Maurice's, I came across a reference to that story of Bedford's, 'Fourteen Fathoms by Quetta Rock.' 'I suppose it is absurd to say of a diving-story that it won't hold water,' he says, 'but will it?' And he goes on to analyze the coincidences on which the published story depends:

'There are absurdities in fiction that (as one of our neighbours used to say), 'I can't abominate.' But I *do* abominate them. If I think a man is fool enough to think me such a fool as to accept such a fake, then all his carefully-built background, and his years of nautical experience and literary work go for nothing.'

The trouble with Bedford seems to be that his values change and his sense of life narrows when he takes up his pen. Didn't he, perhaps, give himself away when he said, 'all that I had to add'? Who said he had to? No one but that ghost of public taste that presides over the magazines. Part of the reason why Bedford's published stories are inferior to his spoken ones is, of course, that they lack the dazzling life he can give them by his miming, his pauses, and his changes of voice; and he tries to replace these by strained, flamboyant description. But there's more to it than that; the difference is a deeper one, of values. Bedford doesn't trust his reading-public fully. He thinks that life has to be perked up in a conventional way to suit them—a click of surprise here, a conventional motive there—and the result is something a good deal smaller than what set his narrative gift moving. If only he could trust his audience more, trust his sense of life more! When you meet him you feel he has streaks of real genius; when you read him you're only conscious of an energetic and uneven talent.

November 20th, 1928 IN Brisbane last Tuesday, I was asked to a lunch given at a woman's club in honour of a Madame Malmgren, who had come from Finland specially to visit the community of Finnish settlers in North

Queensland. She was, I was told, a feminist, interested that Australian and Finnish women won the vote about the same time. She wrote in English, contributed to English reviews, knew Bernard Shaw . . . but something clicked in my mind as I listened. 'Mme Malmgren, a writer from Finland.' I remembered a paragraph in the London *Observer* lately, something like, 'The authoress, Aino Kallas (who is Mme Malmgren, the young wife of the Esthonian Minister to Finland) is now on a visit to London. Elegant and graceful, she speaks excellent English and is much interested in international affairs.'

So Mme Malmgren, now in Queensland, was the Aino Kallas whose short stories, translated from Esthonian, had so impressed me. A remarkable collection, 'The White Ship,' mostly studies of peasant groups finding themselves in a glimpse of freedom after hundreds of years: group comedy, communal pain, always with a wild gleam of poetry . . .

'Oh, so you know what she writes. Well, we'll put you at one side of her, and you can make a little speech all about her literary work; others can speak about her politics.'

I agreed. It would have been a terrible howler to entertain Aino Kallas and say nothing about 'The White Ship.'

Mme Malmgren was there. Looking capable, motherly and intelligent, she was robust and florid in vague hot blacks. So much for journalists' descriptions, I thought. I said her mission to Finns in this country interested me very much; did she find them happy? Oh, yes; her countrymen had settled down here and were working well. (Her countrymen? Wasn't that rather stretching a point for an Esthonian?) And about her writing in general? Yes, she was doing some articles on politics and Australian social life for Finnish papers. And for Esthonia? Perhaps, she granted, her articles would be reprinted in several neighbouring countries.

'But,' I pressed a little, 'what about your distinguished stories, Mme Malmgren, definitely upon Esthonian themes? Your "White Ship" has reached English readers, you know.'

Mme Malmgren looked at me. Evidently I was not the first she had had to look at that way and for the same reason.

'You mean the other Mme Malmgren,' she said firmly, 'you are thinking of Mme Kallas, a visitor to Finland. Yes, I know her stories. I do not like them. They are very morrbeed.'

That was at the salad course. I managed to ask her some questions. By the time strawberries and cream were over, and while more fortunate lunchers were drinking their coffee, I stood up to make my small, my inescapable speech on Mme Malmgren's literary activities.

December 27th, 1928 FROM Keith Hancock, now of Adelaide University:

I'm glad you approve of my *New Statesman* articles. Some of them have caused offence—to the class of people who writhe at criticism and prefer the noisier brands of patriotism. I am not distressed that Australia is not England, nor am I disturbed that England is not Australia; each has its own life, that I like. I put off my English clothes in Australia, and my Australian clothes (some of them) in England. The great advantage of this is that it helps you to get an outside view of both places, while being inside. Of course, this is just what the historian wants to do, and my models are Machiavelli and de Tocqueville. What I write about Australia will be objective and critical, with an occasional unavoidable declaration of my nationality and belief. My job now is to do 'Australia' in Benn's World Series.
So far I've been working through the economical and political situation, and I can't say that I find it particularly encouraging. I agree with you that we must retrace our steps towards—not to—the liberalism of last century. We've put too big a superstructure on our foundations, and we're mistaking the superstructure for the foundation.

January 19th, 1929 FIND that with half of me I'm bitterly regretting our decision to go back to Melbourne. It's necessary because of the children's schooling and other personal matters, but will we ever again find a place so rich in all that makes for happy living? Quiet days of work, with odd hours on the beaches or the flower-plain; and then the breaks at the week-end—tramping up barefooted over the wet sand to picnic at Curramundi, or rowing over to the lee side of Bribie Island. There's been time to read and think, even to enjoy the company of the casual visitors who've wandered in. People don't unbutton themselves so easily in town. What long talks we've had on this old veranda, looking down at Maloney's boat coming in or watching the swans flying up the Passage about sunset!

Strange to remember that we only intended to stay a few weeks when we came here. We've stayed nearly four years, and the place has become part of us.

MELBOURNE
(1929-1932)

MELBOURNE

April 15th, 1929 STRUGGLING and settling into 13, Chrystobel Crescent, Hawthorn. The girls scraping into the P.L.C. well after the rolls have been closed for the year. V. is working mainly on 'The Passage,' begun in Caloundra. (For once a novel begun with its name ready beforehand, almost as wonderful as a baby born with all its teeth).

Lucky this old-fashioned house is so roomy; it has to hold more than we expected. When H.B.H. died suddenly in January and I felt moved to attempt some account of his life and work, I didn't count on so much accessible material. A trunkful of intact family letters going back to the 'sixties in Ireland. Letters from outsiders—personal and political—in a large case of little drawers. Pamphlets and personal documents in pigeon-hole cupboards from H.B.H's. law chambers. Diaries and note-books from all periods of his life. All these things have been assembled and sent to me here. Nothing remains but to write the book.

Yet I'm finding it hard to capture the right attitude of detachment. Perhaps I oughtn't to attempt the book while the atmosphere of family piety remains. Perhaps I'm the wrong person to do it. When I was four or so and they told me about God sitting on a cloud in the sky, I always saw Him with a face surprisingly like Uncle Henry's: H.B.H. being the eldest of a very compact family. On the other hand as the only grand-daughter, I heard any gossip that went around in what, I think, must have been an unusually restrained clan: that is, sometimes I saw H.B.H. *en pantoufles*.

('When you're trying to show a character,' says Louis Esson, 'don't leave out important things like the height and weight. And catch your subject as often as possible in slippers.')

So—to write the book, putting all hesitations behind me. If I had any serious doubts they were swept away by what I found yesterday. Those two large exercise-books, begun about 1925, and containing detailed recollections of early childhood and youth, with my name mentioned in the opening page:

'Nettie has repeatedly urged me to write my recollections . . . A'Beckett wrote his . . . I have no children to vindicate my memory.'

May 30th, 1929 The newspapers announce the death of Barbara Baynton, or rather it is a Lady Headley they are concerned with, the wife of an eccentric English peer and a woman of fashion. There is hardly a word spent on the writer—perhaps they aren't really aware of her.

In truth there do seem to have been two distinct Barbara Bayntons—one a follower of fashion and current values, and the other a gusty, original personality, who nourished her talent on Scandinavian writers and spoke with a forthrightness that had the effect of a strong bush wind on London gatherings. How brilliantly apt was her 'Dingo Dell' for that rather hybrid meeting-place of Anglo-Australians known as the Austral Club!

A pity her work isn't better known; it had real power behind it. As the young wife of a country doctor she had gone through certain experiences that left a vivid imprint on her mind, and instead of sentimentalising them she re-created them with a harsh and relentless irony. The bush-woman alone in the hut with her baby, cowering from the madman who prowls outside; the old shepherd apologising subtly to his dog for letting the ewe and lamb into his hut; the pregnant girl tracking home through flooded country and night-fears to her mother and finding her dead. There is a feeling of cold objectivity in these stories. The writer doesn't go out of her way to win your sympathy for her characters. Her words fall as mercilessly as clods on a coffin.

And yet isn't there, perhaps, sentimentality of a kind, in this detached pose, after all? What is sentimentality but an effort to squeeze more feeling out of a situation than is warranted? and there doesn't seem much difference between doing it with brutal methods or tearful ones. Barbara Baynton's stories belong to a day when the best of the young writers were reacting against rosewater romance. She herself reacted with vigour and emphasis—too much emphasis. Sometimes she leant over backwards in her attempts to strip the idyllic cover from the appearance of things. Going over 'Bush Studies' just now, I came across this description of a railway engine in plain country:

'Suddenly the engine cleared its throat in shrill welcome to two iron tanks, hoisted twenty feet, and blazing like evil eyes in a vanished face. Beside them it squatted on its hunkers, placed a blackened thumb on its pipe and hissed through its closed teeth like a snared wild cat, while gulping yards of water.'

It reads like a feminine straining after power at all costs. And the images destroy one another. The old man squatting on his hunkers, placing a blackened thumb on his pipe, is wiped out by the wild cat. So with a good deal of her writing.

Yet one is always conscious of a strong and original mind behind her stories. Was it because of a false theory of writing that they failed? Plainly the people she wrote about mattered a good deal to her as human beings. She was once half-amused and half-indignant because a critic compared them—characters like Scrammy 'And and Squeaker's Mate—to denizens of the London slums: she couldn't understand it at all. For her those bush types weren't the remote rather sub-human people that actually emerge from her pages.

June 19th, 1929 YESTERDAY the post brought Robert Fitzgerald's first generally published book, 'To Meet the Sun.' It's robust: the poet feels nothing but his own possible limitations and he doesn't let them beat him either. But I found myself saying to someone that F. was modern in his approach. What an avalanche I brought down!

'Modern—not he! Look at his fixed forms, his rhymed stanzas, his iambic beats. Did you never read the Imagists' free verse, or their manifesto? And look at the Americans today—Sandburg as chaotic as Chicago, E. E. Cummings with little spitting lines even breaking at half a word—*that* sort of thing's revolutionary and modern. What's modern about FitzGerald?'

That wasn't a question, merely a challenge. What's modern in him? It's his new naturalness within fixed forms, 'working out a new poetry in the framework of the old.'

In every age, some poets are dissatisfied with those just before them, especially with the swarm of little bad imitators that make their masters absurd. Tennyson was made ridiculous by e.g. the Alfred Austins with their sugared water. So young poets, round 1900, throwing away Austin, threw the baby out with the bath. They threw over Tennyson, Shelley, Milton—abandoned every vestige of the iambic line in blank verse or rhymed couplets as it has been striding on for centuries. Adopting free verse of a broken-off sort, they sometimes—like the Imagists—made a doctrine of their practice: but most of what they actually produced read like notes for poems—perhaps noble and vivacious like those of H.D.—poems that themselves remained unwritten, for fear of falling into commonplace.

To discard traditional forms, with all their echoes in the minds of men, is one way of revolution. The other is to use those forms in a new way—'every age getting the iambic line it deserves'—Shakespearian, Johnsonian, Tennysonian, etc. You can see the line undergoing a new change sometimes in the hands even of a head-in-the-air like Shelley, who can let an emotional current tilt the line sideways yet leave it gloriously afloat. This sort of thing:

and a wind
Shall rush out of a sighing pine-forest.

That line, exceptional for Shelley, is from a passage about an ancient wise man on the Black Sea; a passage that haunted the mind of Yeats in his youth. First the subject of the passage, then the rhythm of the line. Yeats was soon writing his own disturbed, intimate line—a simple one:

And the light wind, blowing out of the dawn.

And that freedom, found so early, to vary the five beats in whatever way seemed natural to him, has made it possible for Yeats to write with the profound, intimate naturalness of his great maturity.

FitzGerald is of course a modern poet in this second mode Yeats has shown him how possible it is to use the freedom he needs, talking to himself, arguing with himself, 'making from the quarrel with himself poetry.' Already in the 'Sea Eagles'

FitzGerald could risk his heroical stance as of a Roy Campbell and change his uniformity of manner for an inward unity:

. . . water from land—and that's my dangerous goal.

In this new book there is the meditative love-poem:

It is not that I am anxious to set aside
The just claim to charm, constancy, grace
Of any slim beauty, but that I trace
In none resemblance to my heart's young pride.

Surely that's what it means to be *inwardly* modern. Contrast it with any challenging free verse, on the one hand, and, on the other, with William Baylebridge's consciously archaic formalism in his 'Love Redeemed' sonnets.

August 4th, 1929 OLD Mr. Y., keeping his habit in making after-speeches at literary gatherings, tonight again led round to the fact that in his youth and as an office boy he once met Meredith. All very well, but there have been more important conjunctions of planets. Someone yawned to me, 'And did he once see Shelley plain, I wonder!' The answer is probably *no*: but it's dawned on me lately that Meredith's father-in-law did.

Thomas Love Peacock lived long enough to have been Shelley's intimate and Meredith's. It's certain that Peacock discovered his satirical vein through living with Shelley and Harriet, among a group of Shelley's followers. Romanticism in Shelley he could bear, provided he was allowed to laugh at it gently: but in Shelley's followers, who had all the faults of romanticism, and none of Shelley's genius, the thing was unendurable. The situation reminds me of Gorky's account of Tolstoy with his humourless disciples. Peacock and Harriet saw the joke together sometimes, and Peacock saw it in line with similar jokes for the rest of his life. In his memoir of Shelley Peacock wrote:

'Shelley was surrounded by a numerous society all in great measure of his own opinions in relation to religion and politics, and the larger portion of them in relation to vegetable diet. But they wore their rue with a difference.'

Rue, it may be noted, is vegetable: nothing else would serve. Peacock created one of these devotees as Mr. Toobad in 'Nightmare Abbey,' who was an impersonation of a single theory, that of opposition to animal food and spirituous liquors. Single theory, though? It was dual enough to serve for two people in the hands of Peacock's son-in-law, long after. In 'One of Our Conquerors' Meredith describes a festivity at which two people confront each other: a man who execrates meat and a woman who abhors alcohol. You are invited to watch their pangs as each contemplates the other indulging in mortal sin.

Vegetarianism was a rarer heresy in Peacock's and Shelley's day than in ours; it would not have gained ground if most vegetarians had been as ethereal and unpractical as Shelley. Finding Shelley in bad health Peacock advised him to substitute for his customary diet of tea, lemonade and bread-and-butter 'three mutton chops well-peppered.' Such was Peacock's advice to most men, except that he always remembered that dine rhymed neatly with wine.

If I drink water while this doth last
May I never again drink wine:
For how can a man whose life is a span,
Do anything better than dine?

After that it is enough to add that Shelley had such a respect and liking for Peacock that he recognised himself as the moony poet in 'Nightmare Abbey' and was not perturbed. Peacock managed to remain Shelley's friend, in spite of deep sympathy with Harriet, and when Shelley died it was Peacock who arranged his affairs.

August 14th, 1929 THIS evening Keith Hancock came to dinner bringing his completed manuscript. V. happened to go to the door when the bell rang, and there was some delay—apologies and explanation in the hall. I could see what had happened—again. When will Keith Hancock, with all his honours on his head, stop looking so young that anyone could mistake him for the youth next door? He's still fair and slight; and year after year it's only the rare inwardness and concentration of his eyes that show how far over twenty he is.

Not that he's at all old. He's the youngest professor in Australia as well as one of our most enterprising scholars, willing to share his good luck—that is, his exceptional knowledge—with every student. His impulse as Rhodes Scholar to extend his opportunities, to study in Italy and write as a thesis his vivacious Risorgimento study of Ricasoli—though it led to his becoming a Fellow of All Souls—Oxford, has still left him with his life, his life-work, ahead of him. Now a professor of modern history, he's made enough time to write this thoroughgoing book, 'Australia.' It was some of the earlier chapters that he came to discuss this evening. We had had them separately to look through before. I felt proudish of one small suggestion. He'd described timber-getters as 'stout fellers of trees.' I was protesting elaborately that in present day dominant jargon the phrase 'stout feller' would infallibly be taken as an agglutination, not to be loosened into normal English . . . but I had no need to labour the attack. W.K.H. just put his head back and laughed on an open vowel, in the way an Oxford scholar permits himself to laugh, the one really Oxford gesture he made. None of the sardonic lipless Australian about it: 'stout feller!'

September 3rd, 1929

IN a letter from Brent of Bin Bin:

I am happy that you think I have achieved 'communicable delight'. *Communicable.* The attempt to make others feel and see as I do the atmosphere and unique qualitics of the landscape which are spiritual breath to me, is half ecstasy—in almost capturing it—half torment in feeling that it is an impossible feat and that I am so feeble for it. How to make strangers realise a beauty in which I am soaked, and enjoy a love of it . . . one must just plunge, trusting to luck not to be merely a bore. At best the greatest geniuses need other hearts attuned to nurture their lay or it is drought-smitten from the start. 'The listening heart' as I heard an unlettered little Italian girl express it.

I find myself capturing a technique to retail the subtleties of Australian life and landscape. It seems to me that a story to be truer than reality (that mirage effected by grouping and selection) should follow natural contours and rhythms. A pulse artificially accelerated, or extraneous outlines because of spurious conventions as to what really is 'action' should be eschewed. The desultory style of pioneer settlements themselves should be suggested, growing up unpretentiously as they did to meet immediate need. An easy unrazored, pipe-smoking—almost casual—method is needed. The old pioneer yarns 'yarned' by the old bush grandads (with as like as not a grandma contemptuous of this inconsequence and deviation from original versions) rubbing their tobacco in their palms and holding up the climax (they mustn't have too much climax) to light and draw, have a charm as characteristic as their environment; but the assembling of a vehicle to carry that easily-evaporated charm into print 13,000 miles away needs ingrained knowledge and loving patience.

September 25th, 1929

'THE trouble about this country,' said Will Dyson last night, 'is its mental timidity. Physical courage—yes, I suppose it's got its share of that, perhaps a little more than its share, but put it face to face with a new idea and it goes all of a tremble. For years we've been boasting that we're youthful and adventurous. It's all boloney. In things of the mind we show about as much spirit as a suburban old maid.'

And he began to lay the blame on our intellectuals. They hadn't the courage of their convictions. They were outspoken together in their little secret corners, but they never came out into the open. They had let the guidance of the country fall into the hands of rich drapers, financial entrepreneurs, newspaper owners, people who in other countries were kept in their place. Here these people were allowed a free run—they had all the resources of publicity at their disposal and they spoke with assurance. Could outsiders be blamed for believing that their crude pronouncements represented the thought of the country?

Furnley Maurice—we had asked him to meet Dyson because it seemed absurd that they should have lived in the same town for four years without knowing one another—was inclined to be gruffly offensive. Did it matter so much what outsiders believed about us? A country's life didn't depend on the notions outsiders formed of it. There was as much thought and creative activity going on in Australia as anywhere, but you couldn't expect the people engaged in it to waste their time in a struggle for limelight; after all, it didn't matter to the drovers and prospectors who were really opening up the back country if Michael Terry, a young Englishman, won fame as an explorer by following in the tracks they had travelled effectively for years.

Dyson, however, was savagely satirical about the retiring Australian who was content to work in silence and let others—outsiders or colonial-minded people—speak with the country's voice. It was sheer mental timidity, he insisted. The intellectuals didn't believe in themselves sufficiently. They were half-persuaded that the rich drapers were the important people after all. It was another version of the treason of the clerks. The intellectuals, with their old-maidish modesty and diffidence, had let the country become a backwater, a paradise for dull boring mediocrities, a place where the artist or the man with ideas could only live on sufferance. It wasn't a question of what outsiders thought, but of the condition of Australia itself. Was it ever to fill its empty mental spaces and become a country fit for adults?

An evening of conflict, with Dyson less witty than usual,

more inclined to use sword than rapier, slashing out wildly at other people and perhaps at himself. More than a hint of frustration in him. As Furnley pointed out afterwards, his charge of mental timidity might easily make a boomerang sweep. In London he won fame by his dash in attacking the whole world of political and social humbug; his dazzling cartoons became known throughout Europe; men like Shaw, Wells, Orage and Chesterton gave homage to him. Yet here, on the home ground, how muffled his attack has been! In four years hardly a line or a word that would penetrate this skin of mediocrity or pretentiousness. Is it that some power has gone out of him or are the odds here too heavy? He is going back to London by way of New York, where he'll have an exhibition of his recent etchings on literary themes.

October 5th, 1929 YESTERDAY Katharine Prichard arrived on her round trip from Perth, a trip that included Singapore. There was some uncertainty about her train. After lunch V. went in to meet her, chasing Louis, who in the meantime, had come out to Hawthorn to invite us to dinner. Finally we all met at the Essons' over a sumptuous lobster meal, the sort of festival Hilda knows how to produce with miraculous speed and gaiety. Stewart Macky managed to come in for an hour in the middle of his medical engagements.

Katharine talked of her journey up the West Australian coast, stopping every day at a port, pausing for a wonderful fortnight at Broome. A crowded month at Singapore and inland. In spite of her long days of travel she looked radiantly alive, physically even more graceful than in the past, her mind teeming with impressions of odd characters, remembered bits of dialogue, her humour and understanding playing about everything like a soft light. She seems to be moving along very buoyantly on a full tide of assurance. In a way she's found herself. Even in those old days in London she knew the kind of books she wanted to write, but she was wavery in her approach to life and unsure of her powers. Now without having lost any of the sensitiveness which made her pace the floor of her Chelsea flat all night after finishing the newly-published 'Sons and Lovers,' she's gained a sort of toughness. She can be deeply moved by the treatment of natives on the stations behind Broome, yet can look at the whole question with clear unsentimental eyes.

December 9th, 1929 THIS afternoon Gerald Byrne brought Shaw Neilson to see us and they stayed on till evening. Neilson could have just managed to travel alone, as he does by train and tram every day to his exacting 'sinecure' in town, but his weak eyes make it hard except on routes he knows well.

Besides, it's clear Gerald enjoys taking this little responsibility, as well as doing more serious things for J.S.N., even to taking down a poem if for once Neilson feels well enough to dictate it. Not that Gerald, that ruddy-faced pessimist, would once omit his formula that life's not worth living—while helping to make life distinctly easier for someone he admires.

As for Neilson, he's a grey wisp of a man now, not exhausted by violent effort as he used to be in the country but regularly tired by his daily job, tramping the corridors to conduct a deputation of Yipp Yipp shire councillors to some all-highest, tramping in another direction to bring the file relating to Yipp Yipp. Not being able to do clerical work he has this as alternative, with the regular three weeks holiday in the year.

And with the week-ends—too short for making poetry but enough sometimes for talk—Neilson has begun to enjoy a few encounters with his more constructive admirers. Blamire Young, as decorative artist and as a manipulator of words, has written some warm pages about his poems and Neilson has been out to his home in the soft valley below the Dandenongs. And Margaret Sutherland, experimenting with combinations of instruments, has composed a setting for voice, piano and clarinet for that most atmospheric ballad 'The Orange Tree.'

When Furnley Maurice dropped in about five, Neilson was talking of the few poets he had been able to read. In his good days, he came on Padraic Colum's 'Wild Earth' and it meant a lot to him, perhaps giving him confidence to use naive rhythms and simple themes that suit him. But through the years the bulk of his reading has undoubtedly been the letters pouring in from A.G.S. Blessing and cursing, admonishing, praising–and sometimes bringing models to his notice, so that he knew what Heine had written, and Victor Hugo, and something of other poets whose names meant nothing to him.

'And you've kept all those letters?' I asked anxiously, knowing Neilson had had to move about and travel light.

'I kept them for years,' he said, 'but in 1917, you know, there was the mouse-plague over the Victorian wheat country. Every scrap of paper went. The only letters of Stephens I own now came during recent years. I haven't been able to take all his advice, but he's been a wonderful friend to me–sometimes a bit awkward, though, when he knocks someone else down with the idea of building me up.'

He made this remark at large and 'to whom it might concern.' It was an honourable disclaimer of agreement with all Stephens' long-standing hostilities or sudden slaughters. If there was anyone in the room who had suffered . . . Peace!

January 4th, 1930 I WONDER if that beautiful lady I knew not long ago who never wrote a letter with anything but a pen she cut from the feather of a sea-eagle was the last person on earth to use a quill pen? A graceful sweeping hand she wrote.

She was not a writer and letters with her were only incidental to more urgent cares. How do writers write? At present from what we hear some novelists use typewriters, card-indexes, even adding-machines of new and newer types. But I like to think of earlier writers. It's on record that the Elder Dumas allowed all Paris to rejoice with him in his magnificent labours. He would boast of 'writing' a book in a month; then would drive out for public homage. Sometimes, causing his carriage to draw up with many splendid curves of *rallentado,* he would enter a stationer's. This moment of selection was most important: his materials were paper and pens, but what paper, what pens! Three shades of writing paper—blue for novels, pink for plays, yellow for poetry; a special pen for each. It was his pleasure so, and did no harm: though only what he wrote on blue paper ever lived. Blake had a simpler procedure:

And I made a rural pen
And I stained the water clear.

The point is that where authors name their tools, whether multi-coloured paper or a 'rural pen,' they are naming secondary things. The whole work has to be planned in the mind before the tools take hold of it. Dumas had his characters all ready—as far as they ever would be so—and straining like greyhounds in the slips, before he let them loose across miles of blue paper. Blake saw his 'Songs of Innocence' in the clouds before he wrote them down in stained water. Nothing matters like this preliminary brain-work, this power, for instance, of seeing the end of a lyric implicit in its opening. Without it a lyric is a mere string of verses fit to be chopped off short at any point. A novel that is not composed as a whole in the author's mind can never be saved by brilliant passages that seem like recoveries.

Yet how many novels do we read that stand up, beginning and ending like a perfect rainbow with an inherent form? How many, on the contrary, have a broken back, collapsing perhaps at the half-way so that thereafter the book 'like a wounded snake drags its slow length along.' When I read a novel whose author obviously believes in his characters to the end, clearly foreseeing in broad outline the last page while he writes the first, I feel I am reading something that (but for the accidents of neglect) will live on. And that book may have emerged either from writing or re-writing by the patient pen, or from assembled mechanisms and card-index cupboards culminating in the alert receptive dictaphone. It shouldn't matter. If the book was great enough, no reader would know.

March 7th, 1930 RE-READING Francis Adams in the Public Library last week, I took down some passages from his 'Australian Essays.' They came in 'Dawnwards: an Australian Dialogue' and the portrait of the young man, Frank Hawkesbury, seems so closely modelled on Bernard O'Dowd in his youth that I'd always taken for granted Adams wrote with him in mind.

'Frank Hawkesbury, the young Australian poet; a socialist delighting in Trade Unions, Religious Revivals (the Salvation Army is a hobby of his) and Secular Organisations, with grand impartiality.'

When Hawkesbury talks about the platonistic Time-spirit and about liking the Booths better than the Bradlaughs his voice has the very rhythm of O'Dowd's. So last night when O'Dowd was here with a few others I took the chance to ask him about Francis Adams. To my astonishment he said that he had never met Adams, and that certainly Adams could not have known of him in 1886 when 'Australian Essays' was published, obscure as he was then and not yet twenty. By the time he woke up to Adams as a writer, he said (particularly through 'Songs of the Army of the Night') Adams was settled in Brisbane. For O'Dowd it might as well have been in Europe, for he was an intensely busy young man doing his University course (Arts, then Law) in evening lectures, organizing and teaching in various ethical societies. He married young. He was deeply-rooted in Melbourne. He couldn't make a journey to Brisbane as Jephcott did, even to meet Francis Adams. By 1893 Adams had left Australia, and a year later he was dead.

But Frank Hawkesbury? Who put that three-cornered pattern into Adams' mind, since O'Dowd apparently didn't? Was it common among the young intellectual revolutionaries of the 'eighties when all kinds of ideas were fermenting? O'Dowd was sixteen when he gave his public lecture in Ballarat, 'The Indictment of Jehovah.' He was already an ex-Catholic, a rationalist, yet with impulses toward organized Christianity—now to that of the church he had left, now to the street-preachers with their songs like 'Dare to be a Daniel.' Like Hawkesbury he had a mystical faith in the future of the People, dedicating his first book to 'Young Democracy.'

Hard to believe he's nearing seventy. A young-looking elastic figure, in pepper-and-salt tweeds, the pockets bulging with papers, and the serious boots of a man prepared to tramp anywhere, town or bush, at the week-ends. His face is normally far less intense than in his early middle-age when I knew him first; and his preoccupation is not the making of poetry but the drafting of laws. (Friends quote his torrential old line: 'Not a law was a boon to the people but a poet dictated its draft.') Yet in a group he's still inclined to accept someone's casual assertion or query as an invitation less to a reply than to an emotional utterance. This is given standing, the rhythmical expression being induced or augmented by a wave of the body, a hum of the voice, a beating of the left foot. In short a bardic prophet still.

As for continuity with his past in other ways, Marie Pitt says that when a Salvation Army group pauses in their suburb, Bernard cannot keep himself from joining it.

April 6th, 1930

NO sooner had I found myself meditating enviously on the power wielded by the publisher of Everyman Books, and noticing too that we are passing through a pro-German period (Lessing's 'Laocoon' being on the new list and his comedy, 'Minna von Barnhelm,' being produced in a recent Irish season) than I was pulled up short! The Everyman reprint of 'Moll Flanders' recently issued has been put on the index by our enterprising but mysterious censor. A classic is to be tossed into the discard by semi-literate officials who probably heard its name for the first time yesterday and scented lechery. The book that George Borrow's apple-woman on London Bridge a century ago used as text-book for flaming morality is to be kept from Australians, even in the sobriety of an Everyman volume—and this when all the salacity of the last irresponsible Naughty Novel is let pass without discussion or mention. When enough Australians are often as angry about this sort of thing as I am tonight something will happen . . .

July 17th, 1930 FROM V. in London:

. . . Perhaps it's because I'm on holiday that everything seems so springy and buoyant. June weather, lively well-dressed crowds in the parks. Every outdoor entertainment thronged, from Lords to the airfield at Hendon, where I went to an international display with Rowland and some Foreign Office people. No hint of the depression that was beginning to throw a shadow over Australia when I left. I may be hyper-sensitive but people here seem rather to gloat over the idea of Australia coming an economic cropper and having to take orders from an agent of the Bank of England. 'This will put them in their place,' is the general attitude.

The sensation of the moment is Bradman, who takes up considerably more space in the papers than Mussolini. Even Henry Handel Richardson was curious about him when I saw her the other day. Was it true he was a country boy? What would this kind of notoriety mean to him?

In literary circles there are faint echoes of the American battle between Babbitt's Humanists and the moderns. At Rebecca West's on Friday she and Amber Reeves were discussing it. Rebecca thought that the conflict wasn't purely literary: that Babbitt and Paul Elmer More were using this rather dead discussion as a defence against the more creative elements in American life. She asked me what I thought of American criticism. I said I regarded Edmund Wilson as the best critic on either side of the Atlantic, and she agreed.

November 22nd, 1930 YESTERDAY morning in the little library he now runs, Furnley Maurice showed me a couple of bare lines in the paper reporting that a girl's body had been found, mutilated and half-naked, in a back lane at Elsternwick.

'That's Molly Deane,' he said soberly.

I gasped a protest. It couldn't be. Such things didn't happen to people you knew. But soon the afternoon paper was out with flaring headlines and all the ghastly details of the murder—at least with accounts of the dead girl's movements, interviews with people who had been with her, and speculations about the crime. There was no doubt the victim was really Molly Deane. She had been with friends to a Shaw play, had caught the last train to Elsternwick, and after waiting a few minutes for a bus had set out to walk home.

The crime has shocked Melbourne more deeply than anything I remember and ever since yesterday morning I have been thinking of nothing else, but in a numb shattered way. I have had no contact with violence before, never imagined it entering my world. Frightful things happen, but to read about them doesn't bring them nearer to you. They remain shut off in their own underground part of life; only people who have a special doom set on their brows are involved in them!

But could anyone have foretold that Molly Deane was one of these? There was that evening a fortnight ago when she came to the Essons' with Colin Colahan, looking eager and girlish in her tight red jumper that went so well with her slim, athletic figure and olive face. Quiet, but with a dusky glow about her. Half-worried about a paint-stain on her flaring black silk skirt, half glad it was paint—not domestic grease. Listening to the talk about pictures with a still alertness as if she had escaped from a suburban background into a new exciting world. Now life begins! This is what I've been looking for!

Somehow I can't help feeling that the meaningless tragedy is part of the cloud that has been lowering over the city this past year—the sense of wheels running down . . . the shabby hawkers drifting from door to door . . . the line of defeated men sitting on the Post Office steps. This isn't a rational feeling. The murder is surely one of those inexplicable crimes that might be committed any time. But it makes shadowy figures in the street outside seem more sinister, awakens a distrust of life in you, sharpens your sense of a violence sleeping beneath the unrevealing surface of these days.

December 3rd, 1930 READING Forster's book of Clark lectures on Aspects of the Novel, and thinking, between chapters, of Professor X., for whom the novel was an occasional holiday subject. As a lecturer to students of classics, Professor X. was superb. He could go over all the variant readings of some piece of text making his students feel that each wouldn't quite do, till suddenly a light—as of new discovery—brightened his eyes: 'But—why not try it this way?' And of course, this happy inspiration opened the sentence as neatly as a nut. We were all impressed, even when, on examination, the perfect reading had first been found by some monk in the twelfth century. It was a grand method of lecturing, letting you see the problems in turn, letting you share in the solution.

But when he left Greek texts and began to talk about the novel, it was another matter. I bitterly remember a newspaper article of his that opened something like this:

'As for the novel, I think when we are looking for masterpieces we must go to the well-known purveyors, Messrs. Scott, Dickens, Thackeray, George Eliot and Dumas.'

And Dumas! This noted classicist who, all his life, had been impressing his students with what they owed to Greece and Rome, could not, when looking at the past century or so, so much as cross the Channel except for a tripper's weekend to bring back Dumas.

Forster, being a writer, is more deeply concerned with literature as a whole.

'My subject is the novel in England,' he begins; 'an unpleasant and unpatriotic truth has here to be faced. No English novelist is as great as Tolstoy—that is to say has given as complete a picture of man's life, both on its domestic and heroic side. No English novelist has explored man's soul as deeply as Dostoievsky. And no novelist anywhere has analysed the modern consciousness as profoundly as Marcel Proust . . . "Cranford," "The Heart of Midlothian," "Jane Eyre," and "Richard Feverel" are little mansions, and we shall see and respect them for what they are if we stand them for an instant in the colonnades of "War and Peace" or the vaults of "The Brothers Karamazov".'

How I would have felt fortified if I'd had this passage to quote to Professor X. at the time! But it would have been sheer waste: I found later on that I had taken his bland pronouncements about the novel too seriously. When we discussed the matter years afterwards, he told me confidentially that the novelist he found most delight in was Agatha Christie.

'I'm afraid I take the novel entirely as entertainment, and who could be better than Agatha Christie?'

January 15th, 1931 FROM Hugh McCrae, in a letter about Archibald Strong who died in Adelaide last September:

Did you see the notice on Archie Strong in the 'Quarterly'? I loved Archie (you didn't) and so I couldn't help feeling grateful to the man who had stored up so many pleasant memories of him.

I can never forget Archie's laughter; nor the clout on my leg at the end of every one of Archie's stories.

Archie's talk, Archie's wine, Archie's tobacco, Archie's fireside.

Another man who has refused to die.

March 9th, 1931 AT the Essons' last night the conversation turned upon criticism. Louis' contention was that for a short sprint, the creative writer was the best guide to the art and craft of writing. He can't stay the course, like a Sainte-Beuve, he admitted; that isn't his own course, anyway; but he has certain things to say that no one else can. And though, when he looks at literature in general, he isn't likely to be catholic in his taste, he has a deeper knowledge of what it is all about.

We went over some of the things authors had written about their intentions and the impulses behind their own work. There was Maupassant's preface to his short novel 'Pierre et Jean,' showing how he read his stories to Flaubert on Sunday mornings for nearly ten years before the master allowed that one was fit to publish; there was Conrad's revelation of how his first novel, 'Almayer's Folly,' was built on a lonely figure he occasionally saw on the wharf when his boat called at a remote river-port in the East Indies; Chekhov's notes on books and writing in his letters; Henry James's prefaces; Synge's small memorable introductions to his plays; all short enough to be gathered together in a single volume, yet worth more than tomes of exposition.

Since the Essons have come to live in our street we have dedicated Sunday night to talk. Louis prepares for one of these evenings, if it is at their place, as if he were setting the stage for a play. The chairs must be in the right place, the fire going properly, the glasses ready. Conversation has always been one of the main delights of life to him, but lately he has come to depend on it more and more. He has a wonderful memory for what other people have said over the years, flashes of wit, or merely some phrase that has lit up a particular situation. The Elizabethans and Lamb are still his chief stand-bys, but he's always curious about what the younger writers are doing. What is to be expected from Brent of Bin Bin? Hasn't the achievement of Henry Handel Richardson and Katharine Susannah given a new fillip to our prose? Is Chester Cobb a real writer, or just a clever journalist exploiting the stream of consciousness? Has the Barnard Eldershaw couple got staying power, or is their novel likely to be all they'll do? Usually he's boyishly hopeful about anyone who has shown promise, but sometimes a writer's style or subject strikes a blind spot in him, and he retreats behind his cover: 'He can't write like Charles Lamb.'

March 19th, 1931 FOR a long time I've been paying, in casual articles and notes, my humble tribute to Edmund Wilson as the most penetrating critic in the modern literary world—the Anglo-Saxon one at any rate—and yesterday an unlooked-for response came from him in the form of a signed copy of his new book 'Axel's Castle.' I've found it hard to keep my mind from it ever since. It has all the brilliant clarity of his occasional critiques, together with the thematic backbone you expect from a book—in this case the idea that the six writers he chooses as significant figures in the literature of today are guided, like Axel, by a will toward refusal.

The six figures are Yeats, Eliot, Joyce, Gertrude Stein, Proust and Paul Valéry. At first you are a little surprised at the choice of names, but Edmund Wilson shows how certain socially-minded writers before the war—Shaw, Wells, Bennett, Anatole France—have lost credit, while his half-dozen have gained by producing masterpieces in isolation, almost secretly.

These books revealed new discoveries, artistic, metaphysical, psychological; they mapped the labyrinths of the human consciousness; they made one conceive the world in a new way. What wonder then that for those who survived the war these writers should have become heroes and leaders?

The more so as they have deliberately cut themselves off from the disillusioning world of action. Edmund Wilson shows how Eliot has 'ineffectual fragmentary imagination, impatience, and resignation'; how much Proust wrote as one who had taken leave of life, and how 'his whole elaborate work might have been based on Axel's contention in regard to foreign travel that the reality never equals the dream'; how Joyce's latest hero remains asleep through an entire novel, and how Gertrude Stein has spun herself an impenetrable cocoon of words, withdrawing into herself completely. As for Yeats and Valéry:

'Yeats with his astrology and spiritualism, his reiterated admonitions (in spite of considerable public activity) of the inferiority of the life of action to the life of solitary vision; Paul

Valéry's M. Teste, sunken also in solitary brooding so far below the level where the mind is attacking practical problems that it is no longer interested even in thoughts which have for their object particular fields of experience—and Teste's inventor, the great poet who can hardly bring himself to write poetry, who can hardly even bring himself to explain why he cannot bring himself to write poetry . . .'

That quirk is almost the only piece of such acrobatics in 'Axel's Castle,' and at the same time it is an entirely necessary piece of lucidity. How else express Paul Valéry's arrested vitality side by side with his great poetic power!

Wilson doesn't attempt to belittle the literary capacities of any of his figures; he is merely trying to analyse what their withdrawal from the modern world means. It is not a withdrawal like Rimbaud's who rejected the civilized society altogether and went off to find the good life in some country where literature didn't exist and mass production hadn't arrived. It is a retreat, he insists, into Axel's Castle, which has only occasional contact with the world around it by the drawbridge over the moat. And for writers who are unable to interest themselves in our contemporary society, either by studying it scientifically, by attempting to reform it, or by satirizing it, there are, says Wilson, only two alternative courses to follow: Axel's or Rimbaud's.

Yet this argument isn't the whole of the book. A great deal of its interest lies in Edmund Wilson's skill and distinctness in showing just how each of his writers has made us conscious of the world in a new way.

May 17th, 1931

THE big Van Gogh print of an old peasant in a yellow hat that Theo sent from London has been acting as a fire-screen all summer. You can stare at it for hours and not grow tired of it. Coming in tonight, one of Meldrum's students gave it a hostile glance:

'Who's your modern painter?' But he eyed it with a sidelong curiosity all evening.

It's strange how that austere old peasant dominates the living-room. It's not the mere arresting colour of his blue blouse and yellow hat; it's the build of the face, subtle as Conrad's, yet direct and earthy above the broad shoulders. A devoted piece of work; plainly the work of an artist who would rather paint than eat. Van Gogh's terrible choice was literally between those two. Years before his death he wrote to his brother: 'My health would be good enough if I hadn't to go hungry for so long; but it's always been a choice between doing without a meal or doing less work, until the time's come when I'm too weak.'

'Up till now' (he's writing from Arles the following spring), 'I've spent more on paint and canvas than on my own living. My money was gone by Thursday and from then till midday on Monday was horribly long. I mostly lived on 23 cups of coffee during those three days—with some bread I still have to pay for. I was so crazy to see the pictures framed that I ordered more than the budget would allow, considering the month's rent was due . . .

'If I'm baffled physically, yet give life to thoughts instead of children, I feel I am part of humanity all the same. I'd rather earn 150 francs a month as a painter than 1500 francs by any other means.'

Lately I came across a different measurement of value. Speaking of 'grumbling, girding painters, musicians, writers and dilettanti—quite a large class,' Arnold Bennett went on to remark:

'These parasites on society cannot, or apparently will not, understand that the first duty of a poet is not to write poetry, but to keep himself in decency, and his wife and children if he has them, to discharge his current obligations and provide for his old age.'

How admirable was Arnold Bennett who knew how to

keep himself not only in decency but in luxury, yet wrote immortal works!

August 18th, 1931 FROM Marjorie Barnard, discussing the biography of H.B.H. I've been working on:

You class your work as not creative: but isn't biography at least a quasi-creative art? The author supplies form and manner. The raw material of a novel is 'given'; the author pieces it together, arranges, edits and synthesises it; only in doing this has he more scope than the biographer whose first duty is to interpret and analyse. I have always looked on history as one of the creative arts, and in my youth acted on this assumption, not without success. Of course one's classification of creative work depends upon whether one places the emphasis on form or content. My natural tendency is to attach much more value to form than to content, and I think I'm right, too, but that it's a mistake to think so—on the analogy of watching pots and loving life.

August 20th, 1931 TO-NIGHT Basil Burdett, who has been staying with us for awhile till he finds his Melbourne feet, read some of his sketches aloud. He's desperately anxious to achieve a mastery over words—partly because he'll have to earn a living at journalism now that he's given over his Sydney gallery, but chiefly, I think, because he wants to find some means of personal expression. He's in the unhappy plight of a man who lives for Art yet can't find full release in any art. In a way he knows more about painting than any man in the country—knows its history, is a keen judge of pictures, has spent happy, devoted days in many galleries of Europe. But he can't make a significant stroke with a brush.

In music, it's the same. It's an intense pleasure to listen to him on the piano any hour of the day, playing some prelude of Bach's, some Scarlatti or Debussy. You feel then that he was meant to be a musician; he feels he was meant to be one. Yet he missed that rigid training European children of talent get almost as soon as they can walk, and knew before he was in his teens that he could never be more than a third-rate executant. Composition? I suppose that depends to a large extent on a tradition, too. The great composers seem to have learnt their notes with the alphabet.

Listening to his sketches tonight I felt he wasn't likely to succeed at writing, either—at least not at the kind of creative writing on which he has set his heart. It isn't a matter, as he thinks, of achieving skill with words, but of seeing things with an individual eye. Basil's scenes were all blurred by what he has read—and he has read most modern novels worth reading in English and French. In spite of some details, it wasn't Sydney episodes he was describing, but episodes that might have happened to some of the minor figures in Proust.

A man like Basil who moves from one art to another sometimes seems as civilised as anyone I'm likely to know—yet he's a hopelessly unhappy being. He is so keenly sensitive to all the arts, yet can find fulfilment in none. And they keep him from seizing the life about him with his full imagination. To him it's dull and dispiriting compared with the intensities of art; he can't see it as material for art, as the real artist can. And he carries about with him a sense of frustration.

If only he could accept his position and use his keen intelligence and perception as critic and entrepreneur! What endless scope there is for both! But for him there's a middleman flavour about such a function. Though he has a strong patriotic feeling he could never be really at home here. In Paris and London there are happy corners where people, not artists themselves, think and talk about art; I've a notion he would feel less a fish out of water there.

September 26th, 1931

WENT across this afternoon to see Bertram Higgins, convalescent from a broken ankle. He was on a chaise longue, in the garden of the old family home, a roomy rambling villa. Three or four people on the lawn—mostly disciples who look upon him as a rare visitant from the world of Eliot and Valéry. Weeks of enforced quiescence have made Bertram's mind keener than ever, even in daytime—usually he begins to warm to a long complete discussion about midnight. Today his slight figure looked fatigued, his face fine-drawn, though he is grimly amused by his mishap.

He was letting people assist him in 'assembling' some background details for a long poem that is taking months to write. 'Not,' he said in a firm severe aside, 'not that the poem is entitled to any special consideration on that account.'

So far as I can gather, the poem's to be in free verse—his own variant of it. A kind of rhapsodic monologue by a Jew, old enough to have witnessed the Crucifixion and to be now experiencing the eruption of Vesuvius at Pompeii. The present darkness over the land recalls to him the darkness of a day forty years earlier. In the darkness of death he feels his way alone, toward an illusory safety, still, *in extremis,* chiefly concerned with the meaning of life for himself.

But the man's name? That's very important. It must show him as what he is—a Jew of Rome, a Romanised Jew. Would he change his original name to Gaius, Caius? But that would obliterate all his origin. Could a Latin ending be put on some Jewish name—David, Absalom? There was Josephus about the same time. Someone ran through great Jewish names: Moses, Nehemiah, Ezra, Daniel, Mordecai . . . Mordecaius! The last part overlapping to give the appearance of a pure Roman name, it makes a wise pun fit for Joyce.

It was forthwith decided; the title of the poem would be 'Mordecaius.' The name need not be used in the actual lines, nor will Mordecaius ever say plainly, 'I am a Jew, now a Roman citizen. I was at the Crucifixion; now I am at Pompeii.' All this will underlie his soliloquy, and the title, 'Mordecaius' will have the task of making what revelation is allowed.

For as a poet Bertram believes in having a strong basis of fact and learning and philosophy (Aquinas and sunspots and spectrum and 'The Golden Bough') but such basis is to remain invisible, implied, never explicit in the actual words of the poem. His readers must dig, dig for their experiences; I heard one admirer say proudly, 'I got that last poem of Bertram's "out" first time.'

This deliberate secrecy (hermetism?) comes as part of the reaction in England against the Georgian poets, the Georgian readers, and their easy hopes that more and more people may read and hear more and more poetry with less and less effort. I can't guess how Bertram would have developed as poet or critic if he had remained in this country. As it is, having spent his years since the age of seventeen in Oxford and London, he dedicated his remarkable powers to a movement akin to that of Valéry's followers in France. This English movement found expression chiefly in the London periodical, *The Calendar of Letters*, in which Bertram assiduously collaborated for its duration, as well as in 'Scrutinies,' a subsequent collection of residual essays, searching and critical. The *Calendar* round 1927 undertook the task of revaluing widely accepted reputations, its withering bleak wind and cold light blasting Galsworthy, Arnold Bennett, Masefield, and other too easy victims—somewhat as Orage had deftly done nearly twenty years before. This habit has led the Scrutineers—led Bertram at any rate—to turn his deadly ray on his own fastidious poems of a few years earlier. There's that poem of his that I cut from the *Saturday Review* years ago and pasted in the back of my copy of the Oxford Book of Australasian Verse, a reproach to the anthologist for his omission. A brilliant poem on conscience, the ancient Demon, the Daimon, written with ease and power, and meaning more each time you read it. But Bertram won't show me any others of that period—say 1923—nor even rejoice in his paternity as regards the Demon. I can only quote the first line of that poem:

Where is the ancient Demon now?

November 12th, 1931 WHEN I answered the door-bell this morning, dolefully expecting some hawker of the Depression, the huge figure on the mat made me gasp. The only other time I had met Paul Wenz was in Sydney at his hotel, where perhaps in the high-ceilinged lounge he didn't look quite so high and broad. That meeting was a lucky accident—he just back from one of his little round-the-world excursions and stopping in Sydney on the way to his out-west station, while I was on my way through from Queensland. And he had got in touch with us because the Red Page had published a note of mine on his writing that very week. One of his novels—was it 'Le Pays de Leurs Pères,' that light war-novel of Australians in England?—had come from Paris that month.

But now he was over in Melbourne on business. In he came, with his Norman blue eyes from Rheims, his fresh colouring under white hair, his broad square shoulders that made you wonder how the man had ever found a horse strong enough to carry him across the miles of his sheep station. What he said seemed to need a great deal of room. Cups of morning tea looked small and apologetic: he should have been offered great bowls of Norman cider as he talked of his new absorbing scheme for making cheap motor-fuel out of charcoal—'there are plenty of trees going to waste here!'

But I had several of his books to thank him for lately: all marked by a spareness, perhaps a slightness. There was 'L'Echarde,' that little novel—all his novels and stories are smallish and schematic—about a frantic woman in the bush who became a burden to the whole district—a splinter in everyone's finger. There was his book about his childhood in Rheims and at school in Paris: 'Il Etait Une Fois Un Gosse.' Pleasant in itself and—what's more unusual—satisfying to your curiosity about what a man expected of Australia before he left home to come here. The Wenz family's special connection with Australia as regular wool-buyers used to fill the children's minds with stories and cram their big storehouses with bales of wool. The children playing among these bales saw them opened and came to expect queer finds in them—a dried flower or burr that had come 10,000 miles. That was Australia: very far, very large, very dry. 'And then when I arrived here in the nineties,' says Paul Wenz, 'there was a drought. And I *hate heat*: and I began with thirteen months of it on the Murrumbidgee.' But at least he had known what to expect.

As a boy at school in Paris, though, was *he* the 'grand Wenz' who shared in a scrape with André Gide? (I was wondering lately when I was reading Gide's 'Si le Grain ne Meurt'). It could be only himself or a brother, equally 'grand.' It was himself, he says: and now Gide reads some of his books, as the chapters or stories appear in French reviews.

The last book he sent me was 'Le Jardin des Coraux'—a pair of Sydney honeymooners on a Barrier Reef Island, their idyllic days broken into by the arrival of a French convict, escaped from New Caledonia, the story ending in horror and death. I felt a little embarrassed in speaking of it; the book read like a sort of synopsis, 'read this and *begin* today.' Lyrical or nothing, the theme as he has handled it is not lyrical, not atmospheric. It needed the hand of a Conrad at least.

But taking it by and large Paul Wenz has had a lot of satisfaction from his books, which after all have been only an incident in his full expansive life. If his gas from charcoal succeeds as well . . .

January 6th, 1932

LAST night, among a crowd of young people, writers or near-writers, I quoted an incident from 'Lord Jim,' and was surprised to see a blank look spread over their faces. Interesting, if painful, to notice how Conrad's reputation has descended; into a nadir, or at least into a trough between two waves. Partly, I suppose, it's mere reaction from the enormous fame he had at the time of his death—the imperial atmosphere of his last trip across the

Atlantic, the interviews and descriptive articles. It was a quite unusual acceptance for a distinguished writer—something more like the fortunes of a shrewd best-seller. Publishers and agents spread his reputation far beyond the minds of those who really enjoyed him.

So now his artificial public has left him and as yet there is no young, eager public discovering him again for themselves. When they do come across him by accident, these young people, they shy away. For them, Conrad is someone who had no explicit social-critical content, no required jargon about ideologies at all. A rhetorical writer, with a belief in the individual and in unquestioning standards of honour and loyalty; abstract virtues, and beneath these a whole dark unconscious world that he saw fit to indicate and then treat only with respect and silence. Leave such jungles to Joyce and others; more significant drama for him lay in those jungles of the Congo where isolated men were trying to hold on to their integrity.

Of course it's natural for young people to renounce the idols of their fathers, but there seems something more than this in the present reaction against Conrad. All the emphasis to-day is on intelligence rather than feeling, on taking the world to pieces and examining it rather than in celebrating the virtues that would hold it together. Isn't that the task to which Joyce, Eliot and the other cerebral writers consecrated themselves? And young people accustomed to this cold analysis look at Conrad's abstract virtues with a sceptical eye. That undiscriminating virtue of his—loyalty, they ask, to what? When Conrad makes his captain and crew slave through sleepless nights to keep their ship afloat in a gale there is a mystical ideal of service at the back of his mind, a tradition of discipline and fortitude that seems sacred. To fail or slacken shows more than a personal weakness; to Conrad it is almost a betrayal of the fundamental laws of the universe. The Lord Jims who crack in a crucial moment carry a brand of Cain across their brows. But what if the ship they are sent out in is some old freighter, loaded down to the plimsoll-line, and intended by its owners to founder so that they can collect the insurance? Who or what is entitled to their loyalty then? The profiteering owners? Or the doomed ship itself? Is there any value in a mystique of service that never troubles about the ends to which it is devoted?

Conrad, with his sharp intelligence, must have been aware of such complications, but he seems to have evaded grappling with them. His world, he persists, was founded on a few simple ideas. But after the simple ideas and emotions of the war-years young people seem to meet anything with a note of interrogation. Liberty, for whom? Loyalty, to what?

March 19th, 1932 IT isn't quite clear to me why the Goethe memorial celebration (Gedenkfeier) last night was so moving. Partly, I suppose, it was because we felt that all over the world, in the parts at all aware of European civilisation, they were remembering that figure of harmony and creative strength.

Here the programme was unambitious, almost hackneyed; yet worth-while. *To remember*:

Tiny statue of Goethe in front of the stage with a huge laurel-wreath flopping round it.

In a pause, the Professor of Germanic studies coming round amongst us near the front, and displaying, as in a monstrance, an authentic signature of Goethe's on an ms. by Eckermann.

The performance on the simple stage of the old Turnverein Hall. Schubert settings of two Goethe lyrics sung gravely, sweetly, by a young conservatorium student, dressed in the tenderest gauzy pink with rosy bows at strategic points, altogether a modern version of a Löttchen or Lili. The sincere applause with no demand for encores; this was a Goethe celebration, not an exhibition of some young girl in pink bows.

A recital, with no lights in the hall and only a candle, real, on the stage table, at which sat Faust to give his first, despairing speech. Generalised medieval costume and the wide black velvet beret of that Eternal Student. How he groaned as he began

Habe nun, ach, Philosophie
Und leider auch Theologie

with every listener ready to give a different sort of groan if he altered a single word.
The singing, by a firm bass, of several Goethe songs, notably the Erl-König, with orthodox emotion and good style.
Acting, with normal platform lighting and no scenery, of a scene from Goethe's Tasso, by a group of young people, mainly of German parentage and obviously used to speaking good German in their homes.
Finally a male choir, mostly elderly men with frock coats and some even with old-fashioned beards, standing in a semi-circle to sing. Young German-Australian 'cellist nudging me: 'The Undertakers' Union!' she giggled, but even to her it wasn't so funny. The men sang several Goethe songs, unaccompanied, in an assured harmony. And the last song was Heidenröslein, to the traditional air, not Schubert's: a delicate national anthem, the audience joining in (unison).

The simple programme, its items too well-done to seem hackneyed, struck me as generous and humane: 'its beauty made me glad.' At the same time, its beauty seemed threatened—precarious.

What is this modern Germany? Does Goethe, leaning forward benignly from the past, obliterate the frantic noises of the rabble desperately following false prophets? Was Dyson right in saying that the humane theme of 'Sergeant Grischa', the satirical reminders of Feuchtwanger and others, had won for Germany in her most difficult days the suffrage and sympathy of the world?

Again, will this quiet evening, illumined by songs and poetry that Goethe gave his countrymen to enjoy forever, will it be repeated everywhere, year after year, like a humanist Yom Kippur, or a poetic declaration of the Rights of Man?

March 30th, 1932 WHAT made me transcribe these fragments of prose, odd poems, into this rather big exercise book during the last year or two? I've just found urgent use for the little collection. It's as if we were getting ready for a march across a desert and found food and drink ready packed, miraculously condensed—portable.

After three years in this roomy suburban house, with books spread about and oozing even into long shelves in the front hall, to plan life in a simple tent on a Barrier Reef island has meant asking, 'What do you use for books?' For books are not to be packed in our luggage, which must anyway contain enough awkwardly heavy things, like blankets and lanterns.

One or two very small books seem to have waited for notice till now. A shabby paper-covered Maximes de La Rochefoucauld—specially good if you've time to peer through their chinks at the world according to Roi Soleil; an old 'Paradise Lost'; a book of Chekhov's stories in Constance Garnett's version.

And there's this exercise book. Some things in it must have been written down quickly, to be considered in some freer future—now in sight? Others are long half-known.

There's no table of contents for this Emergency Ration; but glancing through it I see the kind of thing that has accrued:

A page of masterly cantankerous prose from George Moore. A gleaning of Wells' 'phrases'. Aphorisms from a German review. A paragraph from 'Coonardoo,' bird-song at dawn.

Some poems the girls copied for me in their firm print-script—Yeats' 'Wild Swans at Coole.' A rare piece of Alice Meynell, another of George Herbert. A new lyric Eileen Duggan lately enclosed in a letter. Ruth Pitter's 'The Waters of Paradise' kept from the *New Age* of 1919.

Some paragraphs of literary brooding from Katherine Mansfield's Journal, a sardonic international page from Neumann's Life of Basil Zaharoff.

Well, if we can't live on concentrated nourishment like this, as well as on our own accumulated literary fat, then we must be in worse condition than I think we are.

GREEN ISLAND
(1932)

GREEN ISLAND

April 7th, **1932** THIS island, now we're here, is a flat oval of jungle-covered coral sand (almost forty acres, they say) on the inner edge of the Great Reef. Not even eight feet above sea-level, it's protected from the outer seas by an irregular circling reef that encloses a lagoon—shallow enough to wade through when the tide's out, but deep enough to float a small fleet when the tide rushes back again through the narrow opening. There's always five or six feet of water at the end of the long ricketty jetty that gives a berth to the Cairns launch bringing the Sunday crowd of holiday-makers—and our supplies and mail. Our camp is on the sheltered side of the island, looking toward the mainland. Sometimes at high tide the water softly laps the roots of the great trees that lean over our tent and down over the beach.

Before I came here I'd imagined the Barrier Reef as a great wall running along the line of the coast—a rampart of pure coral rising from the depths. Now, looking out from our knob on its edge, it seems a straggling assortment of honeycomb reefs in all stages of growth, varied by fragments of sunken mainland, such as the great hump of Fitzroy Island to the south. Our island is one of the coral cays that have come to maturity. It has fully emerged from the sea, collected its cover of humus, created a beautiful safe jungle in which you can lie unaware of the sea, though never fifty yards from the beach.

This gleaming little forest of vines and evergreens can seem at times even more wonderful than the coral reef itself. There's a gentleness about it—no thorns, poisonous reptiles, stinging insects. Instead, there are the unafraid birds—tiny silver-eyes, ground-pigeons with lustrous wings of dark-green—and the bright, flickering butterflies, all seemingly sure of being in some forest fastness.

April 14th, 1932 THE IMMENSE apparent nothingness of sea and sky in the calm of early morning! An opaque sheet of silver-grey under a toneless sky. Going down to bathe you've turned your back on all the complexities of the island. (There are these complexities: the elaboration of the jungle-trees and their singing birds; the letters, books, journals from the outer world in our tent, our note-books—those battle-grounds of words.) The simplicity and guilelessness of the sea, then. One white reef-heron stands alone on the pale low rocks towards the east: its long neck is raised, making a question-mark. On rainy windy mornings it stands there just the same, but neckless, its head crushed down into its shoulders, unenquiring.

The one heron, the sea, the sky. No land in sight. The sun not yet up. Void.

With a tearing sound, not a dozen feet out, several small, slender fish—garfish?—leap incredibly high to skid madly along the surface on their tails before vanishing into the sea again. Then, more incredible, a powerful trevally, perhaps two feet long, throws a curved leap into the air after them, striking the water, it seems, just behind them. After that nothing again, except that the sun rises.

April 17th, 1932 BEING driven in early from our explorations by a tide that turned too quickly, we saw near the shore some very attractive figures with poised spears. So that tubbish mission-lugger was in the lagoon! We had seen it from the outer reef as it rounded the island. The three blacks were circling round a rock-cod that they'd driven under a ledge of coral. Hatless, of course, and wearing dark-whitish cotton Jackie Howes (two of them a scarlet loincloth) they all had headbands that looked in the distance like curious liturgical fillets.

These were no symbols, though, no phylacteries. Diving-glasses are worn like that, tied by a leathern latchet at the back of the woolly head, the double discs pushed up high on the brow. When the men go down, they pull them over the eyes, which they fit closely, the thick glasses taking away the glitter and tremolo of the water and giving clear sight.

The oldest of the men is Richard, the captain of the lugger. Middle-aged, in short-long trousers, he has a faint fuzz of greyish beard on cheek and chin, and his eyes are bright under his wispy hair. His companions are young; a tall youth, nineteen, perhaps, deft with the spear, and a younger, smaller boy, Joseph, very bright-eyed, on his first serious voyage.

'Had much luck?' we ask, striding past in the shallows.

'Only cod—and sud-deen,' says Richard.

The sardines they had caught by throwing their pronged spears into the dark, cloud-like masses that gather in the lagoon as the tibe ebbs. But this is only sport for them. Their serious work has been diving for trochus and beche-de-mer in a long, three-months' voyage up the Reef. And now they are on their way home to their mission-station, twenty miles away on the mainland.

Richard talks about their work and its hazards.

'When you see fish you got to go down. Ten feet, twenty feet it might be.'

By fish he means beche-de-mer, lying on the sandy sea-floor. Asked about the depth he can go down, his ancestral politeness constrains him to let you name the number of feet you prefer, while he assents to it, the truth being pushed further and further away, in any direction. Similarly with other questions.

'Is the outer edge of the Barrier Reef near here?'

'Oh, yes, very near.'

'Is it perhaps, ten miles?'

'Oh, yes; close up ten mile.'

'I thought it was further than that.'

'Yes, much further.'

Amiability could do no more. But he is better on measurable ground, his feelings about his work.

'Yes, it give you headache at first, and you don't get much better about that. Shark? No, I don't think about that fella much. I look at it this way: shark want food, but they rather have other thing for beef, not me. The day they want me, that my unlucky day. Not come yet.'

And young Joseph, listening, looks at Richard's faintly-grey hair and nods, feeling that he himself has many years to enjoy before his unlucky day.

As they are leaving, Richard, his eyes bright, his teeth glistening near his flicker of round beard, says shyly:

'To-morrow we go home. To-night we all come ashore to dance. You come along and see?'

April 22nd, 1932

I HAVE been thinking of that dance and song of the mission-blacks the other evening. It was a rehearsal, we found, for the corroboree they would give to their friends at the mission-station across in

Yarrabah Bay when they arrived home—a sort of report of their voyage up the Reef. As we saw it, it happened like this. From their lugger, lightly swinging in the lagoon, they came ashore at twilight, about sixteen of them. They had chosen a clearing where there was grass under palm-trees, and when we went along from the camp they were still sitting on the tiny cliff-edge, running through a few songs as a dreamy preliminary. One of the songs had a few English words let into its pattern:

B-rmm b-rmm across t' water,
Across t' water to Green Islan',
B-rmm b-rmm to Green Islan' . . . .

Then briskly, the time being come, Richard stood up and called the rest in to the dancing-place under the softly-waving palms. There were a few yellow-flamed storm-lanterns and some carbide-flares, acid and white. As the men came forward, you saw they were mostly dressed in their ordinary clothes, perhaps rather heavy when this meant trousers and shirt; yet their mood was not matter-of-fact at all, but very grave. They formed in rows of four, all turned the same way, with Richard in the front row. A 'drummer' faced them, crouching a few feet away. Then they began.

As the evening went on, it became dimly evident that these few men, in dance and song, were presenting the routine of their own lives at its highest points. There was the leave-taking from Yarrabah on the mainland, the setting sail up the Reef. They find a good place to fish and anchor, the boys go down. An alarm! Is it a groper or a school of sharks? Something startling or tragic has happened. They up-anchor and sail on.

One dance succeeded another, each sustained by the singing of the dancers themselves. Or did the dance sustain the song? Both the music and the movement seemed, through many repetitions, to reach some point of climax together, and to cease with strange punctual certainty. There was no accompaniment beyond the steady drum-beating—really a stick on a kerosene-tin, without much variety. It was simply, as called for by Richard, 'one-time' or 'two-time.'

Who made these songs, these dances? They were put together, we found, on deck after the day's work. But there isn't much room to rehearse dances on the decks of a crowded lugger, hence 'to-night we come ashore and dance.' This was a rehearsal for the corroboree they'd give at home, with wives and children and old men as audience—an audience ready to respond to every point. Every point! How much we must have missed! I wanted to hear every song over three times to make sure of the rhythm, the simple but definite melody, and perhaps to remember some of the movements. Their clothes—how ordinary they were—just the flapping Jackie Howes worn outside, and any sort of dingy long-shorts, with sometimes a red loin-cloth over them. Yet somehow these clothes came to seem symbolic vestments almost adequate for their ritual.

Only one man was dressed in character, as if for an occasion. A man? A youth, a boy, young Joseph. It was his first long voyage, and the story of the evening was strung on his initiation and experiences. He wore some sort of headband round his tight black curls and over his red loincloth was a skirt of light-brown swaying reeds. At one point in the evening's programme he was transferred, his eyes shining, to the front row beside Richard. Was it because he then came definitely into the story? Or was it because he was so energetic and expert in the dance, a timekeeper, a model for the rest?

To me it was all darkly-seen, yet a revelation. These people with their simple art seemed so obviously to be satisfying a natural appetite. Are they moved by deep impulses which we, with our mass-produced entertainment, have hopelessly lost?

May 2nd, 1932 THE Sunday mail, coming over from Cairns in the launch, always makes a break in our week. We bear the bag triumphantly along the track from the jetty and dump the contents out on the rough silky-oak table by the tent—letters, papers, books—and for a few hours the sights and sounds of the island are shut out and we are carried into another world. Yesterday V. had a letter from A. R. Orage who, after ten years, has returned to London from America and is starting the *New Age* again, though under the title of the *New English Weekly*.

'This should sound to you,' he wrote, 'like the call to a new incarnation. Many old *New Age* spirits, in fact, will have their being again in the new paper and I hope your spirit in the flesh will be among them. Stay me with sketches, comfort me with articles. Writers are not so many or so spirited as they were before the War; at least I haven't found 'em yet. So keep an eye on us and lend a pen when you see the boat careening (or whatever a boat shouldn't do).'

At night round the fire V. went over some memories of the *New Age* in the days before the War, when Orage came up from the country at the week-end to put the journal to bed and after a hectic Monday morning, the scattered contributors gathered to hear Orage hold forth in the little A.B.C. cafe at the top of Chancery Lane. Katherine Mansfield, with her dark eyes brooding secretly over some alterations in a proof, Ezra Pound, queerly shy and unassuming in spite of his belligerence in print, Wyndham Lewis coming in with a portfolio of drawings under his arm, Dyson ready with some outrageous complex wisecrack when Orage stopped talking. In those days Orage was the best talker in London. Yet he never talked anyone down; he was always ready to listen. There was a humility about him that made him, later, for the sake of his soul, submit to all the disciplines of Gurdieff at Fontainebleau.

For me, memories of the *New Age* always circle round the poetry of Ruth Pitter. It published so little poetry in those days, and her childish verses had a magic about them that wasn't merely a matter of archaic words:

I have a brother, clepèd Fairy Gold
Who dwelleth not in housen nor with men
But in the woods and in the forests old . . .

Perhaps looking so long and often at this strip of lagoon has helped to awaken memories of her poetry, for she has written a good deal about such enchanted seas:

And since that shore is void of Man
No sail about it plies
But hundred-hued Leviathan
Like a prone rainbow lies
And looketh on the weaving waters wan
With stilly emerald eyes . . .

This morning I sorted out a few rather special shells, varied in colour and shape, from pointed pencils to plump cowries, all of them gathered alive out on the Reef and so never abraded by the beach but still retaining their polish and patina. I thought I would like to send them to Ruth Pitter, together with some verses that came to me during the night. The only point in the verses is that the key-lines, addressed to her, are adapted from her successive periods, as I see them.

May 10th, 1932 THIS morning Long Hills, a lean unshaven fisherman, stepped up from the beach with a string of four fine bream, about a pound-and-a-quarter each.

'There y' are,' he said. 'Sorry they're too late for breakfast. Got 'em late last night and didn't like to come in when we saw no light in the camp.'

There was nothing we could give him in return except money, and he shied away from that.

'Couldn't take anything; no, couldn't. Y' see, I was out looking for big stuff, and these aren't worth taking back to Cairns. Weather's bad for fishing these days. We have to muck around the lagoon after grey schnapper to-night.'

He stayed and talked for an hour or two, about fishing, about this bad season with the rains lasting too long, about the mission-blacks from the mainland as contrasted with the Torres Strait boys. As he yarned and drank tea he kept rolling cigarettes, which he often stuck behind his ear half-smoked, forgetting them in his eagerness to make some point or other. He was particularly enthusiastic about the singing and dancing of the luggerboys.

'Them Yarrabah boys can't corroboree,' he said. 'Not like some of the other fellows. Take a good screw at them when they're dancing. They're not sure. Watching one another out of the corners of their eyes to see what to do next. That's not the dinkum thing; it don't come from inside 'em. But if those Thursday Island boys had come ashore from their luggers last night, like they meant to, then you'd have saw a corroboree. Why, they don't know what they're doing when they really get worked up!'

May 25th, 1932 HOW they make themselves felt, these jungle-pigeons with their tranquil ways! You don't see them quite near the camp, but you can follow them, going as invisibly as possible and blotting yourself against some tree-trunk to wait. Their coo is like the hoot of some little owl, a sleepy sound in the afternoon, and it's a very earthy, woody sound as you splash through the water on your return to this land-world after dazzled hours spent in exploring that other watery world, the reef. For most birds the afternoon is a silent time, and naturalists warn you that you can't see or hear much then. Pigeons, though? In every country they seem to be lotos-eaters in their possession of the afternoon, and here it's the same.

It has been interesting to identify the different kinds. We had heard that the big, pied Torres pigeons come here, but their time is later in the year when the nutmegs are ripe.

Looking in vain for them we saw other pigeons, small, dark, less visible because of their colour, but essentially and notably Pigeon, as pigeons have looked to our ancestors. On the ground they step lightly and calmly, as if surrounded by their own tranquillity. At first, seeing them in the shadow, they seemed warm brown; and then the full flush of their rich colouring became clear. Their necks and breasts are more than brown; they have a rich crimson 'shot' through the small, fine feathers. Such was the Gay-neck in India or the 'burnished dove' in Europe. But there's more colour here still. Our gentle brown bird, as it paces, has wings like paniers of bronze-green; a strong green shot with golden-brown. You think of gracious ladies, not so young, dressed in silks that would stand alone. And these green-winged pigeons on the ground, and the slightly different ones in the trees, are the birds that fill the afternoons with their cooing. Let the drumming rain stop and after five minutes' sunshine, pigeons are cooing all's well.

There's a quietly-maddening beauty about a pigeon, as there is about any creature or growth that has been loved and named by mankind since the beginning. (Lilies, from Egypt's sacred lotus to France's formal fleur-de-lys). With pigeons everyone feels at once the grace and the antiquity. There's that passage in Proust describing a chilly but sunny spring morning in Paris when the pigeons, numb and scarcely moving on the lawns, seem like some ancient pottery images that have just been exhumed from a sacred soil. What images would a spade be more likely to turn up! Then in early Nativities, the dove resting on a thatched roof is enough in itself to imprint a tranquil magic on the scene. And now here, to this little windy island, so literally unearthly, pigeons have come from the mainland to link it with the most ancient days and ways of mankind.

May 27th, 1932

AT this season, after the monsoon, and with the S.E. trade-winds behind them, luggers are making their way north from Townsville, where they get their supplies, on their long six-months' journey up the Reef. Sometimes they pass; sometimes they decide that they've found a fishing ground. Day after day one will anchor just outside the lagoon and strike its sails; another will come and, striking its sails, seem to be saluting the first arrival. A fine sight, more especially in this grey, rainish weather; pen-and-ink sketches confronting us on the north.

Sometimes the boys come ashore. To-day, wading in from the reef, we passed along the eastern end of the island, the exposed, windy end, where sea-birds nest in writhen trees; and on a log that was whitened and silvered by exposure sat two men, bearded, dark-bronze. One wore shorts of striped cotton, the other a loin-cloth. They seemed to want to talk but kept to the usual rule: the man who first speaks, he's the one to carry on the conversation. The other approves, nods, smiles, but keeps silence.

The speaker was superb in his bronze stillness; his curly hair and rounded beard were coal-black, but dead-black, like brown coal, contrasting with the sheen of his skin.

Yes, he said, they usually dived for trochus shell and beche-de-mer, but now for trochus only. China's the only country that wants beche-de-mer for its rich men's soup, and now: 'Unless Japan stop t' war, China she can't buy beche-de-mer.'

So they were keeping to trochus shell; everyone needs mother-of-pearl buttons. It had been a good season, he said, and if the price held up most of them ought to make forty pounds each.

'Who owns the lugger?' we asked.

A lift of the chin.

'The *Binabin*? Nobody don't own that lugger—we own it ourselves.'

There was a look of conscious pride in the eyes of both of them. Most of the other luggers, it appeared, were owned by white companies and had a Japanese skipper, but this one, the *Binabin,* was owned and run by the islanders themselves, and they were paying off the cost of it to the Queensland Government by instalments. Each man was credited with his own catch of trochus shell.

'We count our shells, each man his own, but we only count by t'ousands.'

Then each paid his portion of the instalment.

There was steady sunshine now, with light winds across the north lagoon. As we went round to our camp, we saw the other *Binabin* boys, two at a time, get into their dinghies and go racing across the lagoon, manoeuvring their little lug sails. Backwards and forwards they went like swallows, white teeth gleaming in dark faces as they came near the shore and swerved in the shallows. Then they all landed and ran through the island tracks like children, singing now and then, and leaping back to the beach to write something on the sand. All over the island to-night is written one word. It is Binabin.

June 3rd, 1932 CONFRONTED with live coral on the reef, in its endless, subtle rich colours, one is baffled by thinking of the moon-whiteness of all dead coral—all that is kept in museums or housed in glass cases. On the coral growing on the reef, the colour lies like a soft bloom—mulberry, olive, old-gold, hydrangea-blue—along the antlers or the other forms it takes. This colour is the most striking thing about it; your eyes swim with the heavenly tones afterwards. And yet the dead coral that is so much admired is always pure-white like marble; the form is all that remains.

But isn't this exactly like our experience in reviving Greek marble statues that were once coloured, painted and lively? We see them whiter than white, and call that whiteness a classic calm.

June 15th, 1932

TURNING over an old copy of the *Times Literary Supplement*, I came upon a long, portentous letter from Middleton Murry, 'On a Letter of Keats,' following out a certain period of Keats' life when the poet, he says, was haunted by Shakespeare and the sea. In this letter, Keats writes to Jane Reynolds:

'I have found in the ocean's music—varying (though self-same)—more than the passion of Timotheus.'

On this Middleton Murry makes the extraordinary comment:

'Who on earth is Timotheus? . . . Suppose we read "Timon of Athens" for the unknown and unintelligible Timotheus. Timon of Athens who

> *. . . made his everlasting mansion*
> *Upon the beached verge of the salt flood.*

'I do not know to whom the original of the Keats' letter belongs, nor where it is to be seen: but I am prepared to prophesy that, if it is carefully examined, the unmeaning Timotheus will be found to resolve into something like "Tim. Athens".'

Who on earth is Timotheus, whose music in its passion varied only less than the ocean! Anyone who had not determined that Timotheus was to be something Shakespearean and sea-borne would have recognised at once that Timotheus was the famous musician in Dryden's Ode for St. Cecilia's Day, 'Alexander's Feast or the Power of Music.' The special quality of Timotheus' lyre was, as Keats says, the way it could inspire the varying passions, rousing Alexander now to thoughts of war, now to pity, now to love. So well-known is this ode, so consistently included in the anthologies, so much read in schools even, that it is almost beyond quotation. Wasn't there anyone in Printing House Square—proof-reader, office-boy—to whisper to the editor that Mr. Murry ought to know Timotheus?

June 20th, 1932 COMING back from a row in the flattie I found Tinos, the Greek, and another fisherman very intently casting a net for sardines that were moving along just below the flat rocks in small separate dark clouds. Their beached boat was filling with sardines, half-covered in layers with leafy twigs just picked from a fig-tree growing by the shore. I stood talking to Tinos between casts of the net. He has a foreign accent very hard to place but he speaks clearly and forcibly and his precise emphasis of speech has simply no correspondence with the grey, torn and worn non-descriptness of his clothes or the dark melancholy of his cheek. The Sardine King they call him in Cairns. Blue-eyed, used to all the seas of the world—Mediterranean, Black Sea, sardine fisheries of Norway, South America, all round our own coast—he still doesn't seem to be thriving much, for all his energy.

'Tinos wants a bigger boat, more capital altogether,' his mate tells me when Tinos has waded off down the beach. 'Not likely he'll get it though. He's too honest for this game, never over-reaches anyone. And there's always someone to let him down.'

Tinos has thrown the casting net out over a little cloud ten yards out. It falls petal-light, billows out like a mushroom and gradually sinks. He slowly gathers the leads together and brings back his little haul.

'You see I want to catch ton of sardines,' he says, 'but not now. These only for feeshing, about kerosene tin full. If I had drag-net now and got all this mob—about two ton here in clear shallow water, easy to get—then I preserve them. No, not like Norwegian or Italian sardine, tinned with olive oil, but I preserve them in straight salt. No, not sell by pound. Retailers do that: I sell by barrel to retailers. Put sardine in whole, layer fish, layer salt: must have plenty salt. Yes, I preserve them whole, then when person want to use them just take them out, wash salt off, break neck sideways and inside come out, slit along mark, pull fish along slit and skin come off, leave swit flesh. Cook how you like, oil, or vinegar. Nice little feesh, nicest of all.

'People don't understand how good they are: think only good for bait. Last year once I leave three kerosene-tinful here for couple days—worth about two-pound-ten salted down. People feeshing along pier said wotto bait and used them all up, filling tins with sand. But there's enough feesh here to feed us all for years if shops only look ahead. After Christmas, cyclone months come when you hardly go out in safety and people go without feesh because shops won't buy now in good season and preserve it.

'No, shops won't look ahead. If we could sell all we catch in these good easy months, we could live on that all year round like they do in Europe, where there's only four months feeshing at all. But nobody kip anything here. Only Good Friday come round, on top of cyclone season, and then everyone says: "Well, we must have fish now, anyway".'

He gave me a heap of sardines with some subtle recipes for cooking them—or indeed other fish. They depended on having a frying-pan with a lid and keeping the juices well in, casserole cooking really: to be done slowly.

'First put in butter, or dripping, then onion. Keep lid on, frying gently, then put in tomato, fry gently some more, then feesh. Not cook too long after that . . . People eat sardine cooked my way never want beeg stuff after.'

Such tenderness, yet emphasis in his tones. Surely a born cook, an artist!

July 2nd, 1932 COMING back to Cairns after a week down in the cane country, we found that the *Gullmarn* had arrived after a slow passage up from Sydney. She lay tied up at the waterfront, looking very small, squat, and dingy with her peeling green paint beside the

Manunda and the other ships. Somehow smaller and less fit to stand an ocean-voyage than when we made that trial trip on her in the Bay at Melbourne. Yet she's rich in experience, having spent most of her previous life as a pilot-boat in the North Sea.

The crew were in great heart—Hedley and Joyce Metcalf, Dora Birtles, Irene Saxby and a professional sailor called Nick, who is going with them on the chance of picking up a real boat at Singapore. Last week on their way to Cairns they had sailed round the island making signals to us, but couldn't pick up the entrance to the channel. All the better since we were away. And they have a week's extension in which to reach Thursday Island, so can spend the next few days with us at the camp.

This morning we all sailed over from Cairns to the island. A beautiful fresh morning, calm in the sheltered port, but with a stiffish south-easterly blowing outside. The *Gullmarn* has an engine stowed away somewhere in the hold, but it's only for emergency: they have no room to carry oil for it, so they're trusting to the sails. She moved with a long, rolling motion, riding the waves, so different from the launch that butts its way through, quivering in all its tiny bulk.

I lay on the deck, with a mackintosh over me, talking to Dora Birtles. She is using her experience on the *Gullmarn* to do a thesis on Cook's navigation of the Barrier waters. And what experiences they've already had, days of learning to live neatly in a space not big enough to swing a cat-o'-nine tails, shortage of supplies that made them glad of the goat Hedley shot on one of the Whitsundays. The girls are all standing up to it well. There's a professional casualness about them in their shorts and sunburn: they all take their trick at the wheel and are rostered for other duties.

To-night, after a week away, the island seems very snug and comfortable. Through the trees flickers the light of the *Gullmarn*, riding gently in the lagoon, its crew mostly camping ashore.

July 7th, 1932 UP early to see the *Gullmarn* off from the pier, which it passed in fine style, the dull-green boat, the heavy sail with the small human beings moving against it like coloured beetles; then the leap through the channel into the open sea, a misty rain just following. We watched her till she was a speck in the distance and thought of the long voyage ahead, winding through the coral outcrops of the Reef, up through the Dutch islands, to Singapore—and further? Hedley had talked of finally reaching Europe and going up the Black Sea into the Volga. But that seems planning for years ahead. It will be a sufficient achievement to reach Singapore in that stuggy little craft, which looks no bigger than the fishing-boats that come out from Cairns, though its hull is solid wood, built for the gales round Sweden.

The island seems very quiet now they've gone. The last few days have been so filled with voices—feasts at the long table on fish and the salted dried goat they brought from Palm Island, talks round the fire, V. reading Chekhov, and songs on the little *Gullmarn* gramophone, none of them ringing in my ears so continuously as one that seemed to surround the little boat as it shook out its sails for departure this grey morning:

Oh sister don't you mourn
When you see that ship go sailin' over
When you see that ship sail by.

Now the silence flows softly back.

July 10th, 1932 JUDGE Beeby came over for the day in the launch. Obviously he wanted to talk about Joyce and the *Gullmarn*. For all his easy comradeship with Joyce he still adores her as a child, and this project of knocking round the world in a small sailing-boat seems to him a little crazy and quite dangerous. What a foolhardy thing to put your trust in sails, navigating the tropic seas that at one moment are whipped-up by cyclones and the next sink to a deadly stillness that leaves you becalmed for weeks!

Over a lunch of coral-cod, pawpaws and coffee we talked of the Depression that seems to be paralyzing the country and young people's impulse to escape from it. But where was there any chance of escape? The wheels are slowing down all over the world, hopes being trodden underfoot, vitality ebbing. Even in this lotus-eater's paradise—well, look at the tents of the unemployed on the Cairns racecourse.

But as we lounged back afterwards, looking at the tide seeping in over the soft coral, the Judge's natural buoyancy came back to him. He began to talk of his early days, the men he had known—William Morris Hughes, Holman. And then there was that mysterious creature, Price Warung. I'd been asking people for years about him with little result except for Stephens' vague summary: 'A sad rogue, I fear.' The Judge had quite a different opinion of him: 'That fellow fascinated me when I was a youth, just come to Sydney. I didn't know anything about him as a writer—probably he had not written any of his convict-stories then—but he used to appear at political meetings as if he'd stepped down from some other world and was ready to give us the benefit of his wisdom. Well-dressed, good-looking, and in some queer way "distinguished." Yet no suggestion of the charlatan about him. I used to follow him about: I'd never met a man who filled me with such admiration and positive awe. I suppose it was a matter of personality. There were those eyes of his, at once fiery and saturnine. Fred Broomfield said he looked like the confidential agent of a mysterious and hidden power. That was right. He used to urge us to organize, organize, and there was one phrase of his I remember, "the power of the cumulative penny." It sounded impressive at the time. But he had no gift for organizing his own life, poor devil, and he never made use even of the power of the cumulative penny.'

August 3rd, 1932

THE sight of the *Anna Pitt* rocking at anchor in the lagoon this afternoon, left me pondering on the growth of legend. I suppose Anna is the widow of Douglas, but at least half a dozen of the fishing boats that come out of Malaytown bear the name of Pitt. Quite a large proportion of the coloured folk too. Even Charlie Sailor, the formidable king of Malaytown, is related to him in some way.

Yet though Douglas Pitt has only been dead nine years he has already become a legendary figure, so that I can hardly think of him as a real person who trod this beach in his bare feet and steered his shabby boat out through the entrance of the lagoon. Ever since we came here we have been hearing stories of Douglas Pitt from the fishermen—Geordie Ewers, Long Hills, Tinos—and they all have the flavour of an heroic world, slightly larger than this one. There is the story of how, marooned here by a cyclone, he swam out into the lagoon to see if his boat's anchor was holding and was blown over the reef by the gale, but landed safe and sound on the mainland two days afterwards. There is the other story, a little vague, of how in another cyclone he swam to the mainland from Hope Island with a child in his arms. He wasn't merely at home in the water: he was master of it in its most terrifying moods. The matter of his origin is obscure. Some speak of his grandfather, a Jamaican negro, who settled on Thursday Island in the 'forties and made money by piloting boats down the dangerous channel inside the Barrier.

But everyone talks of Douglas Pitt's great heart, his courage, his capacity to handle boats and quotes his proverbial sayings:

For every fish that'll take a bait, ninety-nine won't.

Even old Jorgensen, who fairly bubbles with malicious quips and likes to debunk everyone and everything, grows sentimental about the memory of Douglas Pitt. Hear him describe being out with Douglas after turtles:

'There he'd be, sitting at the masthead like a cat—no, a cat have nothing on Doug—and when we come to a shoal he pick out the one he want. Then flash go d' spear. Doug, he'd dive after it and get d' turtle from behind, holding his flippers and forcing him up from d' sea-floor. Then he snoose d' turtle with a rope I throw him from d' deck. Never miss one—not Doug.'

But he must have his little joke even about his one hero. Doug, he persists, died of eating a whole pint of ice-cream at a shivoo organized by some wealthy admirers who were sending him to Europe to swim the English channel.

It is easy to imagine ballads being written about Douglas Pitt and a whole series of folk-stories about him growing out of the mass-mind. The natural impulse of simple people seems to work in that direction. Before they can feel really at home in any setting they must pour their imagination into it, transforming the natural shapes about them by infusing them with myth. The American lumbermen had their Paul Bunyan and the cowboys their Pecos Bill, and as for our own ballad-heroes, Dr. Souter used to say that they were the subject of oral stories before 'Banjo' Paterson wrote. He remembered, as a young bush medico in the 'eighties, a gaunt old bushman he had doctored telling him that a letter addressed to Clancy of the Overflow would always find him; and he suspected that 'Banjo' had heard many stories of 'The Man From Snowy River' around the campfire as a boy.

August 26th, 1932 TO-DAY, where the shallow lagoon slopes up to the dry reef, V. found a fair-sized stonefish. This is the reef's real terror. Small, banded snakes there are and sometimes huge black flat ones, and eels that can snap like a bulldog and hang on; but one doesn't think of them much. The stonefish is different: the lances along its back can slash through a rubber shoe, and the pain of its venom is so overpowering that it reduces tough fishermen to hysteria. I remember Dr. Duhig, who worked on it for a fortnight while we were in Caloundra, saying that the venom was shattering because it attacked the nerve-centres instead of the blood-stream.

This stonefish was lurking at the entrance of an underground cavern, looking as much like a dishcloth as anything. V. harpooned it with his pronged spear and lifted it to the ledge of a boulder. It was still sandy and hard to see clearly, and when he hit it to knock off some of the sand the sheathed lances along its spine flipped up sending a spurt of venom over an arc of ten feet or so.

Perhaps there was no danger now, but with a stonefish you take no risks. We examined it as it lay there, exposed at last yet hidden with its chosen filth. It was less than a foot long, but nearly as broad, slimed and stuck with sand so that the deadly ridge of its spinal pickets was hard to distinguish even now. Small eyes glared out from deep square sockets. Its long upper lip was mean and covetous; the retreating lower lip sagged, mopping and mowing in idiot frustration. Altogether a most unlovely image of evil.

Tiger-snakes amid their circling spires; eagles swooping down through clear air, or standing in fettered trews erect, even sharks turning on their sides to slash—these can have their own terrible beauty. This creature is nothing but sheer ugliness and horror. Allying itself in the imagination with Spenser's Mammon, or some muckraking figure of Bunyan's, it is enough to disturb the mind of anyone but a Manichee. You never see it move. Usually it squats beneath some reticulation of coral that spreads grid-like over a hole in the lagoon floor; there it half-buries itself till a cod comes in for shelter as the tide ebbs. Then—flick! The blue lances along the spine jerk up as though released by a spring.

We stoned it as it lay on the boulder, and the stones knocked the sand and weed off its metallic form, which finally appeared to have a certain handsomeness of angular outline, and quite a brilliance of varied colour, mostly orange. The face was still vile, the underjaw still shook till the thing was dead, but the dreary slime of the body was all gone. That had been a camouflage, as necessary for its existence as the atrocious armoury along its spine.

September 11th, 1932 V. HAS gone off for a few days on the *Mosman* with his friend, Bill Millard, who carries stores weekly to a river-settlement south of Cooktown. They will probably spend some time fishing around Low Island. Left alone, I've been correcting the last proofs of my book of essays, *Talking It Over,* to go in next Sunday's mail. I find myself thinking about the essay in general. Is it an entirely outmoded form? A vehicle for playing with words and ideas in a dilettante way, suitable for a sheltered corner of society or a leisured and static world, not for this restless, changing one of ours?

Perhaps, but after reading Montaigne I'm not so certain. It was a mere accident, partly of size, that I packed this little selected volume and an even smaller one of La Rochefoucald's Maximes in the luggage, and now at this moment I'd like a *Life and Times* of each of them; a library big enough to cover our long camp table. What exactly was the state of France in Montaigne's day that he so consistently despaired of the present and the future? All, he felt, was fugitive. As for the very language he used in his essays, he declared it to be a temporary one, something that fifty years later no one would even understand; but that made no difference, he thought, because in fifty years, as far as he could see, there would be no readers, no France, almost no human race left. Anarchy and ruin everywhere through fratricidal religious wars! Meanwhile he went softly on, cultivating his garden, meditating on human follies—especially his own—on books and friends and great men of the past; and somehow his work was not suffered to be forgotten, either in those distraught years or at any time since.

September 29th, 1932 PUZZLING about Tinos, the paradoxes of his looks and his mind. I had thought of Greeks as being dark, passionate, and impulsive. Tinos is very fair, with steady blue-flame eyes and with features that always fade away in the strong sunlight. The temper of his mind is judicious and balanced. He reads all the news in the Greek papers from Sydney; he thinks soberly about world-affairs. And his attitude to them is liberal and humane.

Yet he has nothing good to say of the coloured people; he treats them with a perceptible contempt. It is as if a harsh rationalism takes charge of him as soon as you mention them; he can only think of them in terms of mind. This afternoon as we talked on the beach under the hibiscus, Tinos holding forth in his sing-song yet careful utterance, a couple of young blacks came past with fish-spears, the younger one having about a dozen small fish strung on his spear.

'Still hunting bait,' smiled the elder one, a handsome boy with pleasant broad regular features.

Tinos explained that he was Arthur Pitt, a son of Douglas. As usual, the talk veered round to Douglas Pitt.

'Yes, he was the best of the blacks,' said Tinos. 'A better brain than most—a better nature.'

I asked him what he meant: what are the blacks in point of brain and nature?

'The best of them,' said Tinos, 'is the equeevalent of white child of twelve, veree badly brought up. I've had them working for me; I know. Even Douglas Pitt, I was the only one he would work for; he mostly had his own boat. Most of them work pretty well at first if you push them and show them and tell them over and over. But in a few week they die off. The only thing then is—let 'em go. Soon they come back for a job and then you go through the same thing again. Never they use their brain, never they look around or ahead. No political movement or public matter interest them. I tell you they lower than the lowest white man. Yes.'

He went off in his flattie and soon his battered little boat had cleared the lagoon and was trolling up and down the reef, just outside the entrance. Backwards and forwards it went, covering hardly more than a quarter-of-a-mile before it turned, its noisy, coughing little engine making a great vibration on the quiet air. You could see they were getting kingfish, for their trolling lines came in every minute or two, hand over hand.

The boys on the *Anna Pitt* were watching. Soon they had their kingfish-poles out, started their engine, and made their way out of the lagoon in the wake of Tinos. No use, though. In a little less than an hour they had returned to the lagoon, their ice-boxes empty. Tinos had had all the luck.

September 30th, 1932

ALL the luck? No; all the brains. He says so himself! Coming along this morning to where I sat on the sand under the hibiscus, he began to explain about his catch. About three hundred pounds of kingfish, and the *Anna Pitt* could catch nothing.

'Why? They don't use their block, I tell you. They have no brain. My mate, Jeem, and me, we found the sardine shy yesterday, and they not the best bait for kingfish, anyway, so we set to and net some gar. Well, we go out and there's a strong wind blowing. That mean it no good to go out too far: kingfish shoal come in close to the reef and lie deep. We make for the sheltered run and go slow, so that bait can sink well beneath the top of water. Against the wind we go along that part, and then we turn and have the wind with us. You saw the fish how they bite. A big one every two minute.

'The *Anna Pitt* boys see it, too. They come out and follow me, but they get nothing. Why? Well, they don't find right bait to begin and they don't take right track. Because we catch fish they think the sea full of them. But they don't go in sheltered part, same as us, and their lines won't go deep in the rough water; their engine, too, they send it too fast to let the bait sink. I have my engine just half-on, so there's not too much pull on the line. Now that *Anna Pitt* skipper—he's made up his mind that he can't catch fish on this trip, so there's no good trying. He's finished. There's bad luck on his boat; someone put evil eye on it! That's what I mean when I say they inferior. They can't compete with white man. They not on equal terms.'

No use standing up to Tinos and his hard dogmatism when he's in this triumphant mood. I merely say:

'Do you think they know their shortcomings?'

His elvish smile returns and he says with a quiet flash, lifting his chin:

'Oh, only Socrates know that.'

October 7th, 1932 'TO set your heart upon the swallow is a futility.' Yes, Marcus Aurelius, but suppose you were in a place to which the swallow returned year after year? And what is meant by setting your heart? Did you write for people who would want to keep and cage that swallow, curbing both its migration and its lovely swooping flight?

With a swallow, the flight is the bird. I've found a new swallow here lately, an arrival of the Spring, and apt to consort very happily with a little sacred kingfisher. He is a white-breasted wood-swallow. He sat overhead at midday or so; a plump creature, white in front right to the eyes, the wings and back dark so that he looked like a miniature penguin. Plump, almost pursy, rather comic.

But then he flew; an entrancing movement, the traditional swallow curves, light and purposeful, from palm to palm. With the kingfisher he keeps rather in the cleared spaces and the outskirts of the island, though not over the sea or sand. He gives a sweet little call, the sort you would expect from a plump person of long-sustained good habits and kindly ways; but the flight is a grace beyond all hoping.

October 24th, 1932 THE *Mosman* appeared suddenly over the horizon to-day and Bill Millard dropped into camp with a three-foot kingfish, caught just outside the entrance. He had been on a long trip to Palm Island, through Hinchinbrook Channel, and though tired he had plenty to tell about his voyage. It is strange how his delight in these seas never exhausts itself. By now he must know every cay, reef, and niggerhead between Townsville and Cooktown, but he talks as if the life of the Barrier was a half-scanned and exciting book.

Yet you feel it isn't the detail that delights him—the look and shape of things—as much as a vague sense of freedom. After those years in the R.A.N. during the war, and as an officer on overseas liners afterwards, it gives him a sense of release to have his own boat—even if it is only a little tub, making fishing-trips out to the Reef and carrying stores up to Bailey's River. Freedom seems everything to him. To go his own way, to be able to knock around in old clothes, barefooted and with trousers rolled up round his calves, to have no obligations except to provide shelter for his wife and children—this is the good life. With his dark-blue, intent eyes and his lean, rather battered face, he looks like a mixture of Spanish anarchist and lay preacher. There's a quickness and precision about him, though, especially when he's on the boat, that stamps him as essentially a man of action. We spent a long while around the table, poring over charts. It is his plan, when we're ready to leave the island, to call for us in the *Mosman* and take us down the coast through Hinchinbrook Channel. A week's careless voyaging along the Reef, camping on some of the little islands—Fitzroy, High, Dunk—yet with no fixed route and no time-table. It is at once a delightful prospect and convenience for us, but what of him?

'It's my holiday,' he insists. 'We can share the expenses of food and oil. I've been looking forward to it a long time.'

We talked about times and seasons. In about a month

we ought to be ready to leave. There are minor compulsions; no rain has come for a long time, and the water-supplies on the island are running low. Then our tent-fly, in spite of having been treated carefully with oil and wax, is wearing alarmingly thin. The withered vegetation and scant water-supplies make us hope for rain, yet we don't look forward to summer downpours.

November 1st, 1932 THE first issues of the *New English Weekly* came the other day, but it hasn't quite the vigour of the old *New Age*. There has been a slight change in Orage's outlook, and his style hasn't quite that bracing astringency that used to be so marked in both his political and literary notes. What was so striking about him in the old days, apart from his divination in recognizing new talents, was his mastery in so many fields. Men like Chesterton would praise his genius as a political thinker; others said he was the most brilliant talker London had heard since Wilde; while A. E. told people that if anyone in the West knew about Indian mysticism it was Orage.

To me the most interesting thing in these numbers is a long poem by Ruth Pitter. In the past she seemed to live entirely in a magic world; for years I have been haunted by her hundred-hued Leviathan, with its stilly emerald eyes, lying in the shallows like a prone rainbow. This new poem is different, very earthy, full of English sounds and scents . . .

Frost on the grass,
The lonely morning, the still kine,
Grief for the quick, love for the dead,
The little hill's unchanging line
And nightingale so near my bed,
Pass and return, return and pass.
This time like many a time that was,
Many to be,
Swelling and lapsing seasons lulling me.

I find myself, as I read the poem, wanting to underline phrases, yet to keep them well inside the rhythm of the whole. I have a feeling that Ruth Pitter's most revealing phrases are instinctive, and that she herself might take them out afterwards with surprise at their meaning:

Grief for the quick, love for the dead . . .

Daring, a paradox, and true.

November 4th, 1932 IN a letter from Hugh McCrae:

Of course you know Chris Brennan has gone. A man so deep-rooted in the world *couldn't* die easily. From desolate lodgings he was carried to the hospital, where he denied himself to his friends . . . asked for a priest . . . confessed his sins . . . took the crucifix in his hands—and expired. Some of his intimates are hushing up the story; but I don't think they understand Chris, or will ever understand this last most natural act.

I loved Chris. To hear him, as I did, declaim part of a Greek ode, *ore rotundo,* in a street of Elizabeth Bay: with the wind whistling about his body, and without any previous salute when I turned the corner: was to take to myself a treasure for life.

The last words Brennan said to me were my own—written about himself—spoken with a handclasp in King's Cross, Darlinghurst, somewhere about five in the evening:

'*A star in exile*: not *constellated at the South.*'

November 12th, 1932 THIS morning we set out with Bill Millard in the *Mosman* on the first stage of our journey home. For quite a long time he's been talking about this trip; it's his first real holiday since he came north. He has his wife and the children with him, and we're to move south from island to island–Fitzroy, High, Dunk, Hinchinbrook –camping ashore at night and perhaps doing a little fishing and exploring. What wonderful days ahead!

Now, off Fitzroy, the wind has dropped and the stars are out. The harbour is like an enclosed fiord. All the steep shore is covered with finger-long, finger-thick fragments of coral that tinkle with every small movement of the tide. Not another sound from anywhere.

KALORAMA
(1932-1935)

KALORAMA

February 25th, 1933 A LONG letter from Frank Davison, telling about his new work: 'The story threatened to get out of hand. However, I've now got both its shoulders on the mat (for the time being, at any rate) and am sitting triumphantly on its head.'

It's as if he'd just awakened to the excitements and difficulties of writing. Until now, I think, he's gone ahead almost innocently, guided by a natural feeling for life. There's a beautiful eagerness in him. I'll always remember the spring and sincerity of his welcome that Sunday night last November when we came into Sydney from Green Island. His meeting of the boat was so unexpected; what instinct told him we'd get in before the morning? Nearly all the passengers had gone off, and we'd settled down for a quiet evening on the deserted deck when he came with a bound up the gangway. How full of gusto he seemed to us! And what freshness there was in his voice and his general approach to life as we sat talking all through the hot evening, the water slapping quietly alongside, and the lights of Darling Harbour twinkling through the dark.

March 18th, 1933

WHAT is it makes suggestions pop out of your mouth precisely when you're with someone they would shock? Suggestions you'd hardly noticed you were harbouring! Yesterday evening I had to speak to the University Women Graduates' Association about Green Island as it looked to me, and at the dinner beforehand I was sitting next the President, a fine, even famous medical woman, one of a Scottish-Australian family who have been pioneers in both medicine and law. A very serious graduate and organizer of graduates, and a woman who would know how to concentrate on her actual subjects and not go flitting off into the dubious, irrelevant world beyond. I think—I hope—we talked most of the time about her subjects, which were wide and many enough.

Yet, looking back, I can hear my own voice saying something I can hardly believe. It sounds like: 'The next thing I want to do is to learn Spanish thoroughly. I have an idea that the literatures of Spanish-American countries would be very interesting to Australians—new countries in the Southern hemisphere having so much in common.' I must have said it, because I can hear Dr. Jean Greig's prompt reply: 'It is difficult to imagine that the immense labour involved would be adequately rewarded by such a highly speculative result.'

It was as if I had tried the hardest possible surface to see if the ball would bounce off it. It did. But how much is there in that notion for me? And where do I get the literature of the Argentine and Peru?

April 10th, 1933 TO Meldrum Gallery last Monday. A good mixed show: Jorgensen, Colahan, Leason, and some younger ones; also Meldrum himself. All displayed by strong electric spotlights, the rest of the Gallery correspondingly dark. Good method for their kind of tone-values; other painting might be flattened by it.

In the centre of the Gallery I sat looking at a Meldrum interior from a lounge back to back with another one, where a deep, musical voice was speaking in the darkness to Percy Leason:

'No, I haven't heard from my princely friend lately. Not since that letter from China. He thinks I'll do best to publish my book there, in a very large edition. A matter of international exchange, as well as good printing-houses.'

Leason seemed to be feeding the speaker with assent and queries, so that the voice rolled on. Rather Leason than me, I thought, gathering strength to go home, voiceless, with tonsilitis and a temperature. But Percy peered round: 'Oh, it's you!' He brought the man round, a bulky giant with a large, reddish beard, and introduced him. Grant Hervey sat down beside me.

Followed an hour when I strode in seven-leagued boots across remarkable hills and plains, always dominated by an assured, powerful figure, now young, now in middle age, with a deep voice expressing mysterious expectations for the speaker. This was Grant Hervey—in his teens the blacksmith-balladist, writing at great length for the *Bulletin* in thunderbolt prose and hammering stanzas; Grant Hervey, leader in his twenties of the mythical Young Australia Republicans and reporting magisterially on their policies to an important English weekly; Grant Hervey, who always wrote as if his right arm could bring down kings. As years went on, he would 'go to gaol a good deal' for some unexplained reason, not purely political, being master of his fate and making use of the conditions:

(Minds innocent and quiet take
That for a hermitage) . . .

'In Bathurst Gaol I was almost immediately promoted to librarian. My duties began at 6 a.m., but I always rose in my cell at 4 a.m., and during those two hours I wrote my book. I could take time for a nap during the day.'

There were not always such satisfactions in his story. One heard recurrent reverberations of passionate farewells in some dawn: 'For crime unknown I go to my dungeon cell.' There were inherited indignations: 'My grandfather, Cochrane, was a convict—one of the noblest, and one of the most unjustly used.'

And now, here was the present Grant Hervey, by some chain of events, some journey in seven-leagued boots, a lord of the earth, friend of an Indian prince of great power, about to publish his world-shaking book, planning to take a hall in Melbourne and deliver a series of lectures that would set his fellow-men morally and economically free . . .

My temperature, it seems, was nearer 103 than anything; but Grant Hervey was no mere product of delirium. Looking back now, I seem to recognize him as a caricature of those expansive young men of the nineties—Bedford, 'Smiler' Hales, Brady, Edmond, and many others—whose voices echoed so loudly through an Australia that had hitherto been modestly or timorously silent. They had gusto; they made extravagant gestures; they were patriotic and Utopian; they used long, grandiloquent words to express their simple ideas held in common. A pity they laid such value on emphasis that they were easy to parody, and often seemed to parody themselves.

May 2nd, 1933 A LITTLE paragraph in the paper announces that A. G. Stephens has died. Inevitably his name was spelt wrongly. It is one of the ironies of his obscure, significant life that he was known, when he was known at all, by his initials, or as The Bookfellow.

FOURTEEN YEARS

All evening, I have been remembering my first meeting with him, in 1918. An exhilarating afternoon in early summer, the exhilaration not merely a matter of weather. The war was over, V. would be coming back, life was opening up again. In the garden at Killenna the children and I were playing under the flowering gum when Hugh McCrae appeared, with his usual boisterous gaiety; he had with him some of his family and A. G. Stephens, who was on a visit to Melbourne.

A downright, hearty man, not stout, but rather like that mature sea-captain of Conrad's who seemed 'extremely full of healthy organs.' A man who hadn't time to be anything but healthy. One noted that he was bald, his short, neat beard white. But these were not limitations—impossible to imagine him otherwise. The silver beard belonged to his remarkably fresh colouring; his baldness made a dome for his fine, candid eyes—childlike eyes, someone has said, but belonging to a child whose eagerness never let up. No one could believe, looking at his face, that he was pursued by petty financial worries.

He was hoping to revive the *Bookfellow* soon; that was the chief reason for his Melbourne visit. Much of its space, he hinted, would be devoted to Shaw Neilson. The reception given to 'Heart of Spring,' which he had managed to publish —expensively for himself—a year before, made him feel that Neilson whom he had had to carry on his hands for so long was now able to walk alone—or to fly on his Pegasus. A.G.'s interest in our poets was directed chiefly to the makers of lyrics, and of these he put Neilson first. 'He beats the lot of you,' he had said to V. a few years before, showing him the prepared manuscript and wondering when it could be published. He admired McCrae consistently, but I think associated him rather closely with Norman Lindsay, the same thermometer for both rising and falling in his mind.

It was interesting to see him in the garden watching the children—McCrae's and ours—as if they were new creations to him; yet he was the father of quite a long family. McCrae, of course, was acting the playboy. Stephens enjoyed his grace and fantastic gusto, and responded to it. Afterwards, in my little study, crowded as it was with books mostly concerned with my pupils at the time, he asked for French poetry. I had a rather trifling Verlaine selection, containing nothing new to him, and a few studies of Verlaine in German and Italian. He was attracted by a Versailles book (*Cité des Eaux*, by Henri de Régnier), mainly sonnets, but with a few lyrics added. What caught him was an impression of a young girl asleep:

Elle n'a, pour sa tête,
Autre couronne
Que ses deux bras entrelacés . . .

And then out it came, the word of comment, the final accolade of the Bookfellow as critic: 'Ah, that is sung, not merely said.'

It was this criterion, applied always, that made him draw away from O'Dowd, whom at first he published and praised on the Red Page, producing 'Dawnward?' as one of the *Bulletin* booklets. Not that O'Dowd had become less musical with the years; the harsh, stabbing quatrains of his early work had been followed by 'The Bush,' with its own organ-music. But by the time 'The Bush' appeared, Stephens had dedicated himself wholly to Neilson whose song was delicate, Neilson whom he himself had trained to make the most of his lyrical talent. So when he caught sight of Shirlow's etching of O'Dowd on my wall, he turned away to another wall, where there was a photograph of Joseph Furphy. Yes, he had seen the new issue of 'Such is Life' eighteen months before. It hadn't sold three hundred copies for the *Bulletin* when he had published it in 1903—but he had known what he was doing.

In fact, he had known what he was doing all through. For all his humour, he never made jokes about his own judgment. There were so many ways of being hopelessly wrong—he had found the only way of being right. I remember keeping myself from reminding him that, long before, young Frank Wilmot, finding his verse consistently refused by the *Bookfellow*, had invented the pen-name Furnley Maurice, purely *ad rem*, and had been accepted as a new poet. Stephens, when he discovered his identity, never forgave him. Yet the episode gave Wilmot himself opportunities of being magnanimous in ways the tyrant would never know. He was continually acknowledging his boyhood's debt to the Red Page, and recommending people to read the *Bookfellow*.

On the whole the air, when A.G.S. was speaking, was full of possible lightnings, yet with gracious gleams of wit and learning, too. Most of the contacts I had with him afterwards were by letter, but his letters always kept the sound of his voice, as when arguing some literary point: 'You don't agree? Wait till V. comes back and some day we'll go into it hammer and tongs (tongs are married).' He wrote as he spoke—briskly, musically, magisterially—yet with a charming note of play. When his little book on Chris Brennan appeared lately, it ended with a gentle memorial to bookfellowship, the last pages strewing gumleaves one after another in farewell, to Brennan, to Dowell O'Reilly . . . Now let one leaf more fall, with Stephens' name on it. Let it be aromatic, broad, and well-shaped. He should have died hereafter.

June 8th, 1933

ONCE Bernard Shaw spoke satirically of people being so healthy that they'd simply die if they had to sleep in a room with closed windows, and it seems as if the open-air life on Green Island has unfitted me for town. At any rate, after my lingering pneumonia last month, the doctor advised me to find a warm, sheltered place in the Dandenongs. This cottage perched like an eyrie on the slopes of Kalorama is the nearest thing to it that we could find.

As a child, I remember staring at the wall of these Dandenongs across the East; a plain blue wall for the sun to rise behind, a wall to be climbed. But now there's no need to climb; the bus takes you tenderly up a long, graded road; it's all devious and easy. And from the projecting alcove of the sitting-room you seem to be looking down from a great height. The morning sunlight bounces from the clouds below; the distant whistle of the Melbourne train comes from beneath a blanket of wool.

And this spindly cottage clinging to the sheer slope that we've taken for a year or two seems to have a literary tradition. The landlady told me it was once occupied by the Rev. Dr. Boreham, who wrote some of his best essays—'Mushrooms on the Moor,' I think she said—in the alcove overlooking the valley!

June 15th, 1933 LAST night, after a racketty day in town—appointments, radio-talk, shopping—I got out of the wrong train at Croydon and found the last bus up the mountain had gone. A real June night, the air foggy and raw; you couldn't even see the bulk of the Dandenongs against the sky. But I'd keep to the bitumen road on the five miles or so of level, I told myself, and the three miles when it wound round the left shoulder of the hill. No trouble at all; just one foot in front of the other. There would be few cars to blind me with their lights or push me off into the mud.

Once this truth was grasped submissively, a little thinking was possible, was even necessary to take the mind off the heavy baggage—books, food, a framed print, minded shoes, books again. I thought of people who had passed this way before me, their eyes undazzled by car-lights, their feet untantalized by bitumen. Some of them, I remembered, had written to Governor Latrobe in the fifties about their impressions and explorations, the Governor, a wise man, having asked for this, and 'Letters to Governor Latrobe' is in the Public Library. An odd book, filled with the interests of simple men—the size of their selections, the people they met, how they got transport for their stores, what they grew. One of them—the Rev. Mr. Clow, I remembered—had written some long letters about the southern end of the range and the places, like Narre Warren, already being named. His letters had described some sympathetic encounters with blacks and with koalas, and once with the two together, the black consulting the bear about the whereabouts of some lost white man and getting a true reply . . .

Did anyone, I wondered, write to Latrobe about this northern end of the Dandenongs? Probably not. Wasn't it at that time the impenetrable, the inexpugnable? But I need something to think about or I'll remember how dazzling the headlights are, what a crazy load I'm carrying, how heavy my shoes are with mud. Why not write a letter to Latrobe about this end of the Dandenongs—not a hundred years late?

Well, then, your Excellency, one dead winter evening a lubra might be descried at the foot of these ranges, making for her mia mia. Her feet were heavy with black mud; she carried two very full dilly-bags. (What's this little unlit township I'm passing through? Kilsyth, is it?). Some fireflies flickered through the bush—youths with torches, escorting maidens to a meeting. The lubra, your Excellency, had no torch; not even a spark of tribal fire; she had only her dilly-bags. In them, your Excellency, were some rare meats from a special shop in town, shoes strongly mended, grapes from a fairer clime than this, books and—far too many and too heavy—books.

It was after passing that last little township, your Excellency, that the lubra began to wonder about the value of books. Did they enrich life, or were they merely a weight on the mind? Was there one of them in these dilly-bags (to bring the question near home) that would have any virtue when the newness wore off its jacket? Hadn't they been picked up from the counter in the same spirit as a bower-bird seizes on pieces of blue glass? The lubra had reached rising ground and decided to leave the bitumen, with its apparent ease and real perils for one on foot. There was this alternative—the wall of mountain threaded by the old steep, ungraded road down which the bullock-drivers had once brought their timber.

From this point, your Excellency, the lubra says she remembers almost nothing. She rose in the darkness, she climbed that Dandenong wall. Sometimes her foot must have loosened a stone that she heard bounding into a ravine below, but she threw nothing after it, not even a book. She rose. Emerged at the top of the hill and all was intact; only she was in a dream of summer. Would she ever feel cold again? As she entered her home—this lubra has a home—she ceased composing this letter, or even wondering about the value of her load.

July 24th, 1933

THIS Sunday Revitch the Yiddish poet I met in town lately, drove up with a friend. In town I had been the one to ask questions; now he wanted to ask a long series himself. Chiefly about our life and literature, what our cultural aims are, how we regard the future and our place in it. In addition to being a poet he's a journalist, having connection with papers not only in his native Poland, but in the two Americas. His country, you feel, is the world, wherever groups of Yiddish-speaking Jews have gone to live. Bergner's his real name, Melech Revitch merely his writing one, and a good many of his family are artists of one kind or another. All his poetry is written, of course, in Yiddish; he knows no English.

A broadish, dark-eyed man, his approach quiet, his eyes those of an artist, preoccupied. It's curious the interest such Europeans take in the more creative side of our life, when English visitors show hardly a trace of it, even seeming to resent our having any individual character at all. With Revitch the interest was intense and searching. Perhaps because he's conscious of belonging to a people who are also feeling their way toward new expression in literature and the arts. Yiddish literature is still very young, a creation of the last fifty or a hundred years, but men of great talent are contributing to it. Revitch spoke of short-story writers, such as Peretz, whom we know in translations, of many others untranslated, of Sholem

Alechem, the humourist of folk-tales; and then of some new novelists in Poland—Singer and Sholem Asch. When he talked you had the sense of admission to an arena where fine disputations were occurring, fine tales being told or re-discovered, and fine plans being made for contructing the Jewish outlook on the modern world—and this in 1933, when antisemitic waves have arisen and show no signs of being exhausted.

His questions, typed out in Hebrew characters with green ink, would have made a fine skeleton for a literary-social history. One of them ran something like this:

'Australian history, near its beginning, had two great wrongs—the convict-system and the ill-treatment of the blacks. To what extent are these matters reflected in your literature?'

A complex question to unravel in German under the battery of his truth-compelling eyes. How to explain the thinness of our skin and our distrust of any theme that might penetrate to the bone? How to explain our literary bar-loungers and their demand for the light and sunshiny? There was the hostility shown to Stewart Macky's play, 'John Blake,' one professor saying that drama should never touch the convict-period; there was the hullabaloo raised when Katharine's 'Coonardoo' began to be published serially, so many letters of protest arriving that the editor was thrown into a panic. We are still at a stage when any casual person takes for granted he can tell a writer what subjects are tabu and what acceptable.

Before he left, Revitch showed me two of his poems in an American anthology of Yiddish poetry, and as they for once were printed in Latin type, I understood them fairly well. One of them was based on the Hebrew rite of gathering all the pariah dogs of the town in some cul-de-sac, and there was a symbolic overtone in the figure of the pursuer with his whip. He has also written a play on a pacifist theme—'Blood on the Banner.'

August 6th, 1933 BASIL has been here for the week-end, full of his forthcoming visit to Spain. He means to spend a year there, starting from Spanish Morocco and moving gradually north, 'following the trail of the Moorish architecture,' he says. For some time he's been studying Spanish with Señorita Carrasco, and he has always had a flair for languages. Probably before he's been long there he'll pass easily as a Spaniard. When he wears his black beret he looks like one already; there's his darkness, his fluency and vivacity . . .

We talked a good deal about Marcel Aurousseau, whose 'Highway into Spain' we had just been reading. A gay, delightful book by an unusual man. If only the rest of our travel-books were written in such a sensitive and civilized way! Usually they are either full of sentimental gush over scenes the author has come prepared to admire, or they crack jokes about Europe's traditional way of life in the clownish spirit of Mark Twain's 'Yankee at the Court of King Arthur.' Even Bedford's 'Explorations in Civilization' has a touch of this spirit, though Bedford has a real feeling for Italy and the Latin countries.

Basil's pilgrimage, I think, will be fruitful. He has a genuine gift for entering the lives of people other than his own; he would listen to an Andalusian peasant much more intently than to a Dandenong fruitgrower. His romantic nature makes him respond quickly to a foreign scene, or something said in a foreign tongue. He has a sincere desire to enrich this country by acquainting it with the art and thought of Europe.

August 13th, 1933 GETTING back from a walk this afternoon, we found a remarkable youngish German here with Macmahon Ball and his wife. They had been gathering a little waste wood in the hills to take home for the grilling-fire in their Kew garden, and reaching our little side-road they affected not to have recognized our cottage because there were such *neat* piles of cut wood outside it—V. had stacked the split chunks criss-cross to dry them out a bit.

'We admired the piles very much,' said the young German with a twinkle, 'but we thought that if we helped ourselves we would not be able to announce ourselves afterwards—and we wanted to see you.'

He was Dr. Karl Heinz Pfeffer, Rockefeller scholar, who has been travelling in Australia for over a year, collecting material for the enormous book on our social life that is expected of him. Slight, fairish, elastic in movement, he might be athlete instead of scholar, except that he wears rather thick glasses for so young a man. In the modern German way he's inclined to exalt the open-air life, the life of the body. He adores horses: he and Mac go riding a good deal: and he grew lyrical about the healthy barbarism of some Western district station where he was staying—the air full of talk about horses and dogs, 'and, thank God, not a book in the house.'

Yet, though he connects reading with decadence, he has plenty of intelligence and has used eyes and mind to some purpose since he came here, mixing with the black fishermen in Cairns, investigating German settlements, going round Melbourne back streets with a policeman instead of with the Commissioner to whom he had an introduction. Both his experiences and his generalizations were full of interest. The German communities, chiefly in South Australia, he found dull and static. Some of the old families of the third generation still spoke German in the home, 'but, oh, such wooden German; it has no flesh or blood.'

But what about recent events in his own country? He didn't once mention Hitler's name, but the general direction of his feeling was shown when he talked about a ceremony he had taken part in some years back. It was the tenth anniversary of a famous episode in Belgium, late in 1914, when a body of young volunteers (Einjährige Freiwillige), knowing the order to advance from their trenches was given in error, nevertheless stood up on the parapet at zero hour, sang together Deutschland Uber Alles, then charged, every one of them being killed. Now every year on the anniversary, great numbers of boys are taken to encamp on a plateau in Germany. Wakened before dawn, these youngsters dress silently in white shirts and shorts and walk, still in complete silence, through the dim light towards a great stone with one word carved on it—Langemarck. Just at sunrise they solemnly sing Deutschland Uber Alles and salute the stone . . . Pfeffer's voice sank in emotion.

'The old militarism springing up again,' said Mac drily.

Pfeffer grew quite angry.

'Nonsense. You would attack a great spiritual impulse with a dead word.'

He is anxious to regard every impulse in present-day Germany as a spiritual one. There's the impulse of boys to run about the country in bands, inventing dramatic roles for themselves. Not just like the Boy Scouts. Oh, dear, no! 'We have no wish for our boys to wear the same hat as Siam.' Wandervögel. That fits in with the tradition of German romanticism.

And every country must have its own tradition, its own *persona*.

'In England the *persona* is the gentleman. In France it is the citizen. In Germany it is—so far—the field-grey of the last war. Or the Wandervogel of the Youth Movement.'

What would we say was the proper *persona* for Australia? We suggested half-heartedly that there might be something in the idealized figure of the digger—or the bushman. But we couldn't meet him on his own exalted ground. Is he typical of the Germany of to-day? As a type, he reminds me of that young German writer, Walter Flex, whose book of war-impressions and poems I've just been reading (210th thousand). Flex was killed in 1916. He has a queer, boyish Bismarckian ferocity, combined with sweetness, especially in his ballads;

I'm sure Pfeffer must have a feeling of reverence for him.

October 8th, 1933 AFTER being here for the inside of Saturday and Sunday, Leonard Mann has just gone home. In town he had seemed shy and not very forthcoming, but under easy week-end conditions he's perfectly explicit and ready to give himself. You have to get used to his manner; that's all. Long though sudden pauses lead somewhere; his chuckles anticipate something. He has a particularly direct way of looking at you when he's listening, as if he's weighing every word and daring you to fill in the gaps with empty non-sense. Then when he talks you think of words to describe his looks. Fatigued? Tenacious? No, it needs a compound.

Most people would call him reserved, and let it go at that. I suppose he is reserved, but in his case the word isn't just negative. He strikes you as having a reserve of power and being determined not to squander it; it's necessary for the double life he has to lead, a home-provider during the day and a writer in the evenings. He has practically no small-talk. No hankering after social life, either, unless it means an occasional gathering of writers.

I was asking him about his plans. He has one-and-a-half new books written, the first one about the Ballarat goldfields in the fifties, where his people were; the other book he doesn't say much about, but I gather it's modern and political—men facing the Depression, as he has faced it in personal and professional ways after facing the War in his youth (and how slight then was the armour for the flesh!). Yet I don't think he'd ever be argumentative or propagandist in his writing; his interest would be always in truthfully stating a problem rather than in giving an easy answer. I quoted something that Colin Colahan said insistently the other day: 'Art has no predicate: it doesn't say "This is that," but only "This is this": it presents.' Leonard Mann agreed—provisionally, as if he wasn't quite sure of the implications; after all, he's officially and daily a lawyer, though primarily, I think, a poet.

Round the fire he gave us, with his wry, deferring chuckle, some impressions of the writing world he was visiting this year for the first time. There was that evening of amateur plays—'four short plays,' he said, 'and the only one that was at all like a play was like all the plays you've ever seen.'

His second novel will be his test as a writer, he says. But who will decide? He will never accept the bookseller's easy notion that 'Flesh in Armour' was not successful because it did not sell like 'The Rosary.'

As yet, no commercial publisher has taken 'Flesh in Armour' up, but the privately-printed edition has its devoted readers. Last week, Frank Davison wrote to me, very angry because the publisher who, after 'Man-Shy' had won the A.L.S. annual medal, repented of having turned it down and issued it with a flourish, was still refusing to do the same for 'Flesh in Armour'—some wowser of a reader having advised against it. F.D.D. declares that his own father, puritan and ex-soldier, who has some influence, will settle that. I hope so.

December 23rd, 1933 YESTERDAY Flora Eldershaw came up on the bus, having a day to spare while her boat was in port. She's on her way to Europe—her sabbatical year.

Until I met her, I'd thought of Marjorie Barnard as the directive part of that composite, the Barnard-Eldershaw. Chiefly, I suppose, because I'd come into contact with Marjorie first and found she had so definite a personality, in letters and then in talk. There was that day last March, after years of correspondence, when she rang up to say she was in Melbourne on her way to Europe, and would I meet her in town. How musical her voice sounded on the phone, and how it lifted at the end of every phrase: 'You'll easily know me . . . I'm middle-aged . . . I wear brown . . . I wear glasses . . . I'll be watching for you.' (Middle-aged meant precisely thirty-five, or half-way).

Next evening, when she came to dinner, I remember being still conscious of that musical lift in her voice. With it was a sort of demureness that, at every fifth moment, was swept away by a most unusual frankness, often a spontaneous brilliance of expression that made you catch your breath. In her reading (mostly modern cultivated English writers and some Scandinavian) she struck me as being more like an English novelist than an Australian—more English in her literary ideas and range of values, for instance, than H.H.R. Yet there was her personal spontaneity and freshness, her sense of comradeship with other writers here. I knew from her letters that she had all the significant virtues—loyalty, selflessness, industry and, of course, sincerity.

Flora Eldershaw was a vaguer figure in my mind. Yet as soon as she got down from the bus yesterday it was plain that she couldn't be disposed of as part of a composite. A fine head, a broad, generous brow, she's physically powerful, though much too fatigued for her years. She must have called up her reserves and resources continually. Yet it's the extent of these that impresses you. A thinker, a personality in her own right, a robust woman of action, she seems to include the goodness of all her experiences, and her talk, though sometimes using inexpressive words, seems always to suggest the richness beneath.

Having the good inside of a quiet day (the girls were out picking raspberries dawn-till-dusk for a grower down in the valley) she told me something of her past. One of a long family, she grew up on a Riverina station and still knows what country life means, though not with indignant feminist rage, like Miles Franklin. When she reached boarding-school late, she must have shown hunger and tenacity, for she got to the University as soon as Marjorie did. They were history students together under Arnold Wood, English students under the veteran 'little Prof' McCallum—though Flora remembers cutting even one of his vital hours to go to a lecture of Chris Brennan's. French literature wasn't her subject, but she knew what she wanted, knew she was fortunate to hear Chris Brennan once.

It isn't easy for an outsider to understand how a literary partnership is carried on, but in this case it seems to work well. At any rate it has so far, for there are no visible gaps or joins in 'A House is Built.' Any difference in the characters of the two women doesn't make for a difference in their point-of-view or values. They both look at 'A House is Built' itself in much the same way—a solid piece of work made to a standard design, something they rather hope to forget later when they've written a book that's 'all out.'

March 15th, 1934 THE papers this morning bring tragic news of the cyclone that has just struck the Queensland coast, north of Green Island. Many luggers and fishing-boats have been sunk and nearly eighty coloured boys drowned, yet one of the correspondents says that it was not so serious as the 1927 cyclone since, though no lives were lost then, there was immense damage to property, amounting to nearly half-a-million.

Immense damage to property! And property is wood, bricks, iron! McDonald, the Cairns airman, reports that on a flight up the Reef he found the wreck of the *Mosman*, but no trace of Millard or any of the crew. The cyclone must have struck her somewhere near Batt Reef and there is no hope of survivors.

All day we have been talking of Bill Millard—his courage, his camaraderie, his love of independence, and his enthusiasm for that lean rich life of picking up a pittance with a small boat. There was that long, lovely trip we had with him down the Reef two years ago—lying off Fitzroy Island at night and listening to the broken coral fragments fall back tinkling like tiny bells as each wave receded, basking in the sun on the deck as the wind freshened between High Island and Dunk, creeping under the lee of Hinchinbrook looking up at the cascades of greenery that poured down from a height of two thousand feet. The beauty and timelessness of it all! And Bill–good comrade, good seaman–rigging up awning sails to make a patch of shade in the hot afternoons, laughing and telling stories during our picnic lunches on deck, growing serious-eyed as the land neared and it was a matter of making safe entrance through the channel or picking up an anchorage.

Among the casualties of the cyclone, too, has been the battered old boat of Tinos, the Greek. I can still see her clattering out to sea, with her blistered planks and noisy engine– see Tinos standing on the sand below our camp, rolling a cigarette and explaining just why the white man was superior to all coloured people. Fate has played one last ironic joke on him. In the paper he is listed among the casualties as 'Tinos, a Malay.'

March 28th, 1934

FROM Marjorie Barnard, writing of the Davisons who are making a motor-trip up North:

I envy them—passionately. The mind should be well-stocked and driven out into the wilderness every now and then. It is an absolute necessity. But there are so few wildernesses available. Virginia Woolf's £500 a year and a room of one's own is probably the best of them; you could make your own wildernesses anywhere you liked under these conditions—and a flowering one at that. God is sometimes kind enough to intervene, as when Eugene O'Neill developed a tubercular lung, or (more obviously God) when St. Francis was smitten with illness and changed his spots. To be thrown clear of life—like Lewis in the fortress, as anyone may be in a small ship—is the greatest of all blessings.

May 4th, 1934 THIS morning Eleanor Dark's novel, 'Prelude to Christopher,' arrived—the first important book published by Stephensen since he left the Endeavour Press. It is also her first legitimate brainchild (for one gathers that a serial, 'Slow Dawning', is not acknowledged, and is clouded by some family ribaldry about a 'Fast Dark'). Read 'Prelude' to-night. Its literary power gives it a unity, in spite of some unreality in the theme and a good many gaps. How hard a writer makes it for herself in choosing such a tangled, elaborate theme for her first novel! But perhaps that's a foolish way of looking at it. The theme's simple enough; it's the method that's tangled and elaborate. And the method's directed, in the modern way, at squeezing all the inwardness out of the subject.

Eleanor Dark's literary power, besides being what holds the book together, peers in through a few phrases with a hint of the poignancy and glow that were her father's peculiar gift. But how different they are in their stance; she so restrained and withdrawn, and he always ready to give himself away in handfuls. Yet Dowell O'Reilly was one of the most laborious of writers; a story or an essay took him months of work. That dancing, light style of his wasn't achieved easily. Even his letters—there's evidence that he would carry a letter around in his head for days, whittling at it in odd moments and half-arguing with the person who was to receive it.

I've often wished there could be a companion volume to the 'Dowell O'Reilly from his Letters' that contained those written to the woman who was to become his wife. An edited book of his general correspondence and few essays might show all his qualities, or might suggest what he would have done in an ordered world that let him exercise his full talents. His gift was in the direction of 'natural' confession: a Sterne in England, here a Tom Collins. Even in those few letters I had from him in the last year of his life there was a spilling-out of a great range of ideas—humour of an original kind, playful intimacy, fury that, without explaining, he let you feel and share. He ought to have left a fuller record of his difficult, personal, sentimental journey through life.

May 28th, 1934 V. HAS just finished 'The Swayne Family,' a book that, in one form or another, has been in his mind ever since I've known him. Curious how an unwritten novel can change, in time and setting, yet retain its original idea. I don't think the present finished book has much, on the surface, to link it with those first few chapters of 'His Own Household' he showed me so many years ago. The period has been altered, with its particular problems; even the point-of-view has shifted slightly—the conflict between the generations is not seen so remorselessly through the eyes of youth. What remains is the conflict itself—the incapacity of the Swayne parents to see that the life they have built up so carefully cannot possibly satisfy their children—all different, all reaching out for some kind of fulfilment of their own.

The theme, I suppose, has been treated often enough before, but what makes the book seem fresh and full of sap is the way it has been evoked from a living, immediate world. The family really is a family, an organism, in spite of the variety of its members, both of the first and second generations. For instance Anthony, the eldest brother, is a squatter in the Riverina, and Willie, the youngest, a democratic printer in Collingwood, yet when they meet accidentally at the races, you feel they are brothers. Similarly you feel the kinship of any two of the next generation. Yet what differences of outlook and ambition! In this, and in their complex affections and frustrations, the Swaynes are like so many families we've known in Studley Park and Kew.

Now that the book is finished we've been talking of going to Europe for a year or two. There are all sorts of arguments for it. Old friends to see, old threads to pick up, old places to visit, like the fishing-village of Britanny where we lived when we were first married. Then the girls are both ready for a break, an extension of their experiences—A. just leaving the University, H. nearly finished with school. Besides, as V. says, the Europe we knew has since been badly battered by the war of twenty years ago; it may be obliterated by the next.

June 15th, 1934 I'VE often wondered why Gino Nibbi calls his shop of international prints and books the *Leonardo* Art Shop. It's the modern painters that are his passionate care, so why not the Cezanne, the Chirico, the Van Gogh? Or the Gauguin? To Nibbi, as a European lover of art, Australia was a starting-point for his visit to Gauguin's Tahiti, in search of any memories surviving among the people. Having made the journey, he has reverently kept every collected word, whether it fits his ideas of Gauguin or not. Time enough, later on, to see about assimilating them with the tradition of Noa Noa.

When he wrote his account of it all, in his book, 'The Islands of Happiness,' the Milan publisher was probably attracted chiefly by the thought of an Italian's journey from Melbourne to the Society Islands. 'How extraordinary,' as Nibbi says near the beginning, 'to travel northward to reach the South Sea Islands!' Indeed it could be read as the general travel impressions of an eager, unusual man (even if Nibbi reproaches himself, as he did in talking to me last week, his eyes smouldering: 'I feel that certain pages are obvious').

To be 'obvious' is the most loathsome crime in Nibbi's eyes. But the core of the book remains in the few Gauguin chapters. These even seem more simply written, without any fear of being obvious. The material is scanty enough. After all, it is some years since Gauguin died. Young women he painted or loved in Tahiti have forgotten the middle-aged Frenchman. The few still living are tired of being asked questions they can't answer, even about definite pictures. There's that painted fan that Nibbi found, showing young girls in groups; those in grass skirts looking natural and lovely, and those in long missionary Mother Hubbards looking lovely in spite of them—and he couldn't get an old woman to say which kind of young girl she'd been.

Yet there's no sign of disappointment in the explorer's pages. What you do find, at one point, is an extra quickening, for he finds an old derelict Frenchman who actually used to watch Gauguin paint! This ancient sits with Nibbi in an open-air room, the sunlight sifting through slatted blinds. 'Couldn't always understand him,' says the man; 'he used to paint in here. But that big glass bowl standing in the corner—what colour would you call it?' 'Why, dark green of course,' says Nibbi. 'So would I,' returns the other sadly, 'I always did. But he—he called it maroon.'

August 2nd, 1934 FROM Basil Burdett, in Spain:

Strange that you should mention Aurousseau's 'Highway into Spain,' for it came up in a brief, a very brief talk I had with Unamuno. We met only in the street—he had been absent from Valencia and was returning to his son's house to supper, and to make preparations for departure to Salamanca. When I said I was Australian, he replied: 'Ah, I know one Australian who wrote a very fine book on Spain. Muy bien hecho. Muy bien escrito.' Aurousseau ought to know. Such words from the most Spanish of Spaniards ought to mean something to a man. The commendation was really made in tones of unmistakable warmth. It is impossible, anyhow, to imagine Unamuno saying anything he didn't mean. Why should he? I've never met a more direct human being. Even in my few minutes with him I could feel that the man I was talking to was the man whose books I'd read—the man of 'El Sentimiento Tragico de la Vida' and of 'Andanzas y Visiones Españolas,' and not quite the man of the rather caricatured portrait acted for me by a friend in Madrid. I didn't feel he was an eccentric at all. You could almost feel the force of his passage along the street—bareheaded, with a packet of papers under his arm. But there was nothing strange, nothing to excite the vaguest amusement—just a personality of overwhelming force. And the most penetrating dark eyes.

Dora Wilcox Moore knows the Aurousseau family—they live at Manly,

I think. Perhaps Aurousseau knows Unamuno, or knows his opinion of the book already, though. It seems to me that a translation of the book into Spanish should be possible, and even a foreword by Unamuno, except that no one buys books in Spain, or very few.
What interests me, too, about this book of Aurousseau's is the fact of its author being of French descent—he obviously isn't an Anglo-Saxon, apart from his statements about his ancestral Berri—his mother was English, I think. It hints at the possibility of Australia producing a literature formed of the diverse elements of its population, as in America where the mixture of races partially accounts for the vitality of current fiction—for its vitality, if not greatness. Australia—in an infinitely more restricted sense, of course—is also a melting-pot. Aurousseau is a French-Australian. A French-Englishman would be an impossibility.

August 15th, 1934

FROM Frank Davison, who has been on that motoring tour to North Queensland:

I am back now, with 75,000 words done, and am under the need of completing the book by the end of the month. I would like to finish it and then throw it into the bottom drawer for a year; but that can't be done.
The trip (I think), except the Green Island part of it, was something of a fizzle. We took with us about half-a-ton of luggage, but forgot to include a supply of rose-coloured spectacles. It seemed to me, as the map unrolled itself, that we Australians have plundered the delicate beauty of our continent and disfigured it with a careless tin-shanty semi-civilisation. We saw bare little farms without so much as a tree to hide their ugliness, frowsy little hamlets, and big towns that could hardly have been more dreary-looking than they were. I don't know why I should have so suddenly wakened up to it. But there it was. It was painful at times.
We saw a great deal of mutilated natural beauty, a small amount of accidental beauty, almost no created beauty, and a very great deal of created ugliness.
The difficulty is to write of it interestingly and not fail in sincerity—to deal with the subject as it presented itself. That is the only decent thing for a writer to do, it seems to me. The other way is 'to tell only about the good bits.' That, the Devil remarks over my shoulder, is also the sensible thing to do. Unfortunately I possess more sensibility than sense.

September 30th, 1934 THIS week I've been spending a good deal of time, here and in town, with Professor Gustav Hübener. When Dora Moore wrote saying that the Professor of English at Bonn University would soon be in Melbourne, and that one of his interests was Australian writing, I was sceptical. Was she making too much of some polite expression of a visitor's? However there seemed other reasons just now for showing a little hospitality to a German professor and finding out how the world looked to him.

Now his week in and around Melbourne is over, and although his chief reasons for visiting Australia were personal, his interest in our literary scene seems genuine. An unpretentious man, learned, a specialist in Anglo-Saxon literature, his studies often taking him to the British Museum or to Cambridge in vacation, he has been deeply shaken by the impact of Hitlerism. Fair, German-looking, not Prussian, he is unpolitical by nature and habit, but now feels himself expected to have politics of an impossible sort.

Last Thursday evening when we sat talking around the fire he was very forthcoming, and his English is easy and expressive. First he answered questions about German writers, especially poets: Stefan George in his Munich home, Rilke wandering by the Northern Sea; he remembered them from long ago. George, a peasant by birth, with a sense of pageantry and magnificence in living, took poetry as power. Rilke he considered a more genuine poet, submitting to his impressions and letting things express themselves through his words. Hübener's judgments seem personal, first-hand, not going beyond what he has perceived or thought out for himself—never textbook formulae.

Lately in his University the general atmosphere has changed. Opinions in politics prescribed from Berlin, opinions in literature examined for their possible political trend. And what can he make of his colleagues when professors of science and philosophy, traditionally free from bias, now use their talents to demonstrate a purely 'German truth' and justify the Nazi philosophy? He told us, wiping his brow as if after a bad dream, about a social evening in Bonn last year, where a group of academic people discussed Hitler's oratory: why exactly was it, they asked, that when he spoke there appeared a halo round his head? Could it have something to do with that time he was blinded in the war? In merely putting this question, they felt, they had taken all permissible steps in the direction of rationalism.

The radio authorities in Melbourne were glad to have Hübener as speaker: 'we want the national station to catch all important people.' At such short notice the only way to get time, though, was by cancelling a talk of mine: so we were asked to make it a dialogue between H. and me. The morning after his arrival we sat down to draw it up. He didn't want to speak on Germany: he wanted to discuss Australian writing. His interest in it was surprisingly astute. He seized on Steele Rudd, for instance; wasn't there a folk-impulse behind his work, with its comic types and its earthy humour? And this pilgrimage on Saturday to place a plaque on the spot where Joseph Furphy was born—didn't it show a widespread appreciation of the significance of such a writer? Wasn't there evidence, too, of a national literary instinct in the popularity of such a delicate story-writer as Lawson?

This relish of any writing that has come directly out of the life of the country is curious in so academic a man. He is definite about the importance of Steele Rudd—sees Dad as an immense creation of the folk-mind, as much a part of the country's legend as the Man from Snowy River. Inevitably he's a little out in his notions of how widely the Australian imagination has been fertilized by such figures. He's much too ready to believe in a culture that's securely planted, growing from the roots up. But how many professors—home or foreign—would have let the fastidious tentacles of their minds probe into the subject at all?

October 22nd, 1934

HAD expected Brian Penton up for the day, but his Sydney paper suddenly gave him an assignment for the weekend and his wire included a 'curse it' that the postmistress kindly let through intact. He is over here describing the personalities of the Victorian Centenary and he does it as if he were sure of an audience that could read between the lines and understand all the implications. In a way his technique is like that of Dorothy Parker in her relentless stories; he gives people in their own terms, putting hardly a word into their mouths that they wouldn't acknowledge and even admire, yet achieving a sardonic portrait.

There was, for instance, the interview with Sir Macpherson Robertson he told me about when we were having lunch in town the other day. Wearing his professional-vestigial white coat like a sacred vestment and smoothing his wavy, silver hair the millionaire was talking about the £10,000 he had given in prizes for the air-race. Penton congratulated him on his public spirit and innocently remarked how much larger his prizes were than those given for literature. He received a curious stare.

'Literature? What do you mean by that?'

'Well, original writing. Prizes were offered for novels, stories, poems, you know.'

'Oh, books. I never read them.'

Penton talks as he writes. Swift and hard-bitten in utterance he stops when he has finished what he has to say; then he really listens. With his smouldering dark eyes and hair in a crisp dark halo he impresses you as having great energy always on tap. He belongs to that able, precocious group that passed through Queensland University ten years ago, and were associated just after in the temporary quarterly, *Vision*.

November 6th, 1934 FROM Hugh McCrae, after talking about William Moore:

I haven't seen my other William (the Bede Dalley one) for months. I had asked him for a preface to 'Georgiana', suggesting a page and a half, but instead he wrote eighteen . . . all about pies and sausages. Nancy was so horrified that I was driven to protest; however, William agreed, and smilingly stroked out some potatoes. Then, when it came to Mr. Cousins' turn, there was a rumpus and W. jettisoned several bowls of soup and a leg of beef: but refused to sacrifice anything else. Meanwhile he had been going the rounds of the super-highbrows, reading rarebits to Mary Gilmore, Dr. Semple Jones, and others. 'By God, Hughie,' he said, 'this foreword's a corker: Semple blew his nose three times when I went through it last night'; and it happens to be true that the thing has been beautifully written, so I admitted the fact. William, wishing to return the compliment, answered that, since Georgiana could write well, it behoved him to run level with her at the tape. 'One musn't stand before the Pope with holes in one's trousers!'

November 12th, 1934 A PARTY for John Masefield last night at Mrs. Bull's in Surrey Hills. Mostly writers, mostly poets to meet him. Croll introduced everyone to him, using his facetious graceful manner. Made it clear that Shaw Neilson was our poet of chief importance present, and that Furnley Maurice, winner of the Victorian Centenary prize for a poem, and now absent in hospital, made a most 'important absence.'

Masefield was easy and unpretentious in his attitude towards everybody—rising from his chair, for instance, to meet some youths, not writers, who arrived late. On the other hand, he made no movement to talk to Shaw Neilson or to enquire about Furnley Maurice. He and his wife conversed with little knots of people, she about the ceremony dedicating the Shrine of Remembrance in the morning—it was Armistice Day—and the weather on West Victorian sheep stations they had passed through: he about verse-speaking Festivals in England, 'and they spoke so beautifully that one really didn't know which angel to give the prize to.'

Masefield is a good-looking man, though his eyes lack the black fire that seemed to mark them in his youth. As for his manner, his approach, where has he put the grim passion that brought forth lines like—

And the bloody fun of it is, they're drowned!

What would be the equivalent, in maturity, of that fire, that passion?

On his arrival in Australia as guest of honour to the Victorian Centenary Celebrations Masefield had been reported as praising the modern trinity of young English poets, Auden, Spender, and Day Lewis. This was like opening the gates to his successors and slayers, and one admired his detachment. Strolling outside to a camp-fire supper I asked about these modernists:

'Ah, yes, that interview,' he said, 'it was a very leading question.' He thought these poets unorthodox and political; they certainly had their various talents, but he couldn't see that as poets they had much to say. Spender, perhaps? But Auden —well, Auden, he heard, had been a very good teacher before he was a poet: 'and I don't think he'll write much more.' Day Lewis too. His poetic gift was rather different, though he had been a teacher. 'I don't think much more poetry is to be expected from him, either.' He paused, sadly-gladly, then went on with more warmth:

'There's one still younger poet, though, Charles Madge, very promising indeed. He wrote poems already at Winchester and invented a new stanza for himself. Very fertile and original, and he has no politics. He's more likely to bring the general reader towards poetry again as the Georgian poets did, and as I think poets should.'

But they were singing Waltzing Matilda under the trees in the light of the flames as the billy came to the boil.

December 13th, 1934 TO-DAY 'Georgiana's Journal' with an inscription from Hugh:

Praise Georgiana, V. and N.
For courage, virtue, wit . . . And then
Count every grafted fault you find
Well paid with stripes on my *behind!*

In this year of the Victorian Centenary it's astonishing how few family diaries and records have been brought to light: people have used them to light the fire in bygone times of spring-cleaning, or just plain lost them. It took a family like the McCraes to guarantee this Journal's preservation: a family affectionately conscious of its character and succession, and frugally preserving a firm roof, fixed shelves and cupboards, through the generations. And even so this preservation needed a certain amount of care. Georgiana herself, keeping the diary from her arrival in 1839 until 1851 when, with Victoria's stability, her own in the colony seemed assured, or inevitable, must have then laid the diary aside as something no longer crucial in her life: perhaps because she had given up hope of returning to Scotland and showing her diary to the folks. In her old age she came across the papers, dim and dilapidated; and she copied out the whole thing; so it's this copy, on firmer sheets, that turned up in the McCrae house after George Gordon died about 1926. And now it's published, with a sheaf of Georgiana's own sketches in black and white, pencil and wash. She regarded these as notes of their way of living in houses that would certainly not last long, in Batman's Town or Arthur's Seat, as well as notes of a landscape that she was probably the first artist to grasp so naturally.

Praise Georgiana! And praise her descendants for preserving her words and her art. As for Hugh's footnotes and insets threaded through the text, they aren't at all the perfunctory-pedantic work of a mere editor. They're the exuberant comments of a grandson always devoid of a sense of time who feels himself contemporary with his grandmother in her best days. He chucks her under the chin as he explains to the reader who the gentleman was who sang after dinner at Georgiana's home in 1843. He is proud as she travels with her children from Arthur's Seat to Melbourne in a royal dray, 'and all the time as merry as a grig,' as I've heard him say of her, using a Scottish word in her honour. Indeed the task of inter-writing this ms. must have been after his own heart; one could wish he had several Georgianas in his past.

January 3rd, 1935 LUNCH in town with Ella Grainger. She is very lovely; versatile, an artist in her own right, a devout wife. We discussed the compulsion laid on anyone who works in a creative way to follow her own daemon and not to bother about public success. She believes in that compulsion, but also believes, in a half-naive, half-mystical way, that any good work always achieves recognition. She quotes Percy: 'You do what you want, what you believe in, and people come to accept it before long.'

Most of our talk was about Europe, as the problems of living there have been in the forefront of my mind ever since we decided to pull up roots. Where can we find a quiet place to work and to keep in contact with all that is going on in the world of literature, music, art? Paris? London? Spain?

March 19th, 1935 WAITING in Sydney Harbour on the M.M. *Eridan*. This evening, when we were all on board but not sailing until tomorrow, there was a pocket of clear time, and into it stepped, very neatly, Miles Franklin. There she stood on the deck of this little French tub, her deep witty voice roaming in the half-lights; and when she sat down I saw she was bearing gifts, as if we were going out into the desert. A pot of pineapple jam, certainly home-made, and very good: flowers from her own garden, a cake.

In fact, her impulses were those of a generous country-woman; yet she lives in a Sydney suburb. Now I can see why she says, so often, that the life expected here of a woman is too hard for a writer. Living with her mother in the family house, too big for them, she keeps a hospitable homestead—always beds and meals for kinsfolk from the country; fowls laying at the back, flowers blooming in the front, and besides, 'she not know der way to der delikatessen shop at der corner.' An intact country homestead, and therein Miles writes novels about the crowded scenes in such a setting through the generations. In her atavistic devoutness, she goes short of the freedom to write that she believes men writers all enjoy, their good wives undertaking home chores and settling all interruptions . . .

Her talk was rich and energetic, very much her own. I remember Stephensen last year described a train journey to Norman Lindsay's with her: 'all the way, that woman dropping ideas and images like ripe fruit.' Ripe fruit—some polished, some velvety, some prickly. This evening she mentioned an excellent staff journalist who had first resigned, then died; why? 'He got better every year at his job, but he couldn't stand it when all the proprietors used to come and bre-eathe down his neck' . . . We asked her about the old days in the States, when she worked with Alice Henry on the Women's Trade Union magazine. She has never published anything about that, yet she has kept characters in mind; like that young girl leader in a garment-workers' strike, beginning her speeches to her mates, 'You're *plum* crazy,' and carrying them all with her.

Some passengers came up a gangway from a launch, the French liner always anchoring some distance from the usual pier. Miles remarked suddenly, 'Oh, can you get here by launch? That's handy.' And we found she had come by a sort of long back way, walking miles through dark docks carrying her beneficent parcels—and not saying anything at all about it to us nor making us pay the penalty for her trouble in getting here, as some visitors would.

We are making for Europe, and in a way it would have seemed natural to ask for her view of the international scene which at times she has known so well. Yet the evening has passed and she has gone, without any of the talk leaving her Australia—the country where she has known both tradition and character and where she has been so angry about the downfall of young women's careers and yet so furious with visitors who don't see what a fine and peculiar life is arising here.

We are [illegible] would have [illegible]

[illegible] Australia [illegible] tradition [illegible] young women [illegible]

PARIS
(1935)

PARIS

April 23rd, 1935

IT'S really too early in the year to make a rendezvous with yourself—there's nobody else about—on one of the chairs by the side of the Medici Fountain. There's a biting wind, and I feel all the colder from watching the group of little waterproof tent-like objects—some sort of Girl Guides, their hands red-shivery, with sheaves of bluebells from a hike—as they cross the corner of the Boul' Mich' just outside the Luxembourg Gardens. A new type of 'jeune fille bien élevée.'

Yes, it's early in the year, but this is the centre of Paris for me, and here on my first morning I sit for a while. When I used to come here before (1911, was it?) it was high summer, so that every drop of water falling from the superb fountain into its oblong basin was welcome. The rows of chairs on each side were crowded, but I'd manage to find myself one. I had always bolted from lunch after the morning session at Bourg la Reine; the laborious steam tram had seemed as slow as a steam-roller and nearly as loud, and here was a moment of quiet. I was impatient each day for Jeanne to come and lead me away, yet hardly wanted the spell under the thick trees to be broken. Further on in the Gardens, the children's theatres were waking up for the afternoon; outside, the wide rue Soufflot ran shortly to the Panthéon straddling across its square, the great words gleaming across its pediment: *Aux grands morts la patrie reconnaissante.* Punch and Judy—and the Panthéon: from this chair you could have both in view. As well as an occasional small comedy. See if I can remember one, over the years.

(. . . On a chair opposite, across the oblong basin, sits a good-looking young woman. Almost too good-looking, she is profuse in colouring and figure, though dressed with extreme discretion—small, dark hat, dark-blue tailleur, white jabot. Just sitting there. A man, obviously a stranger, takes the chair next to her. Any ordinary, preoccupied middle-aged man. The young woman turns slightly towards him, at the same time staring emphatically into some vast distance. He is looking through some papers, and takes no notice of her; why should he? But she finds this neglect intolerable, and takes steps. Rising from her chair, she sits down again sideways, her back violently turned to the man, as if she had boxed his ears. At the same time she lowers her chin and smiles at him, like a black pansy; but her smile is somehow directed at him through the back of her head—or gradually, relentingly, over her shoulder. It becomes too much, even for a preoccupied, unadventurous man; he begins to respond, his papers now in his pocket. There develops an exchange of contemptuous pleasantries; or is it unpleasantries? No one would know, for a large lady sails into view, not seeking a chair for herself, merely a husband. 'Ah, there you are Adolphe! Sorry I'm late.' He gets up and follows her. As for the young woman, she arranges herself squarely on the chair, with all her work to be done over again.)

Twenty-five years and a long war have made very little change in Paris, except for the women's fashions. And not so much in those. At least it seems so to me as I sit here, trying to remember what was worn in those days, and particularly what it was to be a student, coming in every afternoon from Bourg la Reine with a breathless eagerness for new experience.

April 25th, 1935 SPENT most of yesterday looking at bookshops. One at the Odéon is marked Larousse, as a watch-maker's might be marked Greenwich, where time is made. Poking into its shelves, rich not only with dictionaries, I said to the young salesman, without first noticing his languid eyes, that it must be wonderful to be where knowledge comes from—Larousse! He wasn't pleased by my bungling enthusiasm.

But how many ways there are of bungling in a foreign city! It's a long while since I shopped in Paris, and I'd forgotten about the business siesta from twelve till two. Walking from that Larousse down the narrow, neat, quiet Rue de l'Odéon, I came on Sylvia Beach's bookshop and library—Shakespeare and Company, in distinguished lettering. An impressive shop-front showing American and English classics and moderns in good editions; Shakespeare, Hemingway, Gertrude Stein, Whitman, Quixote (English), Christina Stead, Thackeray. In a frame, a striking piece of embroidery, showing a ship, a sunset . . .

I made to enter the shop and found myself banging at a shut door, my bump sounding like a knock. The door was opened by a dark-eyed American woman, with a forgiving voice: 'Did you *specially* want anything?' Of course not: I wanted everything in time and nothing now: I'd come later.

In the afternoon I found that the gentle dark woman was Sylvia Beach herself. The photograph I'd seen of her discussing proofs with Joyce had made her springy hair look fair, her eyes blue. (These preconceptions!). As she told me the story of Shakespeare and Company from its beginning in the twenties when American and other English-speaking people came in droves to Paris, I soon understood that from the first it was no perfunctory library and bookstore, but a workshop and a treasure-house. A leaflet she gave me, explaining library subscription terms, carried a brief testimonial, signed 'A.M.' Who? It was cautiously translated, its French bones showing through:

'. . . Is the student eager to pore over the great Elizabethans? He need not cross the Channel; in the rue de l'Odéon he will find them all . . . English novels from the earliest to 'Ulysses,' writers of the Victorian Age and the Irish Renaissance. Those who follow the latest literary events know that the book that London and New York is discussing is always to be found at the same moment at Shakespeare and Company.'

So it seems that from being an English library for the foreign colony, it has become an institution for French readers, its value recognized by the French Government, which gives it a small subsidy now that bad times have come and the American invasion has receded like a tide.

Sylvia Beach's biggest single exploit has been the publication of 'Ulysses' a dozen years ago, when both American and English publishers were afraid to touch the book. She has done other publishing, issuing novels (not only Lawrence's), and then, the tiniest exploit, that perfect book with a dozen poems by Joyce, 'pomes penyeach.' I remember ordering half-a-dozen copies of this shilling book when we were at Caloundra, seeing it mentioned in the *Times*. Sylvia Beach agreed that, of course, the title as spelt was taken from some kerbside barrow in Dublin, laden with perhaps penny broadside ballads. It was all part of Joyce's memory—Dublin photographed in his eyes, echoing in his ears, till he's made the whole world aware of this old shabby city on the Liffey.

Sylvia Beach has a good many of Joyce's papers—transcripts, corrected proofs, letters about details of production—the kind of thing that would gather in the course of publishing such an extraordinarily complex work as 'Ulysses.' At the present crisis she'd be willing to sell them in England for the sake of Shakespeare and Company, taking them to Christie's herself, but a very high authority has assured her this wouldn't be possible; any Joyce papers would be seized by the Customs and burnt! So Shakespeare and Company limps along gloriously, providing not only the most stimulating books in the English-speaking world but a rendezvous for writers. Not only for foreign ones. As a dark black-hatted, heavy-shouldered man enters the shop and begins moving round the shelves she whispers: 'Excuse me a moment; there's Paul Valéry. I must see if there's something he specially wants.'

As a library and a place for the interchange of ideas the shop has its definite functions. Sylvia Beach said she didn't pretend to handle French books much; she's going to show me why to-morrow.

April 26th, 1935 AS I crossed the little street from No. 12 with S.B. this morning, she said: 'There really ought to be an underground tunnel here; Adrienne and I go backwards and forwards so often.'

Adrienne, I found, was M'lle Monnier, the proprietor of No. 7, with its sign, 'La Maison des Amis du Livre'—a woman as markedly French as Sylvia Beach is American. And if the one is twentieth century in her looks, the other is deliberately medieval. Adrienne Monnier's full gown of heavy woollen grey stuff (duffel grey?) seemed a habit of some order—oh, a secular order. Her round face with its large lambent eyes and good brow looks what is called spiritual—in a secular way again. As for the habit, it wasn't austere and lank, but bunchy and merry, not worn by a 'sainte triste.'

(. . . I've often wondered if the rationalists, the humanists, the defenders of the rights of man—if they couldn't develop a secular-religious approach. There was that secular monastery in Henry James's story, 'The Great Good Place,' but it was too much like a gentleman's club. There was Guyau's, 'Esquisse d'une Morale,' mapping out a moral equivalent for orthodoxy—equivalent, not ersatz. All this zig-zagged through my head while I looked at Adrienne Monnier, with her world-rejecting clothes, her lambent eyes, her illuminated face.)

She explained the various functions of her Maison; the recent publication of pamphlets on folk-lore (olk, as in polka); the occasional publication of literary reviews, especially, ten years ago, her monthly, *Le Navire d'Argent*, edited by Sylvia and herself—Sylvia the gatherer of foreign material, the two of them often collaborating as its translators—Whitman, Blake, Disraeli (letters), young Americans like Robert McAlmon; and Adrienne Monnier collecting rare work, often work-in-progress, from French writers of the time.

But what interested me most in the old copies of their review that they gave me was the standing statement on its back-covers about the final, basic function of the Friends of the Book:

This House stands as the unchallenged initiator of the present library movement. Its two great principles have by now stood the test. The first is moral: that a librarian must not only be well-read, but must conceive his task as a sacred one; the second is practical, and consists of the management of selling and lending.

This Library is the most complete and well-stocked of all lending libraries. It contains many out-of-print books, all the moderns right up to the vanguard, and all the old classics.

What an achievement! I have been thinking of my feelings in the presence of Adrienne Monnier—and not merely because of her duffel-grey, either. 'De savoir prendre sa tache comme une véritable sacerdoce'; and Sylvia Beach is equally consecrated to her task. They are the two vestals of the rue de l'Odéon, and their undying fire is the spirit of the book.

April 28th, 1935 IF I hadn't known about the world depression, *la crise,* I'd have guessed it from Paris, where it's wave actually broke later than with us—and is lasting longer. For instance, there are the books in English for sale, mostly printed for emigré Americans, remaindered now for next to nothing. Little Crosby editions—Kay Boyle's short stories, Hemingway's 'In Our Time,' Robert McAlmon, and then Saint Exupéry's 'Night Flight,' excellently translated by that remarkable man, Stuart Gilbert.

Who is Stuart Gilbert? Translator, into English, of 'Vol de Nuit,' and much else. Translator of 'Ulysses' into French. Author of 'Ulysses—an Interpretation.' And a convinced admirer of H.H.R. I've something in a notebook he wrote to the publisher of her 'Two Studies' a couple of years ago: 'There is no book previous to "Ulysses" that I have read so often, and so often recommended, as "Maurice Guest." To my mind, it is the best novel written in the twenty years preceding the war . . .'

But still, who is he, this perceptive critic, this bi-linguist, translator, interpreter? Every country needs such men.

These nuggety American books, in paper covers and with excellent print, are now to be found heaped up in the most unlikely places. This week I've bought perhaps a dozen copies of 'Night Flight' (with Gide's preface) at about fourpence each. Their primary public has left France; no wonder Paris shivers a little. 'Good Americans when they die go to Paris'; not now. New Dealers will hope for some different Champs Elysées, with a valuta more tempting for men in hard times.

April 29th, 1935 THESE haunting open-and-shut book-barrows, guarded by old men, that stretch along the Left Bank! This morning, rummaging among them, I came across a selection of Australian short stories from Dr. Mackaness's anthology, translated into rather prim French. A little further on, a very clean copy of Léon Daudet's novel of 1922 about a military dictator, 'Sulla': too clean, hardly cut, and with a clean visiting-card inside: *Léon Daudet, Deputé de Paris,* 12 *rue de Rome.* Did he name that street in his image: was it part of his *action* française? And who sold his book unread—a friend or a reviewer? Anyhow I bought it. I'm prepared to believe that Daudet wrote the book with an eye on his own rue de Rome rather than on Sulla's city: in fact, he has pointed this out before the book begins. On the cover, 'Sulla et son destin'; the subtitle, 'A tale of long ago and always'; and the dedication, 'To Frenchmen who can see, this true tale is warmly dedicated.'

June 15th, 1935

WITH daylight saving, and in June, even the most determined late-diner can't dine after dark. So in sunset light you recognize Heinrich Mann in a Boul' Mich' pavement café. He is dining alone, thoughtfully, and with a napkin tucked amply round his neck. In another café is Alfred Kerr, looking like a dignified poet of 1860—wing collar, black cravat, sideboards, frock coat; exiled in time as in place. Then in a bistro near the Deux Magots there is a group of youngish people, mixed French and German, gathered round little Gustav Reger, anxious and passionate; probably speaking of friends, worse off than himself, left behind in Germany. In an Italian group is Gaetano Salvemini, challenging beard raised with his voice, his head gleaming in baldness after his exile that began more than ten years ago.

You wonder, as you move round, if there are no writers but exiles—refugees—in Paris now. Maybe the French ones are invisible, dining in private; but it's certain the refugees are very many. How do they live? Heinrich Mann, I suppose, can keep on with his novels wherever he is, and they'll be translated and published. Writers of literary criticism, like Alfred Kerr, or political opinion, like Gustav Reger, contribute to the various free journals that went into exile when they did. Ossietsky's *Weltbühne* left Germany in 1933 for Prague, Zürich, and, I think, Amsterdam. And here there are German periodicals—some short-lived—a *Weltwoche*, a *Wochenblatt*, written for and by refugees. There's also at least one anti-fascist Italian weekly.

But what is life for all these refugee-writers? 'By the waters of Babylon I sat down and wept.' It's true they're not captives; they're guests in a country still free; yet how can they sing the songs of Zion in a strange land! What they write will surely be a poetry militant—not triumphant—and tragic, revolutionary tales like those of Anna Seghers.

Her memorable face is one you will not see among refugees in the cafes. A friend of hers tells me that with a husband and two lively children she keeps house in a suburban flat, somehow managing to write her books, too. With her political record, she'd have long ago reached a concentration camp if she hadn't come away from Hitler's Germany. As it is, her parents in Germany are apt to be endangered if she's conspicuously outspoken here, in writing or speech—which she wistfully remembers when she opens her sewing-basket and looks at their photographs fastened inside the lid.

June 21st, 1935 TALKS at odd intervals with Christina Stead. I feel rather ashamed of having brought her, with some others, to this Hotel des Grands Hommes, just because I knew it and they asked for a suggestion. It's suddenly burning midsummer, and the Panthéon makes this the hottest square in Paris. Christina, who knows her way everywhere, would have chosen better. But it has meant that we've seen a good deal of one another, going out for meals and walks, as well as sitting together in conference sessions. Her voice is easy to remember:

'My father wanted me to be a scientist like himself. When I was very tiny he used to tell me the names of what interested him most—fishes with frightening faces. It was all right, but when he saw I learnt easily he took me to science meetings. I suppose I was about ten by then. I wasn't frightened of fish with ugly faces, but those science women who didn't know how to do their hair or put their clothes on! I ran away from science forever.'

Or on Sunday morning, as we set out on a walk from our hotel, which is near an important police headquarters:

'Now *why* are all these gendarmes being sent out in lorries from the barracks to-day? What meeting of the people are they going to break up? Would it be that big communal picnic at St. Cloud? Look, there's another lorry being loaded with them. Who's going to be crushed?'

And later, in the Luxembourg Gardens, coming back to the dread science-women:

' . . . I was determined to make enough money some day to have the right clothes. I must admit that I've got rather a weakness for shoes. And gloves. Yes, and hats. I buy my hats in London, but it does seem a pity not to be able to take one back from Paris now. It's not the best part of the season, though; it's too late. You see, in Paris when hats come in at the beginning of the season you don't think of buying those. Hats in the first wave are bound to be exaggerated, put out to attract people who are bound to be caught by anything showy. You just wait till that short wave's over and then the good hats appear—the serious ones; you simply must have one of those. Yes, of course there's a third wave later in the season, as now; it consists partly of failures, rather cheap. It's not safe to buy one of them, but it's not at all safe to buy from the first wave, either.'

All this carefully-adjusted wisdom uttered by this lightly-elegant young woman in a voice of homely realism; a voice without accent, but slightly coloured by her recent pan-European years.

June 24th, 1935 GETTING out of a taxi at the Mutualité for yesterday evening's meeting when André Gide was to speak, I was arguing with the others about paying the fare and didn't notice a little woman standing on the pavement. But she had noticed me, recognized my back view—after twenty-one years—and when I turned she looked hard at me and said in English: 'Ar-re you Nettie Palmer?'

Of course I knew her at once. Jeanne! Jeanne Billard. Hadn't I been looking for her half-consciously ever since I came to Paris, here where so many things reminded me of her—streets and gardens we had explored together, cafes where we had discussed the Universe over our coffee. But that she should have known me! Blessings on her old friend who kept her waiting so that she lingered there outside the door, watching people arrive.

In the fine split second before I bridged the gap of years I saw her as I'd never be able to do again. (For as soon as I knew she was Jeanne, the girl of 1910 came flowing back; I saw her in the form and colour of those days, coming triumphantly along to meet me at the Medici Fountain happily clutching some art-books she'd bought with her last francs—colour-prints of the 'Après Midi d'un Faune,' and other ballets with Bakst decor. The eager spring in her figure, the gleam of mischief in her eyes.)

Now I saw a compact little woman in her mid-forties, dressed with an elegant shabbiness, few of her francs being put on her back, and yet her needle not rusting. Her face absorbed, yet humorous; her body a little thick but vigorous; the whole figure that of a woman who chose what she wanted from life yet gave herself away with both hands.

And this was Jeanne again! Her friend, Pierre Charreau, arrived and we drifted in to hear Gide together, full of excitement. Now it's next evening and I have moved into Jeanne's flat in Montparnasse until next week. I feel as if a door had been opened, letting in the past, making everything I look at mysterious, familiar, a little more than itself.

June 25th, 1935

THIS morning in a couple of hours we both had free, Jeanne and I told each other the story of our lives since last we met. The midsummer sun poured in through the big trees in the courtyard: Jeanne had just played some recordings of Monteverdi that she got from a special society in Italy.

Her life has been much more accidenté and difficult than mine, but she speaks of it with her own verve and courage. How does it go? . . . 'and then for a long time I had to get home early every day and cook the dinner for us two—without anything to cook . . . ' and 'the year before my eldest brother died, he used to call for me in his car every Sunday morning and take me to some part of Paris he'd just discovered—a special view, or some little old church—and if I kept him waiting he'd play scales on the picket-fence down in the courtyard, like a little boy: he a solid architect and father of four . . . I adored him, Nettie.'

Intermittently since 1920, when she first worked for Henry de Jouvenel, in his political campaign, Jeanne has been his confidential secretary. Now she smiles, 'I am the chef de secretariat!' Jouvenel, I think, would be an unusual politician in any country. You could see this even by the subjects of the newspaper and review cuttings that he expects from his confidential secretary. Not just politics, national and international, which obviously concern him in his job, but the arts, literature, general ideas. And his chief, special objective? Nothing less than the impossible, in recent years: the maintenance of a friendly link between France and Italy. Which Italy? As Député, as official visitor, Jouvenel can communicate only with Italy's official authorities.

Jeanne's loyally intent on his hopes: though doubtful. Outside of her work for him, she maintains her own life and interests (she's no Prossy). Watches, on her own account, what's changing in the arts and in society. Sometimes she writes a critique of a picture exhibition, with a strong feeling for what is fertile and original: a sort of vicarious shame when confronted with the derivative, timid or spurious.

Among her friends is Diego Rivera. He has painted her several times—for some mural? And Jacques Lipchitz, the sculptor. People come to her flat a good deal, as if to a friend's studio. She's not a frequenter of cafes now.

Books are often sent her by friends. A new one has just arrived, by an Italian journalist, paying incidental lip-service to Roosevelt, which Jeanne felt was unpardonably false. It hurt her like an insincere painting; she is capable of robust moral indignation on a great variety of planes. I can't see in her any of that deep seated scepticism, the social neurasthenia, that seems endemic among so many French groups since the exhaustion of the war.

June 26th, 1935

THE Russian Embassy, 79, rue de Grenelles, is incredible in its contradictions. The traditional crimson carpets everywhere; elaborate visitors' books on ormulu tables in the hall; well-hung lace curtains on the enormous french windows of the reception-rooms, kid-gloved waiters at an elaborate buffet. All this surviving in a continuous stream from the Czarist days of the Embassy. But now the Ambassador's name is Potemkin—'the name of that famous revolutionary battle-ship,' everyone reminds everyone. There are no pictures: only one very large photograph of Lenin. The Ambassador's wife is dressed with what looks like a demonstration of matter-of-fact—a short yellow sponge-cloth frock, as if she were pleasantly going gardening or marketing.

Yet again, among this visiting crowd of international writers, the young Madame Koltsova, wife of the editor of *Pravda,* wears a most delicate dress and make-up, like a good fairy, very modern style. When she offers a plate of sweets to Lion Feuchtwanger how can he refuse her? This slight but nuggetty little man, tanned and toughened in his Riviera exile, must have spent much of his life refusing sweets and concentrating on his novels, written with the aid of a card index. I had been asking him about his books; he spoke in French, sometimes in English, but when the Koltsova came up he went into German, a common meeting-ground: 'You say you haven't read my "Ugly Duchess." On the whole I am glad. It is my weakest book. Except perhaps "The Oppenheimers"; that was written too near the events it describes—the Nazi coup d'état of 1933.' I suggested that it must have been written as soon as the events occurred. 'We had it in Australia by the end of that year. Translated from the original German.' He stopped me: 'Ah, no, I must explain. There is no original edition in German. I write, as I think, in German; but chapter by chapter as I write, copies are sent to translators in, perhaps, eight languages. So when I have finished the book, the translators have only the last chapter to handle. I assure you it goes very smoothly. The only exception is when I have to make some changes in an early chapter: then I am really sorry for my secretary, who has to notify all the translators. But I try to avoid that sort of thing, once I have begun seriously on a book.'

What a picture of literary and secretarial activity he called up, this alert little man whose books are published simultaneously in every country but his own! Surely book-making on this scale has never been carried on before? Tolstoy spent more than five years on 'War and Peace,' Flaubert even longer on 'Madame Bovary,' and they were not translated into other languages until long after they were written. How far is Hardy's 'Jude the Obscure' known even now to readers other than English ones? But the present interest in world-affairs has allowed the novel to become a sort of international clearing-house, dealing with political events at a public level of thought and feeling. Feuchtwanger admits that even historical themes are only of interest to him in so far as they can be used.

'I find that Josephus, the Jew of Rome, sheds some light on the present-day situation of Jews in a hostile world. It is largely for the sake of such oblique commentaries and contemporary overtones that I chose the historical novel as a form'.

I could not help wondering how, amid the clatter of typewriters, he found quiet to think and develop his themes. But perhaps it isn't necessary. His novels, basically, are much the same; his card-index seems to yield only a certain constellation of characters, problems, relationships, and these can be varied by small changes in background and personal habits.

June 27th, 1935 THE sudden midsummer heat has broken down. Near seven this evening, sheets of warm rain. I was making for the Metro, rue du Bac, when like everybody else I bolted for shelter. But the porch of the small watchmaker's shop simply gathered the rain that slashed sideways, and the watch-maker asked me inside.

Except that I kept dry what followed was the worst kind of mauvais quart d'heure. Just on closing time, with no more customers possible in such weather, the man wanted to close the shop. But I had to wait there, and he sat on bitterly, demurely, and the rain roared. He morally couldn't push me out into the street, cannily couldn't go into his back parlour, leaving his precious shop with the annoying foreign body in it.

The foreign body, for once, was speechless—with shame. Yet could I have believed, say in the Dandenongs last year, that I'd be in the presence of a Parisian following an ancient and thought-provoking trade and not ask him, in fifteen spare minutes, what happened near his shop, rue du Bac, in 1794, or in the '48! To say nothing of February, 1934.

When the rain stopped, it was a giant tap turned off. The bad quarter of an hour was over, and mumbling heavy thanks I bolted for the Metro through the steamy surprised street.

June 28th, 1935 AT the Charreaus' yesterday evening with Jeanne. Flat a La Fourche in a quiet street of old-fashioned houses, set back among heavy trees. They had planned dinner in the summer-house by late twilight, but the rain came. There was another visitor, Mme Jeanne Bucher, a subtly graceful woman.

Vivacious astringent talk, accepting those present without reservations, and even, with some reservations, accepting quite half-a-dozen people—politicians, artists—in the world outside. When the evening was over, I knew probably as much about each member of the group as I could have got by direct questioning, and I had the good of the spontaneous talk besides.

Pierre Charreau is about fifty, quietly observant, sensitive but sceptical. An architect (among other things a famous glass house, not a glasshouse, on the Left Bank) and interior decorator. The room where we sat, harmonious and functional, showed his hand: dining-table in steel and black glass, with a long hollow for flowers, and glass shelves underneath. I remember a couch with three high sides, so that you looked over the edge as in a bath (a Roman bath for suicide? one for a murder by Charlotte Corday?). It was covered in some heavy green silk, a tissue woven to order by Jeanne. All modern, logical, yet personal.

Dolly Charreau is English-born, fresh-looking and robust. She cooks a subtle meal and likes it. She came to France as a girl ('since when', she says expansively, 'France became my lover'). Completely bi-lingual, she sometimes translates English short stories, by Manhood, by Coppard, for French weeklies. But that's only a side-line. She runs a business (very capably, I should think) and writes social articles for magazines.

Mme. Bucher, rather self-effacing in manner, is certainly a woman of experience and knowledge. I gathered she has a studio and holds exhibitions.

Both the Charreaus are devoted to Jeanne and in touch with all her activities. One part of the evening was spent in enlarging on what she had done since I last met her.

The talk turned to politics—Laval, Eden, Mussolini, Abyssinia—and shuddered away. To Léon Daudet, Colonel de la Rocque, the Croix de Feu—at which it took a square stand.

To architecture—private, public, Le Corbussier, Francis Jourdain. To writers—wasn't André Malraux rather forcing himself to draw a new political moral with every book? Look at those prefaces of his. Didn't a more natural voice for today come from a writer like André Chamson, traditional peasant, traditional revolutionary?

Altogether the kind of evening one dreams of—everyone alive and alert and if anxious, not for petty personal reasons. As Jeanne and I walked to the Metro with Mme Bucher, the summer stars looked large and full of conditional promises.

June 30th, 1935 THIS morning I came across an ironic account of last week's Writers' Congress with fleering references to Gide: 'Culture is in danger and must be saved. From all corners of the world writers rush to the rescue. And, as President, they have a great, a dangerous artist, who in his writings has ceaselessly portrayed a universe of unrest!'

The picture of Gide was that of a subtle and disturbing sceptic, troubling the waters of humanity's spirit. But André Gide of 1935 is a man of peace. Permanently? Who knows? The communist faith, or his acceptance of it, has mellowed his deep, exceptional voice and the ironic outline of his unforgettable face that could seem like a reproduction of those stone faces scattered over Easter Island. (I remember two of these placed at each end of the British Museum portico. The inscription showed that some poor sailorman of last century, thinking to please Queen Victoria, brought them to her for a present. The encounter would have been worth seeing—the proud, satirical, ancient colossal faces confronting the Queen who by definition was 'Victorian' and by tradition unamused. I wonder whose idea it was to bundle off the two heads and place them confronting one another from the ends of the cold portico, where they can watch scholars hurrying in every day to study questions like the mysterious origin of Easter Island heads.)

Gide's present face could not disturb Queen Victoria. As for his ideas—well, that's another matter. 'Communism restores to the writer his fertility.' It was Malraux who wrote that in a recent preface, already famous, but it was Gide who quoted it the other evening in his long address on the individual writer and society. His critics get nowhere by acidly remarking that, since his conversion, he has shown no signs of a new fertility: the truth is that he was never to be judged by quantity. 'Fertility' for him, means being able to write for an audience, small or large, that is willing to be interested, such an audience as he now feels himself to have, perhaps for the first time. You can see this in his gestures—easy though few: in his speech, gliding remorselessly from popular propositions to others he knows will be harder for his listeners to take. He pays them the compliment of assuming this breadth of mind.

His gestures: As he prepared to give his address ('a r-read sairmon,' but read as if spoken, and spoken as if thought out on the spot), he hesitated with the microphone. Too low for him standing, for he's a tall man, with easy movements in his roomy tweeds; too high for him as he sat behind his part of the table that stretched right across the platform. Smiling his arcane smile, he screwed the mike down a trifle and sat to read as if at his leisure, the mike familiarly carrying every bend of his meaning right into the separate minds of the audience.

His speech: For the most part, this was an alternation, a zigzag, of warm, forthcoming admissions of literary 'communism,' and then of astringent reminders—e.g., that to have immediate literary communion with an audience wasn't enough, that a great writer goes ahead of reality, opens up new ways of seeing, thinking and feeling that may alienate him from his contemporaries. (Gide showed how, in days past, many a good writer had had little communion, except with posterity—Blake, Herman Melville, Stendhal.)

But it was at the close that he came nearer to his audience, as if someone had anxiously asked him what would be left to write about in a society that was satisfied, one in which basic human needs were at last met:

'I cannot accept the view that a man will cease to be interesting when he is no longer hungry, tormented and oppressed. It is true that suffering, when it does not defeat us, may strengthen and toughen us . . . yet I like to think of–I long for–a society in which joy will be accessible to all, and await the coming of men whom joy, rather than suffering, will ennoble.'

. . . *et de grandir*: With those last words he jerked his head a little, like a swimmer coming to land. There was a gleam on his bald head, on his glasses, and on what was behind them. At that moment he did not seem at all 'a great, a dangerous artist': his demand on the universe of man seemed so small, so reasonable, so possible, and his spirit so benign.

LONDON
(1935-1936)

LONDON

July 4th, 1935

SETTLING down to life in Bloomsbury, and picking up some of the threads dropped twenty years ago. In a way Bloomsbury has the atmosphere of a small town, with the advantages of a metropolis. You can walk home from the theatre or concert hall; most of your marketing can be done on the kerb or just round the corner; you find people you know popping up at every turn, though they're mostly birds of passage like yourselves. There is a homely feeling about those greyish streets and green, enclosed squares. English? Yes, in every stone and railing, yet with none of the English stiffness towards outsiders. Already I feel more at home than I ever did out at Muswell Hill, where we spent the first years of the war.

At Edith Young's flat to-day we were talking of the gibes flung at Bloomsbury in recent plays and novels and trying to find out what the word conveyed to most readers. Long-haired men and short-haired women? An 'arty' approach to life? An un-English cosmopolitanism? Is it true that Bloomsbury has become a refuge for rather hard-up writers and painters? Edith's own circle has a fairly large sprinkling of Indians—Mulk Raj Anand, Iqbal Singh and others—and she herself still slaps vivid colours on her casement frames and skirtings as soon as she moves into her latest hospitable attic. A malicious satirist could picture Edith as typical Bloomsbury. Yet what freshness she has, what eager absorption in life! As much now as when, years ago, she used to try to adapt herself to Australian ways of thought and feeling, flinging herself into our dramatic movements, learning whole pages of O'Dowd's 'The Bush' by heart, wandering absorbed as a child through the fern-gullies of the Dandenongs.

July 8th, 1935 YESTERDAY, Sunday, Ruth Pitter came to welcome me to London, a tweedy, powerful young Englishwoman, square-cut hair, firm, good features. I was alone. She asked me to go back with her to supper; she wouldn't be so free during the week. Bus to Chelsea talking all the way—of Orage and his death in harness last year; of Denis Saurat and her other French friends who published 'Persephone in Hades' in France. She told me about her workroom, where she and her partner, with eight girls under them, produce art-and-crafty things for a living. I couldn't see the workroom; it wasn't open and was some distance from her flat.

A clear fire was burning as we came into the living-room; a room in the fresh light colours—lilac, off-white—that courageous Londoners most affect, in defiance of soot, *quia impossibile*. The wooden chimney piece was painted cream. On it were no flowers, only a vase like a large bubble of glass, on a stem. It was full of . . . 'It's just a brandy goblet,' said Ruth, 'and inside—your shells from Green Island, of course. I just put them back when I've washed them and they take what places they like.' And that was what they had done, the white fluted, the maize-coloured round, the lilac pointed, the curved white coral, making a harmony due to their origin. I was overwhelmed, as if all the birds were quiring and harping among the blossoming trees on Green Island, or as if—what was more—I were with a remarkable poet, whose dreaming boy could

> *Send forth his soul to the Antipodes*
> *Of palm and coral and the flower unknown.*

Over the chimney-piece hung a painting, a seascape, the chief colours being lilac and cream—little breakers creaming in froth, with children dancing through them to the shore. But it wasn't hung there for any accident of colour; there was something ecstatic, possessed, in the happiness of those children. 'A painting of A.E.'s,' said Ruth gently. 'He gave it to me in Ireland last year.' So this very English poet, Ruth Pitter of Essex, knowing the English airs and seasons in all her limbs, has affinities with the Irish national poets. And she showed me some mock-heroic pen-and-ink sketches she had made, of herself on the heights of a bony Donegal cliff with A.E.

There was a poem of hers in the *Observer* the Sunday before last. 'Oh, yes, the *Observer* will publish anything if it's short. So that tiny poem was sent in with its middle verse cut out, which left eight lines exactly. Remember it? Yes, I remember everything I've written. This was the way it went.'

She stood up to say the poem, this capable, good-looking muscular young woman with the haunted eyes; and she spoke the twelve lines beautifully, uttering the words like ever such a good little girl, but like Sybil Thorndike, too.

But what a memory for her work Ruth Pitter has! Even this poem published last Sunday might be hard to remember if she had worked on it a lot—the different versions might emerge from her mind with the ink that scored them out in turn. But hers is not a photographic memory. What she remembers and reports so heartily is the poem in its final form, as good as she could make it.

July 12th, 1935 ANOTHER hot July afternoon. London people, plunging into shorts, seem to feel the pressure of it. I had to go up to see Christina Stead with a message. Up. I remember, when we arrived in London from Paris, and people were sharing a taxi to Hampstead, Christina was emphatic that it would take in her place in Baker St. A huge building of flats, and hers on the seventh storey—a long corridor from the lift. Lightness, modernity. One room given up to a gramophone with masses of records on shelves, and to a typewriter, with masses of files in pigeonholes. (File of *Humanité,* for instance, on account of its *faits divers,* Christina surprisingly said.)

She looked flushed, emaciated, romantic. She had been writing a long, elaborate account of the Paris Writers' Congress, as well as her usual work, and taking it out of herself. Her husband, William Blake, came in, a powerful, rather nuggety dark man, and his mother, a little lonely expatriate from Germany. He speaks English with a cosmopolitan accent, rather bent by the U.S.A. Christina would make tea for me, gracefully whisking out pink serviettes, but adventurously, as if making maté in honour of a Uruguayan; and offering me some wine as if for relief.

From one window there was a view of Westminster, not only the spires but the parks. A sense of rolling carriages in golden afternoon dust (motors, I suppose). The London season in flower. Much accumulated glory. I said, 'And he called this city The Wen.' W.B. quirked, 'I haven't read Cobbett for a long while,' pronouncing it Cubbitt, as Christina would say, 'It's hut to-day.' They were speaking of Ralph Fox, who comes regularly to read economics with W.B., and what a serious, versatile fellow Fox is. And what a linguist; they declare he can talk Russian with peasants in their villages, and of course he's in Paris every few months making speeches at workers' meetings in the suburbs.

W.B. had a bit of a hangover from too many cocktails somewhere yesterday evening. I happened to mention being to dinner at the fantastic-serious Boulestin's, where R.D.W. took us last night before the ballet. 'Boulestin,' said Blake with heavy caution, 'Boulestin's not entirely trustworthy with his *plat du jour;* that can be commonplace. But with someone who knows how to order, as I gather your host did . . .'

He's like that—a connoisseur in all the arts, an epicure to whom even Boulestin's is not the last word in cookery. When we moved back to the next room, Christina put on a special recording of 'The Sunken Cathedral.'

July 19th, 1935 WHEN Pamela Travers drove her car to our door this afternoon, I took for granted she'd come up from her cottage in Sussex. But the first thing she said was: 'I've been to Dublin, to A.E.'s funeral.'

So they've taken him from Bloomsbury to be buried on his own soil! We had known ever since we came here that he was dying. There had been his note to V. saying he was too ill to see him again yet; then Ruth Pitter had a note early this month in a tone, she said, of unmistakeable farewell. Pamela Travers hadn't much to say about the funeral. The part of Irish life to which A.E. gave so much is submerged at present. When his *Irish Homestead* came to an end, it could grow again through the *Irish Statesman,* but when the *Statesman* itself died and groups broke up there was nothing left of his familiar world. I don't think he was very much at home here in London. Ruth Pitter described him as seeming vaguely lost and solitary in a shabby boarding-house with dingy stairways and fly-specked aspidistras on the landings. Orage's death last year must have been the worst kind of blow to him, and his own long illness and death seem like one of those strange, half-voluntary departures.

Pamela Travers is a tall young woman; fair, vigorous; not at all what I'd gathered years ago from a photograph of her as a poet contributor to the Sydney *Triad,* which made you think of her as small, shy, fey. I owned up to her that earlier still I used to think she was just one of the pen-names of Frank Morton.

'I'd have taken that as a compliment, then,' she said. 'I used to admire him very much. But, do you know, I simply can't remember my life in Australia. My childhood in the North, in the tropics near Cooktown—yes; but not the years when I was busy growing in Sydney. Life seemed to begin when I came here and went to Ireland.'

She was accepted, surprisingly, as an Irish poet by Yeats, James Stephens, and especially A.E. And there is no doubt she has written some real poetry in the Irish 'peasant' tradition, though I remembered, rather wryly, a fragment of one lyric in which she, perhaps, bettered the Celtic instruction:

And I pray to the ewes of thought
To let down their milk . . .

This later work of hers is a strange, intense flowering. In a sense, her development is like that of Jack Lindsay, another *Vision* poet, who once campaigned against local associations in poetry, and has now returned to earth—in his case English earth.

July 26th, 1935 YESTERDAY and to-day I was at 'Green Ridges'; my first time of meeting with Henry Handel Richardson, except by telephone a month ago (a firm voice, recognizably Australian still) and by letters for the past ten years. And by her books.

All was accurately arranged. Miss Olga Roncoroni ('my friend and secretary') drove me out from Hastings along the high road; we passed through a tight little village, then along the road to this lane near Fairlight. Miss R. sounded the horn as we drew up near the gate. As we entered the front door, the staircase was on the left; H.H.R. was standing on the bottom step to receive. Formal, yet making her own rules; a slight and perhaps—as the press says—'diminutive' figure, yet commanding. She wore a velvet house coat and dark slacks, wore her clothes as if she meant them.

Tea in the big room downstairs: grand piano: Böcklin prints—'Maurice Guest' period. The french window opened on the rather formal garden; beyond that, there were miles of empty green ridges to the Channel cliffs. (Hastings was further to the right). Summer haze; timeless summertime, 'all the long, blest, eventless day.'

Long talk with H.H.R. after dinner in her study upstairs. Here was another piano, a radio ('it's the only way you can hear modern music without making the journey to London'), a stylized bust of H.H.R. by the Roumanian, Sava Botzaris. The huge windows gave a wide view over the ridges, the bay, the Channel. But I sat with my back to the window, by some shelves nearly filled with books by Australians. H.H.R. on another sofa across the room.

The talk wandered like a quiet river around themes raised in our letters during the years. H.H.R. said she was glad I had never hesitated in the use of her pen-name, her name. There was that time in 1929 when the press at home had sudden headlines about *Ultima Thule*: 'Australian Woman Writer Leaps to Fame.' (Leap in slow motion; it was 21 years since 'Maurice Guest' had first appeared.) Two editors, knowing I had written about her books for years, now wired me: 'Who is Henry Handel Richardson?' I said she was H.H.R. and a great writer: I gave literary particulars. It wasn't my fault that, after all, sundry relatives and friends had come to light with personal information the editors wanted; her looks, her likings, and that she was Mrs. J. G. Robertson, her husband being Professor of German Language and Literature and director of Scandinavian Studies at University College, London.

'But I've worked more than twenty years to establish my own name,' she said. 'Why shouldn't I have it? After all, Richardson was the name I was born with—and perhaps I place an almost oriental valuation on a personal name; any way, why should a woman lose her name on marriage? As for Henry, well, "Maurice Guest" appeared at the time of feminist agitation, and I wanted the book to be a test. No one, positively no reviewer, spotted it as "just a woman's work." Handel—an uncle in Ireland, rather musical, adopted it, and I took it over. My husband rejoiced that I wasn't merely Mrs. J. G. Robertson.

'Those who begrudge me my H.H.R. are all of a piece with the journalists and librarians greedy for identifications. I insist that "Maurice Guest" and "Mahony" are works of fiction, not just essays in autobiography. There's that German baron, botanist and musician, in "Ultima Thule." Of course I had Baron von Müller somewhat in mind; but all I knew of him was gathered from an old photograph, found in a family album. The rest was imaginary. I believe my father knew the Baron in earlier life, and his botanical studies were common property, of course. As for the music, well, all Germans of that date had it in them. His face, with its brown beard, might have been that of my counterpoint teacher in Leipzig . . . So much you see' (she spoke very firmly), 'for the "facts" in "Richard Mahony".'

Some time during the long evening the blinds were drawn, the lingering light shut out. All I remember is that H.H.R.'s face across the room was first shadowed, though still firm, then clear again. Her alert talk is what stays in the mind, its vigorous questions, its firm outlines.

I didn't expect to see her this morning, as she usually sits down at her study-desk at 9.30, takes up a well-sharpened pencil from a dozen on her tray, and works till lunchtime, when she hands the result, whether pages or sentences, to Miss R. for typing out. To-day, though, there was a walk for three, further up Tilekiln Lane and out of it, climbing to the old Coastguard station on the rise, and looking over towards Romney Marsh and, again, the sea. H.H.R. walks lightly and strongly. It's hard to remember how uncertain her health is: easier to grasp that lately she played tennis nearly every afternoon; that was, I think, till her husband died two years ago. Then she left their house in Regent's Park, placed her husband's collection of books in the University as he wished, found this house and made a few alterations, and built up a way of life here—so that she could write steadily, as before.

Here is her house, alone and self-contained, with Miss R. to keep visitors and inquirers away, in person or on the telephone. Visitors, if they must come, can be received in the drawing-room, which looks intimate and hospitable enough, being within the shell that H.H.R. keeps round her. But the drawing-room, for her, is almost a public room, and on the ground floor. She needs to retreat and retreat into perfect solitude for work. It's only by passing through her bedroom, and then through a muffled baize-door beside her bed, that you reach her own study.

People call this secretiveness, but it's rather economy of effort, all for the sake of her writing; she finds it exhausting to meet more than one or two people at the same time, and she can't afford exhaustion, so she keeps withdrawn. She knows where she's going; she has known it ever since she was a child. When they flattered her about her music, and sat her at the piano, a child of eight or so, to play at country concerts, she wanted to play with her pencil, too; wanted to write poetry. When she went to study music at Leipzig, she worked at it hard enough—six hours' practice a day—but while she practised her scales she'd prop a book before her, one of the classic novels of Europe. At last her ambitious, energetic mother gave in and admitted that, for all her marked inborn talent, her training had come too late to make her a concert performer, and H.H.R. was overjoyed; it left her free to write. Married and in London, she settled down to write; her husband took this utterly for granted. 'But then,' she says, 'when I actually read him the first twenty pages of "Maurice Guest," no one was more amazed than he was. He hadn't guessed I could do so well. I'll never forget that day.' Ever since, except in illness or when taking a holiday for health's sake, she has regarded every day as a working day. To live is to write.

After lunch there was still some time, and we went for a dazzling drive. Up and then past Romney Marsh, yellow and luminous with summer, inland to the old sea-cliffs of Rye. We didn't stop there for any of the 'olde' places, nor for Henry James' house, and when we drove back through little white Winchelsea, we didn't look for Beverley Nichols' thatched roof; we went into the old church, but H.H.R. felt it cold and went outside in the sun. 'We're walking on the graves of infants,' she said in a tone of fatality when we joined her across the grass.

A swift drive back to Green Ridges, swift enough even for H.H.R., who's curiously modern in some of her passions, and then indoors for tea, looking out on the brilliant summer garden. Miss R. drove me to the five o'clock train—a smooth train, its quietness filled for me with the last twenty-four hours.

August 28th, 1935 THE summer days go quietly in this old Sussex house that R.D.W. has lent us while he's holidaying in Italy. He has lent it to us—generous man—in full running order: with housekeeper, supplies, well-stocked wine-cellar, and the suggestion that there ought to be plenty of room for our friends at week-ends. So some of them have been coming—Leslie and Coralie Rees, Ella Dunkel, and Theo Sproule.

This midweek it was Stewart Macky. Stewart so rarely gets to the country now that to-day we arranged a long walk. Drove first to a point beyond Steyning and then climbed up the Down, passing through a hangar (nuts and maples) and finally reaching level ground. Examined Chanctonbury Ring (a round mound, all trees) and the Dew Pond next it. Boiled the billy on a spur near a hangar of beeches and sat looking at the Weald below.

A lovely crisp, cool, sunny day. Stewart still walks with a slight limp, a legacy of his old football days, but to-day, coatless and hatless, he had the spring of a boy, wanting to throw stones and run races. We talked of his playwriting. He admitted that when he decided to concentrate on his medical work, he had burned the only copy of *John Blake*, as a sort of gesture of renunciation. Probably he could re-write it if he had time, but he hasn't; he has a Harley Street practice and a regular series of hospital rounds. When he first came to England, he showed his short play, 'The Trap,' to Walter Turner, who was impressed with it and tried to get it put on as a curtain-raiser at one of the theatres, but the day of the short play had gone, even then. I think Stewart still feels the call of the theatre strongly. Almost as strongly as when he was a young doctor at Streaky Bay, putting aside every penny he could save in order to give the Pioneer Players a flying start.

In the middle of the afternoon clouds blew up and we descended to the Weald in the edge of a shower. Using the map, we found an old footpath to Henfield, but it ended in a track grown over by waist-high nettles, very wet. Took refuge from another shower in a great haybarn. By nightfall we struggled into Henfield and secured a taxi home, drying ourselves before a roaring log-fire.

September 9th, 1935 LIVING here in Dickens country, with the quarter-hours chiming from Clerkenwell Green, balconies like Miss Tox's on all the first floors, Bagnigge Wells around the corner, and an 1830 coal-grate with the politest of little hobs in our own third-storey sitting-room, I wonder why I've delayed till now to visit the authentic Dickens House just a street away. There, at 48, Doughty Street, you have the big basement-to-attic house that Dickens and family occupied, near the beginning of his career, about the time he wrote 'Pickwick,' say, 100 years ago.

My first visit this afternoon won't count, after all, because most of my interest was taken by Dr. Shelley Wang, who arrived at the same time. In spite of his thick glasses and short sight he remembered me at once, and we went round the house together. The old curator drew his attention to some foreign editions: 'and these,' he said, 'are the Japanese translations.' Shelley Wang blinked, then remarked genially: 'Indeed. My wife has translated several of Dickens' books into Chinese.' But the curator remained intact.

I asked S.W. what he had been doing. Some organizing work, demanding journeys abroad, he said; and a few articles and poems he had had translated for London reviews (I had seen some poems in free verse in the *Mercury*). But mostly his hands had been full with his mass of reportage and comment for the Chinese underground press, the continuous task he had described to Christina Stead and me that evening in Paris. It pays abominably, of course, but as an exile since the Japanese attack on Shanghai in 1932, he feels in duty bound to keep in touch with the movement against Japan. It's hard to see how he and his wife manage to live.

He was telling me that as an editor in Shanghai he kept going during that dreadful March till all was over, and moreover recorded his experiences almost from hour to hour. He wants some day to publish that record in English, and wondered if I could collaborate in it with him. His own English is a struggle—full of fine Chinese idioms, proverbs and foreshortening. The wrench in crossing such enormous gulfs in expression would be utterly fatiguing in working on a swift narrative; he would need help.

A grey day, a cool London light on the Dickens bust in the library. Just then S.W. said: 'I should like to take your photograph, please.' I think he spoke to Dickens, whose whiteness will certainly have come out better than the dark hat and suit of the woman beside him.

September 29th, 1935 THE first blows in the Abyssinian War have been struck. I'm not sure that most people grasp the fact; there have been so many months of what seemed like hesitation since we saw those shiploads of young Italians giving the Fascist salute and singing Giovinezza as they passed us in the Suez Canal last April . . .

But one person has noticed it, and bitterly. In a letter to-night Marcel Aurousseau quotes Claudel, giving the words of a *poilu*:

Puisque pour arrêter un homme il n'ya que du fer et du feu,
Tout ce que vous voudrez, mon général!

That patience, that obedience without question, because you have to 'stop a man,' on one side or the other! I think Aurousseau feels a little responsible for all soldiers, since he was in the last war and did not suffer greatly. 'For me,' he said once, gaily enough, 'it was a comfortable war, as wars go'; but to-night's note was written from bed with an attack of pleurisy, which usually gets him for a week or so at the beginning of London's smoky winter—the result of a war-wound, something to do with stopping a man.

October 1st, 1935 BASIL came in for the evening, after his enormous European tour, so long and curly that, as he says, it got out of hand a bit. He's sure now that he really does enjoy pictures. Looked at them everywhere, from Moscow to Vienna and ended by chasing the Rembrandt exhibition to Amsterdam. Russia he found strenuous within and ultra-formal at the borders.

October 11th, 1935 LAST night to the Westminster Theatre—Auden's 'Dance of Death' and Eliot's 'Sweeney Agonistes'—with Anand, Edith Young, and Philip Henderson.

In both plays the words didn't seem to matter so much as the miming and the general movement. Auden's play, in particular, seemed an allegory which could be understood almost as well if acted in dumb show. I'm wondering if the ballet and the drama are approaching one another. There isn't much difference between these plays and 'The Rake's Progress' at Sadler's Wells, which is being put on with Rex Whistler decor (after Hogarth, of course) and modern music by Gavin Gordon.

I was interested last night in the comments of Anand and the others. The modern taste is for what is abstract and symbolic. In spite of the success of 'Hamlet,' both long and short, at the Old Vic, there's not much interest in the analysis of individual character, or the conflict of individual wills. Auden's play suggested robots moved by mass-impulses and mass-ideas, and it depended on skilled production rather than good acting; yet it kept the audience (mainly young people) in a simmer of excitement: 'this means ourselves.'

October 15th, 1935 A COUPLE of weeks ago, I had addressed the society of Indian writers (with Anand, as president, looking more than ever, in profile, like a hieratic small dark bird, his head raised thankfully) when I was accosted by a young Englishman with the surprising name of François Lafitte, who asked me if I had read Havelock Ellis. Of course I had. Would I like to meet him, then? Havelock Ellis was his grandfather and he would like to talk with an Australian writer; he was interested in Australia, having spent some early years there. Most certainly I would like to meet him.

So this afternoon, at four, I climbed down from the Herne Hill bus at Holmedene Avenue, guided by Havelock Ellis's very precise directions, sent me in his own handwriting from the country. Rows of rather fussy, identical, ninetyish two-storeyed houses in red brick. The door of No. 24 was opened by an attractive, middle-aged Frenchwoman who welcomed me, remembering who I would be. She took me upstairs to her room to lay my parcels and fur down, then across the landing to Havelock Ellis's study.

'Monsieur, this is Miss Nettie Palmer.'

Havelock Ellis rose from a lounge, saying before Madame left:

'And this is François' mother.'

He invited me to a chair by the fire and sat down on his lounge again, leaning rather against the end with his legs crossed. I saw him thus in profile most of the time, his own eyes turned to a fine French impressionist landscape on the wall (the work of Madame's brother, he said, an artist who died with his life-work unfinished). His profile was fine and balanced, with his white mane, his white beard not hiding the firm lips, large, clear-blue eyes almost untroubled-looking, almost childish, with a slight unstrained cast seeming to give a personal quality to them, as in Louis Esson's eyes. He was dressed as if he had ordered his suit perhaps forty years ago, and—his figure and habits not altering—had had it copied in some very uncrushable tweed, soft and silky-surfaced. Like a grand Whistler portrait he sat there, but not silhouetted against the wall; more fluid and ample, with the October light coming through remote bay windows behind him.

His voice, high-pitched and a little jerky, was the oldest part of him:

'No, I'm not Australian-born, but it was a pardonable mistake for you to make in your little book. Others have done it before you. I've been to Australia twice, the first time when I was a child of seven, going round the world with my father who was a ship's captain. The second time I was sixteen and stayed four years, the most important years of my life—chiefly because I was so much alone.'

We talked of 'Kanga Creek'—it was really Sparkes Creek, across the Liverpool mountains where the plains begin. Two girls in the Mitchell Library (Bertha Lawson and Marjorie Ross) had lately gone there and taken photographs to send him. There hadn't been much change, he said, since the days when he had taught there, keeping two small schools going that were four miles apart. All the details of his little idyll were exact, but not the story. There was no girl, for instance—didn't he wish there had been!

His memory seemed to move easily among the old scenes: teaching in the two tiny schools left him some leisure and much solitude, through which he found himself.

'All young people should have a spell alone. I'm grateful to Australia for having given me that quiet time.'

There was Grafton, a fine, wide-spreading village on its beautiful river, where he'd taught for six months in a private school: there were his friends, the Kennedys, with whom he had corresponded for many years—Lauri, the 'cellist, was the descendant he had known best in London since. When he had left the country, he had kept in touch with it through its literature, at least till the beginning of the century. Then a few years ago, A. G. Stephens had sent him his little book on Brennan, and Randolph Hughes sent his, also.

'What they said about Brennan was interesting enough until you came to quotations from his poems. I'll admit I can't see much in Brennan; he seems so imitative of the French, doesn't seem to have any new vision of things. I can well believe he was remarkable as a man, and if so many of his students became distinguished scholars, that's a good sign.'

Life in Australia seemed free and homely to him in the seventies and early eighties, somehow natural. There wasn't any insistence on freedom, but neither were there any attempts at repression. People took things as they came. Australia still seemed to him a beautiful, primitive continent, where an eccentric man could go his own way and find solitude if he wanted it. Chidley? Well, perhaps they had been rather stupid about Chidley. He was an unusual man, an original, a philosopher in his way.

'He sent me his extraordinary Confessions, a most valuable document, not only because it's so ably-written, but because it's an account of Australian life of the time—Australia's social-sexual life, I mean. It couldn't be published then; the day when it can be is still far off. It must wait in the Mitchell Library, where I sent my copy.'

It was growing dusk. When I got up to go, he accompanied me downstairs, talking all the way. His love for keeping things. How his wife had differed from him in destroying letters as soon as they were read, 'though' (with a twinkle) 'she did keep mine.'

From the street I looked back as he stood a moment at the front door, a vital figure in his springy tweeds, rich with wisdom, but a little faun-like. Was he 'modern,' or was it ageless? I thought of this as I waited for my bus, slightly chilly. But where were my fur and parcels? Upstairs in that room opposite the study. Dared I slink back for them?

A maid opened the front door and I mumbled my confessions. But from across the hall came Havelock Ellis and took me upstairs himself.

'When friends of mine leave something behind,' he said laughing, 'I like to think it's because they're loth to go.'

It had not needed his long association with Freud to bring him to that bit of kindly analysis.

October 24th, 1935 TO lunch with Rowland and Asta Kenney to meet their friend, Margaret Cole. A seriously happy woman. Warm brown eyes and a good physique; you felt she lived easily on many planes. Overworked, of course. Running three professions, whatever she calls them. But not showing strain, not riding for a fall. It's as if all her jobs—wife-and-mother, collaborator with G.D.H. in whodunits as well as in his 'Guides,' a journalist-adviser in her own right—as if all these jobs, joining on with her principles as Fabian and feminist, each acted as a relief from the others instead of adding to the sum of effort.

A matter of temperament? A matter of planning, more likely, from her youth up. Which must be one reason why I've found myself taking even the slightest of her recent articles on the training of girls as expressing genuine thought and principle, and even the lightest of the Coles' pretty murder-stories as giving a coherent picture of some social scene.

The feminist in her is on the alert; why not in a world of woes for women still? Last week, she said, the *Manchester Guardian* (I think it was) opened a series of annotated photographs of writers from Manchester (Mancastrians?) with G. D. H. Cole. About three inches of his activities; Oxford professor, publicist, writer. At the close this complete sentence: *Wife assists.*

One of her articles on careers for girls suggested that parents shouldn't force their daughters to go straight from school to the University. But suppose the girl over-rode all her parents' reasons and plans, I queried. There was that girl I'd been interested in, wanting to let her experience a little 'life' after school, but she broke her neck (I must have paused a little jerkily, for I noticed Margaret Cole and Asta exchanging a horrified glance) 'broke her neck to go to the University,' I hurried on, 'not being willing for a year's delay, though she was barely seventeen. That meant she'd finished with the University, Honours and all, before she was twenty.' Margaret Cole hadn't a solution at the time; she even accepted the girl's eagerness as a valid impulse. But she'd have a reply later; perhaps in print. I even think she might write one that the girl, as well as her parents, could accept.

Her mind works in its spare time. 'Coming into town by car,' she was saying, 'when one can't read, it's sometimes been my dreary pleasure to collect appropriate names for businesses, and take them home. That estate agents', Waite and Waite . . .'

November 8th, 1935 TO live near the British Museum gives you more than the Museum itself, though that's inexhaustible. As I go past the notice-board inside the front door I have to turn my head away, there are so many announcements of lectures I want to hear. Some at Farringdon Hall—mostly science, by great names, Jeans, Haldane, Dunne. Some at King's College, mostly literary and historical, for students and public.

This week at King's College, Jules Romains, with Denis Saurat in the chair. Romains is like a middle-aged business-man, but then what is a French business-man like? Saurat, frail, fairish, small-boned, with hollow temples; utterly bilingual, though he, like Romains, spoke this time in French.

Two lectures, aimed primarily at students; one on Romains' own poetry, one on Victor Hugo. As a child of Paris (this brought back the first section of his 'Men of Goodwill') Romains had always had a sense of crowds, and his early unanimist poems were experiments in crowd-expression. I remember Bernard O'Dowd telling me about the idea emotionally at the time. To be a poet was a hard life, though, even with ideas ready. Romains recalled, affecting a little romantic melancholy, the writing of one poem on a freezing night, the room heated by a little oil stove he'd bought for fourteen francs; no light but a shaft from the moon; and he wrote with a pencil on blotting-paper, couldn't see to make corrections. He read us the poem.

At other times, he said, the poet's difficulties were spiritual. There was his own long poem, 'Europe'—a special kind of crowd-poem—written as a gesture of peace during the War. He read it to an audience of anxious friends in Adrienne Monnier's bookshop. It was the year of Verdun. 'Europe' depicted the

River Rhine, Father Rhine, and all the races of Europe that had passed along it to the sea.

I remember Adrienne Monnier's pride as she told me about the reading of this poem in her 'Amis du Livre.' I don't know whether this was what led to the formation of that French pacifist library we used to hear about vaguely: Furnley Maurice's 'To God from the Warring Nations' was said to have been placed there.

But poetry was an activity of Romains' youth. I think he abandoned it since becoming a dramatist and novelist. His second lecture—but you need a different word—would causerie do? His French is so natural, yet it's comfortably formal; like extremely good talk from someone used to great quantities of it, used to reciprocity, to good listening. For his address he had a few notes, but never read from them. When he quoted lines from Hugo, it was done as an engineer would mention a construction well-known:

Waterloo! Waterloo! Waterloo! Morne plaine . . .

The King's College students rejoiced, half-laughing in recognition.

As he was speaking, with his fine phrases held in suspension, his climaxes so built up, and his whole theme clear, down to its last illustration, I found myself wondering what English writer could be confidently sent to Paris to speak about, say, a revival of Tennyson, which may easily occur. Could an Englishman count on French students' delighted recognition of the chestnut:

Where freedom slowly broadens down
From precedent to precedent?

When Jules Romains closed and put away his papers, it was like a pause, not an abrupt stop: and I think Saurat meant this when he said that Monsieur Romains had shared a great many of his ideas with us but was certainly carrying a great many more away with him in his bag.

November 13th, 1935 TO Rebecca West's for lunch in her flat somewhere behind Selfridge's. I'd been looking forward to meeting her since her friendly letter of some years ago, in response to a review I'd written of 'This Strange Necessity.' No, long before that. How well I remember Rowland Kenney talking, in 1912, about this Hampstead girl, fabulously young and clever, who wrote under a pen-name she'd taken from one of Ibsen's heroines; from then on, I'd followed her essays in *The Feminist* and then in *The New Republic*, marvelling at her growing power and assurance. There was her little book on Henry James, about 1917, as notable for its penetration as its wit.

She came in, a little late, to the drawing-room where the butler had asked me to wait—breezy, and with the brilliant dark eyes I'd expected.

'Excuse me, I couldn't get away sooner: I've been working.'

And as we went in to lunch through the folding-doors she lightly gave me an inkling of the extent and variety of her work. There were not only her regular assignments—book-reviews and causeries for this country and America—but her short stories and her occasional novels. Then much of this year has been spent in travel, giving literary lectures for the Foreign Office in North European countries.

'Lately I lectured in Finland, Lithuania, Latvia, and Germany—in that order. Not the most convenient order for travel-arrangements. The worst of the F.O. is that it knows nothing about geography.'

She was responsive and forthcoming, but when we came to literary matters several dark little snags cropped up in the current of our talk. We disagreed about Henry Handel Richardson, about the achievements of Orage as an editor. When I spoke of the young writers he'd helped to find their feet and direction, she challenged me abruptly:

'Tell me one writer of any quality he helped—tell me one.'

A dozen names were on the tip of my tongue—from St. John Ervine and W. L. George to Ruth Pitter—but it's hard to give chapter and verse in such matters. And I suddenly remembered a long, seemingly-malicious attack by Randolph Hughes on R.W.'s 'St. Augustine' that Orage had found space for in the *New English Weekly* before he died. Evidently there were antagonisms working that I knew nothing about. The difficulty of coming into this London literary world from outside is that one fails to remember it consists of fallible men and women, with their accumulation of likings, antipathies, imperfect sympathies. Judgments always look so impartial when committed to cold print and read in, say, Green Island.

November 26th, 1935 ANAND came here last night. The bell rang just after nine, and when I ran downstairs he was standing below the steps, his head half-under his wing, somehow, and staring up at our second-floor windows to see if they were lit, or in hopes we'd drop the key down to him, Bloomsbury fashion. He was wanting to know if we'd read the manuscript of his new novel, 'The Coolie.' We had; we'd enjoyed it, but felt it wasn't brought up enough; in many senses there was a blurred, furred-at-the-edges feeling. His English is good, sometimes even brilliant, but his descriptions and dialogue aren't taut and clear enough.

V. went over the manuscript with him pretty thoroughly. If only Anand had unlimited time! He's willing to do a month's hard work on this before it goes to the publisher, but really can't afford more than that—can't afford time to re-shape anything or meddle with the structure.

'I was just in a hurry to get things down plainly . . . couldn't think of spending myself on fine writing.'

But 'getting things down plainly' is a matter of clear vision, not of fine writing at all!

'The Coolie' is a more complex story than 'Untouchable,' with changes in the point-of-view that Anand doesn't always know how to manage. He's best with a simple theme that he can deepen and enrich. Then there's the problem of giving information (that his coolie couldn't possibly know) about the life through which he passes—the life of an industrial Eastern city. Is it this interlarded information that blunts the sharpness of the young coolie's impressions and robs the story of some of its freshness? V. read Anand the analysis by Vernon Lee of a passage in 'Kim' where Kim lifts up the flap of the tent and sees the officers at mess, with their gold bull as mascot in the middle of the table: Kim imagines they are pouring libations to their god. All well and good; you live in Kim's mind and see the scene through his eyes; but the omniscient Kipling can't leave it at that—he goes on to explain that the little gold statue had been looted from Pekin. At once your clear vision of the scene passes; the magic is broken.

Anand took the point well, but said he couldn't forget he was writing in English, mainly for English readers who didn't know the background, and there were many things in Indian life it was hard to convey without giving the information direct. The difference between class and caste, for instance. There was that time, in real life, when an untouchable was a rajah. His subordinates would take orders from him because of his rank, but would never dine with him because of his caste.

The difficulty of having to write with one eye on a foreign audience! It disturbs the state of deep absorption in which books should be written, subtly ignores the integrity of a work. This jumping about from one point-of-view to another is just an outward sign of inner disharmony. Anand is so intelligent, so sincere, so anxious to live up to the good opinion E. M. Forster and others have formed of his work. And he has such rich themes tumbling about in his mind. If only he had a little more leisure. If only he could write all-out in Urdu and be well translated into English.

December 5th, 1935 FOG after frost, penetrating the house. Stewart Macky dropped in at midday, between his Moorfield hours in the East and his afternoon practice in the West. V., by exception, out. We had lunch in the sitting-room, pushing the table near the fire. Stewart was saying this week's frost has been so beautiful; it's worth paying for in cold: the trees in the garden behind his home at Wembley were like blue glass. (Glass, is it? Hadn't I slipped and fallen twice in Gray's Inn Road, to the polite derision of three taxi-drivers?)

Stewart was full of good experiences as usual—experiences snatched in his few spare hours—but first he wanted news of Louis. News or memories, Louis will always be of first-rate importance to him. 'There's no one like him to listen to,' he said. 'His talk's simply the best I ever heard.'

And when Stewart mentions good talk, he does it against the background of the circle he's been meeting almost ever since he came to London five years ago, when Walter Turner, his kinsman by marriage, invited him into a remarkable little group, representing nearly all the arts. Just a dinner and talk, weekly, fortnightly; James Stephens, who seems to have brought his voice and mind to London for keeps; Huxley; Mark Gertler; Koteliansky, now turned publisher.

And Turner himself, concerned almost equally with literature and music—a lyric poet, a critic, a biographer of musicians. It seemed characteristic that when we met him at the Mackys' one afternoon last July, Turner, having been to the great Mozart festival at Glyndebourne, was absorbed in demonstrating, contrary to many press comments, that the libretto of 'Cosi Fan Tutte' was noble and significant. Most of us had never heard the opera. It was getting late, and Turner's pretty French wife, after protesting about a train, alighted on the arm of a chair like a despairing little bird, since it was apparent that Walter had begun an important dissertation and would finish it. And finish it he did, by sheer concentration. The sort of concentration that makes him able, they say, to write his *New Statesman* articles in a roomful of people talking.

But what a grand member of such a group Stewart must be, responsive to each of the others' special interests in turn, listening with a generous gusto, able to report finds of his own. I like to imagine him in some masterly painting of them all—as you once had Johnson, Garrick, and other names with perhaps one extra figure, unnamed but attractive. In the new picture there would be Turner, his hair slicked back tightly as if to let him leap into a dispute, his face lit with emphasis; Stephens, gnome-like, with remarkable eyes and the enormous brow that explains, among other things, his strange power in mathematics; Gertler, Kot, and the rest. And the unnamed figure that adds so much to the picture? How can the painter show this man watching, listening, enjoying, and all the time giving himself out—his eyes smouldering and gleaming, his hair dishevelled by some inner force, for the fellow has a good share of 'chaos in his cosmos' . . .

To-day his talk was of some less-known French impressionists, on show this week in a small gallery, some part he has just seen Flora Robson play, an Adolf Busch solo in the Queen's Hall; and always with human zest. I suppose the word for him is 'integrated.' If he admires Flora Robson or John Gielgud in Shakespeare, he also wants to know what his friends at home are painting or writing—wants this all the more. He ought to be an artist of some kind: I hear he's a very good eye-surgeon. But he shows none of the bitterness, even spite, that marks so many men who feel frustrated by a career they chose wrong.

December 19th, 1935 JUST back from another couple of days at 'Green Ridges.' H.H.R. is perhaps more revealing, because more concentrated, in midwinter. The chunky house, with its central heating, cut off from the creeping cold of the Downs and the sea-mist, seems a little dynamo, humming with long-stored energy, carefully-husbanded.

We went out, drove along the foreshore, then inland to the glorious town of Battle, returning through countless other little country places they had visited before H.H.R. decided on 'Green Ridges.' We walked to the highest ridge above the Lane, heard the fog-siren on Beachy Head a dozen miles away, saw the nothingness of distance over the Channel. Always I felt her tautness, like a coiled spring.

She is working now on another book, highly documented. Nothing to do with Australia this time. Her general ideas on writing have never changed. More than ever she is determined, for her part, not to interfere with her characters but to let them work out their own destinies; to keep the author out of it. It was the same when she began, in 'Maurice Guest'; to the confounding of the critics who wanted, for instance, to represent the controversial passage on Mendelssohn as her own opinion. Later on, people quoted Richard Mahony's view of Australian life, people, and landscape as her own; this in spite of the brief aside at the opening of 'Ultima Thule' where she speaks as a 'native born.'

I listen to her out-of-doors, where she shows me, on the misty Downs, some grand stuggy horses, Suffolk Punches, actual importations of a farmer who had once travelled abroad to Suffolk; or indoors, in the study all the evening, the mild central heating quickened by a fire, the mental atmosphere warm and fluid. She asks me about some Australians on her shelves. What is this novelist likely to do next? Hasn't that one rather the over-emphasis of a journalist? What poems are to be expected from So-and-so?

So much of my own life has been spent watching writers at work, reading in manuscript their poems, stories, novels, listening to their ideas—or guessing at them; trying to come to some conclusions about the special nature of each. But what makes up the special nature of this writer, H.H.R.?

First of all, concentration: her life planned to fertilize those hours of creative work. But concentration to what end?

Economically free, she has never thought of writing for money, never been tempted to please a publisher by writing a novel for the new season. Her impulse to create has all along come from a passionate interest in human relationships and character; perhaps a lifelong absorption in a few figures that have touched her feeling and imagination. Her need for human contacts is mainly satisfied by the people in the world she builds up. She seems to have few close friends, and has no love at all for large groups.

To write is her joy. Suggest to her that a writer's life is a hard one, an agonizing struggle with intractable material, and she will deny it. 'But I love every moment at my desk. How else could I have kept on writing all these years, getting nothing for it but starvation-fees and obscurity?'

Success, immediate and retrospective, came, ironically, with 'Ultima Thule,' her most intransigent book (one that had to be published privately). It might never have come in her life-time. She would have kept on without it. She is a writer.

December 27th, 1935 A SMALL, interesting party at Rebecca West's flat, very cosy and Christmasy. Central heating for warmth and a log fire to provide a centre, with Christmas cards spread round in their hundreds and everyone conscious of the timelessness that is part of this season.

We rather expected a crowd, but there were only Vera Brittain and her husband Prof. Catlin—he gently ex-cathedra and professorial, with that falsely-youthful exterior of Harrison Moore and Keith Hancock—John Beevers and his wife, a young, fair-haired Mlle. de la Tremblaye from Switzerland, and Mr. Henry Andrews. ('I am the husband,' he said with a twinkle, as he met us on the landing).

He is very much more, though, than a literary woman's husband. A banker, he knows his London, knows his Europe, and not only its languages. He was brought up in Germany, and seems to have had a very liberal education there. One doesn't expect an Englishman (or a Scotsman) to be so familiar with both the arts and sciences as he is.

There was plenty of good talk, of a quiet group kind; no wild revelry. Rebecca West, offering sherry, said: 'There isn't much to drink, but that's because our butler's so stern. At our party last Christmas a young man got excited and insisted on embracing that torso'—a fine modern nude—'saying he thought it was me.'

Came home through mawkish, mild weather, V. going on to another party at Colahan's. Read Dorothy Richardson's 'Clear Horizon.' It wasn't clear, but rather rich.

January 10th, 1936 JEANNE in London for a week and staying with the Paresces. Paresce himself is a handsome, uncertain, restless fellow, a brilliant journalist for *La Stampa,* but not a fascist. How he separates his private attitude from his public one is a mystery. Perhaps the difficulty accounts for his occasional moody look; he seems slightly uneasy with Jeanne, in spite of his affection for her, as if he were continually searching for common ground. Mme. Paresce is a witty, friendly woman, devoted to Jeanne; a Russian, but with six languages.

This evening Jeanne was talking about her task of editing the papers of Henry de Jouvenel. She's had great difficulties. There are complicated personal matters—his impossible and rich second wife, wanting all the limelight of his death as 'my right'; and there are the children, anxious that the portrait shall be a satisfactory family one. For the present Jeanne is also ghosting a young, inarticulate politician, publicist for a University League of Nations, and getting his articles into the Paris press.

January 17th, 1936 FROM Hugh McCrae, after describing the delights of the Camden Show:

> I frankly hate your damned old London; and how you can stick it out there, fresh from Green Island, passeth my limited understanding. My own simple wants are satisfied at the

local Plough and Harrow, where I was given my first *free* drink one day last week, in recognition of ten or twelve years of heroic attendance. And I saw what you have never seen on the way to Claridge's—a pair of magpies dancing in the dust. We have willows, too, almost within a foot-length of the bar doorway; and a backwater of the Nepean with great Dutch-looking draught-horses sucking up tadpoles while they drop manure in oblation at the same time.

February 5th, 1936 V. AND N. to dinner with Ruth Pitter in her Chelsea flat. Her mother and her partner are on a three weeks' cruise to Algiers, shaking off the chills of a long London winter. Ruth perhaps more responsible-looking in winter, her hair cut squarer, her clothes more tailor-made, her low-heeled house-shoes like boys' dancing-pumps. She has been absorbed in business detail: I haven't met her all winter—nor since A.E. died in July.

She was discussing with V. the recent memorial dinner held by friends of Orage: Herbert Read, Philip Mairet (writing the biography), Will Dyson, about thirty more. V. went with Rowland Kenney. As they talked it over, I sank into the typescript of her next book, called, after the first poem, 'A Trophy of Arms.' She has had no book out since the 1928 'Poems,' except 'A Mad Lady's Garland,' mostly grotesque, decorative gargoyles in archaic or pseudo-archaic language.

The new book contains those ample, flowing odes, like 'Thanksgiving for a Fair Summer' from the *New English Weekly* in the year of its resurgence; pieces so 'true' (like 'true' singing by someone with absolute pitch) that they used to distress critics who believe that modern poetry should bristle like the fretful porcupine with difficulties intended to mislead. There will be some of her brief lyrics, final in form like a circle or a star. And some experiments in sapphics, the form used intimately: unrhymed, of course. She read us the poem in sapphics that ends, 'and the soul, the housewife'; and that other 'Fair is the water.' Sure in every phrase.

Her poems have been produced gradually, in chinks of time, the first jottings made with the pencil that all day long does the mysterious necessary work of costing, as well as some of the designing in the business.

To-night she was absorbed by an idea; that people nowadays dodge suffering, by anaesthetics, by comforts. Won't they have to pay some time? Denis Saurat had lately written about this in a book, 'The Three Conventions.' By evading our natural fate we leave a mass of pain about, unendured, unexperienced; and this mounts up until it explodes in a crisis or a war. Saurat's mystical theory of balance derives perhaps from the scapegoat, certainly from the Gaelic figure of the Sin-Eater.

Ruth developed the fantasy. Was death on the roads due to an accumulation of evasions? Did she agree, I asked, with the anthroposophists, that the giving of artificial chemicals to the earth—instead of natural humus compost—was bound to lead to famine and plague in the end? And where did you draw a distinction between natural and artificial? 'Natural' suffering! 'Artificial' relief out of it! I felt her meditative, for the idea was taking her further than she knew. Perhaps she was just 'going with the ship'; it might carry her into some intensity of expression—*ça a sa vérité*—and then leave her free.

February 27th, 1936

TO the superb Chinese Exhibition for the third time. It's well arranged historically, and by taking room after room you flow naturally through the countless centuries. Near some Bodhisattvas I met Will Dyson, debonair in this month of gnawing cold and looking round him with his usual pugnacious twinkle. I congratulated him on Betty's work at the Old Vic.—designs and costumes for 'Peer Gynt' and for Chekhov's 'Three Sisters.' Astonishing that temptress in the Norwegian mountain scene, a scaly, greenish, moonlit horror; and those sisters in varying densities of grey and black, as if in degrees of mourning for the Moscow they were never to reach. There was dramatic intelligence as well as artistic skill in the designs.

But Dyson would not be pushed into the position of proud father. In his fantastic way he began a long harangue about how the writers and artists of our generation were being elbowed aside by youth.

'Betty's all right, but isn't it just because she's young they're making such a fuss about her work? These young people—all of them cocksure and ready to run the world for us. Time we made a real stand against them and refused to be driven from the stage. Don't you find your own daughters like that? Quick to bully you and tell you your ideas are old-fashioned? Well, let us all stand shoulder to shoulder and resist this contumacy. Close our ranks.'

He had mounted his charger and was riding a-tilt with comic bravura. The ruthlessness of young people. Their poise and arrogance. The way they would gang up against all the accepted leaders of the day before their own and drive them out into the desert. Suddenly he looked at the clock, with an affectation of the timid hireling, and said he would be late for an appointment with his editor.

'Don't forget,' he grinned at parting. 'We must close our ranks.'

When he left me among the timeless Bodhisattvas, I thought of the evening last July when I was taken with a little group of the editor's friends over the huge *Daily Herald* office and shown all its modern gadgets that I couldn't understand. There was special telegraph-apparatus for dragging news out of darkest Africa, a front-page photograph of the Aga Khan with his latest racehorse being printed for the delight of two million working-class readers, and a teleprinter to inform the Manchester office that some friends of the editor were being shown over the London works, repeating the news back to London in half-a-minute.

They showed us everything, it seemed, except to-morrow's cartoon by Dyson. Yet Will Dyson it was, in his startling youth, who had given the still younger, the newborn, the embryonic *Daily Herald* its almost fabulous force in 1913.

March 1st, 1936 THIS time in London we've come across several young men who follow the curious, unhopeful craft of publisher's reader. A few do it all the time, like professional wine-tasters, tea-tasters—and don't they just remember to spit it all out every time! I remember T. told me he hadn't come across, in three years, one manuscript worth recommending until he struck G. B. Lancaster's 'Pageant.' That one he recommended as *first-class*. He must have been unfortunate—and his publisher.

Some men 'read' as a side-line to nourish their serious activities. Philip Henderson is one of these. I had known his work as literary critic and literary historian for years before I met him. There was his edition of Skelton, his Everyman prefaces, e.g., to Spenser's minor poems, and, more recently, his study of the Novel in the Twentieth Century Series. It seems that all these important tasks don't, in modern Grub Street, keep a man going. A publisher pays a fee of thirty or fifty pounds down in advance, and by the time the book appears the money has been used for rent and food; and that's all. So a writer looks for reading to do. Reading a manuscript novel means not merely handing in an expert opinion ('This ms. is quite unpublishable,' 'This one is worth talking over with the author') but a typed summary of the plot, however foolish, and the subject-matter, however banal. So that to read and treat a manuscript takes at least a day; and three manuscripts a week only bring in thirty shillings! *Behold what ills the scholar's life assail!*

But in the rest of the week Henderson does his books. And he has just shown us a formidable one in manuscript, 'The Novel To-Day,' reading us the preface. Or rather giving it to

Edith Young to read while he listened. Serious, sensitive, with a very slight and intermittent stammer caught in his years of struggle, Henderson is aware of himself as standing between the classes in English society. Is he the modern version of a Gissing young man, I wonder? But with what Gissing's characters omitted—a sense of the general basis of society, a concern for the safeguards of civil liberty, a hope for fundamental, necessary change. This concern, this hope, have taken him at times to places like the distressed areas in Wales, where he found that his modest beard (familiarly accepted by young people in London as a Jesus beard) aroused a certain sympathy among the miners; it seemed that he, like some of the rest of them, couldn't afford a shave in years. He has kept his beard.

The theme of his new book is an analysis, not to say an arraignment, of the principal novelists in England and Europe. To what extent have they shown a response, in their books, to the unrest and changing forces of to-day? Virginia Woolf he sees enclosed in a narrow world, or, if peering out, using special glasses for the purpose; the same in some degree with E. M. Forster, for all his liberal breadth.

Among continental novelists, Henderson seems to measure social alertness according to their consciousness that many liberals and radicals, as well as Jews, are now in Nazi concentration-camps; or that is the effect of his chapter appraising the work of Malraux in France, Döblin in Germany, and speculating about the novel in the U.S.S.R.

Yet his theory of the functions permitted to the novel to-day is so much clearer than his actual investigations, that I can only write down here the remark that closes the long prefatory chapter, 'The Function of the Novel' and think it over:

'If the novel to-day is to have any other function than recording the doings of the decadent descendants of Moll Flanders and Robinson Crusoe, it could scarcely have a nobler function than that of awakening man to a consciousness of his destiny as a social being.'

March 3rd, 1936 JUST as I was preparing dinner Brian Penton looked in after several months in the South of Spain, writing his sequel to 'Landtakers'. He has handed it over, completed, to his publishers here. He looks brown and springy.

Malaga for him has been a place of strict work, and pleasantly cheap. Rent very low, the house even over-supplied with everything, including quantities of fine linen. The food was good, if you liked Spanish cooking. The only expense was drink at week-ends; you stopped working and kept open house. I couldn't tell if the cheapness was just *valuta* or held good in Spanish currency. Climate good, he said, for the winter; it might be restlessly hot in summer.

We discussed Spain chiefly as a place for foreign writers to live and work in, as Basil always recommended. For some time we've been thinking of going there when A. comes back from Vienna. Penton recommended Andalusia—he was lyrical about the people with their marked character, their abandon and love of life. But we've nearly decided to make for the north-east coast, the Costa Brava, if we can find a place that's quiet yet handy to Barcelona.

Nothing was said of the political situation in Spain. Was this because Malaga was sleepily unpolitical, or was Penton preoccupied with his compulsory return to Sydney for his job? 'And it means being cut off for years'—that was the way he looked at it: 'here in London last night I was able to hear a whole recital by the Lener quartette.'

March 11th, 1936 THIS evening Marcel Aurousseau admitted that one of his ambitions was to edit a definitive collection of Charles Harpur's poems. He feels Harpur has always been taken in an uninformed way, the same few short poems being transferred from anthology to anthology and his longer work, often his better work, passing unnoticed. The subject should be settled, he said: the poems should be accessible, so that the Australian Muse can be placated by a correct vision of the poet whom Kendall praised as 'her first and her favourite child.'

But—the cat's out of the bag—one of Aurousseau's incentives in the matter is geographical, or at least topographical. If he edits the poems, he'll write a biographical preface; and lately, somewhere in mid-London, he came across a Harpur Street, spelt in this way. Is that a clue to Charles Harpur's origins?

I've never met anyone in whom literature and geography merged so significantly as in Aurousseau. One evening here he said he had more hope for Australian geography than Australian literature—though the geography, so far, had some appalling faults and gaps. As a geographer, I think, he has an idea that a separate and fresh view of man's earthly life might be drawn from within the borders of that island of the South, the Last Sea-thing . . . But methods of discovery and statement must be organized, must be thorough. His mind turns to the 18th Century astronomers and navigators who exercised their rapidly-expanding scientific knowledge in drawing up Australian charts and maps that are still valuable. The responsible outlook of those scientists was a new religion, humanist and rational, and he bitterly resents any cheap sneers at their limitations.

Aurousseau's own writing, the more you examine 'Highway in Spain,' stands firm in both spheres, literary and geographical; his slighter papers, such as some unpublished impressions of his Sydney childhood, could give geographical chapter and verse for each scene. In spite of his definite interest in all the arts, he's primarily a scientist, yet in his position at the Royal Geographical Society he's humorously aware that the officials often hesitate to ask him to review a book for their Journal for fear he'll be 'literary,' by which they vaguely mean decorative in style. (As if, I suppose, he might drag Quixote's Duchess into a review on a book on Spanish geology, or quote Keats in a book on Darien).

There's bound to be a slight conservatism, and even old-maidishness, about such venerable institutions as the R.G.S. Aurousseau was telling us about that stalwart explorer, Ella Maillart, when she lectured there lately. It was an important occasion, and the Society attended, together with its wives in evening-dress. Some of the chief wives sat on the platform, or at any rate just in front of the table Ella Maillart was using. After speaking brilliantly of the famous journey through inaccessible parts of China she and Peter Fleming had made, she suddenly, as if introducing a pleasurable climax, said: 'And now I'd like to show you just what Peter and I had to eat.' And there, on the polished mahogany that is the apple of the secretary's eye, she lit a small spirit-lamp and, still speaking, cooked a very small mess, rather like office-paste. She stirred and spoke, stirred and even waved the spoon about so that it dripped hotly—down some of the wives' decolleté backs, Aurousseau is inclined to believe, and (what was ultimately worse) on to the mahogany table, the secretary's pride and joy. The explorer had demonstrated her point. Their rations for some long, difficult weeks, had been nasty, brutish, and *short.*

April 5th, 1936 YESTERDAY met Jean Young in Cambridge, and she took me to see her old friends, the Leavises. Mrs. Leavis, a friendly, dark, young spectacled woman, welcomed us and, after we had dropped our cloaks, ushered us in to the sitting-room where Dr. Leavis was handy-man, watching the tea-kettle on the fire. He was tallish, baldish, with brown hair and side-whiskers; brown, sensitive humorous eyes, with a droop at the corners. Mrs. L., with her high, very rapid utterance, and Dr. L. with his slight drawl broadening his vowels, were both of them fatigued, and utterly aware of it all the time—admitting it in words.

Coming along, I had asked Jean Young about their position, which is known to be unfortunate. She explained that Mrs. L. had been L.'s most brilliant student while he held a University post as English lecturer for six years. Then they had married. At the end of the six years the post came up for revision: L. had expected re-appointment for another period, thereafter permanently. Nothing of the kind. Through some hostility of the academic authorities he lost the post and has now to live on giving lessons, though he has also a tiny post as lecturer in a specially hard-up college. Yet he publishes *Scrutiny*, which is eagerly read by his old students all over the world, and he is overwhelmed by students who make their way to him for advice and training. As for his wife, she wrote her brilliant, searching book, 'Fiction and the Reading Public', as a thesis years ago, but has not had leisure to do anything else except articles for *Scrutiny*.

Dr. L. has fluency and pungency in talk, though he finds writing a slow, difficult matter. 'My wife's the making of *Scrutiny*, you know. She's a born journalist, and comes to the rescue, especially when a promised article fails to turn up at the last moment. Incredible to me how she can write straight off like that. With me, writing's a long struggle . . .'

Again and again he confessed: 'But I'm so tired. I'm undertaking too much. Even now I can't speak as I should because I've got my eyes on that boy over there. There's no need, as his mother's here and at leisure. But we're so used to the need for watching him.'

The boy was little Ralph, terribly nervy and delicate, physically unable to 'tolerate fats' and mentally alert enough for the age of six instead of two. He didn't sleep, his father said, and he had been very ill.

While Jean and Mrs. L. talked on the sofa about their common friends, I asked about *Scrutiny*, in which (March) I had just been reading his grand revaluation of Keats. What relation was *Scrutiny* to the two volumes called 'Scrutinies,' collected from files of the *Calendar of Letters*? He said it was in direct descent. He had immensely valued the *Calendar* while it lasted, and had admired the critical intelligence of the young men—Edgell Rickword, Garman, and Bertram Higgins—who had run it:

'The *Calendar* was an important review, and I couldn't help regretting it should be forgotten and unused. It was very little known or circulated at the time, and complete sets are now unobtainable. I had my set bound and kept it safely; but I thought something could be done about it and, two years ago, I got Wishart to publish a volume compiled from the *Calendar*—"Towards Standards of Criticism".'

He showed me a copy, with an essay by Bertram Higgins in it, which he much admired; said Bertram was a wonderfully sound and shrewd critic and wondered how that little *Calendar* group had got themselves 'educated'—had they educated one another by good conversation? He asked me how old Bertram was, and when I told him thirty-five said that made him think all the more of him—he must have been under twenty-five in the days when he had followed him and found him so sound.

'As for Rickword and Garman, it seems they've gone all to pieces. Call themselves marxists, but are really just Bloomsbury, knocking round at cocktail-parties and not doing any thinking.'

I told him I thought he was misinformed—that Garman was in poor health, lived in the country and came to town every week to deliver a careful literary lecture, while Edgell Rickword had just taken over the managership of an important publishing business. But L.'s apt to suspect a young writer of turning Bloomsbury, which means for him—I asked for his definition—'an acceptance and bandying about of current fashionable notions on literature.' He complained that the Indians he had seen lately were hopelessly Bloomsbury, and I found he meant Iqbal Singh and Anand.

'I've known Singh for years and have been disappointed in him. After a term at Cambridge he decided to leave. He was to be a genius; the University could give him nothing. Then lately he brought me his long story, "When One is In It"—you've seen it?'

I certainly had: a tense, imaginative story of life among the cotton-spinners of Bombay.

'Well,' said Dr. L., 'that, of course, was so hopeless I hardly knew how to tell him. He has no sense of writing at all. It's not as if he were a beginner. He's quite twenty-five and doesn't know more than that.'

(Leavis's tha-at has a dying fall; he never bites his words off with a snap. He is tired, neurotic, never indecisive, though; the dying fall finds its angle of repose.)

I demurred about Singh, admitting some turgid passages in the story but insisting on the strength and pattern and sincerity; L. said he would read it again, but I'm afraid he knows the answer. From Anand he seemed to hope for nothing, though he knew that E. M. Forster had prefaced his 'Untouchable.' When it comes to new material, entirely new material, I feel, L. is just as academic as the other academicians. He told me, innocently, that when he found a New Zealand student of his, named McCormick, doing a thesis on Tudor literature that bored him, he proposed that he should investigate something nearer home—'The Reason Why There is No Literature in New Zealand.' An investigation with the answer known beforehand, x = o! The little modern continuity he admits in literature is nearly all very safe—Eliot, Forster, Virginia Woolf, Lawrence, Joyce and (I hear incredibly) Charles Morgan!

But time was going; Ralph was being put to bed; day was closing. Dr. L. sauntered down to the bus with us, hatless and without overcoat. 'I'm Cambridge-born, but my wife's Mediterranean and never gets used to this cold.' Jean was advising holidays in the Scilly Islands if they couldn't get as far as Greece or the South Seas. He shook his head. The child needed his regime, his doctor; he himself needed his books. The vacation was the only time he could do his own work, and if he didn't produce a new book regularly his reputation would drop; he couldn't afford that.

We missed a bus or so; at last caught one. A short ride. We hopped out, in the middle of Cambridge, near the Market. Can you run like a hare? Jean asked. Not very. Dodging evening shoppers and promenaders, still possible in a town of narrow streets and few cars, we passed the Market, reached King's Parade, and raced down to the Bull Hotel.

April 14th, 1936 A FROSTY evening, with people's footsteps echoing like steel along the pavements. I went alone to Colahan's studio. Good talk around the stove —Mrs. W. and her French god-daughter, John Farmer, Colin, and his little boy, David. Talk of disarmament, Colin quoting Norman Angell, Mrs. W. saying with her soft accent. 'Once we had hop'. Perhaps we are better knowing now there is no hop' of peace.' She left with her friend at ten; then Colin showed me what he had been doing lately, dancing about the studio and placing the canvases on the easel in his apt, vigorous way. They included a new portrait of V., unfinished.

'Last time he was here,' he said, 'I did some good work on that. I was so pleased with that work that I painted it all out for fear of being limited by it next time and led to develop it without regard for the whole. "No, you don't," I said to myself, and out it went.'

He showed me a portrait of Mrs. W., her graceful bent head and smooth hair over a red velvet cowl and black tunic. I had seen it before, in a different state. 'Too perfect,' Colin had sniffed. 'I've been putting in certain delicacies I *know* about her, not giving force to her complete appearance.'

So this time, after further work on it, he has let an inconsequent blob of shadow appear on one cheek, to counteract or counterbalance the exquisite finish of the brow and hair.

'You know she *has* queer high cheekbones, that Basque woman, and they're bound to make a certain distortion on her face somewhere.'

(But does this harmonize with his determination not to 'know' more than the perishing mortal eye can see at one stage or another?) His insistence on Leonardo's 'innocence of the eye' is the chief theme of his brief essay that he means to use as a preface to his catalogue when he holds his exhibition soon. Brief, did I say? He had it in about 10,000 words, and was tearing his hair over it: the arguments recurred, overlapped, collided; the connecting links were shadowy. How could he get it down to a short clear statement?

'Tell you what, V., if you can manage to reduce this to a thousand words I'll give you one of my very best landscapes.'

Which was done, with more immense toil than Colin will ever know. His funny, cussed acknowledgment was chiefly concerned with what had been shorn away.

'I feel like a dreamy cow-cocky who's called a bloke in to do some clearing and wakes up to find his paddocks immaculate, but all his nice trees gone . . . Can't I have *one* more page?'

Anyway, we've got the landscape, an Eltham bush-track, very unpretentious and sound. And a lovely frame that Colin made from an ugly gilt one, letting his little David do the patina that gives it distinction.

BARCELONA
(1936)

BARCELONA

May 15th, 1936

HOW clean everything is here after London! Not merely our sparsely-furnished cottage itself, which we have taken for a year, but the air, the fishing-boats drawn up on the sand, the strip of beach that runs in a long curve to the docks at Barcelona.

Our irregular but continuous row of houses—the Calle Monsolis—stands against a hill, and the concrete walls of the courtyards behind the houses are even higher at the back than at the sides, so as to support the sheer clay cutting over which hang trees belonging to a wide farm immediately above—a fig over us, a cherry further along. Just as these houses almost lean against the hill and face the sea, so I find myself leaning back against Spain and looking out on the Mediterranean: I orient myself, that is, I face the East.

It is good to be in Spain these days. There is a feeling of sap stirring, of life beginning to bud, and not only because of the Spring. I feel that the young people who come pouring out to the beach in their shorts or coloured frocks are heady with the sense of a new world opening up ahead of them. It is partly a political, partly a social liberation. They are discovering the pleasures of 'sport,' of hiking, of tramping over the hills with picnic-baskets, boys and girls together. A good many of the conventions of Old Spain must have pressed very heavily on youth. But now—every Sunday seems to be a fiesta.

Not for everyone. Things are going badly for Roca who keeps the fonda at the corner, and for his prim, pretty little 'Aragonesca' wife from Saragossa. It is going to be a bad season, they say, and many of the big houses, like the Torre Monsolis, are closed up; the rich people have gone to France and there will not be the parties of theatre-goers and concert-goers driving out along the beach-road from Barcelona for supper. At least so Roca says dolefully. I feel sorry for him, for he has been very good to us since we came, though we spend very little with him, doing most of our own cooking. He has sunk a lot of money in this fonda of his, making it gay and modern, and he is a wonderful cook. But he takes the bad outlook very lightly; a buoyant, intelligent man, he is more concerned with the general welfare of the country than with his own personal prospects. His wife, though, stands at the door of the empty fonda watching the youthful holiday-makers and their picnic-baskets with narrowed, resentful eyes.

May 18th, 1936 DAY begins here with Arasco, our oldish, wrinkled neighbour on the right—which is the side of Barcelona. No need to sing to him, 'Awake, Arasco, and begin the dawn.' Who could be early enough to call him? He has begun the dawn almost in the dark, clopping about in his wet-day wooden shoes, winding up his well-buckets in his resonant courtyard, dealing with cans and basins that clang against the whitewashed tiles. He lives alone in his whitewashed house and does his housekeeping in an exemplary and early way, banging a rug or two against the garden railings opposite. If the mornings are at all fine, he takes his breakfast out to the stone ledge beside those railings. Breakfast, is it? Nothing in the world but a large slice of bread, half an oval long. On the bread, perhaps, a stroke of oil, or with it an onion, tomato, or orange. Nothing to drink, nothing hot for breakfast.

But I forget. Arasco usually has one more thing to his breakfast—a book. Sometimes it's a very thick novel—mysteriously he always seems to be on the last page when we see him—sometimes a magazine with close type. A thoughtful lonely man, Arasco, his lean face wrinkled with long disregard of sun and wind, his lean body stooped but nimble. What is he; a retired peasant? Yet not so definitely retired; look at his tiny front garden, the same size as ours. From its top gate on the *calle* to the lower one opening out on the beach road, every inch is crammed, and with serious vegetables—great walls of tomatoes splayed on bamboo-poles, stretches of potatoes, compact groves of onions. He hates a weed, visibly suspects our morning-glories of climbing his fence. His garden is cunningly irrigated by pipes passing under the narrow *calle* from his back-courtyard. It's exciting to see him turn on his garden-sluices suddenly—'in Xanadu did Kubla Khan'—a rare excitement, so far, since the sky has been sluicing us all so well this spring.

June 4th, 1936 I HAD thought Maria rather a weak if noisy reed to lean upon, but how she blossoms out when she begins to feel at home! Her gaiety, her whirlwind energy, her capacity for talk! Her husband is a fisherman, very poor. He goes out at night with the others in the mosquito fleet, but since he can't afford a licence he's not allowed to sell his catch in the market, so must take what he can get for it outside from the other fishermen. Maria, when she's not cleaning for Roca or for stray people like us, goes out to work in the fields, picking peas for something like fourpence an hour and her midday meal.

Hard going, but what a zest for life she has! Her body's thin and her long hair's straight; her dark eyes have a slight squint, yet they have no lack of expression. While we have a cup of tea together (Té Lipton, in a flat muslin bag as big as a penny) during a pause in the washing, she pours out everything in her mind leaning forward eagerly to batter through my density:

'I've been here near Barcelona now for five years with my husband and my two little boys. It's all very well, but ah, I used to be in Andalusia.' (Fluted accent on the *i* as in *Maria*). 'In Andalusia you really live, if you can get food or keep alive at all. Here it's different. A woman can get work to do—yes—but it's not living. Everything's so dull, *muy triste*.'

Dull? In what way, I ask her, looking out at the scarlet geraniums of the courtyard. She twists her arms and body about in the effort to make herself clear. Catalonia faces east and even gets winds from the cold mountains of the north. Life here, the people here, seem to her all chill, canny, serious.

'In Andalusia it's different. Many flowers in the streets always, people dancing, people warm. I can't explain. Here it's often cold; no, not very cold, not much colder in winter even than that first week you were here: but it *seems* cold. In Andalusia it's never cold in the same way. People are warmer; they laugh and sing more; they wear flowers in their hair.'

Of course; hadn't I seen the ghost of a red wreath on Maria's hair when she sat down to talk? Andalusia, Sevilla—aren't they perhaps a dream of vanished youth?

June 6th, 1936 IT'S pleasant to work here, looking out on the dancing tideless Mediterranean. I'm occupied, at present, on a translation of Helene Scheu Riess's novel that she gave A. in Vienna. Helene wants it finished before she leaves for America at the end of summer. It's a light, rather flimsy story with brilliant passages of dialogue that are, perhaps, suited to a different book.

V. is engaged in preparing an abridged version of 'Such is Life' for Cape, a much more delicate business than anyone could have imagined. We had difficulty in getting a copy to bring here, but Henry Handel Richardson willingly lent us the one I'd sent her years ago. I'm afraid that Edward Garnett didn't realize all the difficulties when he insisted that 'Such is Life' should be cut down by 50,000 words if it were to be introduced successfully to English readers. He admires the book, but thinks that parts of it are so local as to be unintelligible to anyone who doesn't know the period and the background, other parts so wordy that they act as a drag on the book. And he quotes the case of W. H. Hudson's 'Purple Land that England Lost.'

'When it was first published it went absolutely flat. Hudson's special interests had led him to linger in odd nooks of the story and wander up pleasant but irrelevant bypaths. After it had been out for some years, I persuaded him to let me cut it down by nearly a third, and since then, nearly thirty years ago, it has been steadily in demand: one could say that it had become a classic.'

But surely 'The Purple Land' had not such a subtle pattern as 'Such is Life.' Tom Collins seems to have taken a sly pleasure in planting tiny keys to his plot in the most casual and apparently irrelevant bits of dialogue.

June 8th, 1936

THERE'S no shop selling newspapers in this village at all. To get one, you have to walk to a place opposite the station (a kilometer away, as Roca says in his advertising posters: his fonda is twenty meters from the beach, a thousand from the station). Yet the number of papers published in Catalonia is very large. They are of every shade of politics, from off-white (not so very far off, either) to carmine.

To-day in Barcelona, while I waited for A., I bought a *Vanguardia* to glance at under the plane-trees. An easy paper to read—such fine sepia photographs and clear letterpress. In former days it was a conservative paper; it's still as far to the right as it can stand, and though it is fairly well-written, it wavers between culture and a rather stuffy pietism. On its leader-page, it publishes the name and attributes of the day's saint and in a prominent place there is a discussion on why women should never go stockingless. The reasons, supported by suffocating details, come under three heads—hygiene, aesthetics, and religion. Bare legs are unhealthy, they might pick up germs; they are ugly (this is where the details become most morbid), and at the same time they are sinfully attractive; it is irreligious to expose them to view. Finally, on the other side, if some say it is cheap to go with bare legs they are wrong, or as near as knows no difference, for passable stockings can be had for two pesetas at Jorba's Great Store. I don't know who owns Jorba's, but I have heard rumours.

The attack of the past on what is modern or liberal goes on in all sorts of obscure ways, and it is most noticeable in the area of women's interests. The women have no clubs where ideas can be exchanged, as even the workingmen have, and I suppose they are naturally pious and conservative. So much of the colour of their lives has always been associated with the Church's ceremonies and fiestas.

June 15th, 1936

YESTERDAY, coming out from town, I was carried express past Mongat railway-station and was suddenly roused by a ticket-inspector. It ought to have been a simple matter to pay the excess and get out at Masnou, but the inspector was an officious little person, obviously fond of scenes. He made a drama of the situation, brought the attention of the whole carriage on me, demanded extra fares as a minimum penalty—and when I looked in my purse I had no change.

Luckily a workman, watching us from a couple of seats away, came to my help and after rating the inspector in vigorous Catalan brought out a handful of coins. Then, as we alighted at the station, he kept on making almost personal apologies to me in Castilian for the official's discourtesy.

'Such an incident,' he finished up, 'couldn't have happened in France. Never!'

His naivete made me smile.

'No,' he repeated, 'Such things don't happen there. These officials are stupid. Not enough education.'

A thick, vigorous man with hair *en brosse* and lively intelligent eyes, I took him for a Southern Frenchman, exasperated at the people he was exiled among—but, no! When I went over to-day to thank him and pay my debt I found he had merely worked for a time in France. His wife keeps a little shop on the outskirts of Masnou, selling charcoal and a few vegetables. Her name is Dolores Pla. The man had learnt the trade of a hatter in Lyons but no one wore hats now.

'And they never will again. These young fellows! Afraid, more than anything, to be thought señoritos.'

His wife, a tall, thin woman, has her husband's restless intelligence and vitality. She is a native of Vilasar, two villages up the coast, but like her husband has a nostalgia for France: everything there was civilized, everything here stupid. Politics —well, one didn't bother with politics here; they were of no importance. People talked a lot but they had no ideas for improving the country. Spain was a poor country, and would remain poor. The woman brushed aside the chatter of the children coming in for a small copper's worth of sweets to back up something her husband had said:

'School? Yes, but how can one talk of school here without mockery? They have got rid of the Jesuits, but who is to take their place? Look at these children—little animals with no sense of discipline. There is no one to control them. The teacher is satisfied if he gets the day through without them throwing things at his head.'

Her concern was for Pedro, an only son, with dark eyes and bristling hair, the image of his father. He had a bent for mechanics, she said, but how was he to satisfy it in Masnou? Even in Barcelona—wasn't it true that anyone who wanted to follow a profession had to go abroad to some other university?

'In England,' her husband said, 'every boy has the same chance. Whether he is the son of a roadmender or a marquis. All sit on the same benches together.'

No use trying to dispel their illusions. All their energy seemed to be devoted to finding out things in other countries that were superior to their own; yet, in spite of its pessimism, their talk had an exuberance that made it feel like a cool fountain after that hot walk along the dusty beach-road.

July 2nd, 1936 FROM Mulk Raj Anand, very happy about the success of 'The Coolie':

. . . The Press has simply burst into an hysterical paean of praise for the book. *The Spectator, The Daily Telegraph*—everyone has been most sympathetic and understanding. I am sending you a copy of the chief reviews.
And I have suddenly been lifted from obscurity into notoriety through a speech I was asked to make at the Gorky memorial meeting. I don't know if my head has swollen, but I am going to buy a new hat. But if my fame has been made, my fortune hasn't been.
All this has been very strenuous, especially as I have the Indian Progressive Writers' Association work to do, arrangements for a Fifth Indian Political Conference (on the 10th-11th) to make, a Civil

Liberties committee to bring about, and what not. On top of this, I am in the middle of the Indian peasant novel, 'All Men Are Equal.' 'An Indian Tragedy' is finished, but it is a very blatant book, and will have to be toned down before it is published. And, at any rate, I will have to tread the ground warily, and perfect everything before it comes out, especially since 'The Coolie' has been such a thundering success. I don't know whether you have read Ralph Bates, the proletarian writer. He is going to Spain soon, and I have asked him to meet you.
I wish I could come to Barcelona myself, because your letters have such a contagious high-spiritedness about them. And I imagine from what you say that life is simple and open there and one could work all day. If only I could come I would. I shall certainly come in February for the next session of the Writers' Congress in Madrid. But you may have left by then.
I can see V. at work all day. He is an example of perfect serenity and patience to me, and please tell him I am emulating his example.

July 4th, 1936 WITH A. last night to a demonstration in Barcelona on behalf of the young Brazilian officer, Luis Carlos Prestes, who had been imprisoned in Rio de Janeiro for working-class activity. Usually people seem so self-centred here, so remote from the international scene, that I was curious to see how many would participate in this meeting. I was soon enlightened. When we found the Gran Price after going down the narrow Street of the Hospital, a curved slit between high old houses, people were pouring into the building from all sides.

What a gathering! The hall had a wide, circular floor, then three galleries, the widest at the top. Very quickly it was packed. People of all ages and sexes—and, apparently, all classes—though the tone of the meeting was set by the youths and girls in uniforms of shirts and shorts, or shirts and grey trousers, very militant young people of the Popular Front parties.

Señora and Señorita Prestes (mother and sister of the imprisoned man) appeared on the platform and were given the central seats. Everyone rose and cheered them wildly; it seemed that everyone knew the story of this young Brazilian revolutionary. The mother was a dignified woman, dressed in black with sufficient care, sufficiently absorbed and tragic. The daughter, in light-grey with a rose-coloured scarf, was more alert and responsive.

A spirited meeting, with vigorous speeches, mainly in Catalan; but long drawn-out. It had been timed to start at ten; it was ten-thirty before it really started; and when it ended our last tram had gone. That meant a considerable trudge home, but when the outer city had been left behind it was full moonlight and a nightingale was singing gloriously in the tiny wood near our house.

July 5th, 1936 A LOVELY, hottish day, with little striped tents appearing on the beach and the sea full of bathers—girls playing with rubber golliwogs, young men skimming about on their water-skis. A.'s friend, Lise Gidenke, came out for the day, and we bathed before lunch. She's a Finnish girl, full of languages, full of exuberance.

'Oh, I li-ike it too mauch,' she said, as we lay looking at the gay beach and the reddish, flower-filled hills behind.

V. came home late, having spent the afternoon at a bull-fight in town. He had wanted to see a famous matador from Gerona, who had been advertised as coming out of his retirement for this special occasion; but V. had an uneasy feeling that he had been helping to preserve an old and rather esoteric ritual. A very impressive ritual in its way, but with all its gaudy accoutrements smelling of the moth. Some of the cruelty had been eliminated; the horses of the picadors were padded to the eyes and seemed more likely to pass out from their age and debility than from the horn-thrusts of the bull; there were no casualties among the matadors, either, the bull being reduced to a dazed and helpless state before the matador approached for the final coup de grace.

Yet there seemed something dark and evil about the whole pattern of this surviving sport. It had been so obviously designed for the entertainment of another age, for the occupants of royal boxes, for elegant, cold-eyed people who felt a renewal of their security when they watched the slave's blood pour out on the sand. There is something almost aggressive in the effort to keep the game going now. V. said he felt that for most of the men and women in the boxes around the arena the bull symbolized the dumb and dangerous People. They were nearly all middle-aged—wealthy tradespeople and rentiers. Most of the young people were hiking about the hills in shorts or sunning themselves on the beaches.

July 19th, 1936 AWOKE to the dull sound of firing, but took it to be celebrations connected with the opening of the People's Olympiad at Montjuich Stadium. Not till the milkman came did I notice how still everything was—no trains running, no cars on the road, hardly a soul on the beach. The little milkman's face was very serious: 'A military rebellion's broken out in Barcelona.' Women and men were gathering in the calle, looking across the bay to the city and listening to the faint rattle of machine-guns. There was uneasiness in their faces, but it was no use asking them what the trouble was; they were emphatic that no one could know anything. Soon cars with determined-looking men in them came tearing out from town; barricades were hastily thrown up along the road and preparations made to blow up the little stone bridge between here and the station.

It was terribly hard to grasp what was happening. Everything echoed with vagueness, nothingness—nada, nada . . . Yet into the bright morning some evil seemed to have suddenly entered, violently shattering the quiet, threatening all the future. The big, empty houses up toward Tiana appeared in league with it, as if they had been waiting all summer for the attack, harbouring conspirators behind their handsome stone walls. I found myself thinking: 'This feeling of liberation here was an illusion. The dark forces have struck back; there'll be war all over the world.'

But what affected us directly was the thought of A. in Barcelona among the fighting. She had stopped in town to act as interpreter for a huge group of French athletes coming in at midnight, and was to meet us at the station this afternoon. We tried to get in to Barcelona by walking along the railway-line, but were stopped by young men with rifles. All afternoon there were awed groups in the calle, listening to the firing across the water. The loudspeakers on every window sill gave no real news, merely buzzing like cicadas: 'Tranquilo, Spaniards, tranquilo: we are winning.'

After tea this evening we sat on the stone coping near the church, watching the cars being searched for arms as they came in from the Costa Brava, and wondering what was happening across the water. Suddenly the lights came out on Barcelona city (everywhere but on Montjuich Height) and things seemed more hopeful.

July 21st, 1936 NO way of getting news of A. yet. Maria came in yesterday with the most bloodcurdling stories: 'The dead are lying in heaps along the Ramblas.'

She was half-hysterical because her mother is living in a little street off the Ramblas, yet she seemed to have a feeling that life had become dramatic and interesting. Señor Ness, next door, was reading what seemed to be a public bulletin in the calle—when I asked for the loan of it he said rather curtly that I wouldn't be able to understand it, that it was in Catalan; but in a little while he sent his daughter in with it—a very clear Government statement about the attack on the city by rebel troops in the barracks around. General Goded, it seems, arrived from the Balearic Islands a few days ago, and organized the revolt to time with others in the garrison towns all over

Spanish Morocco and Spain—Ceuta, Seville, Saragossa and Madrid.

Our house was searched yesterday by a string of solemn young men like those who man the barricade down the road. Someone had fired on a military lorry during the night, apparently.

July 22nd, 1936 NO trains or trams are running yet, but trucks tear down the road, full of men armed with the new rifles taken from the surrendered soldiers.

Roca advised us to try to get into town by one of the lorries carrying vegetables. After some trouble we secured a pass at the Mayor's office and climbed into a lorry packed with a mixed crowd—unslept men carrying rifles and revolvers, two women with babies. Countless barricades to be negotiated, but the pass with the C.G.T. stamp on it carried us through.

We searched for A. at various hotels and at the Montjuich stadium; but while we were lunching at the Hotel del Centro she appeared, gay and grubby, in the blue cotton frock and white shoes she set out in last Saturday. For her the actual attack on the Spanish people has given them a mandate to set their house in order as they dared not do before; and now to be young is very Heaven. She had been busy helping to interpret for the little groups of athletes who were marooned here when the rebellion broke out, helping them to send telegrams home: All safe.

Barcelona is in a ferment, the streets broken by barricades built of road blocks and sandbags. Not much military damage, but churches and big buildings gutted by fire and crowds milling about, searching for Falangists, waiting excitedly for news from other parts of Spain. An outburst of cheering in the middle of the afternoon. It was for President Companys, a quiet, confident little man who was making a tour on foot along the Ramblas, giving reassurances. No shops or banks open yet; at the British Consulate the head-clerk said he had *heard* of a man who was successful in changing a cheque yesterday at the International Banking Corporation by going round to the back. Still there are signs of life becoming normal again, and we will be able to walk home to-morrow.

July 25th, 1936 WALKED over to Masnou this afternoon to see the Plas. Maria had stories of violent happenings over there, and we thought that Pla, with his hot head and his outspoken contempt for everything around him, might have landed himself in trouble. But when we had successfully penetrated half-a-dozen barricades with our C.G.T. pass, and had reached the outskirts of Masnou, we were stopped by a shout from across the road:

'Salud!'

It was Pla himself, hatless, in sandshoes, talking to one of the men on guard. He hurried across and greeted us, his eyes shining with friendliness, with sheer joy of life. What did we think of the Spanish workpeople now? Had we heard Prieto on the wireless yesterday, or read his speech in *Vanguardia*? Had we seen the young men marching off to take the barracks at Saragossa?

He brought us across to his shop where his wife was standing behind the counter, putting quick stitches into some garments of Pedro's. She was exalted as he was, and their talk gushed out in parallel streams. Zaragoza . . . Azana . . . Zaragoza. The wonderful organization of the syndicates. Their promptness in getting the food-supplies into working order. Even the bakers and charcoal-sellers going round already with their carts!

The shop was empty of everything eatable except for a few wilted lettuce, but strewn around were newspapers of all kinds—some with illustrations—and it was plain they had been feeding on these. They knew how the campaign was going in every part of Spain; they had the names of all the chief generals and loyalist leaders at their finger-tips. And Pla was confident about the outcome.

'We Spaniards,' he said with a smile, 'we don't ask much. We can live on bread and a few onions, but we must have our freedom. Yes.'

July 28th, 1936 COMING up from a bathe this hot afternoon, I met V. returning from town. Bad news: we must make plans to leave almost immediately. He had been talking to the British consul and could get no reassurances about the changing of travellers' cheques. The consul was jumpy, convinced there would be bloodshed here, surprised and a little irritated that anyone should want to stay. 'If you do, I can take no responsibility for you.'

It is exasperating to have to go, since (for one thing) the house is taken for a year, but the rebellion may not be as successfully quashed as we imagined a few days ago. Can we depend on the fragments of news that filter in to us? Even Roca, usually so optimistic, has been looking gloomy for the last couple of days. 'Better go,' he says, 'Bad hours are coming. There are twenty-five major towns in Spain still in the hands of the rebels.'

Yet the real question, for us, seems to be one of money and mails; in spite of the way the tomatoes are coming on, we could not live on our little garden! I had no notion this situation would face us as I loitered on the beach this afternoon, watching the little boys playing at trench-warfare while their mothers sat sewing in the shade outside their houses.

MELBOURNE
(1936-1939)

MELBOURNE

September 14th, 1936 P. & O. *Moldavia,* on deck, early morning. Glad to know I'm moving homeward, but for once I can't help feeling a pang for the Europe being left behind. No, not for Europe so much as for this country whose dim coast we've passed without seeing. Gibraltar was hidden by a thick fog at evening. Almeria, Valencia, Barcelona—they were only visible to the mind's eye. Yet they've had a deeper reality for me, as we've coasted past, than all the personal, fugitive life of this ship. What has been going on over the horizon there during the last few days and weeks? The ship's wireless gives a little discreet information that means nothing: the passengers, so far as I can see, are quite incurious.

Last night I hung over the rails, calling up a vision of Mongat as I saw it last, close in, from the destroyer's deck.

The mosquito fleet, homing after a night's fishing; the white houses of the village itself; the bulbous domes of the vacant Monsolis mansion on the ridge, the houses of the level Calle Monsolis below. Almost Roca's fonda, almost Maria's home in the village.

This morning I woke up before dawn, looking forward to the day ashore at Marseilles. In the dim light these famous limestone islands were in receding shades of purple, until a nearer one shot into sight, almost black. But now the day's garish with light everywhere; the islands stark white, Marseilles a tumult of buildings, Notre Dame de la Garde incredibly high and golden.

September 16th, 1936 THIS one-class boat with its thousand-or-so passengers ought to make encounters easy; but the shapeless crowd is anonymous. Except for one immense, striking polyglot group—Colonel de Basil's Monte Carlo Ballet, going on its first Australian tour. Carrying with it the myth of Europe's peace, beauty, and harmony.

Complicated accidents are required to bring people together. Some old friends happened to mention an Englishman named Haskell at their table, in a different saloon from mine. Arnold Haskell? They didn't know. I first saw the name over articles on ballet in the *New English Weekly*—1932, and then on until Orage's death.

Meeting A.H. to-day, I found a small, dark man, wistfully observant. He told me he had listened to Orage—used to spend an evening a week with him in London. He had felt Orage's extraordinary qualities of wisdom and divination, but, I think, had been rather puzzled by the range and depth of Orage's interests. Haskell has some touch with all the arts, but is essentially a specialist. Perhaps Orage wouldn't, of himself, have 'covered' ballet in the *Weekly*. As it was, I remember Haskell not only wrote steadily about it but stood up to several controversies with readers who took ballet less seriously than he did. And it's ballet that brings him here; he's a roving journalist accompanying this one *in partes infidelium.*

A born liaison officer, H. has watched and listened effectively. There's his book on Epstein; conversations yielding Epstein's ideas, and done on the principle of Gsell's book of Rodin's talk (L'Art) long ago. Yet I doubt if H. could do a comprehensive book of Conversations with Orage; he would deal quite expertly with studio-talk, but his mind has its limitations.

September 22nd, 1936 IT seems ironic that the ballet's practice should have got well started just as we're in the Red Sea, where nobody works except, of course, the stokers in their cellar cool. ('I can't help wondering how the Israelites had the energy to cross over at this spot, even when the waters were rolled back for them,' someone yawned just after Suez yesterday). It's hot now, but there's a blessed breeze from somewhere. I've known the Red Sea far more sultry.

The practices were held at first with tarpaulins down, making a large private room amidships; but now it's opened up for air, and rows of knitting-women in deck-chairs make a sort of involuntary audience against the sea-line. Actual observers cluster round the piano, which is near the director of the ballet, Woizikowsky. The dancers are in skin-tight, jersey-wool bathing-suits, mostly black. W. himself in white shorts and open shirt. Round his neck hang two objects: a whistle on a thick, white cotton cord, and a gold cross on a thin gold chain. As he starts off a group of the corps he first trills on the whistle, then beats time—Rás, Dva, Tri . . . Rás, Dva, Tri. If one never learns Russian, there will be at least those pregnant words.

The young English pianist—he told me he was recently conductor of a small German orchestra—obediently plays a polonaise belonging to the 'Sylphides,' swerves suddenly to a part of the witch music from de Falla for a solo by Kirsova, the Dane, then to a rushing passage from 'Scheherazade,' with all the dancers engaged. Impossible to guess how much the dancers know of what they are building up. Woizikowsky and his whistle, they have to know. Sometimes when he leaps and stamps to clarify the movement, the whistle leaps and hangs down his back, till I'd swear he nearly blows the gold cross instead.

To see the dancers working in practice-dress is like being inside the works of a piano, accurate and infallible. One girl, not at all well, was resting on a deck-chair; 'but of course I'll join in and dance when they need me'; and she did.

To Haskell, after years of devoted association, every dancer is personal as well as professional. 'That's Sonia Woizikowska —a beautiful little thing, with great promise . . . That man will do a very good duet part in "Aurora's Wedding".' H. knows just what is being taken to Australia. I can't see that he wants to know anything in advance about that country—at any rate, not from me, or at present. I suppose a ballet creates its own world around it; a globe of glass.

November 18th, 1936 TO the Collingwood Town Hall, to see 'Till the Day I Die.' Found the doors locked and a great crowd surging about in the street outside. 'No performance,' someone said, 'the councillors have got cold feet.'

It seems as if a spirit of funk had descended upon the whole country, at least upon those at its head. 'Don't say or do anything that could possibly offend Nazi Germany,' is their cry, as it was on the *Moldavia,* when a young man was officially rebuked for wearing a Hitler cartoon costume for the fancy-dress ball. 'Till the Day I Die' has been banned by the Government after a protest by the German consul in Sydney; and now there's an atmosphere of something subversive and thrilling about it. People who wouldn't ordinarily go near a play of any kind want to see it. Apparently the councillors of this very democratic suburb were afraid that something devastating would happen to them if they let it be played.

Came home with Furnley Maurice and Ida, whom we encountered among the crowd, and brought them in to supper. Even Furnley is bitter about our determination to turn a blind eye to what is happening in Europe—neither to speak nor hear any evil of Nazism, and to see no evil in it. It's a slight change of front for him. For years he's been insisting that we should cultivate our own garden and not bother too much about affairs overseas. There was that poem of his describing the Australian soldier returning from Europe after the war, troubled because his countrymen were

Brooding on the Romanoffs, the Syndicats, the Boyne

and not planning for the future of their own country.

In those days so many people were inclined to suggest that nothing here was important, that any interest in our own life was a preoccupation with the parish pump. I think Furnley's isolationism was a reaction against that.

But since the Depression and the raising of the black flag in Europe, he's altered his stance a little. He was keenly interested in all we could tell him about Spain.

March 12th, 1937 THIS evening Hartley Grattan and Furnley Maurice to dinner, after a rather hard and hottish day. As Carnegie scholar, Grattan is soberly preparing for his great work on Australia. 'One year of travel, getting a look at every part of the country,' he says (he's had some months of that already), 'then a year of studying the documents and writing.' But he's savage about the lack of documents. We simply haven't kept our documents, and except for Sydney (and perhaps Adelaide) there are no archives worth mentioning.

Grattan has immense confidence in himself and he may produce a really valuable book. It shouldn't be hard for him to outdo our previous visitors, for most of them haven't been really interested in the country, and have looked at it with a trivial or journalistic eye. There's no doubt about Grattan's interest, and he has a tough faculty for breaking through the political and newspaper façade that hides our life. He's always probing for the economic roots of things, and when it's a matter of history he reads Brian Fitzpatrick rather than Ernest Scott. He can be rude to the right people.

Perhaps it's that forthrightness in him that makes it so easy for him to get on with Furnley Maurice. He sincerely admires Furnley:

'I wonder if the young people of Melbourne University know what an interesting poet they've got on their campus?'

During the evening he tackled Furnley about what he called our pre-war Utopian outlook and our ignorance of sociological developments here, past and present. There was some hammer-and-tongs argument, but more understanding then when they met at Mrs. Bull's ten years ago—he unaware that Furnley was a writer, and Furnley taking him for an uppish American tourist, out to 'knock' everything Australian.

June 15th, 1937

FROM Ruth Pitter giving some news of people in London:

'I was talking to T. S. Eliot lately—he said that his admiration for Orage (which I asked about, as it puzzled me) was on account of his calm and fearless independence of idea. I like Eliot. It's the followers who make the racket.'

Curious how many people like Eliot when they meet him personally, and even talk about his modesty, though the quality that comes out in his work, especially his criticism, is a kind of arrogance. I have just been reading Arnold Bennett's journal, in which he describes Eliot coming to him and asking for an article in reply to an attack by Virginia Woolf. Bennett's note would make you picture a rather humble young man, deferential to the famous novelist, and keen to get his advice on literary projects—especially on the possibility of writing a drama of modern life in rhythmic prose. Yet this was at a period when Eliot had already made his reputation and was editing the *Criterion*. 'I liked him much more than ever before,' Bennett concludes.

July 29th, 1937 AFTER dinner Alan Marshall dropped in with the manuscript of his novel, 'Factory,' and read parts of it. He has such a good, resonant voice and such a strong mimetic gift that I couldn't help feeling he might have been a successful actor if he hadn't been handicapped by his lameness. But perhaps it's more important for him to write. There's no doubt about his talent; he's got an eye for detail and an ear for the rhythms of everyday talk. Some of his little bits of dialogue have such a lyrical swing that they sound like poems.

This novel has a very good theme—the rise and fall of a small boot-factory in an industrial suburb. The whole venture only lasts a few months, but there's time to get to know a large number of people and to watch them at work. I've some doubt about the mechanics, though. Alan's interest in modern literary experiments has led him to try a lot of devices that aren't necessary and tend to make his factory-hands seem a less natural crowd than they are.

During the evening he was telling us of his long fight to make a life for himself, crippled as he was from the age of seven by infantile paralysis and bad operations. In the country he got along well enough; the other youngsters were decent to him and he taught himself to ride and swim almost as well as any of them. But, coming to town about eighteen, he felt bewildered and lost, and for a time sank into a pit of depression. One day, studying the face of a man coming toward him on crutches—he was always on the look-out for other cripples—he asked himself:

'Why is it that if I saw that man's head, cut off from his body, I'd know it belonged to a cripple?'

It was the way the face had become stamped with self-pity, he decided; and he made up his mind not to let anything of the sort occur to him. It hasn't. Surely not even Roosevelt has achieved a more robust triumph over his disabilities. This evening, while we were talking, I'd so completely forgotten his lameness that a little shock passed through me when he groped for his crutches by the side of his chair before rising to go.

October 15th, 1937

A STRANGELY attractive figure, this Dick Whately—in some ways as typical a bush-Australian as Lawson was, yet a windblown waif of a man, drifting around the world, not much concerned about food or shelter for himself, belonging to no time or place. You'd hardly notice him in a gathering, with his frail figure, brownish colouring and self-effacing manner; and yet you'd never forget him after talking to him for five minutes. It's his mixture of innocence and experience, I think: everything he says is interesting and his own. I'd been curious about him ever since reading Esmond Romilly's 'Boadilla.' He figures in it as 'Aussie,' and though you get no full-face portrait of him, his subtle, flickering, friendly personality haunts the whole book. Obviously that young Englishman, Churchill's nephew, had a deep affection and admiration for him; whenever he speaks of 'Aussie' a glow comes through his words.

Yesterday Whately came to lunch, and at six o'clock we were still talking over the meal-table, no one conscious of the time. It was eleven before he finally left the flat, and even then you couldn't be sure he wasn't drifting off to other friends. He seems to ignore the clock and create some timeless world around himself, and while he's there you live in it with him; what do meals or chores matter? Yet he's the most unassertive of men, not wanting to impose his personality or make much of himself.

It was only by adding one casual story to another that I could fit together the facts of his life. Apparently he was born in Melbourne but had gone off as a youngster to earn his living up around the Murray and had gradually worked his way over the continent, turning his hand to one thing after another. Then he'd gone to sea for a while, leaving his ship in an American port, drifting down to Mexico, where he'd picked up a little Spanish and adapted himself to the Latin-American worker's way of life. Altogether he stayed eight years in Mexico and the South American countries and it's easy to imagine him bending his back with Chilian and Argentinian workers and joining in their talk at meals. I don't think he found himself less at home there than he would anywhere else.

What made him go to sea again I don't know, but at his first English port he came across an article of V.'s in a London paper giving an eye-witness account of happenings in Barcelona. Immediately he set out for Spain, getting there, after many shifts and adventures, in about a month. He must have looked a queer bird to Esmond Romilly when he turned up in his little English company; it says a good deal for Romilly that he could recognize his rare quality so quickly.

All day I've been thinking about him and wondering what that rare quality is. It shows in his talk about men and places, a delicacy of feeling, a deep humanity, a flickering humour. If he could write, he'd be another Lawson, though not so self-absorbed and sentimental. In his halting way he can hold you and move you by his intimate penetration of life.

November 13th, 1937 YESTERDAY'S press announced obscurely that Paul Montfort's statue of George Higinbotham, robed as Chief Justice of Victoria, would be unveiled at 3.20 by Chief Justice Mann, a successor. I persuaded our small committee for Spanish Medical Aid that it should break up early and go—all three of us—to the unveiling. The others were a little vague about Higinbotham's significance. As we bustled out I begged them to disregard the text-book history where he is mentioned only once and then merely as a party politician ('McCulloch's pugnacious attorney') and to study instead the high benign brow ('Greek-browed Higinbotham' was O'Dowd's phrase): I reminded them of his erect courageous bearing as tribune of the people and the quixotic originality of his public acts up to the time of his death

Rain came on. I found I wasn't sure where the statue had been erected. 'Near the Exhibition Gardens,' someone had said, so we pressed on. A big procession was passing there, but it was the funeral of a very popular fireman. Back on our tracks, we found a handful of people gathered near the old Treasury Building; this was the place of homage, then. The speech of Mann, C. J., was almost over, the tiny audience beginning to melt away. This great occasion had been merely the assembling of a few umbrellas! Extraordinary absences included not only the mass of the people but individuals like O'Dowd, Maurice Blackburn, and J. V. Barry—the three men one thinks of as finding inspiration in Higinbotham.

The statue? Looking rather bundled and anonymous, the old Chief bends his heavily-wigged head as if to catch the words of some faltering witness. 'Simply photographic,' said McC. of the *Argus* to me admiringly, and I let it go at that. He and his colleague were curious about my presence. 'What on earth brought you to this ceremony?' he inquired as we drove back to town together. And when I told him, he began to ask for some facts about this man, who had once been the editor of his own paper and whose portrait hangs upstairs in the editorial office. This morning, I see, he speaks in his gossip-column of my 'enthusiasm' for Higinbotham.

But the whole affair makes me wonder if there isn't some essential lack in us, something missing that keeps our life from having meaning and depth—interest in our past, reverence for those who have shown outstanding qualities of mind or spirit.

When we look back it is on great empty spaces; the significant dead have no memorials; the few statues in our parks are mainly of forgotten grandees and kings. It must be because we have no sense of ourselves as a people, with a yesterday and a to-morrow. I can't help remembering that little fishing-village in Britanny where we lived when we were first married; on some rock rising from a wheatfield a bronze plaque, in memory of a local poet or hero. How these simple memorials added another dimension to the day-to-day life of the village!

January 23rd, 1938 NEWS of the death of Will Dyson in London. I have been going about all day with a feeling that something extraordinarily vital and irreplaceable has gone out of the world. Dyson was one of the few people I've met who seemed possessed of that rare thing, genius; there were mysterious powers in him that made his mind able to leap at least two bounds ahead of other people's, and you got the effect of this in his piercing divination and crashing wit. It was hard to feel intimate with him. There was that air of playful toughness he met you with; a pose, I always suspected, that he adopted early in life as protection for a very sensitive spirit in a rough-and-tumble world. It must have been adopted so early that it impressed itself on his features; his knowing, challenging grin reminded you of men standing on the corners of back-streets in Collingwood. Yet the play of light and warmth on his face when he was really moved!

I think he was unhappy during his last years here. Few people knew of the staggering reputation he had made in London before the War, when men like Wells, Bennett, Belloc and Chesterton united to pay homage to him. The savage power of his cartoons had taken the easy-going tepid world of pre-War London by storm, and he had always in reserve his wit as a talker and his astonishing ability as a public speaker. But in Melbourne there were hardly any opportunities to use these gifts, and he didn't go out of his way to make them. I think he was overcome by Ted's long and painful illness. He had always had a deep affection for this elder brother of his who had brought the whole family up and was now withdrawn and almost inarticulate. Yet he rarely visited him: he would say (with a stab, partly at himself, partly at life):

'When I look at Ted I see myself as an old man, and I can't bear it.'

I have been recalling the first evening I met him, at his place in Chelsea, nearly twenty-five years ago. He was describing in his comic, extravagant way a situation that had brought the whole street buzzing round like a swarm of bees the day before, when Betty, aged three, had put her head through the iron railing and couldn't draw it back. There had been a clamour of advice, people rushing hither and thither, Dyson himself tearing up in his shirtsleeves to the ironmonger's and bringing back a man with a hacksaw to cut through the iron railings. No one—no one in Chelsea—remembered Dickens and Mrs. Jellaby's little child who got caught in the iron railings. But Betty, before the sawing commenced, must have had an intuition of how the situation was solved then, for she said calmly:

'Daddy, I fink I could get my tummy frough instead of my head.'

And, turning her shoulder, she wriggled back quite easily through the railings.

It was Dyson himself who held the floor that evening, but I have an even more vivid memory of Ruby—surely one of the most generous, radiant and beautiful women who ever walked the earth—'Ruby Lind.' Some of Dyson's gusto for life, even his power, leaked out of him when she died in 1919, and his wound was still open when he wrote a couple of years afterwards:

There is no soft beatitude in Death,
Death is but Death;
Nor can I find
Him pale and kind
Who set that endless silence on her breath . . .

April 29th, 1938 FROM Marjorie Barnard, discussing questions arising out of Huxley's 'Ends and Means':

Politically, I'm afraid, I'm an irresponsible. I have no politics, only a political Philosophy, held (at places) with passion. It is conditioned by extraneous and impertinent circumstances, that is by subjective rather than objective reasons. A puritan inheritance and a natural eclecticism cancel out and leave me without a perching-place on any of the patented political creeds. Rigidity, eclecticism, and a fondness for abstractions combine to edge me toward lost causes. Huxley presents the very paragon of lost causes. That book, 'Ends and Means' is like a chock under my mind. This is my lost cause. Something settled, anyway. As for non-violence, has violence ever been a success? How can intellectual problems ever be settled by violence, or by turning them into emotional problems? Isn't it thinking that the world needs to get it out of its mess, and doesn't violence make thinking more and more difficult? That's its charm, of course. Cutting Gordian knots, and what not. *And* being in things together. Being out of things together isn't the same thing. I've always rather fancied the Roman senators who put on their best, sat in the Senate, and quietly waited for the barbarians to kill them. They did kill them, which is, I suppose, the point. I've not the faintest doubt that you'd win on points if we embarked on a political argument, or that I would remain obstinately true to my (unbloody) blood.

June 14th, 1938 RE-READING Shaw Neilson's poems this week I've been struck particularly by 'Let Your Song Be Delicate.' What led this poet half-blind, living in a remote Mallee settlement, to write a tiny Art of Poetry, as if he were a Horace or a Boileau? Did the impulse spring from some deep need within himself, or did it arise from his discussions of his poetry by letter with A. G. Stephens? 'Let Your Song Be Delicate' was published in 'Heart of Spring' in 1919, but it had appeared in the *Bookfellow* many years before, and was written as early as 1909. At that time Neilson had written little but easy balladry, and had certainly not read many of his fellow-poets. What made him lay the kind of injunctions upon them that are to be found in Verlaine's subtle and difficult 'Art Poétique'?

The problem set me turning up old letters. In 1907, I remembered, Bernard O'Dowd had asked me to make a translation of Verlaine's 'Art Poétique' for that little Melbourne quarterly *The Heart of the Rose.* He himself was obsessed with it; its call to music first, its insistence on delicacy, on the need for 'rime' to be unemphatic.

'I had A. G. Stephens here on it one delightful evening last year,' he wrote, 'and between us we knocked some sense out of it, as well as lost some butterfly-dust from it. But I can't reproduce it quite satisfactorily for others' use.'

For use? That was how he, and probably A. G. Stephens, regarded it. I don't think my translations—one in prose, one in O'Dowd's own stern stanza—were very successful. O'Dowd admitted that he missed something.

'I would say that I missed from it that strange hovering between life and death, here and hereafter, reality and unreality (vice versa, I should have put it) that comes from Verlaine's poem like an emanation, and to me explains the Symbolist movement more than any words I have read about it.'

But if my version failed to catch this 'hovering between life and death,' Neilson's did not so fail:

Let your song be delicate,
Sing no loud hymn,
Death is abroad . . . O, the black season,
The deep, the dim.

We shall never know how conscious Shaw Neilson was of being influenced by translations from Verlaine, but we can be sure that Stephens made the Symbolists' 'Art Poétique' real to him, gave him some inkling of Rimbaud too. How else account for this quatrain (like an incredible foreshortening of a recollected Bateau Ivre) in 'The Scent of the Lover':

I am assailed by colours,
By night, by day,
In a mad boat they would bear me
Red miles away.

It is strange to think of this simplest of poets, this half-blind recluse of the Mallee, being led into the symbolic world of Rimbaud, that world of colours substituted for sound, sight for hearing.

August 14th, 1938 REHEARSALS of 'The Cherry Orchard' are nearing their end. The more I watch them the more my admiration for Dolia Ribush grows. He's not merely a producer; he's a creator, keyed up in every nerve to bring something living out of the void. There's a beautiful intensity in those dark, implacable eyes of his as he watches some scene gather momentum. He knows each sentence, knows exactly the emphasis it needs, yet he won't impose anything on the actors from outside. The feeling, the emphasis, must come from inside them. 'Should I sit down after I say that?' someone asks. His eyes snap. 'If you feel it is right—yes. But don't—don't always ask me things like that. It is for you. Think what is happening; don't think what you have to say or do. Let it come out of yourself.'

With his coat off he dances over to illustrate something. Immediately, in spite of his broken English, the character comes leaping into life—man or woman, Lopahkin or Ranevska. A being that is not himself, but separate, projected by the force of his imagination, the subtlety of his intonations, and imposed on us. Yet he won't let the actors copy his movements or gestures; no, they must get inside the character themselves, feel the words they say.

Have I ever met anyone to whom Art means so much? His general methods may be Stanislavsky's, but his delicacy and exuberance are his own. He can be deeply hurt by a false note in any creative work, whether writing, painting or acting; and the theatre is a sacred world. I had never had much understanding of Chekhov as a dramatist: as produced by Gregan McMahon twenty-five years ago, 'The Seagull' had seemed a solemn piece of futility; but every one of these rehearsals I've seen (and they've lasted over a year now) has filled me with excitement. A sense of being enriched, a deeper belief in what Art can give to life.

December 1938 THIS afternoon Esther Landolt was talking about her first impulse to write. It was a translation of one of Lawrence's novels (I think, 'Sons and Lovers'), read when she was a girl in Switzerland, that awakened her to the life about her. She suddenly felt acutely aware of the shapes of things—clouds, trees, animals—emotionally aware of her relationships with other people. But her first serious book was written under the excitement of a brown-shirt parade in Dresden, in 1932. That solemn assemblage of stony-eyed fanatical youths struck awe into her, gave her a vision of what was happening in Germany. The book was accepted, but not published, as just then Hitler came into power.

Her later books have made a name for her in Switzerland, where she is now regarded as the leading German-Swiss novelist. She admits that Switzerland treats its writers well, but is sceptical about any plans to encourage literature here.

'Money, security, literary movements—no, these are not so important. Lack of them will not keep people from writing. Not those who are meant to write. They write because they have a live coal inside them.'

Undoubtedly she has the live coal, though it takes something to fan it into a glow. Often, in spite of her early experiences, she seems indifferent to what is happening overseas (in Spain, for instance), unaware of political events. There's her natural gaiety, her appetite for the cosy, friendly side of life, as when she gathers parties round the candle-lit tree at Christmas-time. She's lyrical about the station-life of the Western districts, where she goes to stay sometimes, and is making that country the setting of her next novel. There's very little about the actual working of a sheep-station she doesn't know; she has a passion for the work of the land, its sounds and smells, and wonders why the women she meets there take so little interest in it. She's more at home with the men—but feels it's easier to get to know the horses and sheep here than the people.

February 10th, 1939 LAST night Mr. Justice Evatt to dinner with news of A. in London. He had met her at the Loutits', and had afterwards gone to see her in Charlotte Street. He has a great admiration for her, partly communicated, I think, by Dr. Loutit, who was the head of her unit in Spain. Did we know she was writing a novel?

'She promised to let me read the manuscript,' he said.

He seems to be drawn naturally to young people, as if he found their attitude to life and their general interests more stimulating than those of the old or middle-aged. He was questioning H. about all the details of her escape from the crown-fire that caught her and her two friends in the Baw Baws last month. It really might have been a fatal affair for them. Few people have lived to describe the passing of a crown-fire over them, and a good many lost their lives in this one.

As for E.'s own experiences, the encounters and discoveries of his sabbatical year had given him plenty to talk about. The grandeur of Egyptian art, as revealed by the large stylised statues at the Louvre . . . his renewed enthusiasms for the moderns and primitives, with their sure handling of fundamental colour and rejection of irrelevant detail . . . his long talk with Roosevelt . . . discussions with Frankfurter. He brought a copy of the *Harvard Law Review* with his article on Judge Carvosso, comparing him with H.B.H.

The man leaves you with a sense of the fulness of life. It's partly physical; the broad, powerful shoulders of a former footballer, the gusty voice and laugh; but partly his management of energy and time. Ever since—at that fabulously early age, under forty it must have been—he accepted an appointment to the High Court Bench, he has taken for granted that, in this Olympian calm, he can do what he wants. His leisure when it comes is complete—at the close of the day, in vacation. But lately he has been filling it effectively with the writing of significant books, like 'Rum Rebellion.'

April 12th, 1939

FROM Marjorie Barnard, on a public funeral:

I was in Darlinghurst on the morning of the funeral, and the whole Cross was reeling with the pontifical mass. Men, iron railings, turned into snakes and knotted together; the walls bloomed in fungus, grey and purple; trees that had died half-a-million years ago came back again, their black leaves turned against the sun, and somewhere, out of sight, Man, as small and naked as Moses in the bulrushes, lamented his future. I am not exaggerating, Nettie.

May 25th, 1939

FROM Hugh McCrae:

Carrying books and papers upstairs to their new cubby-houses at Double Bay, Nancy happened on a packet of your letters. She smiled at the quantity and said:
'You never hear from Nettie Palmer now. Has she put you on her black list?'
'The Spanish War,' I replied.
'The Spanish War is—over!!'
'She mightn't know . . . Do you think I ought to tell her?'
Spain indeed! 'Tis the um-um- indeterminate state of Denmark.

May 30th, 1939

FROM Marcel Aurousseau:

Have you read Ortega y Gasset's 'La Rebelion de las Masas?' He has something to say about frontiers becoming inflamed and hypersensitive *perhaps* just as they are about to disappear, and I begin to feel that there may be something in it—that we may live to see the thing called Europe emerge as an organic whole. Yet I am really terribly afraid. I used to think our aristocracy was done for, and that the international interests had become the real power, but Chamberlain shows that the two are almost identical, and that our decadent first families are still terribly powerful through their money. We have to get rid of that with determination. Old English families rule Australia by drawing immense dividends, and they control a lot of the rest of the world. But *la noblesse*, as Proust shows, is one big European family, quite prepared now to enslave the lot of us if it will make the money safe.

Yet how far does the decay go? It seems certain now that the population of England and France will dwindle perceptibly in our time, and so may that of Germany; but Italy, Turkey, Russia, Japan, America, will go on growing, and where does all that land us in the next fifty years? I see little chance of a 'programme,' and a great need for the dissemination of correct information on all sorts of subjects; but even a small voice is not allowed really to speak, unless the statement is quite harmless, and my own experience was more shattering in Australia than here. Nobody must be offended—and one can't live in the wilderness. My line, at present, is simply to see what I can get away with . . .

August 4th, 1939

FLAGS flying in the city. Someone said: 'Outbreak of war. And on the anniversary of the last one.' For a few moments I was carried back to Trégastel—those days twenty-five years ago when the order for mobilization shook our village and people gathered half-dazed in the square; fishermen tramping in to put away their nets for the duration, white coiffed women making plans to gather in the harvest . . . But this time the flutter of flags was only for Queen Elizabeth's thirty-ninth birthday.

There's no doubt, though, that the idea of another war has been accepted by people who would have rejected it strongly a year ago. People like M., who seemed blind as images of stone. For me, the war is something that has been going on remorselessly since July, 1936, when that sudden attack came at Barcelona. Looking back over my journal, I can't help noticing how little it has been concerned with purely literary questions since then. But is there, I wonder, any such thing as 'pure' literature? Isn't it just a conception of people who look on writing as an escape from the living world? Perhaps a painter or musician can cut himself off, in his work, from what's going on around him, but a writer can't. I remember thinking, when we came home from Europe, that our writers were trying to do just that, but lately all I know have had this sense of the ground quaking beneath them as acutely as I have. There's that manuscript of Leonard Mann's, 'The Impending Crisis'—impending whether war breaks out or not; there's Frank Davison's 'While Freedom Lives,' with its sense of urgency; there's already in nearly every letter I get the feeling of Kipling's footslogger, 'there's no discharge in the war.' And what a ghostly unreality hovers over those who either seek a discharge or pretend that they're above the battle.

To-night I've been reading over the 'Anatomy of Melancholy,' with its marvellous 'Digression of Air.' Easy for Burton, dreaming by the Isis three centuries ago, to speculate remotely about us in our non-existence: 'That hungry Spaniard's discovery of *Terra Australis Incognita* . . . cannot choose but yield in time some flourishing kingdoms to succeeding ages.' These are the kingdoms, no longer *incognita;* this is the succeeding age, and a difficult one; here are we, a part of mankind, and being forced to face the fact.

Part II

The Poet

EDITOR'S NOTE

Most of Nettie Palmer's poems appeared in the two volumes she published in London: *The South Wind* (1914) and *Shadowy Paths* (1915). The last two poems included here, 'Gray Light' and 'Art Poétique', are previously uncollected and form part of her small output of poetry in the twenties. They were published in July 1921 and June 1922 respectively, in *Birth: A Little Journal of Australian Poetry*. Most of Nettie Palmer's verse was consistently represented in the leading anthologies appearing in Australia in the 1930s and 1940s, but her main energies went into literary journalism, and she wrote very little poetry in the most productive decades of her life.

Poems from The South Wind

THE SEEKER

Whip-bird, whip-bird, calling through the deep-dawn
  Calling through the chill time before the break of day,
Lone bird, sweet bird, flying down the mountain,
  Stay and let me hear you, beside the almond spray.

Seek her, seek her; ah, you rise up early,
  Hoping you may find her, the mate that went away.
Early, early, I would rise before you,
  Had I any hope left, beside the almond spray.

Onward, onward, search the mountain over,
  Call her where the creek calls and quiet shadows play.
Only, only, come again at evening,
  You and she together come, beside the almond spray.

VISITANT

Who is he that understands
All the power of Beauty's hands?
By the mercy of the Lord
In her right she bears a sword;
Though the thrust thereof is deep,
Stabbing hearts from sodden sleep,
In her left she carries dew,
Easing hearts that waken true.
Till the world of wonder die,
Beauty, look! is passing by.

When the blackbird sings alone,
Pouring forth in raptured tone
Through the dark before the day
Praise of star and bursting spray,
By the leaf that faintly stirs,
Surely all the hour is Hers:
Phosphor reigns in sapphire sky.
Beauty, look! is passing by.

All day long the dust may beat
Through the wide and windy street
Till the steadfast evening comes,
Enters little dreary homes;
Then the baby free from harm,
Laid within its father's arm,
Droops the head for quiet sleep,
Where a heart is throbbing deep.
Soft the baby's fine-spun hair,
Hearts are soft that linger there.
Ere the tears of joy be dry,
Beauty, look! is passing by.

Under gums and sassafras
Aged tree-holes fall and pass,
Mingled then like mouldering bones,
Through the fern and over stones
Purls the little creek and sings,
Ever young from secret springs;
There the land-crab's gray-blue claw
Huddles to his furtive maw
Matted leaves and sinks again
Toward a deep and marshy den.
Overhead the fronds of fern
Spread their covert, and in turn
Sassafras and gums that rise
Meet the blaze of summer skies;

While this gully down the hill
Works its dark and quiet will,
Sheltered close, and you may seek
Every reach along the creek,
Ere you find a space of sun
Where the ripples laugh to run;
Only here and there a frond
Waving feels the light beyond:
Did you see a Presence flow
Tranquil through the sudden glow?
Did you hold your heart and cry,
Beauty, look! is passing by.

THE FAMILIAR PLACE

City roofed by highest heaven,
Rooted in the earth we love,
Place of call for every spirit,
Those who circling from above
Enter human souls and wrestle,
Then departing seek their place,
Where Creation's flaming ramparts
Guard the furthest rim of space:

City where the tales of poets
Every hour are coming true,
Love, transforming, daunting, swaying,
Death, creating souls anew:
Where the skies are bright with visions
And the streets on every hand
Spell a mute, appealing message
For a saint to understand:

Other cities, voices tell me,
Age-old beauty consecrates:
Other cities glow with colour,
Stir with mightier loves and hates:
City, little world of wonder,
Only world I ever knew,
Hell may gape or heaven may open,
I'll know all through knowing you!

Melbourne, 1908

THE PRISONER

It seems the world would set itself
  The task of still reminding me;
So many little hints of you
  Keep crowding in and finding me.

Today absorbed I passed along,
  And town was only town to me;
A crossing woke my sight; I thought
  'Just here, two eyes laughed down to me!'

Sometimes I think outside my door
  There sounds a footstep known to me,
But passing on. Not so would pass
  The step that brought my own to me.

Familiar things, the dawn, the dark,
  The trees, the stars, are binding me.
Forget? How can I, all the world
  Reminding me, reminding me!

WATTLE GROVE

Because the little street was foul and dank,
 And factories glowered upon it from above,
And low fogs filled it from the river bank,
 Or hot winds through its narrows burst and strove,
 Because it missed the westering star of love
And dawn's cloud heralds rising rank on rank,
 The stolid burghers named it 'Wattle Grove'.
The very board they wrote the words on shrank.

STROMBOLI

We passed at night by Stromboli,
Across a rapt and moonlit sea,
The island-mountain glimmered white
Beyond the waters' pallid light,
So pure it seemed, a place apart,
And yet it keeps a burning heart.

The night we passed by Stromboli,
Was it yourself came near to me?
The Southern day began for you
While moonlit dark was all we knew:
Did you awake and rise and work,
Till I could feel you through the mirk?

The lightnings haunted Stromboli
From foamy clouds beside the sea,
The moon would chill the burning heart,
But lightnings make the demon start,
Who dwells below the mountain caves
And darkly stirs the summer waves.

The night we passed by Stromboli,
Both Near and Far were known to me,
And vanished both; and you and I
Flashed in the lightning through the sky
And felt the mountain pure, apart,
And knew, ah *well*, the burning heart!

BEFORE

Lights of Berlin in the Northern sky behind me,
Wintry dark and an empty road before,
So with the wind I drift, for a great wind shouting,
Tears at the high, bare trees, at the planes and lindens,
  All day long it tore.

Trees in a line by the road, and beside, beyond them,
  Wide, dim fields in the old year ploughed and sown;
Now with the winds of the early spring-time throbbing,
See them there by the lamp at the long road's turning;
  Rough and brown and lone.

Out in the dark they roll with sods unbroken,
  Stalk nor blade to be seen, but the earth is quick.
Yearning, passionate power of the dark earth waiting:
Soon, ah soon, comes the lark and the green blade starting,
  Juicy stems grown thick.

Whether I drift with the wind or I turn to face it,
  Still I behold my heart as a waiting field,
Stretching far in the dark while it longs for summer;
Come, strong wind, and quicken the growth within me,
  Cause me to stir and yield.

Clearer heard than my feet on the metalled roadway,
  Comes to my ears the rustle of crops to be,
Comes to me now the voice of my mate in summer,
He and I to be strong, sure, ripe together. . .
  Wind, blow long, blow free!

Poems from Shadowy Paths

THE OMEN

Though I have seen the still snow furred along the bough,
And I have seen a sapling glade in sunset molten red,
And heard a lonely summer creek that purled when day was
  dead,
Not all these haunting fair things have power to hold me now.

And can it be an omen to keep me free from harm,
Or can it be that him I love on earth has never been?
For leaning back against the wind I pace the living green
And the sun about my shoulders is like a lover's arm.

THE VOW

All the hot night I could not sleep,
  Beneath the jacaranda lying,
I saw the late moon climb and creep,
  I felt moths flying.

All the hot night I did not dream
  Save only of a word unspoken,
A faltering faith, a vow supreme
  Scarce made, then broken.

A SEAFARING

To wake this summer morning
And feel the boat move lightly,
The sea a silken wonder,
The far cliffs rising whitely,
A stretch of sea to cover
Before I meet my lover.

To catch the light of sunrise
Flung on the seaward ranges,
To see about Kiama
The heights all gleams and changes,
To guess their forests gleaming,
Their fern-hung cataracts streaming.

To move along this coastland
Where silver gulls are wheeling,
The prow with rush and ripple
Still to the northward stealing,
That when the daylight's over
I there may meet my lover.

To hear our voices faintly
Because the sea has held us,
To feel the glory bringing
Strange comradeship to weld us,
As happy pilgrims faring
To some great joy for sharing.

To see far breakers flashing
By league-long cliffs and beaches,
Until, the coastline breaking
In countless radiant reaches,
My heart will rise and hover
With joy to meet my lover.

THE MOUNTAIN GULLY

Bracken breast-high beside the winding track,
  Sometimes a fallen log to bar the way,
A steep descent, the footing wet and black,
  The gully dewy-dark in burning day.

And there the hill-fed creek makes hidden play,
  A naiad half-discerned with smouldering eyes,
She holds a harp whose few slow notes betray
  The passion whence the ferns and mosses rise.

What ferns about the harp! What water plies
  In drops to make the music, on and on!
What deep content across the spirit lies
  Till all the world like floating dust is gone!

And you and I are here, and breathed upon
  By one enchantment. . .Ah, the hours betray!
And all the moving fingers of the sun
  Invade no more and tide-like shadows play.

We seek again the place of outer day,
  The long ascent, the footing wet and black,
Uncanny fallen logs to bar the way,
  Bracken aglow with sunset by the track.

BRITTANY

The crops were yellowing that July
  In light that could not waver or fail,
  In winds that guided the blood-red sail
Of homing boats by a sunset sky.

And that was the Month of Pardons there,
  In village and village round about
  The sacred emblems were carried out
For Sunday processions in dreamy air.

And the tides that month ran blue and high,
  They lapped the stones of the low church wall,
  And softly bit where the rushes tall
Had dyked a garden in years gone by.

I sketched one day by a banked-up field,
  The tide came in, full, soft and blue,
  And shone beside me: I gazed and drew.
And fought with colours that would not yield.

There stood a cottage beyond the wheat,
  A heap of stones well-piled, no more,
  It watched the boats as they neared the shore,
The grass about it was long and sweet.

A peasant woman had passed and said,
  'In yonder cottage a sick man lies;
  'I think by the one black rook that flies
'Before tomorrow he lies there dead.'

I painted on, for the lights elude,
  And life's too short to entrap that glow,
  That splendour of summer, that overflow
Of beauty there in its matchless mood.

But then, as an old wife hobbled near,
  And said, 'In that house my son has died.
  'His child has gone for the grave-cloth wide
'And cross and candles to guide his bier' –

Why then, by the westering sun I saw,
  And then, by her old, sad eyes I knew:
  As the water shone there, wide and blue,
She felt but Heaven, no break, no flaw!

She went. I stayed on the narrow ledge
  Between the field and the radiant tide.
  And old tunes rose in the air, to glide
Across the waters that lapped the sedge.

I turned my eyes from the dazzling West.
  A man came out from the village street,
  And pacing with steady, solemn feet,
He carried a cross before his breast.

The cross of the church, to stand all night
  By him who had died that day of days,
  It flashed and gleamed in the level rays,
And the man who bore it was close in sight.

He trod the dyke and our glances met.
  Now he was a man and I was a man,
  But I made way for the sacristan . . .
For God's in Brittany, living yet!

THE FISHERMEN

Why do they lay their nets away?
  The tide runs blue, the tide runs well,
And summer day to summer day
  Calls like a silver bell,
And yet they lay their nets away.

Why are their women dumb and still
  When each man carries home his net
The little granary to fill,
  'Neath every roof-tree set?
The women watch them, dumb and still.

Along the sands with steady feet
  The men come in at break of day,
And pace the winding village street
  To lay their nets away:
Where now must fare their marching feet?

At sunset comes a bugle-call,
  The village square is filled with men,
Their children climb the churchyard wall
  And shout farewell again
To men who hear the bugle-call.

Because the happy soil of France
  Is trodden by an ancient foe
With martial pride and circumstance,
  These quiet men must go
To prove your soul immortal, France!

Trégastel, August, 1914.

THE MOTHER

In the sorrow and the terror of the nations,
In a world shaken through by lamentations,
    Shall I dare know happiness
    That I stitch a baby's dress?

So: for I shall be a mother with the mothers,
I shall know the mother's anguish like the others,
Present joy must surely start
For the life beneath my heart.

Gods and men, ye know a woman's glad unreason,
How she cannot bend and weep but in her season,
Let my hours with rapture glow
As the seams and stitches grow.

And I cannot hear the word of fire and slaughter;
Do men die? Then live my child, my son, my daughter!
Into realms of pain I bring
You for joy's own offering.

FULFILMENT

Nights before you came
(My little, little child with gentle lips)
I had a dream of sailing ships,
Shadow ships, lordly ships,
And one small coracle without a name;
I cried, 'You little boat across the foam,
'Row well, row well, and bring your burden home.'

Watching open-eyed
(My little, little child with wavering croon)
I saw the trees that held the moon,
April moon, Easter moon,
And one small star she had with her beside;
I prayed, 'Great moon within the poplar tree
'Send down your star to bring my child to me.'

Now I hold you here
(My little, little child with hair so fine)
Whether by dream or deed of mine,
Child of mine, safely mine,
You sweet, small magic in the budding year;
No anxious longing more: lie, little head,
Against the heart that hope-come-true has fed.

THE SQUARE

I am haunted by the little stony square,
  Close beside the ancient ramparts and the sea,
And its trees are in a pool of sunny air.

But shadowed, shadowed now it comes to me,
  When I see through the midnights or the days,
Something's fettered in the place that would be free.

Could I seek the town again, the cobbled ways,
  Could I find a certain steep, ascending lane
That would lead me to the square and let me gaze;

Just a moment by the gateway, faint but fain
  I would linger, fearing Something; then to pass
Scanning all the silent houses, pane by pane.

But there never shines a candle through the glass,
  There are no faces watching at the door,
And the trees tremble guilty in a mass.

I shall seek this terror out and not give o'er;
  Must that pool of sunny light become a pit,
With a dreadful presence lurking at the core?

Yet here must I remain and dream of it,
And dream the church-door opens till I find
All the desolated shrines with lamps unlit.

Is it there the horror lurking, to unwind
Of a sudden like a many-fathomed snake?
Ah, no longer may I falter, deaf and blind!

For I know it. . .And in dreams a heart can break:
There is nought to find and vanquish in the square,
There is ruin, and eclipse, and thunderquake.

For they say, the news is borne upon the air,
How that three times the surging tide of war
Has invaded, and destroyed, and laid it bare.

They will never ring the vespers any more,
And the old homes are dead, the trees are gone,
And the place is like a waste of sandy shore,
Or a desert the simoon has breathed upon.

THE ESCAPE

Her life is all a burden like the ticking of a clock,
Her feet must move in city streets, her days are counted all,
To beat against her life would be to strike on living rock,
Alas, she owns no heavenly powers to bring the waterfall.

But while her days are passing like the ticking of a clock,
I know the world she wanders in for moments clear and few,
I know the dawns she clambers through to meet the vital shock
Of mountain winds that wake the day through wattles hung
with dew.

Her steady hands are moving like the ticking of a clock,
But ah, her heart is dancing for the dreams within her eyes,
The mountain tops, the valley trees that waver like a flock,
And gods beyond the mountains and incense through the skies!

Her work is brave and faithful like the ticking of a clock,
And still her soul is rhythmic with the timeless wind and sea,
And when the world that binds her now is all a broken lock,
Through worlds long guessed and conquered she will wander,
being free.

WONDER

Child, what beauty wraps you round?
How should one discover it?
By your tiny, eager hands
Curved like shells on ocean sands,
Or young ferns that wave and flit
Where a creek makes lyric sound?

Should I name your beauty all,
How your hair, the shadow-soft
Shadow-dark across your brow,
Melts the heart within me now,
While your croon, alow, aloft,
Sweeter comes than hill-bird's call?

Not by hands, or voice, or hair,
Shall I name your beauty clear,
Child of mine, ah, not by these!
Fair your body lies at ease,
Seen and held, so near, so dear,
Yet your beauty lies not there.

Fairer than the child I hold,
  Lonelier than the child I bore,
You within your world apart
Spinning dreams around your heart:
  Wearing still that look you wore
Sheltered in some starry fold.

THE BARRACK YARD

A sack of straw suspended from a tree,
  Soldiers with bayonets in the barrack yard,
  In turn they lunge and thrust and stand on guard,
Their faces rigid, fraught with destiny.

A summer wind is moving dreamily,
  The sack a hundred times is gashed and marred,
  In the tree-shadows by the railings barred
The city children stare and laugh to see.

What of life's glory, what of memory's glow!
What of the boon of song, the great word written,
  The highest peak our dreamers ever saw!
We learn to slay our kind. Ah, might we know,
Dying, that every foe our hands had smitten
  Was but a mute and soulless man of straw.

PROCNE

Like a swallow seems my Love,
Thus would I her semblance prove:

See her eyes so softly blue,
Such the swallow's wing in hue.

Hear her laughter, lighting swift,
So the swallows fare adrift.

See the smile that curves her lips,
So the lurking swallow dips.

Watch her swallow-thoughts that soar,
Yet come home to me once more.

Ah, but pray thee, mark one thing,
She deserts me not with Spring.

THE FLUTE

I sat fluting,
Fluting on a fallen gum was I,
Fluting, then I sang: and one came by
Dragging wearied feet, but his eyes shone;
'Whence, my friend?' He rested, I played on,
'Whence, my friend?' 'I came,' he slowly said,
'Where the shadowy gullies led;
'Ah, that mazy twist and turn,
'Where by banks of moss and fern
'Still the creek runs cool!
'There I bathed in pool and pool,
'Nameless like the birds, now few,
'Now a jargoning chorus, sweet and long,
'In wild young saplings where the sun was strong.'

I sat fluting,
Fluting then I sang, 'But cease,' cried he,
'Your songs from lands outworn beyond the sea,
'Your May-time full of nightingales,
'Your roses, all your sunny dales,
'Each rill berhymed these thousand years,
'Each flower bedewed with lovers' tears,
'Leave them all; come near and sing
'This great nameless, new-found thing,
'This Australia. . .Feel the perfumes fling
'Out across the gully and the height,
'Sing of trees ashine in starry night,
'Their light-hung leaves, their peace, their naked might.'

I sat fluting,
Fluting, but with heavy heart was I,
My songs went withering out against the sky,
They died: I sang no more:
But he with visage brighter than before,
Took my flute and played, then sang;
The hillside like a temple rang.
Ah, my heart, he knew, he knew!
The sunlit winds about him blew,
And he played on; the dappled shade,
That downward-drooping gumleaves made,
The creaking drag of loosened bark,
A far bird soaring like a lark,
All these he sang of, for he knew.
I saw a little cloud across the blue,
It paused to hear,
The wild bush hearkened near,
My soul was all one ear.

Fluting,
Fluting and singing after sundown still
He glorified the glorious virgin hill;
Then came the tide of evening chill;
Upon the eastern height
Trembled a sapphire light,
The shining of the summer moon to be,
I turned to him, 'Ah, see!'
But he against the darkness of the West
Sang of his songs the last and loveliest;
Looming he rose, became a part
Of all that Bush whose key was in his heart:
Humbly alone his raptured songs I try,
Ah, must I lose them! Must their memories die!
Falter not, flute! Beneath the moonlit sky
I sit fluting.

Uncollected Poems

GRAY LIGHT

Out in the Bush, this night,
Fear tapped chill on my wrist,
Fear in the quiet light;
Why, when there came no mist?
Why, when the track showed white?

Something was gone, withheld;
Over the moon's clear face
Soft clouds gathered and swelled,
Quenching the lit world's grace,
Leaf and bracken unspelled.

Worse than the darkness it seemed,
Light, with the splendour gone.
No branch beckoning gleamed,
No leaf quivering shone,
Sheenless the ferns' hair streamed.

Fear laid hold on me fast;
So, I said it, comes death,
Not the shattering blast,
But a sudden fading, a breath –
All the magic is past.

There while the world was gray,
Clear and gray and bereft,
I saw brothers betray,
Never a nation was left,
Never a cause held sway.

THE POET

I saw bitterness kill
Men and leaders of men;
Lands lie suddenly still,
Broken ploughshare and pen,
Others falter for will.

Truth, I said it, is here.
Let me behold it now,
Plain in a gray light drear;
Truth I bind to my brow,
Cold on my wrist lies fear.

Gray of the moon, ah, light,
Light most cruel of all,
Dulling the spirit of might,
Letting the dead thoughts call,
Lifting griefs to the sight.

Gray of the moon, you pass!
Light's like stars in the trees,
Leaves are shining as glass,
Fern-fronds gleam in a breeze,
Fine dews glint on the grass.

Beauty's tide's at the full
Floating thereon, I cry,
All my sins are as wool,
As the fleece-white cloud in the sky,
That delicate breezes pull!

Steeped in the rippling peace,
How I behold this world,
Rounded in rich increase,
Hang like a bubble pearled,
Where shadows would fail and cease.

O moon, thou gentlest star,
Soothe me, but set me free.
Thy joy is a dream too far,
Cover thee, let me see
Truth where the gray paths are.

ART POÉTIQUE

(From the French of Paul Verlaine)

Music, music first of all,
And in it choose the broken kind,
Melting in vagueness on the air
With nothing to impede or bind.

And when you come to seek your words,
Do it in some half-slighting way.
What's dearer than the twilit song
Where Certain and Uncertain stray.

'Tis lovely eyes behind a veil.
'Tis noonday trembling with its light,
'Tis autumn's sky of mellow blue
Crowded across with starry white!

For Shade is what we still desire,
For us not Colour, Shade alone.
Oh, Shade alone can link in love
Dream with dream and tone with tone.

Take Eloquence, and wring its neck!
And Rhyme – well, when your mind's at heat,
Subdue her lightly to your will;
Unwatched, where will she stay her feet?

THE POET

The sins of Rhyme, who'll name them all?
What child was deaf, what negro mad
To forge for us this penny gem
The file proves hollowed out and bad?

Music again and evermore!
Your verse the wingèd thing that moves
Before us when a soul departs
To other skies and other loves.

Your verse must be the happy chance
Scattered where morning winds are pure,
Bearing the breath of mint and thyme –
The rest is – literature!

The Literary Critic and Historian

EDITOR'S NOTE

This section contains a selection of Nettie Palmer's writings on the subject of Australian literature. 'The Beginning of Australian Literature' appeared in Hassell's *Australian Miscellany 1921–22*.

Modern Australian Literature 1900–1923, published by Lothian Book Publishing Company Pty Ltd in 1924, was, with Hartley Grattan's *Literature Australia* (1929), the only summarising survey of its kind to appear between *The Development of Australian Literature* (1898), Henry Gyles Turner and Alexander Sutherland, and *An Outline of Australian Literature* (1930), H.M. Green. Limited to a precise period – the years nominated in the title – the book is significant for what it reveals of the expectations and hopes of the time. Its concern is for writers who 'add a new factor to the literature of the country' and it maintains that 'literature depends for its existence on an individual note in the writer, while the individual for his power depends on possessing more or less harmony with the life about him'. Nettie, like Vance, was concerned with the relationship between a national literature and the national experience behind it, but both explored this relationship in a tentative, unprogrammatic way and had no readymade formula to account for it. The value of Nettie Palmer's *Modern Australian Literature*, apart from the stimulus of its crisply formulated opinions, now resides in the way it presents the range of Australian writing as it appeared to one informed and observant reader at the time. As well as comments on the novel and short story, the book covers children's literature, non-fictional prose and women poets. If in places it is barely more than a list of names and titles, these have a permanent interest for literary scholars and historians; but the whole is enlivened by a sharp alertness in the writing and a sense of discovery as Nettie Palmer reveals the extent of her reading in Australian writing after her return from overseas.

Nettie Palmer wrote a number of pieces for the *Illustrated Tasmanian Mail* on individual authors. For this section I have chosen a few of these, but mostly her more general articles. She wanted to help create an awareness of the difficult situation Australian writers and intellectuals faced at the time, but above all to show that Australian writing has an importance for Australians which they should recognise. In the interests of consistency, subheadings and paragraphing have been retained as they appear in the *Illustrated Tasmanian Mail*.

The articles appear in order of publication, and the dates are given here: 'Australian Literature', 1 December 1927; 'Dramatic Writing in Australia', 4 April 1928; 'What Is an Australian Book?', 13 June 1928; 'Australian Novels', 15 August 1928; 'A Melbourne Chronicle', 26 September 1928; 'Literary Censorship', 23 January 1929; 'Australian Literary Journals', 20 February 1929; 'The Need for Australian Literature', 17 April 1929; 'Lawson's Stories', 24 April 1929; 'Barbara Baynton', 26 June 1929; '*A House is Built*', 21 August 1929; '*Coonardoo*', 4 September 1929; 'The Arts in Australia', 11 September 1929; 'Literary Standards', 25 September 1929; 'The Truth About Australian Poetry', 16 October 1929; 'Australia Leaks In', 26 February 1930; 'An Outline of Our Literature', 23 April 1930; 'Building Jerusalem', 14 May 1930; 'Some Foreign Relations of Australian Literature', 13 August 1930; 'Creative Writing in Australia', 13 May 1931; 'The Australian Scene Today', 8 July 1931; 'Mary Gilmore's New Poems', 16 September 1931; 'Ten Years Ago: "Dark Ages" in Australian Writing', 13 January 1932; 'The "Olive Schreiner" of Australian Literature', 16 June 1932.

The Beginning of Australian Literature

You know the mental tumult that comes when you are faced with a phenomenon like this. A large box with a picture of a girl on it, holding a similar box with a picture of a girl on it, holding a similar box. . .but the subsequent girls and their boxes are already out of sight among germs and other infinitesimals. In the same way a glimpse of endless progression comes before the mind when faced with the question of, 'Who came before Homer?' It is like peering over a precipice into the world of Atlantis. Homer, you see, survives, in two great epics of twenty-four books each, and his predecessors, good and bad, are gone.

There were predecessors, of course. Even if we had no evidence of them, we would know that the world we call Homeric could not have been built up at the first attempt. There were bad predecessors and good, because art involves selection of the best from all sorts. As Burns said of morals, so it is in art; when we survey a work of art 'we know not what's resisted'. Every line an artist writes or draws might have been worse if he had listened to the worst of his mental counsellors. But those pre-Homeric poets must have been better and better as time went on, so that when Homer began to build up from them he had countless lines completely made, like the archways in a child's blocks. More than this, he had his subject-matter all seen for him, though maybe it was himself, as well as his goddess, that made the story to bind it together.

How long had it taken his forerunners to see their world as epical? Who first saw that the way a little sailing-boat leaps forward when the wind fills its sail is not casual, not trivial, but a thing of eternal beauty? No actual talk of beauty, of course, but the unmistakeable presentment of it! Every one of these things, once seen, then captured in the wave-music of the hexameter, was a creation, a conquest, part of a world built up.

The world was built up, then, and at the moment of its completion it was also a limitation. Homer provided later Greek poets with their ambit, no small circle indeed, and it was taken as fixed that what Homer had seen fit to see and to recognise in his poetry was the subject-matter for Greek poets. There came the three tragedians. Aeschylus abode by Homer's standards, Sophocles too. The third, Euripides, questioned Homer's themes as a model for Athens of centuries later. He said, in effect, that new seeing was now needed.

With us, of course, there is no danger that we should see our Australian world through Homer's eyes: not enough likelihood, indeed; for his simplicity and magic would be revealing for us in face of seas often bluer than his own Aegean. Our tradition comes through Chaucer and his predecessors, who also made a world. Hard work they had, too! There was that England where they lived, the place and the people, and how was it all to be made into literature? Was it to be seen with the eyes of Normal earl or Saxon churl? Whose language was to describe it? It is such an odd story now, but who could have guessed that Chaucer could do so much, writing good plain Saxon with strong verbs, homespun phrases, and yet enriching it all with Norman French till the language was like an antique silk dress that could 'stand alone'.

As soon as Chaucer had performed his miracle, English poetry went singing on its way, and there is no reason why it should ever stop. Gradually the whole English landscape has been revealed in this poetry, and there are countless aspects of it that have only to be named and a nerve is touched that throbs with memories of great literature and art in many centuries. Such a word is nightingale, or meadow, or oak. For us in Australia these words have no association other than literary. We inherit Chaucer's tradition, but not his subject-matter. How are we to see a eucalypt except in terms of an oak that failed? How can we see a romantic bird except as a nightingale? The earliest writers in Australia found no difficulty in this matter, for they cheerfully described Australian phenomena in terms of the phenomena that they had already seen described in literature. Wentworth's famous prize-poem 'Australasia' was even praised for its correct local colour, but one gathers that the correctness lay in such vivid statements as that Parramatta was near Sydney, and so forth. His description is of this kind:

> Theirs too on flow'ry mead or thymy steep
> To tend with watchful dog the timid sheep.

There was that friend of Charles Lamb's too, by name Barron Field, who used to send Lamb nervously facetious verse about this continent, a bad joke at the best! But the question is, would Wordsworth himself have been able to bring out the essential character of the landscape at first? Would Constable have been able to paint Sydney Harbour so that it did not seem a faint reflection of Portsmouth or Southampton? As for Jane Austen, to mention another contemporary, she would merely have shrunk with horror from our 'untidy' bush, and left her Marianne, the maiden of 'sensibility', to revel in its haggardness.

As late as the 'fifties we have Richard Rowe, in his *Peter Possum's Portfolio*, finding, after much else, something that he considers picturesque:

> A little rural bit worthy of the pencil of a Gainsborough. A flock of bleating lambs are descending to the stream. . .In front of an English-looking inn stands an English-looking landlord. . .

This is obviously derivative; it is to seek a dolphin in the woods! As Rodin in his Boswellised book was made to say:

> In art nothing is beautiful except what possesses character, and character is the essential truth of any natural object whatever, whether beautiful or ugly. In art there is no ugliness except in whatever nervously seeks to be pretty or beautiful, instead of being expressive.

It is not easy, of course, to see anything honestly, or describe it in a way that brings out its essential character. It was hard for the first pioneers not to see a tangled scrub track as an English lane *manqué*, or a blackwood as a sort of inferior oak. Gradually though it has become possible for people in Australia to see just the beginning of the simple truth in the life about us, and to recognise that it has a beauty of its own. It is as if we saw the thinnest, gold eyelash of a moon, and by its light divined the orb. Who have made us this crescent? Those who have painted or written of Australia, taking it as their natural subject-matter, not as a mere foreign place from which to make quaint copy. We may say that the man who first grasped that the term 'antipodean' is relative began the salvation of the Australian consciousness (for after all Europe is merely our antipodes).

It was hardly before the sixties that the writers began to perceive the difficulties of their task, the intractable nature of their subject, its rich freshness. Marcus Clarke inverted the question in his well-known dictum that 'Lycidas' could not have been written by an Australian. Good, and in the same way it might be said that even Milton's eyes, trained to English contours, could not have 'seen' the Australian landscape.

Extraordinary honour is due to Kendall for his nature poems and their degree of freshness in utterance. His rhythms have a freedom, the nature he sees refracts light, it begins to be Australian. But his words are seldom Australian, for he moves in a mill-round of brook, rill, and dell, words that hang a spurious sort of muslin mist over the scene. He was not close to the soil, and much was to be hoped from those who were. In the nineties came A. B. Paterson, gathering rough rhymes from camp-fires, and showing, when at his best, something of the ballad simplicity that ends by bringing new and concrete words into the language. He was one of a group, and they might have gone far and produced some ballads that would live, but the touch of journalistic ease was on much of their work, and the final seal of this superficiality and slickness was set by Ogilvie, who, while seeming to beat Australians at their own game, really destroyed game and all in the end.

The point is, though, that all these past developments have enriched the language and enlarged the scope of a writer who begins now. On the one hand we have Kendall's dancing rhythms and haunting names as well as Gordon's galloping rhymes, and on the other hand it is now not merely possible but even necessary for an Australian writer to use words like creek, and gully, and paddock.

All the time the other mediums, prose, painting, music too, have to wrestle with the same problem and contribute their own solution. Prose was at first helpless in its attack on Australian subjects, and only existed as a vehicle for what may be called cosmopolitan subjects. Almost unwillingly, writers like Richard Rowe came to attempt the impossible, and produced:

> Like a mighty army of Huns in never-ending march, the gloomy trees sweep down from the far distance to the never-ending shore. Here and there, it is true, the sombre mass is enlivened by a break that beams in cultivated beauty and tells of the sweet charities of Home; but even on its enlivener the black bush casts a shadow from its superfluity of shade. . .

Then on a neighbouring page:

> Laying down in the Brummagem shade that Australian trees afford. . .

No great sureness of touch in that scene-painting, but still he has tackled his theme.

Later on Marcus Clarke, with a real gift for prose, wrote brilliantly on general subjects, but could not use his brilliance when he turned to normal Australia. His 'Bullocktown' sketches are self-conscious and provincial, squeezing superficial oddities for their last drops of farcical humour. Such writing is born of blindness, and in spite of a certain popularity will disappear when people find they can have a better laugh elsewhere. By a better laugh I mean, of course, one that as well as giving a tickle under the ribs gives nourishment to the imagination. It was Lawson who, in the nineties, gave this particular nourishment, and his stories of sheer humour would in themselves reveal the ways of 'men coming and going on the earth'. His stories are of all kinds – yet they join to make a kind of corporate achievement, and with all his airs of careless colloquial writing, he has a sense of form and hardly ever misses. It is a pity, though, that in some of his volumes the harmony is broken by the introduction of some story written for an overseas review. In such a story he abandons his personal style and pipes a barbarous journalese, referring, for instance, to a certain person, whom as a good journalist he will not again call 'Dr Smith', as 'the clever but inebriate doctor'. In the same volume is found a masterpiece like 'A Hero of Redclay' (elsewhere thrown into rather heavy verse under the name of 'Ruth'). This is mostly a matter for his publishers, though. A volume of perfectly-chosen Lawson stories would be a revelation.

Another writer, less known but equally broad in his sympathies, appeared by literary evolution or dispensation in the late nineties. When Tom Collins's *Such is Life* appeared over our skyline, the natural attitudes of simple men became clearer, lit by humour and tragedy, and the ways of slowly-moving bush days. Tom Collins never once writes as an onlooker at a freak show, but as a civilised Australian among his own countryfolk. He has suffered from his publisher, but differently from Lawson. Lawson's stories have been published in indiscriminate batches: Tom Collins's have as yet mostly been left unpublished. Yet he is, and will be, a vital, pervading force, and has opened many doors for later writers.

Here only a few names can be written down, such names as are in the succession and have successors today. In every generation there are others who occupy solitary places of their own, writing or painting about some glamour-world, not here yet nowhere else. For our purposes we are speaking of those who have hung their castles in the air above definitely Australian soil, illuminating it and taking its colour. Among the authentic interpreters came Francis Adams in the nineties. He was the most valuable of our few visitor-critics, and added immensely to our stock of self-knowledge, both directly in his book, *The Australians* and indirectly in many striking essays. He discussed Australian institutions, personalities, ideals, in a kind of friendly, persecuting way that helped to crystallise a good many nebulous hypotheses! Criticism like his helped poets to affirm that 'beauty is truth, truth beauty', and thus, bringing out passionately the truth of a scene to know they were at length evoking beauty. It helped also the other potential creators, novelists, essayists, painters, by emphasising the special nature of the civilisation surrounding them.

It can never be too emphatically stated that a literature can only grow from within outwards. 'Local colour', splashed on as though by an outsider, will never make a picture, though it may make an amusing sketch (all kangaroo and boomerangs, like some of the prints in the Melbourne Public Library) for an early colonist to send home to people who have no means of verifying the production. No one who has ever lived in a place as his own, and loved it, can feel that its salient features make up mere local colour. They are part of a man's life, and he will render them with feeling or else remain silent. It is the tourist-mind that seizes on any superficial queerness, and this of course becomes boring when handled by many tourist-minds in the same mechanical way. The genuine interpreter, though, will be drawn not to the easy picture-postcard kind of description, but past this to the intimate, difficult things. A wattle and a gumtree grow up together, mingling their boughs. Although akin in colour, their forms are unlike to the point of sheer infinity, the gum with its polished leaves hanging downward, while the wattle's feather-fine leaves stretch out like hands. Who can begin to render these ecstasies of contrast! Yet themes like this cry out for utterance in every part of the wide bush.

One speaks naturally of scenery, as in thinking of Homer one quotes his lines about sea and storm, or of Chaucer with his 'frische floures'; but after all a scene is only the symbol of the whole national life that has to be displayed or evoked. The Homeric world meant laws, institutions, and works and ways of men and women, their speeches and quarrels and buildings and horses and wars: so did the world of Chaucer, and so will ours. But it may be ventured as a dogma that not until the Bush has been truly indicated by many interpreters will there come any full expression of our general life and character.

> For Great Australia is not yet: she waits
> Where o'er the Bush prophetic auras play. . .

Modern Australian Literature 1900–1923

The opening of the twentieth century is a convenient starting-point for the examination of tendencies in Australian literature. Turning a corner in time is often a tonic, but this milestone was for Australia a point recognised by poets, politicians and patriots. That 'Australia is the unit' was the refrain of some hammering verses by Joseph Furphy. Others looking at the Commonwealth less in the spirit of propaganda than of prophecy saw:

> The peeping glories of her opening page.

Indeed a sense of expectancy was in the air.

Perhaps the chief possession of Australian writers in the year 1901 was this consciousness of nationhood. Australia was no longer a group of more or less important colonies, hanging loosely together with the Bermudas and Fiji on the ample bosom of Britannia: Australia was henceforth Australia. What that name was to mean it lay in the hands of her writers, above all, to discover. There were more or less official odes written on the subject at the time, but the inquiry is not even yet complete.

The literary influences surrounding anyone who began to write in 1901 were not what they would have been a few years before, in the time of the solid novels of Rolf Boldrewood, Marcus Clarke, and Mrs Campbell Praed. At that time writers had neither found their right relation to their audience nor to the life about them. Boldrewood's greatest novel, *Robbery Under Arms*, was written with a deep simplicity and directness that he never showed again. It was written for Australia, where it was first published in serial form, and the writer took for granted that his readers were familiar with the life he described. The success of the English edition, though, led to his writing for an overseas public, and his other books were subtly but certainly different from *Robbery Under Arms*. They were more occupied in showing off Australia to an outside audience. This was a tendency not wholly absent from Marcus Clarke, even in his masterpiece, *For the Term of His Natural Life*, while it was persistently present in the novels of Mrs Campbell Praed and lesser writers. It may be called the colonial attitude, and was almost inevitable in writers of that earlier period. Yet it implies a self-consciousness about externals that is against any deep revelation of life and character. Instead of investing their subjects with atmosphere, something the writer has absorbed and has power to give out naturally, they were inclined to daub their pictures with 'local colour' to please eyes likely to be attracted by an unfamiliar surface.

In the nineties this kind of writing was suddenly superseded by the short story of the intimate and natural type, written as though for people who knew their own country. In these stories the writer never apologised, never stepped outside the picture. The young writer of 1901 would not fail to be powerfully affected by this growing revelation of the life around him as something important, something worth expressing for its own sake. The tradition in prose of this kind was established by Henry Lawson, Price Warung, and other writers for the *Bulletin*, who were guided by the genuis of J.F. Archibald. In verse there were the bush and sea ballads in long-lined verse, valuable mostly for their immense range of subject-matter, and their intimate attitude toward it.

THE PERSONAL VISION

In an appreciation of Lawson's stories, the English critic, Edward Garnett, said that they expressed a continent. That phrase may suggest what we have to demand from our literature, that it shall to some extent express our virgin and inarticulate continent. If Lawson has indeed once expressed it, life still needs repeated and varied utterance. Which of our writers have found a meaning in the life about them and been able to write down what they found? Capable work, produced with the eye fixed on the market, may be interesting enough as showing the writer's industry or adaptability, but it does not add any new factor to the literature of his country. If that man had not written that book or that piece of verse, another would have written its equivalent! Let us admit that though the machine-made product has its uses it has no relation to what is done with spontaneity for its own sake. It is no concern of ours in this inquiry.

What does concern us is work that has its own vitality on one plane or another; and that vitality will be shown by a personal relation between the writer's style and matter. De Goncourt said once: 'But there is a personal language, a language of which every page, every line, is signed for the intelligent reader, as much as if the writer's name was at the bottom of that page or that line.' He spoke of a living and growing literature. Using that test and looking at our own writers, would we not say that a page of Dowell O'Reilly's prose at its best was distinguishable from that of Randolph Bedford or of Barbara Baynton at its best? Would we not agree that four lines of Bernard O'Dowd could not be mistaken for four lines of Hugh McCrae or Chris Brennan, even when in the same metre? Such writers do prove to have individual distinction, and when we add to these names many others, it is equally clear that they have a great deal in common. So much so that their work is stamped with a definite Australian character.

That, then, is the pardox. Literature depends for its existence on an individual note in the writer, while the individual for his power depends on possessing more or less harmony with the life about him. The writer with a distinctive style is simply he who will write nothing that he has not observed and made his own — as Velasquez vowed to paint only what he saw. As for the writer's unity with his fellows, there is little in Australia to suggest a conscious school of writers, and the headquarters of our literature is more elusive than Canberra. Any common characteristics, then, must have been caused by the sharing of some common depth, which it is the task of prose-writers and of poets to reveal.

THE SHORT STORY

Most of the best work that Australia has done in prose so far has been shown in the short story. It would be unlikely for writers of the natural kind to begin with what are called well-made novels. Their subject has been the enormously varied life of people drifting about in Australia where social conditions are, to a large extent, still fluid. In pondering, for instance, on men who exemplify the mobility of labour by tramping from one shearing-shed to another, a writer is not apt to see their lives steadily and whole. What he sees is perhaps deep, but sharp and sudden. He would be more likely to see a novel in the lives of English villagers, and indeed in *Triangles of Life* Henry Lawson wrote a more connected series of chapters than elsewhere, his theme being precisely an English village, where he lived for a while many years ago. His usual stories, though, were of people who met, touched, separated, and if he had written a novel it inevitably would have been a picaresque one, dealing with the inconsequent adventures of Joe Wilson, Dave Regan, or some of his other characters.

Lawson seems to have led the way to the real short story in Australia. A real story is one whose writer believes in his subject, and wants to express it with the fullest truth and sincerity. The unreal story is a matter of mechanism only. Its writer is concerned with working out some smooth pattern, and like a Procrustes he will maim or distort his theme to bring it into shape. Lawson had too deep a respect for the life he described to falsify it for the sake of mechanical effects, and it can be seen now that his early 'Drover's Wife', although not his best story, was a definite standard of truth, and opened the eyes of other writers to what was really poignant and dramatic in the life around them. That lonely mother, sitting in her dreary kitchen with a club beside her watching for the snake that does not emerge till dawn, has come to be a large and symbolic figure.

Deaf from his youth, Lawson was yet endowed with a great sensitiveness to whatever succeeded in reaching him through the ear

– the turns of speech that show character, children's voices, noises made by work done clumsily or delicately. His other senses were almost painfully alert, with a pain that was confined to the writer; for, before writing down what he saw, he steeped it in sympathy. Although his stories are sometimes rough and defective in detail there is a fine freedom about their general form. Their loose, easy look is not due to limpness, but to perfect control. In such a way the bushman has been described as riding, 'sitting loosely in the saddle all the while'. Lawson sits loosely in the saddle, and this gives his best work the air of naturalness that most modern writers of the short story, from Chekhov onwards, have tried to attain.

In later years Lawson's reputation suffered a little from the promiscuous publication of his prose and verse, and the high quality of the work in *Joe Wilson and His Mates*, for instance, is in danger of being forgotten. But though he became diffuse, his style never altogether lost its naturalness and integrity. This could not be said of Louis Becke and other writers of the period who gained a wide recognition. Louis Becke's stories of the South Seas, published in *By Reef and Palm*, were remarkable mostly for directness of approach to their subject-matter, which was light and macabre by turns, but always vivid. His later work was done in England, at a distance from the audience who might be expected to have some knowledge of what he described, and it became more artificial and thin-spun. Although he wrote much, these later stories were mainly of the evanescent kind supplied to magazines, and have no permanent literary value. An English publisher is at present preparing a collected edition of his works, but it is not likely to be an important addition to our prose.

The same kind of fate has overtaken Albert Dorrington, a writer of vigorous, clean-cut stories. Showing freshness of invention rather than of vision, his *Castro's Last Sacrament*, published near the beginning of the century, opened the way for a romantic treatment of the unexplored corners of our life. He had a talent for investing everything he touched with an exotic atmosphere, whether a fight between domestic animals in some Sydney suburb or the work of divers on the Barrier Reef, but the few books he published since leaving Australia lack the concentration and direct appeal of his earlier work.

Barbara Baynton's short stories are confined to one small volume, *Bush Studies*, published in 1905. They attracted attention by their terseness and realism, and that acute critic, R. B. Cunninghame Grahame, singled the author out as one who could be compared with Gorky or some of the Russian realists more easily than with any English or American writer. Yet for all her clear and cold objectivity there is a bias toward harshness that injures the truth of her studies. Raw colours are flung on the picture, and there are no soft shadows to give it tone. Her characters – shearers, station-folk, bushwomen – move about in a hard, white light, as relentless as the noonday sunlight of the Bush.

Fivecorners, a book of stories and sketches, was published by Dowell O'Reilly in 1920. In the great variety of studies in this book, the most striking quality is the author's use of a personal notation. His characters are frank with him, and he has the power to write down their more significant words. The stories range from farcical sketches to poignant studies like 'Twilight' and 'His Photo on the Wall', that are full of a delicate pathos, always lit by humour.

Most of these stories, before being collected in bookform, had been published in the *Bulletin*, and it is only fair to say that that paper had a great deal to do with maintaining the standards of the short story. From the days of Edward Dyson's comic epic-in-little, 'The Golden Shanty', to the last grim little vignette of life in the trenches, it has succeeded in evoking a large number of stories that are memorable. There have been Randolph Bedford's fantasias of tropical Australia, heaped with passion-vines and termitoria; the pungent subtleties of James Edmond, wrapped in a kind of parable that is his own; the whimsical character sketches of Ernest O'Ferrall; and numerous little wedges cut from life by men to whom writing was not a habit. It is unfortunate that so few of these have been rescued from their fugitive form. At present there is a rising interest all over the world in the short story.

American and English selections are published every year with very solemn, classified census-lists, and they receive as much attention as was bestowed on poetry during the years of war. Australia has been found to produce stories of the unaffected and valuable type in surprising numbers, but they are usually left in the periodicals where they first saw the light. Apart from the books mentioned here in detail, hardly any stories of value have been collected, except J. H. M. Abbott's sketches of the South African war and Edward Dyson's tales of the mines.

THE NOVEL

We can take for granted, then, that the qualities of the Australian novel, after 1900, are mostly those of the short story, with its vigorous and pointed ways and its lack of roundness and suavity. The influence of the early solid novels of Boldrewood and Clarke was weaker than that of the intimate and naturalistic writing of the nineties. Looking for the significant novels since 1900 we come upon Miles Franklin's *My Brilliant Career*, published early in the century. It was a vehement, irregular, and somehow unforgettable tale of a young woman's life in a country district of New South Wales. At the time, and later, it had its own success, but it was not what the circulating library expects a novel to be. It lit up a new landscape by showing what manner of human beings could be tortured or enraptured under that sky. In the same way, Arthur Adam's early novel, *Tussock Land*, with its doctrinaire enthusiasm about the primitive life in New Zealand, as contrasted with the artificial life in Sydney, had its own lyrical impetus of exuberant youth, with little else. One can only say that if such books were better made they would probably be made worse! The first thing that a renovator would prune away would be their luxuriant utterance of zest and wonder. With this gone, little would remain. Arthur Adam's later novels are formal, and built, as their diagrammatic names show, on an abstract idea of irony: *Galahad*

Jones is one, another *Grocer Greatheart*. But this abstract idea does not provide them with enough life to carry them successfully through their course.

Early in the century Randolph Bedford also published two novels of the exuberant kind, *True Eyes and the Whirlwind*, and *The Snare of Strength*. They have no outline to speak of, but there is a great deal else. *True Eyes and the Whirlwind* is a naturally-written, picaresque novel describing the adventures and experiences of a boy as he grows to manhood. It is filled with a very real vitality, and gives true pictures of different phases of our life at different periods, the glimpses of early days in Broken Hill being particularly fresh and vivid. In its general style it is distinguished by a lack of sentimentality and a delight in the richness and abundance of life. Not quite so good is *The Snare of Strength*, a novel planned on more conventional lines, which break down in the end and are effaced by the author's spirit of indomitable gusto. It deals with politics in Victoria and mining in Northern Queensland, but most of its value lies in the lyrical beauty of its descriptive passages.

Turning to a very different writer, Barbara Baynton, we find in her novel, *Human Toll*, a kind of inverted gusto, an enthusiasm of bitterness, like the scent of burning bracken. The writer lets her relentless observation loose in some scarred part of the bush, and it finds strange quarries among fire and drought and disasters of the spirit. The important thing about such a book is its general effect on the mind of the reader. *Human Toll* is, after all, conceived with largeness of spirit, and its writing is clean and exact. The effect is one of strength.

Louis Stone, in *Jonah* and *Betty Wayside*, deals with Sydney. *Jonah* is a fierce, strong study of the Sydney larrikin when young, and is the best novel of its type that has been written in Australia, but the type has definite limitations. Its realism seems less derived from a personal point of view than from adherence to a temporary doctrine, and this gives it a rather mechanical air. *Betty Wayside* has a slight story, but plays eagerly with interesting matters, such as Australian music. It shows Sydney as the lively and romantic city that it is. Another city book, this one set in Melbourne, is *Painted Clay*, by Capel Boake. It is lumpy and uneven, but it gives good pictures, in the round, of life in shop, office, and city street that had not hitherto found their way into imaginative fiction at all. In the same spirit Katharine Prichard wrote her novel of a mining township, *Black Opal*. A freer and deeper book than her earlier novel, *The Pioneers*, it creates the life of an isolated but self-contained settlement – its problems, characters, struggles, and humours. The direct appeal of *Black Opal* arises from the fact that the little world it presents is not viewed with the eyes of an outsider. Its values are those of the men themselves, and this gives it an atmosphere of freshness and truth. The skill with which the author makes her male characters move and talk is surprising, and there are some remarkable group scenes. Above all the book reveals the significant landscape of the interior, varying with season and hour.

Though 'Steele Rudd's' [Arthur Hoey Davis] books are strung together loosely, they have to be considered as novels rather than as selections of short stories. Perhaps they hardly come within range of this inquiry, though the first, *On Our Selection*, showed an undoubted vigour in creating farcical types that yet had a real connection with the soil. Unfortunately its humour sprang less out of character than out of physical accidents, and so was unable to set a pleasing tide of laughter flowing that might have provided a relief from the harsher studies of bush life.

For a different reason it is unnecessary to examine the work of some recent novelists of the conventional type. They have written books as capably constructed as those of their English and American counterparts, but their work lacks the personal vision that makes *My Brilliant Career*, for instance, worth considering in spite of its crudeness and immaturity. In literary criticism the intention of the writer has to be taken into account as well as his achievement.

It is important to mention, though, that there have been some really good children's books written in Australia. Without them our children might grow up in the belief that they lived in a country not fit to be put into a book. Even those who felt a private affection for the world as they saw it would suspect their emotion of vulgarity, since all beautiful and interesting things had been shown to happen in countries that had snow at Christmas and spring flowers in May! It is not inspiring for people to believe that they live in some abnormal antipodes, for which they must apologise. The writers of children's books have nearly all taken their Australian setting for granted in a very healthy way.

Ethel Turner began the breezy family story, and her charm of narrative and character has held good through a great list of her books, as well as helping to set the tone for succeeding writers. During the last twenty years Louise Mack, Mary Grant Bruce, Lilian Pyke, and others have written fresh and interesting stories of town and bush life. A more important vein, though, was struck just once by Mrs Aeneas Gunn. *The Little Black Princess* was a book made from simple sketches of Northern Territory life, and centres round the figure of the little black Bett Bett, who took refuge for a while with the writer. The book delights the tiniest children, and yet intrigues the anthropologist. Bett Bett appears, stays awhile, learns a little, laughs much, wonders much, expresses herself in quaint yet competent pidgin, and finally decides to go bush again — aged nine or thereabouts. She goes back to her kingdom and the book ends, leaving the reader aware that he has been in the presence of something that has the permanent quality of literature.

PERSONAL BOOKS

Leaving the novel, or the near-novel, as some of these have proved to be, we touch on a group of books for which it is not easy to provide one really accommodating category. It might, perhaps, be said that all they have in common is their unlikeness to one another. To this doubtful home we must consign such a personal record as *Such is Life*, by Tom Collins [Joseph Furphy]. Appearing in 1903 in its surprising bulk, this book of solid whimsies and ingenious bush history at once took rank as a classic of its kind. It contained stories of droving, long and straggling as the mobs of cattle themselves, meditations on Shakespeare, remarks upon the geology of the Riverina, and personal narratives. The book was in the form of a greatly expanded and annotated diary, and it is said to have originally contained the whole of *Rigby's Romance*, since published separately as a full-sized novel, but its undoubted unity is achieved by the power of a formed style and a rich and varied personality.

Among these personal books are some that contain memories, like Mary Fullerton's *Bark House Days*. The Bark House was the home of a large and happy family, growing up and clearing the virgin forest in the wilder part of Gippsland. Perhaps the frontier has moved a little further out by this time, but such families must be growing up all over Australia. Pioneering is not a matter of remote history, and books like *Bark House Days* are not out of date. They are needed to remind us of one of the most constant elements of our life.

In a starker and more adventurous setting, this pioneering is again the theme in Mrs Aeneas Gunn's *We of the Never Never*. The book is a series of simply-written chapters, portraits of men who thought nothing of themselves and their most impossible tasks in a trackless and waterless country, and the naive yet spirited style conveys an effect both of charm and truth. Mrs Gunn shows her characters in their habit as they lived, and they emerge dignified by their simplicity. Again, another kind of pioneering, in the islands north of Australia, is set down by Jack McLaren in his book, *My Odyssey*, published this year. Using a style that is clear like glass, he lets the scenes of extravagant horror, or strange beauty, or sheer humour, appear in their completeness, but almost without comment. The result is something that has the effect of creative work. Writing from his island retreat within the Barrier Reef, E.J. Banfield has already revealed the charm of our tropics, but his interests were primarily those of a naturalist. He reported facts rather than created a world through his individual vision.

Randolph Bedford has at least one of these personal books between covers, though he probably could collect half-a-dozen. *Explorations in Civilisation* is the provocative title, civilisation being Europe. It is not the Europe of the globe-trotter that he explores, though. When he goes to Italy, for instance, he looks not at museums, but at mines, where he notices that the miners are underpaid and overworked. An amusing and observant book, it still fails to entrap more than a fragment of the author's abundant literary personality.

E.J. Brady, the balladist, dropping into prose in a friendly way, wrote *The King's Caravan*, and *The River Rovers*. These spirited books cover a wide field of adventure and observation in a light way. Heavier work of a more journalistic kind was performed by C. E. W. Bean in his books, *The Dreadnought of the Darling*, and *On the Wool Track*. They are slightly lifted above journalism by the freshness of their subject-matter and the unity with which they have been conceived.

Dowell O'Reilly's *Tears and Triumph*, published about 1912, though it actually contained an objective story, was expressed in one of the most personal styles ever known in Australia. Less than a hundred pages long, the story glances from 'God's eye views' of evolution to the insistent realism of a lonely little woman in a glaring, empty and remote suburb of Sydney. The book is threaded with a glancing wit, and weighted emotionally with a rather double-edged kind of feminism. His zest for the poetic idea at the heart of the evolutionary theory never left him, and on this theme he wrote his last published essay, 'Wings and Song'.

DRAMA

Drama does not exist as literature until it has been published, therefore the only plays that concern us are those in book form. These are few enough. In 1910 Arthur Adams published a volume of three full-length plays. One was *Galahad Jones*, the dramatised version of his novel of that name; another, *Mrs Pretty and the Premier*, was a semi-political play that had been produced both here and in London. Not quite firmly fixed in the realm either of fantastic farce or realistic comedy, these plays lacked character, and in a preface the author rather disarmed criticism by affirming that they were designed for the commercial stage. A more definite gift for social comedy was shown by Adrian Stephen, whose fugitive dramatic work was published in 1919, after he had been killed at the war. It included a two-act play and some shorter pieces, all the work of a very young man with talent. There was no positive achievement about these plays, though. They were without atmosphere, or any marks of an individual view of life, and can only be regarded as promising experiments.

Louis Esson's two volumes, *The Time is Not Yet Ripe* and *Dead Timber and Other Plays*, belong to a different category. *The Time is Not Yet Ripe* is a farcical comedy, satirising the political and social life of the day, but the volume of short plays has more permanent substance, and contains by far the most important dramatic work yet published in Australia. Eschewing sentimentality of any kind the dramatist gives stark little pictures of life in the town slum, on the country farm, and the Western droving camp. Louis Esson is a more objective writer than Lawson, but he deals with the same subject-matter in his own form and from his own angle, continuing the tradition of naturalism, and somehow allowing the harshness of his treatment to be tempered by a poetic vision of life.

CRITICISM AND BELLES LETTRES

Books of essays and criticism have seldom appeared, except through some accident of academic or journalistic affairs. It is a far cry from the days when a man like Hazlitt would produce a book of essays as one makes a table of polished wood and expect to receive his price for it. Hitherto much of the best Australian criticism, original and constructive, has only appeared in fugitive form. The varied and often important critical opinions of such men as Arthur Adams, Hilary Lofting, David McKee Wright, P. I. O'Leary, and Frank Morton are constantly covered in an equal snow. In 1904 A. G. Stephens published a book of critical essays, alarmingly named *The Red Pagan*, the title simply showing that the work was reprinted from a weekly Red Page. With a distinct bias toward the use of scientific ideas in treating of literature, he covers a large range of subjects, sometimes with a creative touch. The last essay is on Australian poets of that period, who are criticised by the application of original parodies that stick like burrs. Hugh McCrae, in dedicating a volume of poems to this critic, quoted Spenser and defined his functions:

> Ne spareth he most learned wits to rate,
> Ne spareth he the gentle Poet's rhyme,
> But rends without regard of person or of time.

A pleasant enough tribute, but it is only fair to say that A. G. Stephens, using the light rapier of an inexhaustibly easy style, has done as much to help and cherish as to destroy.

Poetry Militant was a challenging lecture that was issued as a small volume in 1909. Until then Bernard O'Dowd was the author of poetry that was wholly bare and austere in form, however luxuriant intellectually. In this essay he declared that this world of ours was not yet fit for Poetry Triumphant, the joyful, calm songs of Olympus or Elysium. 'An Australian Plea for Poetry of Purpose' was his sub-title. Beside the eloquence of the main argument, a kind of historical-critical interest is given to the little book by the inclusion of a long paragraph beginning, 'By the way, we already have an Australian poet', and naming and qualifying many poets of the day as forming one composite Australian poet. In a country where there are no reviews to put on record, sans intermission, all works of value that appear in book form, a list like that can give a few much-needed clues.

Several lectures of Professor T. G. Tucker's were published later as books, some like *The Supreme Literary Gift* occupied with matters of general literary interest, others dealing with special classical studies. Of these his *Sappho*, published in 1913, shows his peculiarly successful expository method at its best. Taking for preference a nut that is very hard to crack, he touches it, for what seems the first time, in the one right spot, and it flies open obediently, 'disparts three-fold to show the fruit within'. It is the style of the perfect lecturer rather than that of the essayist or original critic.

Professor Walter Murdoch's essays have appeared only once in collected form as *Loose Leaves*. Fortunate in his extraordinary appearance of naturalness, Professor Murdoch always manages to write an essay that flows from beginning to end, no matter how many turns and bypaths of thought it follows. Their size rather suggests their origin as articles, but not many articles remain so fresh after a space of years.

Peradventure, a solid volume of essays on literary subjects, was published by Professor A. T. Strong about 1912. The book shows an extraordinary familiarity with most of the European literatures, past and present, but as in all similar books what the reader receives is rather information than the aesthetic pleasure that comes from more creative criticism. In 1920 the same writer published a study of Shelley, written with a more revealing enthusiasm.

Romance, by Furnley Maurice, was a book of essays, personal and critical, published in 1923. The book is chiefly memorable for certain phrases, such as that W. B. Yeats 'held down the warm body of Irish poetry with a marble hand'. As a statement that may or may not be true, but its beauty is disarming and suggests what is the fact, that the book is the work of a poet rather than of an essayist. The writer is obviously more interested in these vivid ideas than in the logical flow of an essay.

Opinions less about literature than life were set down with economy and force in *Annotations*, by F. Sinclaire (1920). The book provides also a nucleus for a collection of Australian aphorisms of the quiet kind:

> Many liberties do not constitute Liberty.
>
> Beware of the man who talks about Art or Religion without giving the particulars.

As a glancing, philosophic attack on Rationalism the book has an importance out of all proportion to its size.

Mary Gilmore's book of essays, *Hound of the Road* (1921), was the spirited utterance of a woman whose life has been wide and full of adventure. It shows, no less than her poems, a delicate sensitiveness to all varieties of human experience.

HISTORY AND BIOGRAPHY

What should be a vital department of Australian prose is history and biography, but in spite of the immense field of research the result has been scanty. Anyone interested, though, might compare the cost of printing a slight book of lyrics with that of a closely-printed volume of history, maps, illustrations, indices and all. Among the books since 1900 that have surmounted these difficulties are those of Ernest Scott. He first published a short and fascinating study of La Perouse, which showed the author's special interest in the revelations of topography. Next came a comprehensive *Life of Flinders*, and in 1915 a standard *Short History of Australia*. Such competent books were urgently needed, and they themselves need some rivals that would express different points of view, unless history is to be considered an exact science.

Recent historians have had for their theme 'Australia in the Great War'. Books written about it from different standpoints, according to the writer's experience, but all more or less official in their status, are those by Sir John Monash, C. E. W. Bean, and Henry Gullett. Of these Sir John Monash's account of the last phase is marked, not merely by its authority, but by its unpretentious clearness in dealing with complex issues. This use of a classic restraint allows episodes like the winning of Mont St Quentin to come out in their real grandeur. Yet it is rather remarkable that, except for these exact records, the war has added almost nothing to our literature. An unofficial record of the Gallipoli campaign, however, was written by Sydney de Loghe in *The Straits Impregnable*, a forcible book that had distinct literary quality, in spite of the occasional self-consciousness of its style.

Of biographies the most important since 1900 is *Alfred Deakin*, by Walter Murdoch. The subject was a vital one and well-documented: the book shows that its author considers biography a form of literary art. A book like Ambrose Pratt's *Life of David Syme*, on the other hand, is useful but not immediately connected with literature. It may be said that many other lives are waiting to be written. Sir Thomas McIlwraith, of Queensland, has not been given to the nation in a book, nor has Chief Justice Higinbotham, of Victoria, been adequately treated in the only biography that has appeared. Indeed, the lack of good biography is a fundamental weakness in our prose literature.

LITERATURE AND OTHERWISE

Having come so far in this outline of prose work without giving a definition of literature, perhaps we can be content without one altogether. The word 'literature' is often distorted and degraded at the present time, being even unctuously used for the printed matter available at propagandist meetings. Still, it remains the only convenient word we possess for writing that shows a more or less intense and imaginative view of the world, or some portion of it. Apart from such books, though, there are others concerned with the matter-of-fact discussion of technical, economic or legal problems. Necessarily overloaded with statistics and formulae, these books for all their interest are not to be counted in with literature. They have their own value, and a good account of them is badly needed in this country. There are the small textbooks on wide subjects, for instance, such as Professor Gregory's monograph on Australia, which is content with being broadly suggestive in its interesting political and social comments. Anthropological books, too, like those of Spencer and Gillen, have their vast and increasing value, but have only potential literary quality. On the other hand, Dr C. McLaurin's *Post Mortem*, brilliant enough on its own plane, has rather an anti-literary point, occupied as it is in explaining artistic capacity in terms of physical science.

It would not be needful to emphasise these distinctions except that, in some columns devoted to books, a work is taken as serious according to the subjects treated. A treatise on housing or cotton-growing is serious, for instance; a collection of Dowell O'Reilly's short stories is a bright flippancy! It is true, of course, that housing and cotton-growing are important subjects, and so are many others, but the recognition of this often leads to confusion. Things should be kept on their own planes, and the test of value on the literary plane is not importance of subject but creativeness in the treatment. With this in mind we must pass over many weighty tomes in order to seize on those with the creative spark in them, 'the few, the fruitful few'.

POETRY

In some ways it is easier to follow the course of poetry than of prose in Australia. At first the difficulty is only that of seeing wood for trees. A bibliophile reports that he has read some 2,000 books of Australian verse, many of these published since 1900. In addition there are numbers of fugitive pieces that cannot be considered here, though some of them are more memorable than much that is in books. Then, again, for short-cuts that often prove to be no more than blind alleys, there are a few anthologies.

In this large mass of verse what we want to discover is the work that has permanent value in itself, and not merely as a stepping-stone to something else. When the century opened, the bush ballad had been established as a popular form of poetry. The ballad-makers of those days, writing vigorously but carelessly about the life of the bush as they knew it, would use each other's metre and manner more readily than borrow a horse. The great value of their work did not lie in a characteristic and individual style, but in its range and zest.

About 1900, E. J. Brady had developed his ballad-form, and was filling it with the sea, the 'Grey Water'. Since then he has published books of sea songs and bush songs, and other books that contain not songs but enormous and exciting facts. Edward Dyson had a store of tales from the mines that sometimes went into a flowing ballad-form, and sometimes into crisp prose. A. B. Paterson had a steady popularity, alternatively through vigour, as in 'The Man from Snowy River', and through sentiment, as in 'Black Swans'. The fourth star in this often-named constellation was Henry Lawson, whose ballads were above all things touching, filled with the intimate revelations of obscure lives that formed the core of his prose, as well as with humanitarian emotions and lightning-flashes of rebellion.

John Farrell, Barcroft Boake, and many others wrote in the nineties, but it is these four that concern us because they carried on into the present century. They were joined by a brilliant colleague, Will Ogilvie, who in his *Fair Girls and Grey Horses*, ended by destroying their simple craft. With more skill than the others, he had less real simplicity, and imported into the bush themes a light romanticism, and a touch of facile sentiment. Where the bush ballad had been like a man striding across open country he made it into a waltz in a barn, with lamps and flowers. As far as mere form went, this meant the substitution of smart stanzas lit by epigrams for the long, loping lines and sparse rhymes. But in spite of the troubadour easiness of most of his work, there was a hint of real poetry in it, and perhaps he may be said to have formed a link between the sheer balladists and Victor Daley, who at this time was touching his last notes on his instrument of few but sweet strings. Roderic Quinn took it up for a time, but played his own songs on it. In *The Circling Hearths*, but still more in the earlier, mystical *Hidden Tide*, Quinn sounded the note that caused him to be hailed as Celtic at a date when the Celtic twilight was beginning to be descried overseas. It was not that he borrowed the imagery and landscape of the Irish or Scottish poets. With an impulse akin to theirs, he used images from the life he knew, as in 'The Camp Within thc West', where the sundowner becomes a strange and symbolic figure.

And how are these wayfarers called
And whither do they wend?
The Weary-Hearted — and their road
At sunset hath an end.

Roderic Quinn's two books were published by the *Bulletin* in a series that included small books of poems by Hubert Church, James Hebblethwaite, Bernard O'Dowd, and Louise Mack. Then all these books were bound up in one solid volume with photographs, and unusual biographical notes by A. G. Stephens, so that the public for once could know what was what. Here you had the scholarly Hebblethwaite's *Rose of Regret*, a volume of musing, written in Tasmania but threaded by memories of England. Louise Mack in *Dreams in Flower* made her bubbles of song, many-coloured and vivid, in Sydney sunshine. Hubert Church in New Zealand wrote *The West Wind*, a volume of verse that was sometimes stately and a little remote, sometimes directed by a firm melody. Bernard O'Dowd, in Melbourne, but passionately conscious of Australia as a whole, cut like ribbed lightning across the calm of the book with his *Dawnward?* using short, harsh stanzas, and often long, harsh words.

This book, *A Southern Garland*, looked like the beginnings of a definite literary movement, for all the variety of its contents, and much was expected of the poets in it. While the balladists have had for their successors 'Gilrooney' with his *Land of the Starry Cross* and John O'Brien, with his more recent volume, *Round the Boree Log*, the poets of the *Southern Garland* were to continue the purely lyrical tradition that came from Kendall through Victor Daley. Their development, though, was individual and apart. Hubert Church published longer volumes, *Egmont* and *Poems*. *Poems* included two long pieces of blank verse, as well as some of the best lyrics from *The West Wind*.

Thou wilt come with suddenness
Like a gull between the waves.

That is a fine, lifted opening for a lyric. Sometimes the concluding lines hold the balance of power, as in 'Fields'.

The Summer light it goes,
    The bird away it flies,
And Love is one with those:
    The rose that never dies
Never was a rose.

James Hebblethwaite published two more volumes within the last few years. He seldom startles, but never disappoints. His later books could have been foretold from the *Rose of Regret*, but they were welcome and beautiful. As for the others, Louise Mack soon exhausted her small spring of poetry, and Roderic Quinn, though he has continued to write over a long period of years, has not been able to maintain the distinction of his first two books. The best work in his *Poems*, collected in 1920, was that already familiar.

Readers of Bernard O'Dowd's *Dawnward?* though, with its fierce austerity, could hardly have foretold his fifth and greatest book, *The Bush*. In it he forsakes the bare, ballad verse for an original ten-lined stanza of great beauty, that suits his theme. There are between sixty and seventy of these stanzas, and in them lives the Bush.

As many, Mother, are your moods and forms
As all the sons that love you. . .

And one aspect after another is rendered. The Bush is the mountain forest, it is the box-tree dotted plain, it is tropical jungles where 'the yang-yang screams through cactus wilderness', it is even 'the Bush where no tree grows', and it is the spiritual home of Australians, the source of their visions. The close-packed yet seldom crowded verse fills with exultation, yet with questioning and fear; such questioning is of this poet's nature. Can Australia be the dawn of new hope for the world after all? Australia can inherit all the dreams and discoveries of Europe, but will she inherit nothing evil? With all the intensity of the author of *Dawnward?* the poet looks at the life of factory and farm and again wonders and fears, seeing only a repetition of the old world's mistakes and sins. Then with a gesture he renounces fear:

She is a prophecy to be fulfilled.

She is Eldorado, Eutopia, Hy-Brasil – if we make her so. The poem ends with affirmation:

Love-lit, her Chaos shall become Creation:
And dewed with dream, her silence flower in song.

Taken in its breadth and its great depth, this is a poem so notable that it is hard to look for its fellows in English since 1900. The task to begin with was immense. No easy phrases about roses and nightingales and the accepted European poetic subjects were adequate. New lines, new phrases had to be made for the 'delicate amber leaflings of the gum': new words had to be drawn into the service and suffused with the poetry of the whole.

Many stanzas are autobiographical, but only in such a way as to relate the man to the Bush. When he remembers his boyhood it is to call up images of old mining-places:

Where lithe indignant saplings crowding claimed
The digger's ravage for their plundered queen.

One idea that takes up too much space near the beginning of the poem is a whimsy that has something in common with the idea of Macaulay's New Zealander on Westminster Bridge, but goes further on. To the people of a million years hence, we and Homer and the Nibelungs will all be so remote that we shall seem to have been contemporaries with one another. Follow this up, and you will have the people of that remote future doubting whether the Australian Gilbert Murray wrote Euripides, or vice versa. Further, 'The sunlit satyrs follow Hugh McCrae', and 'O'Reilly's Sydney shall be Sybaris'. A succession of stanzas filled with these ingenious inversions and associations is amusing enough, but only for those who use the surface part of their brains when reading a poem. These illustrative stanzas could well enough be omitted when the idea itself has been already magnificently stated:

Forgetful Change in one 'antiquity'
Boreal gleams shall drown, and southern glows.

Yet the poem remains great. Written in the grand manner, it never lets the manner carry on without content, and seldom without sheer poetry. Here are some of the final lines of the stanzas:

> Remorse unbaring slow her barbed tooth.
>
> Thin desolation on your haunted face.
>
> Eyes that were ours before the world began.

Whatever the value of Bernard O'Dowd's other work, and it is considerable, *The Bush* is his most important contribution to Australian literature itself. It is the book a young nation needs, a meditation, a prophetic book, and a seed-bed of poetry!

Before *The Bush* he had published that rich and significant book of sonnets, *The Seven Deadly Sins*, giving each 'sin' a sonnet for the prosecution and one for the defence. Then in his most recent book, *Alma Venus!* (1922) the long title poem, in heroic couplets, is again a passionate putting of the case, for and against. There are some questions, though, which a poet, if he raises, must answer. In *The Bush* the poet was The Answerer, which according to his master, Whitman, is the poet's chief function. But it must be said that it also took a poet to see that a question existed.

Another poet who, like Bernard O'Dowd, has bidden the English language achieve feats unknown before, is Chris Brennan. Not that he aims in the same direction! Devoted to French poetry, above all to that of the Symbolists, Mallarmé and others, Chris Brennan has found himself almost alone in making something of the same kind in English. He would seem to have by heart Verlaine's lightly-moving yet profound poem, 'Art Poétique'. Music, music, first of all, cried Verlaine, then insisted that the words used should be suggestive, not complete in themselves. As for the grand manner, he went on:

> Take Eloquence and wring its neck!

Rhyme, also must not be allowed to overmaster the poetry, and in Chris Brennan's work it certainly does not. His rhymes are unemphatic; they make only a flicker. The music is present everywhere. Sometimes, indeed, he seems to be working in the medium of musical sounds rather than of intellectual words (as Verlaine wrote poems called *Songs Without Words*):

O white wind, numbing the world
  to a mask of suffering hate!
and thy goblin pipes have skirled
  all night, at my broken gate.

The minuscular beginnings of each line are the poet's own, not a slip in transcription. He writes them in that way all through the big book of *Poems*, published in 1911, and the high level of his delicate work gives him a right to any finesse he may exercise. His exactness with regard to elusive ideas makes him able to express simple things perfectly when they arise:

The quiet hour awaits the moon.

I am shut out of mine own heart
because my Love is far from me.

Such lines have the naturalness of flowers opening.

A book published during the war contained 'The Chant of Doom', a long poem in heavy, short trochaics. In this poem the music is absent, unless it be that of a drum, and the neck of Eloquence has not been wrung. It is the great body of lyrics in his earlier books that has made the impressive record of Chris Brennan.

When Hugh McCrae's original book, *Satyrs and Sunlight*, appeared in 1910, it proved to be the expression of several different poetic worlds that he, as a poet, inhabited at different times. Sometimes he would seem to be most conscious of his name and conceive a ballad in the Scots language and kind. Here was vigour and warmth and gaiety, but not the startling originality of his world where he found the title of his book. When he returned to satyrs and sunlight he moved in a kingdom that was his own because he alone knew it. It is easy to say that his satyrs, naiads, gods and centaurs can be found in the Classical Dictionary. They can; and many poetasters have tried to revive these beings with results less interesting than those afforded by the Classical Dictionary. Hugh McCrae, though, writes of Pan and his nymphs, or Apollo and Daphne, or Silenus and his old songs, for no reason but necessity. These subjects are more real to him than the twentieth century. He has, in a sense, experienced them; his assured rhythms and clear-cut images make this certain. Sometimes, indeed, the poems are like marble statues seen by moonlight, but the marble always comes alive, the gods appear. There is at least one of these poems so strange in its imaginative veracity as to seem a miracle. That is 'The Unicorn'. Its few simply-formed quatrains compose a world:

> O never more I'll hear him call to me,
> Or spy his peak come travelling o'er the sea,
> Swift as a kestrel on its tented wings,
> Between the conches of the Triton kings.
>
> My unicorn. . .my unicorn is dead.

There have been those who would ascribe Hugh McCrae's terrific centaur poems to some vision of prehistoric Australia: actually, though, the poet seems unaware of any special country. Sunlight he needed, and a hard, flinty soil where hoofbeats could resound; from these he made his 'Sicily'. Some of his other poems are traditional in a stately manner. As Hilaire Belloc said of another: 'He worked upon verse as men work on the harder metals.' In his smithy he can make delicate tracery like this:

> And O awake, Elizabeth,
> The dawn is in the aspen-tree.

Another volume, *Colombine*, published three years ago, had less satyrs and more Elizabeth. The marble groups of figures, it might be said, were replaced by scenes on tapestry. The reciprocity between Hugh McCrae, the poet, and Norman Lindsay, the illustrator, could go no further than that. McCrae's later poems have been published in a form inaccessible to readers who were not also collectors of expensive art-books.

Though Arthur Adams's most important poetical work was published just before the century opened, he continued writing verse for some years, though perhaps with less spontaneity than at first. Coming to Australia as a young man he made it his home, and his most poignant lyrics have sprung from his nostalgia for Maoriland:

> Her fresh young figure, lithe and tall,
>   Her twilight eyes, her brow benign,

She is the peerless queen of all –
  The maid, the country, that I shrine
  In this far banished heart of mine.

This tightly-packed verse is typical of his style. Rarely moved by a definite lyrical impulse his work is nevertheless terse, firm, and characteristic. Perhaps these qualities gained their fullest expression in a volume, *London Streets*, which aimed at evoking the varying atmosphere of the more notable London thoroughfares; yet the attitude is too much that of the aloof, alien poet for the book to achieve complete success. There is hardly enough surrender to the spirit of the place. About 1912 Arthur Adams collected all the work he cared to preserve in a single edition and signified his intention of retiring from the poetic field. This volume of careful and rounded verse makes a distinct addition to our literature.

Another writer who, like Arthur Adams, came to Australia from New Zealand must be included in our range of inquiry for various reasons. The critical writing of David McKee Wright has had an effect on contemporary verse, and the bulk of his creative work has been done here, although he had already published a couple of volumes in New Zealand. A careful student of metrical forms, his technical versatility has always been very great. In *An Irish Heart* (1916) his rhythms, as well as his title, give proof of his racial origin:

Proudly, proudly will the tall men go
  Working a clean plough and a new spade,
By the way they carry their heads shall all men know
  There is a light in their hearts that will not fade.
But they will build well with good stone
  And they will dig well in free land;
And the fair thing and the rare thing that is theirs alone
  Will be singing till the world can understand.

Here he cleverly uses stress instead of accent, as in the line, 'Working a cléan plóugh and a néw spáde'. Such a variant in verse is especially valuable in Australia as giving the death-blow to the idea that a good line is to be made by the counting of syllables. We all know the painful results of this old theory among the balladists, where a verse would often be full of long syllables that had to be gabbled because they were unaccented. 'So they lîved through hard séasons and tróuble' would be a typical line, with the long syllables, 'through hard' of no more value than 'in a' would be.

In 1920 David McKee Wright won the Rupert Brooke Prize for a long poem on 'Gallipoli', but this, like the bulk of his later work, has not yet been collected in bookform.

The varied books of Furnley Maurice's [Frank Wilmot] poems bring to mind one of G. K. Chesterton's formless plaints:

> He seems to think nobody minds
> His books being all of different kinds!

An early book, anonymous at the time, was *Unconditioned Songs*, a modern type of book, filled with brief visions and broken melodies. The word 'unconditioned' seems to mean that the songs end when their first innocent motif is spent. The book is a revolt against the bondage of forms. For contrast came a book of tendencious poems, *Eyes of Vigilance*, including a long, formal meditation, since famous, 'To God, from the Warring Nations':

> God, let us forget
> That we accused of barbarous intent
> The foe that lies in death magnificent.
> How can we hate forever, having proved
> All men are brave and bright and somewhere loved?

There are sonnets in this book, too, sonnets used with a personal twist, not merely forced into their shape and rhyme. There followed a yet larger volume, *Arrows of Longing*, sonnets and lyrics and reveries in free verse. This lyric is characteristic:

> Give me rivers to cool my hands,
>   Give me hills for stay.
> I have a fear an' a little fear
>   I hurt my love to-day.

Furnley Maurice is most himself when he achieves this exact rightness in hyperbole. He has imagination and poignancy, and he knows his mediums. His imagination broods to discover something clear and sure, such as this about the sea floor:

From the drowned gardens where slow water-gales
Wash unknown jungles and world-weary hulls.

It is not easy to name another poet who could have found that astonishing phrase, 'slow water-gales'. Once made and placed in the easily-fitting rhythm, it is a jewel that delights as much by its setting as by its own beauty. Such beauty, almost hidden by its harmony, Furnley Maurice can at times provide.

Shaw Neilson is now represented by two volumes of poems, *Heart of Spring* and *Ballad and Lyrical Poems*.

Let your voice be delicate:
  The bees are home;
All their days' love is sunken
  Deep in the comb.

By such a verse Shaw Neilson, and none other, is to be recognised. Sometimes his pictures are literal, sometimes frail with the burden of imagination. This, for clearness:

Across the stream, slowly and with much shrinking
  Softly a full-eyed wallaby descends
To the blue water's edge. . .I see him drinking
  And he and I and all his folk are friends.

He has an affinity, at his simplest, with the Welsh poet, W. H. Davies, and though less unfailing in his innocent freshness has occasionally a deeper magic of phrase. He is apt to cling with gentle fanaticism to his own subjective names for things seen, till the words become an abstraction to the reader, who can, however, for comfort, always return to lines like:

And a young foal spoke all his heart
With diamonds for eyes.

A poet with a peculiar kind of talent, well developed, is Frederick Macartney. His first natural quality is a freedom from vague extravagance. Taking advantage of this immunity, he can let his fancy wander safely to its limit, using fine, firm craftsmanship the while. The result is a body of poems nearly all expressing what they set out to express, which is a rare achievement. Here he outlines his aim:

Skyward – a little way,
  Going up straight and blue,
Amid green bracken to the purple day,
  Ascends the safe smoke sweetening a gully through
  With resinous eucalypt odours: thus pervadingly accrue
The pungent native meanings that my diligent rhymes essay.

That is from *Poems* (1920). A more recent book, *Something for Tokens*, shows that he has not swerved from the mark. It has been said of him: 'When he has added to his extraordinary sympathy for words an equal sympathy for things, he will bring, gently, a new note into poetry.'

The war has found curiously little expression in Australian poetry. There was the picturesque pageant of *Sonnets of Empire*, published soon after the war began, by Archibald T. Strong. Using what has been called his 'bridled intensity of epithet' in this volume and in his *Poems* (1918) he made a body of work that showed fine craftsmanship and a trained sensitiveness to words. His sense of form is complete enough to pass unnoticed. He has also the power of surrendering to an occasional mood that can lead far, as when in a sonnet he wrote: 'The light that fills lost causes'. Furnley Maurice's meditations in wartime have already been mentioned. In sonnet and elegy form, they were a notable contribution to such poetry. As a contrast came Leon Gellert's *Songs of a Campaign*, published in 1916. A body of vivid lyrics, full of the passionate realism of an imaginative soldier, the book made a deep impression. Sometimes the words seemed to be forced into shape by what they described, as in this:

Every morn I wake
  And every morn I stand
And see the shrapnel break
  On the smashed land.

It must be said, though, that a large group of war sonnets, which in the second edition were bound up with the lyrics, have a less eager and personal, if a more decorative quality. After the war the most competent 'digger' verse was a book of soldier songs from Palestine, by 'Gerardy'. In most of the pieces, though, the concentration of vision and phrase that might have made the galloping lines into poetry was missing. There remain the war poems of William Blocksidge, but what he wrote about the war is so intimately bound up with his general outlook and philosophy that some account of his whole poetic work must be given.

William Blocksidge has published several volumes of poems, but *Selected Poems* (1919) may be taken as representative. Chosen in groups from the work of many years, including those of the war and after, the poems were personal both in utterance and philosophy. The early poems were a love-cycle, set in the sea-air and hard sunlight of Moreton Bay. Most of them were formal, though in great variety, but a firm kind of free verse sometimes appeared. A group of profound and original love sonnets in Shakespearean form was followed by another sonnet sequence, 'A Wreath', a memorial to a friend fallen in the war. The heart of the book, though, as of the poet's philosophy, lay in a free verse poem, 'Australia's Dead'. Of these men he cried:

> Divining that life lives by death
> They spent their breath in that magnanimous purchase.

This was the theme of the last part of the book, 'Life's Testament'. In it the verse is often heavy, but with the burden of thought. Sometimes it moves like a Latin hymn, yet not smoothly, as if it dreaded the too easy, the soporific:

> The term, the flower, the consummation
> Of my elected transmutation
> Into my Utmost Self I fashion.
>
> I drive my dead to the dust; I put
> Off whatever yields no fruit –
> Thus my duration's absolute.

The book ends with several prose chants on the idea of this immortality. It is a far cry from the early 'Moreton Miles' to these heady precipices where the poet seeks

> Thought that builds
> Another outpost in the universe.

The effect of the work of William Blocksidge is cumulative, one poem revealing and supporting another. A high distinction of style and thought is never absent.

The most distinctive thing about *Bells and Bees*, a volume published by Louis Esson in 1911, is the way a note of folk song is sounded, even in pieces that seem to come from the dark lanes of city slums. This is rare in Australian poetry, where even the bush ballads have a touch of sophistication that destroys their effect. Louis Esson has the art of picking out rich phrases from the vernacular and building them into his work, as in his cradle-song:

> Baby, my baby, fain are you for bed,
> Magpie to mopoke, busy as the bee.

A later volume, *Red Gums* (1912), was not quite so striking in its revelation of this particular quality, though it contained one slang poem, 'Back ter Little Lon.', that is a perfect thing of its kind, and in its sheer reality and lyrical impulse makes most other attempts to put verse into the mouths of our slum-dwellers seem false or insipid.

R. H. Long's modest *Verses* (1918) contained the work of a real poet, and included some sonnets that could only have been written by a man who knew the Bush and loved it with all his senses. He has a rare faculty for weaving the names of places into significant lines. This has been a special task for poets in all ages, and Australia needs it as a foundation and a background. The quality of his general work may be shown by this sestet:

> Give me a road that winds among the hills,
> Some mountain myrtles in a cloudy sky,
> And be not niggardly with wayside rills
> And cool retreats for all things moist and shy,
> And let me hear the lyre-bird's luscious notes
> Thieving the ballads from his neighbour's throats.

Frank S. Williamson in some of the poems of a volume, *Purple and Gold* (1910), also evoked the atmosphere of the bush, particularly the atmosphere of early morning, with its jodel of magpies. He has made some lyrics that float easily into the mind:

> She comes as comes the summer night,
> Violet, perfumed, clad with stars.

Robert Crawford through a large number of poems in several

volumes, *Lyric Moods*, and *The Leafy Bliss* (1920), has maintained his own qualities of grace and finish. Finding a special pleasure in the artificial forms of French origin, especially the triolet, he has let them bind him, and it may be suggested that they have shorn his locks.

In *This Green Mortality*, and his two previous books, Louis Lavater has shown a sensitiveness to the half-revelations of Nature. Such an elusive mood could perhaps best be captured by music, but his vision shines out serenely enough in some 'dew-filtered underlight'.

Rupert Atkinson, in a very different spirit, has poured forth fiery cataracts of verse in his books, *By a Midnight Sea* and *A Modern Magdalene*. Sometimes he appears in a personal mood of 'fleering' at the Universe. More often, as in *A Flagon of Song*, he spends much of his energy in exotic themes, 'Egyptian Lyrics', 'Omar Dead', and 'A Viking's Death'. He has an easy mastery of form, and an imagination that would seem even more powerful if he strained it less, and avoided constant assertive words like 'ecstacy' and 'passion'. His sonnets are his own, conversational, argumentative, often sardonic and effective like a cartoon.

Coming just on the borders of poetry is the work of C. J. Dennis, whose first book, *Back Block Ballads*, was published in 1913. He has altered his characteristic vernacular style very little since, except in *The Glugs of Gosh*, a satire that was not vernacular but 'straight'. The ballads were very well done, as well as C. H. Souter's, with quiet fun, tuneful if rather mechanical metres, and plenty of well-managed, unobtrusive rhymes that charmed like juggler's tricks. The only thing he added to the books that followed, *The Sentimental Bloke*, *The Moods of Ginger Mick*, and so on, was a story to bind the pieces together and hints of sustained character. As poetry his work has little meaning, except for an occasional happy lyricism, but he has a real humorous and satirical power that is never used harshly.

In this survey of twentieth century poetry, most attention has been paid to writers whose work has been entirely embraced by the period. It has been thought unnecessary, for instance, to refer to the work of George Essex Evans, a capable, rhetorical writer who greeted the opening of the Commonwealth with an ode that is still remembered. Nor can we touch on the work of George Gordon McCrae, whose *Fleet and Convoy* (1915) was the graceful and dignified tribute of a veteran to crusading youth. Sydney Jephcott, again though publishing *Penetralia* in 1909, a book filled with rugged but real poetry, more properly belongs to the earlier period when he was hailed by Francis Adams as a writer of individuality and promise. It is many years, too, since Arthur Bayldon, whose latest volume of poems is not more than three years old, began to be known as the author of rhetorical and powerful verse that reached its climax in the well-known sonnet of 'Marlowe', with its last line:

> A scullion fleeing with a bloody knife.

Then there is the work of John Bernard O'Hara, whose *Songs of the South* (first and second series) were the prelude to a long succession of volumes. His verse, though without any very strong character, showed facility in the treatment of a variety of themes. Thus a poem about a wind would have long, loose lines, while an apostrophe to 'Homing Crows' would consist of taut verses with five brief lines each. At the time when he did most of his work, technical excellence and versatility were qualities of some importance.

J. Le Gay Brereton's work ranges from his *Song of Brotherhood*, published in the early nineties, through his *Sea and Sky* (1908) to a small volume, *The Burning Marl* (1918). His standing as an Elizabethan critic lends weight to his poetic play, *Tomorrow*, dealing with the poet Greene. In the poems in *Sea and Sky* he uses suggestive epithets in strange places:

> The phantom waves still fret and foam
> And sigh along the visionary sand.

Those lines from a lyric, 'The Robe of Grass', suggest his range of expression. In *The Burning Marl*, which is chiefly concerned with emotions roused by the War, he is more didactic, and not always so effective.

WOMEN POETS

For sheer convenience the women poets since 1900 may be grouped together, although they are quite varied and usually without influence one upon another. Louise Mack has been mentioned with the poets of *A Southern Garland*. Mary Gilmore, first known by the book called *Marri'd and Other Verses*, had something of the same ease and poignancy, but her roots have always been deeper in the earth. Few women have been so much the poet of women, as in the poem 'Marri'd', which ends:

> An' feelin' awful glad
> Like them that watch'd Silo'm;
> An' everything because
> A man is comin' Home.

In her largest volume, *A Passionate Heart* (1918), she has used a great range of metres, including a personal free verse, and there are a few poems like the very original, 'Botany Bay', with the wayward lilt of old ballads, whose irregularities are simply those that show the potter's thumb and its excellence. Her most constant idea, though, is a kind of mystical human sympathy:

> I had forgotten how much I owed
> To one, and two, and three;
> I thought I travelled a lonely road –
> But the whole world walked with me.

Marie E. J. Pitt, whose *Horses of the Hills* contains all the work she has collected so far, has power of another kind. It would not be fantastic to suggest that her verse has the steady rhythm of galloping horses. It maintains the same rhythm always for the length of a poem, never turning aside from even a difficult metre, which indeed Marie Pitt seems to enjoy. Her best-known poems are those about places, where the names are woven into the tune of the words:

> Wild and wet and windy wet falls the night on Hamilton,
> Hamilton that seaward looks unto the setting sun.

Robbed of some intensity by a too-easy alliteration, the poem still remains memorable. The recurrent line of another is:

> Kurraba by the North Shore blue.

But it is not easy to do justice to a writer whose more subtle and important work is still in fugitive form.

Zora Cross began her poetic work by a book, *Songs of Love and Life* (1917), that included sixty love sonnets and a group of young-hearted lyrics. The sonnets were less original than the other poems, but the remarkable thing about them was their easy movement, as of some slender animal with strong, silken muscles.

> For all the echoes of the horn and shell,
> From Jubal's harmony to Pan's shrill lay,
> Your soul has gathered through your ears, made strong
> By timbrel, harp and little singing bell.
> So come, my love, make melody today,
> Be swift, be swift to sing me into song.

An enviable style! In her second volume, *The Lilt of Life*, blank verse moves with the same freedom.

Lala Fisher, whose slender books, though privately printed, are well-known, rose to her highest in the lines to her father's memory. *Grass Flowering* is the name of one book, and her work has indeed a likeness to the 'silent-seeded meadow grass'. This is from a lyric, 'Secret':

> To guard her nest
>   The bird, outwinging,
> Leaves it unsought;
>   And singing, singing
> Guides the stray guest
> On a false quest.
> So laughs she lest
>   Someone, not caring
> Should chance on grief
>   Almost past bearing.
> Safe is the nest –
> The heart may rest.

Nina Murdoch in her *Songs of the Open Air* (first series 1915, second series 1922) shows the possession of something called sincerity. Her words seem to come from a centre, and her utterance is clear and personal in each mood. Sensitive to the Bush, especially by the sea, she welcomes the sensual impression, the warm wind laden with spray, the 'scent of crushed lantana'. Her love poems, too, are laden with the images of sea and sky.

The work of Dorothea Mackellar, beginning with the volume, *The Closed Door and Other Verses*, has been chiefly vivid and enthusiastic landscape painting. Sometimes the whole palette is thrown on the canvas; that is, the colours are named, not evoked. She is better at sterner moments, as in describing a strange lake in South Australia, whose waters are:

Warm, warm as blood
Not enough to cover
The quaking mud.

Mary Fullerton published first a book of thoughtful sonnets, *Moods and Melodies*, and later in contrast, *The Breaking Furrow* (1921), a book of rough ballads and lyrics. On account of some democratic chants in it, the book has been described as 'palpitating with humanity', but it is not merely that. It has literary quality as well. This of a wild-flower:

A spory wonder singing with the sap,
And all around the uncomprehended Bush.

M. Forrest, whose firmly-wrought *Alpha Centauri* appeared about 1910, has since collected very little compared with her enormous production. Technically dexterous, she delights in the treatment of romantic themes. A book of fairy verse in 1916 and *Streets and Gardens* (1922) give characteristic examples of her fluent and ornate work.

The Mountain Road and Other Verses (1912), by Enid Derham, contained lyrics that were very fine separately, but rather disconcerting when taken together, the extreme naiveté of one seeming to defy the rich sophistication of another. One notable lyric, with strong images, is 'The Gum-Tree':

Through all thy height
  How dost thou blossom, giving back the sun,
Each leaf a light!
  Thou unconsumed one...

A stanza from 'Star of the Sea' is one that other poets have tried to write:

As Love in some supreme despair
  Can cast aside the bonds of space
And glimpse upon the empty air
  The one Beloved's form and face...

Winifred Shaw, beginning to write in quite recent years, has already three books of verse to her credit. Most of the poems are tuneful ballads on the model of older ones and with similar themes – Gipsy queens, minstrels, castle walls, and a good deal of such reliable paraphernalia. Still, her capacity in imitative and decorative writing is remarkable, and every here and there she achieves a more personal image, as in the 'Fine Clay', from her first volume, *The Aspen Tree*:

O white clay, O fine clay, of the earth cold
  Him I fashion cunningly surely will be sweet.
Godlike I am moulding him in the god's mould,
  Hands, lips, feet.

This poem with its strange, almost perfect rhythm and its stranger depth of thought is such as to make one fear for the writer that she should ever overlay it with an accumulation of average work. The writer was probably not meant to spend herself on quantity, but on intensity.

In some but not all of her fugitive verse, Elsie Cole has sung native wood-notes wild. Her lyrics of the bush are her most characteristic work. The skilled and thoughtful sonnets and nature-poems of Clarice Crosbie remain not only fugitive, but hidden under a pen-name, 'Syd C.'. Dulcie Deamer has written much in rather vague but powerful stanzas upon large themes – Death, Love, Life. The verse of Alys Hungerford has only recently been collected in a book. Her affinities are definitely Irish, but her rhythms are rather personal than national.

In general it may be said that the Australian women poets have contributed less than their quota to that stream of really vital work which it is here our purpose to study. Of efficient verse they have made a great deal, far more than it would have been possible to mention here, even by the omission of everything else; but romantic associations, spread out over long, shapely verses, do not make poetry. It is originality, or perhaps intensity, that has been lacking.

A further complaint is a negative one. Our women writers who have written so much and so capably have not added to our store the kind of poems one might expect from them. It is a man who has written the best cradle-song, and two men who have written the best child poems – L. H. Allen in *Billy Bubbles*, and Furnley Maurice in *The Bay and Padie Book*. In such directions women may be said to have a kind of inside knowledge. If they have neglected their chance in this kind of verse, though, it should be remembered that the particularly good and varied supply of children's prose stories has been almost entirely provided by women writers.

GENERAL SUMMARY

In trying to give a glimpse of the significant work that has been done in this century, one is met both in the domain of poetry and that of prose with the same obstacle. There is practically no record of such work but in the scattered books themselves. There are not even groups of writers, each group gathered round some centre. Except for the accidents of journalism Australian writers remain isolated, and often their books are issued from obscure presses. Sometimes they are only privately printed, and distributed spasmodically, as usually happens with the work of William Blocksidge, one of the most vigorous and suggestive of our present-day writers. In these anarchic conditions it is hopeless to search for signs of definite literary movements or influences.

From time to time shy attempts have been made to create a centre. For many years there had been the Red Page of *The Bulletin* which had acted as a unifying force in recording all important books published in Australia and focusing attention on what was being done; but it gradually changed its nature and abandoned this particular function of a consecutive index. In 1907 a small body of writers gathered round *The Heart of the Rose*, a Melbourne quarterly with purely literary aims, but after four issues the review died, and the company of writers dispersed. Later, in 1916, a monthly magazine, *Birth*, was issued in Melbourne with the object of attracting good poetry and of recording and reviewing new books as they appeared. It lasted for six years, and succeeded in publishing two small annuals, containing the best poetry published in its ordinary issues. Yet neither of these two last ventures could be described as literary movements. The writers concerned did not subscribe to any aesthetic dogma, and were not swayed by the same influences.

Something that might be given the name of a movement did, in fact, make its appearance last year in Sydney among the group of young contributors to *Vision*. In a definite pronouncement in the first issue of the review they put forth the articles of their doctrine. These, briefly stated, were that good poetry was based on clear images, and that its subject-matter should not be 'local' but should come from worlds evoked by the imagination. The first proposition is familiar enough; most poetical movements have started off with the same affirmation. But literary theories are only of importance to us when we can judge their results, and those of *Vision* have not had time to produce much fruit in creative work. A volume, *Poetry in Australia – 1923*, was, however, published by the *Vision* press last year with a preface by Norman Lindsay. Besides containing the work of older men, like Chris Brennan and Hugh McCrae, it gave prominence to some younger writers, particularly Jack Lindsay and Kenneth Slessor. On the two last-named the chance of this movement developing vitality in the future would seem to depend.

Perhaps Hugh McCrae may be credited with having fathered this school of young poets. If so, it would be almost a unique instance, at least in recent years, of an Australian writer's work having a direct influence. The most unfortunate thing in our literary history is the way promising movements tend to run into the sand. There has been no one to follow Henry Lawson. His work remains the most intimate revelation of our life in prose, in spite of all that has been written since. It would seem to have been very easy for later writers, using the tracks he pioneered, to explore further and perhaps open up a wider prospect. The tendency, though, so far as there is one, has been to turn back to the macadamised road. Most of the stories appearing recently have been of the competent, rather mechanical type from which the young writers of older countries are proudly trying to escape.

In the same way there has been no development of the loose, individual novel that seemed to promise something at the beginning of the century. It has been left to an English writer, D. H. Lawrence, to continue this tradition in his own way. In his *Kangaroo* (1923) he has written a novel, shot with a wayward beauty, which will be of permanent value to our future writers. In its pictures of our landscape, seen through friendly, alien eyes, as well as in its revelation of our national character and social habits, it is a boon to us, and we may consider it as a brilliant gift from overseas. Or perhaps we may take it as compensation for the loss of those of our writers who have been forced to go abroad. Many of these become absorbed in another life and only occasionally, like Havelock Ellis in his recent *Kanga Creek*, remind us of their origins.

This brings us to one factor that cannot be overlooked in glancing at our literary development. The facilities for ordinary publishing hardly exist in Australia. It has not been found possible, for instance, to publish novels here, except those of the cheapest kind, and numberless short stories of value lie buried in the files of newspapers. We are dependent, so far as these things are concerned, on the taste of English publishing houses that apply their own tests to an Australian book, and select what they want. The value of this selection may be judged by the fact that almost all the books it has been thought worthwhile to mention in this survey have been issued in Australia, in spite of the difficulties that surrounded such publication. Lately, it is true, art books of various types have been produced here successfully, but they have a public of a special kind, and such publishing has its limitations. It is only likely to be favourable to such literature as presents the world decoratively in terms of apes and peacocks.

With all this, the truth remains that since 1900 a large body of important work in prose and verse has been produced. It has been penetrative rather than conspicuous; and there is this consolation in looking at the difficult conditions under which it has been done: if our literature has had to struggle with a stubborn soil, it may make for ultimate hardiness in the plant. Australian writers have somehow managed to keep their craft alive. The average of their work is higher than it was at the beginning of the century; it is wider in range and more varied in style; a great deal of mere rhetoric has been cleared away. The books sketched in the course of this enquiry have, in spite of their scattered origins, a combined and cumulative power, and they have left a sense of vitality in the air.

Articles from the Illustrated Tasmanian Mail

AUSTRALIAN LITERATURE

Poetry First

In most societies and circles where Australian literature is mentioned, you find that the discussion nearly always circles round the matter of Australian poetry only, as if what appeared in prose could not be literature at all. It is a queer and unfortunate habit, leading people to imagine that if they can string some or any words together into verse lengths they are being serious writers! It leads also to the enormous crop of 'spring poets' who make the standing joke of our philistines. Think of it, there were five hundred poems entered for the Canberra Ode competition in May. With this superabundance there comes a levelling-down, and so it happens that all our poets are in danger of being considered comic spring poets, and all our prose writers are almost ignored. The fact is though, that our good poets are few, and that they are genuine and important: and our prose writers have contributed immensely to our growing literature.

The Wave of Poetry

In reporting on the present state of our poetry, we can only say that it is at a low ebb. The usual output of verse is probably being kept up: that is, the verse columns in our few magazines are filled, and the short pieces required as fill-up in other pages are supplied. Little of this, though, is anything more permanent than 'copy', and even its writers seem to think so, as almost no verse is now being issued in book form, either from journals or fresh manuscripts. A few years ago, soon after the war, there were many books of verse produced, here and abroad. Here *and abroad*: so then the wave that encouraged poetry here and the wave that floated it abroad were probably one and the same wave. Each Australian poet who, since then, has not been publishing, perhaps not even writing, would probably give you quite personal reasons for his recent inactivity: mainly economic reasons, in most cases. Yet he is also a part of the world wave, which is now depressed everywhere, except, it seems, in America. Here our poets from whom we might have most to expect have all published their latest books about 1920.

Some Names

Take a few of the names. Bernard O'Dowd, after writing *The Bush* in 1912, has given us nothing since his *Alma Venus!* with its wide visioning of our destiny and desire. That came about 1921. Furnley Maurice's two large volumes, each important in its different way, *Eyes of Vigilance* and *Arrows of Longing*, have had no successor during these several years. Unless indeed one were to mention, enthusiastically too, the new editions and expansions of his famous book of Kiddie Verses, *The Bay and Padie Book*, which is probably one of the few genuine expressions of the elusive child point of view that have ever appeared. Hugh McCrae, the exhilarating poet of *Satyrs and Sunlight*, has been silent since the appearance of his dainty *Colombine*, except for his inaccessible volume of *Idyllia*, published for connoisseurs, with valuable drawings by Norman Lindsay. (A connoisseur, unfortunately, does not merely mean a person who knows what to like, but one who can pay for it.) Again, it is some years since the appearance of James Devaney's striking book of verse, *Fabian*. Shaw Neilson's second book of ballads and lyrics came in 1923, later than most: his frail, beautiful notes will ever mellow in our minds.

It is the white plum tree
  Seven days fair,
As a bride goes showing
  Her joy of hair!

A contrasting poet, working more strenuously with what is

recognised as the mind apart from the emotions, is Frederick Macartney. He again has published nothing since his *Something for Tokens*, a book several years old. It is said that the philosophical poet, William Blocksidge, has a new century of sonnets on the way. It must be remembered, too, that it is only a year or so since Louis Lavater edited a solid volume, *The Sonnet in Australia*, containing sonnets from very many hands. None of these, though, were recently written: the wave, we observe, is flat. All we can do, and it is a good deal after all, is to use the facilities afforded by Authors' Week, and hunt out the poets' past work that has been revealed. Suppose we reread O'Dowd's *The Bush*, and feel its high organ tones again: Hugh McCrae's *Satyrs and Sunlight*, with its marble strength: Louis Esson's book of folk songs, *Bells and Bees*: Shaw Neilson's *Heart of Spring*. We might do much worse!

Present-Day Prose: The Novel

When it comes to prose, our contemporary report can afford to be much livelier. It is noticeable, though, that when our verse does appear it is usually published in Australia (whether at the publisher's or the writer's risk). Our novels, on the other hand, which are more expensive to print and distribute, are almost all published overseas. There is no need to emphasise the misfortune of this: it means that our novels have to satisfy the desires of an English publisher, who chooses what will be likely to please his English public. For a book to satisfy that condition, and at the same time to emerge as a valuable part of our authentic literature, is something of a marvel, but it has occurred, and more than once. The outstanding success in this way for 1927 was Katharine Susannah Prichard's novel, *Working Bullocks*, a book full of shimmering impressionism, conveying the life and struggles of timber getters in the south-west of West Australia. Appearing at the same time, but with more of an appeal to the merely modern and urban in the reader, came Chester Cobb's sombre, dull yet sincere book, *Days of Disillusion*, set firmly in Sydney. There has also been a quota of average popular novels, given out in a mechanical way by the mass-production type of English publisher. This at least shows that Australians can produce marketable fiction, in its competent unimportance, as well as the rest of the world.

General Prose

In the matter of what is called general literature, we have seen some strides taken lately. There was Jack McLaren's remarkable book about his hermitage on Cape York, *My Crowded Solitude*, a book that followed on the heels of his other one, *My Odyssey*, which recounted his years among the South Sea Islands. Mr McLaren is not a globetrotting writer of travels: for instance, his sojourn on Cape York covered about seven years. Seven years, and one book about it! Most of the travelloguers make seven books out of one year's rushed experience. More recently has come Harry Burrell's book on the platypus, a masterpiece of patience and even charm. Nobody quite knew before what an insoluble beast-bird-fish this ornithorhynchus was, but Mr Burrell has gone far towards answering most of the riddles he raises. Perhaps he would like to be reminded of the late Dowell O'Reilly's summary of the case, from his essay on evolution called 'Wings and Song'. He wrote, 'By ambition fell the platypus: he wanted to be everything at once, and missed the bus. . .' Coupled together because simultaneous, like twins, though not alike in manner or opinion, are two books of essays, one by Francis Jackson, of Sydney, and the other by Alan Mickle, of Melbourne, the latter already known as the author of *Said My Philosopher* and other volumes of essays.

The more one names the books that do exist, though, the more the phantoms of those that ought to appear dance round the point of the pen. Almost more than new books, we need collected and sifted editions of what work exists already. We need some volumes of the Best Short Stories of Australia, collected over thirty years, from this country where short stories were always a forte, before the form had a vogue elsewhere. Then we want an anthology of Lawson's best stories. After that, a book of collected Australian essays. But there is not time to say all we want. Australia has produced few books, perhaps, but such collections would help to show that we have had more and better books than most Australians ever know or imagine.

DRAMATIC WRITING IN AUSTRALIA

At present what may be called the 'Little Theatre Movement' in Australia is in every sort of throes. The whole aims and principles of the Repertory Theatre societies, in Melbourne and Sydney at least, are being canvassed in meetings and press. The organisation of a professional company with what would be called repertory programmes is apparently determined. The politics and theatrical meaning of the change have nothing for this [article] to discuss. What does interest me, though, is the question of the quality of the plays to be produced. What will be a repertory play, as opposed to a commercial one? What has been a repertory play hitherto? Again, when the promoters of the scheme announce that they will include some Australian plays for certain, what plays of 'repertory' quality will they be likely to find?

The Name 'Repertory'

Although I have used the word 'repertory' several times here, I am aware that it is about to be dropped by the new organisation. It is felt to be an outgrown shell or a misnomer, what you will. The name has had a strange history. Used first on the Continent, it meant a theatre where plays that might or might not have commercial value were tried out. (In this way it resembled Mr Leon de Lion's recent 'Q' Theatre, at Kew, London, where experiments are made.) When the Repertory Theatre movement began in England, though, round about twenty years ago, the name had already received a slight but significant twist. The Repertory Theatre, for instance, run by Charles Frohman and Granville Barker, was one in which plays of definite literary quality were put on in quick alternation by professional players. There were no long runs; there were no stars. The play was the thing. It was such a movement that brought out Barrie, Galsworthy, Shaw, and lesser men; and it became recognised as promoter of a native drama. It might and did produce some established foreign plays, such as those by Ibsen and Hauptmann. But it was felt that if the Repertory Theatre had not first produced Galsworthy, Shaw, and the rest, introducing their work to an expectant and prepared audience, those dramatists would have remained unknown. Thus in England the Repertory movement came to have two significant phases; it was known as uncommercial, definitely so, and it was known as being ready to produce native dramatists with literary quality. This literary quality was, of course, 'literary' in terms of the stage. Some mistakes were made, but on the whole the 'literary' play in the narrow sense of being fitter to read than to act was rejected. These literary dramatists were genuine playwrights; they wrought plays for the theatre, not for the study. A few years after its inception in England, the Repertory Theatre movement, with small or capital letters, reached Australia, beginning in Adelaide. Here the name again slid a little to one side.

'Repertory' in Australia

What happened in Australia, generally speaking, was that the history of the English movement was studied, and its list of plays borrowed. In a few rare cases an Australian play was started, but it would be billed, usually, as an Australian play, while the other plays, Barrie, Brighouse, and the rest, would be called, 'repertory'. The English scheme of a season of quickly changing plays was hardly adopted at all; it made too great a strain on the resources of an ordinary amateur society. Thus the two chief meanings that 'repertory' had had in England were lost in Australia. There was no succession of changed plays, and there was no predominance of native drama. What the repertory movement did achieve in Australia, though, was something important enough, though different. It meant the formation and retention of groups of people interested in plays that were not merely commercial successes. If sometimes the Australian repertory societies have produced plays that were more suited to the commercial stage, it must be said that this was due to neglect of those plays by our commercial producers who had been occupied by an interest in a 'wider appeal' still. Into the repertory programmes, too, there did leak a few Australian plays from time to time, such as Louis Esson's *Dead Timber* and Mrs Dale's *Secondary Considerations*, which are still remembered well.

Promised Plays

The new movement promises, as its first two Australian plays, *Brumby Innes*, by Katharine Prichard, and *A Happy Husband*, by Harrison Owen. A curious pair, for those who say Australian dramatists have a sameness about them! Katharine Prichard's literary power is well known, and in *Brumby Innes* (which has been compared with Eugene O'Neill's work) we gather that she has let herself be fascinated by the vivid native life in the wild, northern parts of West Australia. The symbolism of corroborees will clash with white people's laws. Harrison Owen's play, not yet published either, is known as being an exciting success in a London West End Theatre last year, and news comes now of a very prosperous season in Vienna. Harrison Owen is a man who has known what he wanted. It has taken him eight or nine years in London as journalist and dramatic critic to begin to get it. His passion for the stage and his desire to write plays has made this second venture of his an international success, of an artificial sort. A Viennese critic writes of it, after saying that it is a delightful comedy providing excellent opportunities for fine ensemble work:

> An English comedy? It is more exactly in the French style of comedy, only with English society figures and with a shimmer of Wilde paradox over the whole. It turns on the entrance of a conventional gentleman-burglar (who has studied at Oxford and learnt Latin and a little Greek,

> and who can smoke or offer a cigarette in the most elegant way) or a conventional triangle scene. The lover, who is where he ought not to be, refuses, for his own sake, to denounce the burglar. The plot gets thicker and thicker, but seems to clear by sheer convolutions and wit in the third act.

Obviously it is a very competent play of its kind. As an Australian onlooker, one can only hope that Harrison Owen's extraordinary skill and wit will someday be used in the portrayal of some scenes less conventional and also nearer home. As someone wrote lately:

> Universality is, as a rule, a writer's reward for fidelity to his native culture, and Ibsen has made the peoples of both hemispheres hang with him, enraptured, over his parish pump.

It is to be hoped that the new development of the 'repertory' movement in Australia will attract writers like Harrison Owen back to their parish pump. From the point of view of literature, few Australian plays exist yet in book form. Katharine Prichard's new play will probably soon be published, together with some earlier work of hers. Of recent years there have appeared two volumes, each of four short plays, Vance Palmer's, *The Black Horse* and Louis Esson's *Dead Timber*. I think I saw lately that the name play of Esson's book was being adapted for the films as *Tall Timber*. The setting of the play was exactly the very tall timber of the Gippsland hill forests.

WHAT IS AN AUSTRALIAN BOOK?

Lately I have been watching some people who were having quite a lively and ambiguous time, chasing a satisfactory definition of an Australian book. They wanted an inclusive, not an exclusive, definition; they wanted to make a list that would be as rich and full as it ought to be. Somehow it was not easy. A Norwegian friend of mine, to whom I mentioned the difficulty, said, 'Well, at least in Norway we know where we are. A Norwegian book is one written in the Norwegian language.' Australia has no such language barrier. An Australian book is written in the language that is the most widely-used on earth. An Australian book must show its nationality in some other way, except that now and then it may use certain general English words in a way that has a special Australian meaning. On the whole, though, language is no help in our search.

The Safe Books

It is easy enough to define a purely Australian book, one well within the pale, which can be triple at least. The triple parts are these: That the book should be written in Australia, by an Australian, about an Australian theme. There are many books answering to all these demands, with the further detail that they are also published in Australia. For instance, there are Henry Lawson's stories and ballads (faintly complicated, but not in any way disabled by the circumstance that some of them were first published and others republished in England.) There are all Bernard O'Dowd's poems, seven volumes published by Lothian, Melbourne: the first *Dawnward?* first published by the *Bulletin* company, Sydney. There are Louis Esson's short plays and poems. All these books are Australian in theme as well as in author. Even when O'Dowd is most abstract, he may at any moment draw a simile from the bush. As someone wrote of him once:

> His feet are on the solid earth,
> His head is in the silent land.

And his solid earth is Australian. In the catalogue of Australian books his works give no trouble. Where does the trouble begin? It begins with those books that break any or all of the canons, being perhaps not written in Australia, or written there by a foreigner, or having an overseas topic. What books remain Australian in spite of these *buts*?

Incompletely Australian

The number of different ways in which a book can be partly Australian is as many as the permutations and combinations of those four conditions will permit! A book can be possessed of the first three qualifications, only, or of one only. The search cannot here be detailed. It is enough, perhaps, to quote what I think an interesting and typical test case, that of the novel *Maurice Guest* by Henry Handel Richardson. The author, having left Australia, her birthplace, before the age of twenty, settled abroad, and after fifteen years or so published this formidable and famous novel. It is not written about Australia; it was not published in Australia (Heinemann published it, and it was translated into German, and, I think, into Scandinavian languages); it was not written in Australia. Is it an Australian book because of its author's nationality? I think it is, after all. My opinion does not rest on the fact that the calamitous heroine was an Australian, for one feels that she is merely made Australian so as to seem as foreign and mysterious as possible in the cosmopolitan music student life in Leipzig. No, I call the book Australian because the author makes the slip of letting Americans speak of their home town as a 'township', a very Australian word. Finally, the author has subsequently shown her Australian origins by a reversion to theme in her *Richard Mahony*, the altogether Australian triology whose third volume is due to appear in a few months.

Maurice Guest

Accepting *Maurice Guest* with enthusiasm, then, as one of the very highest products of Australian literature, let us see how the book appears to English critics who have never thought of it as Australian at all. It will be seen that it is taken as a great novel on its merits. It is not said to be greater than other Australian novels, for it is not noticed as Australian. First published in 1908, with two editions, it was reissued in 1922, with a remarkable preface by Hugh Walpole. He gives its history, from when it first appeared:

> Its publishers advertised it most ably, many reviewers were enthusiastic, but it had none of those immediate glories and sensations that fall every once and again to a remarkable first novel. It was talked about a little, it was admired intensely by a few, and then at the end of the three months that are supposed to be the average span of a novel's active life, it apparently vanished, and was no more seen. It was only then, however, that its real history began. From that year of 1908 until this of 1922, it may be said that no week has passed during which someone somewhere has not said to someone else, 'Have you ever read a book called "Maurice Guest"? If not, you'd better.'

Continuing, Hugh Walpole says that the book has had an enormous influence on the writing of the younger generation of novelists. Yet he seems to admit that the influence has often been ignored. That is, while he expounds the kind of truth and vitality that are found in *Maurice Guest*, he perforce contrasts them with the realism of many recent novels in which:

> An insistence on petty detail has often been thought to be all that is required, and the more you fill your bathroom with accurately-described sponges, tooth-powder, and cakes of soap, the more truthful your vision of life. And, further than that, in order that you shall trust your imagination in nothing whatever, it has lately been a gospel that you shall never leave the inside of the cranium of your leading characters, shall tell only what they themselves are actually thinking, and if by that you end in being nothing but autobiographical, what matter, since you yourself are the most interesting person in the universe?
>
> This sort of truth was not Mr Richardson's. His book appeared before these later fashions, and considering its immense influence, among other writers, it is remarkable that the path down which it points has not been more generally followed. The reason why it has not is, I think, because it is an extremely difficult path. *Maurice Guest* is founded, one cannot doubt, on actual experience . . . but that is not to say that Mr Richardson has for one moment photographed his acquaintances. No true artist photographs anybody; the act of creation is something much more composite and mysterious. Some passer-by suggests a mood, some sun-setting or sun-rising a situation, some conversation a motive, and the creative work has had its beginning, but the end is far away.

Standard Novel

It is a curious history for a first novel to arrive at being a standard work, and to be republished on that basis. We can only be proud that it is an Australian's novel that has reached that eminence. It will be noticed that Hugh Walpole, in accordance with the masculine pen-name, speaks of *Mr Richardson*. If I have spoken of the author as 'she', it is not with a view to breaking down the well-known pen-name. The sex of the writer is, however, more than an open secret to those who noticed that her second novel, appearing about 1910, was a brief volume, *The Getting of Wisdom*, giving a wild and exact account of four years spent as a boarder in an old-established girls' school in Melbourne. The book is hopelessly out of print. Luckily for us *Maurice Guest* was reclaimed and republished. It is time for its successors to share that good fortune.

AUSTRALIAN NOVELS

The announcement by the promoters of the *Bulletin* novel competition that manuscripts to the number of five hundred and thirty-six had been actually received is a matter for national astonishment. Reader, if you have ever written a novel, remember how easily the first few pages ran, and what an uphill fight you had for the rest of the way. How the pages of rough copy flew about and transposed themselves! How the fair copy became unfair and had to be revised and re-written! What a cumbersome affair of slippery sheets the completed book was; and how unlike a book it looked! Then please multiply your formidable experience by 536 and think what has been happening all over Australia during the past months. All of these books have been made, with great effort and usually with little experience, by people who felt that at last a door was opening to their energies. Everyone knows that the actual winners must be few: but the lift in the status of the novel in Australia will be considerable. An Australian novel, until quite recently, and indeed (for many people) today, has almost seemed a contradiction in terms, like a white blackbird. Now that some of our novels will actually be finding eager publishers, instead of being as unsaleable as blank verse epics, there is more likelihood of their finding readers also.

What is a Winner?

In any competition there is an element of chance. No judges can be godlike and judicious at every moment, never relaxing in their intensity. In judging such a huge number of books, it is almost certain that their fatigued minds would be attracted by what was 'striking' rather than what was merely solid, allowance of course being made for other qualities at the same time. It is interesting to look back, though, and see what kind of work other competitions have evoked from authors. The fact emerges that the chief literary prize-winner in Australia has been that rather esoteric writer, Katharine Susannah Prichard. Added to her other qualities, she has had the quality of – luck, is it? She has caught the judges' eye repeatedly; she caught it with her first novel, *Pioneers* (published by Hodder and Stoughton, and rewarded by a prize of £250), with a brilliant short story, chosen by *Art in Australia* for a £50 prize some years ago; and last year, with a play *Brumby Innes*, that came first among a hundred others. Onlookers are rather holding their breath to see if, among all these pseudonymous novels, Katharine Prichard will have one that is as well set for fortune as her other work has been. Whatever successes she has had in the past, she has always added something fresh and original to our literary store.

Variety in Australian Life

One thing that I hope the 536 novels will emphasise is that there need be little monotony in the subject matter used by Australian writers. Lately I have been examining a great many Australian stories in magazines, journals, books and manuscripts: and nothing stood out more clearly than the immense variety of geographical angles from which Australia can be regarded. A Victorian speaks of 'The North-West' and means the Mallee country, with its acres cleared for wheat, running up to the irrigated country with Mildura and its fruits and close settlement of semi-urban, rather 'American' homes. In South Australia, they say 'the North-West', meaning the interior, near the transcontinental line, given up to sheep. In West Australia, the North-West means the country used by H. E. Riemann in his book of short stories, *Nor'-West o' West*, set in Broome and its hinterland. The North-West of Tasmania would be quite a different type of setting, and will indeed be inexhaustible for writers. This is just to name one half-point of the compass! It would be amusing to follow up some of the others and notice the hiss in a West Australian voice that alludes to the 'Easst', and the yearning in a Queenslander who says 'the South'. The point is, though, that the life and problems of various parts of Australia show immense contrasts, from pearling at Broome to legislating at Canberra. Our writers have the task of gradually revealing it all to us.

What is a Novel?

Like most English publishers, the managers of the present novel competition have decided that a novel is something well over fifty thousand words, indeed nearer to a hundred thousand. French publishers have more elastic ideas. More than one novel in recent years, like that West African black fantasia, *Batouala*, has been quite short, 'lightweight', as the nervous English publishers say. As if a reader, borne down by the essential force of a book like *Batouala*, would ever count the words! No: to me it seems that every book has its essential length, the length it ought to be: and that many a book, born to be short and clear in its utterance, is spoilt by the dilution of a hundred thousand words to make it the length of a novel! E. M. Forster, in his recent *Aspects of the Novel*, accepts some Frenchman's definition of a novel as 'a fiction in prose of a certain length'. But everything hangs on the meaning of the word 'certain'. When we say 'certain' we usually mean 'uncertain'. Forster says that for practical purposes 'certain' means more than fifty thousand words. Good: and then we come to the line to be drawn between short stories and novels. Is a fiction in prose of forty-nine thousand words a short story?

Hardy's Minor Novels

It is only within the past twenty years or so that the 'short story' has become recognised as a respectable part of English letters. In the 'nineties, indeed, the Yellow Book in England and certain collections in Australia began to give it an importance: but to most people it remained either a mere magazine distraction or a novel that failed to develop. Hardy's publishers have just brought out, in one of those large omnibus volumes that are so usual and welcome nowadays, *The Short Stories of Thomas Hardy*. Was Hardy then a forerunner in the art of short-story writing in English? Not at all: that is merely the publishers' blurb on the cover. Hardy himself, in the prefaces to the four volumes here put together, refers to his 'tales' and even to his 'minor novels'. Some of them are tales in the sense of being collected folk lore, from Hardy's broad 'Wessex.' Others are undoubtedly best described as 'minor novels'. 'The Changed Man', for instance, the name-story in the particular volume of admitted minor novels, is something like a skeleton-novel, in several thin chapters, a novel which Hardy did not see fit to develop into full length. They are interesting to read, as all that Hardy wrote was interesting, but they have no hint of the fullness and vitality of a good short story. Henry James once confessed that his usual method in writing a full length novel (and some of his, like *The Golden Bowl*, were very full length indeed) was to write it out first in thirty thousand words, and then to write *into* it, bringing it up to more than a hundred thousand. Hardy's minor novels read rather like unearthed copies of some first brief draft like that of James. Only they have no other developed form. This book of Hardy's short stories should however, be read for what it is, another glimpse of the rich, ironic spirit that brooded for nearly a century over the length and breadth of Wessex.

A MELBOURNE CHRONICLE

It has been exciting this month to come upon a new novel, *The Montforts*, in which, with the bare allowance of average novel-length (three hundred and fifty pages) the author has rendered the complex, developing life of a Melbourne family from the forties of last century up till now. The author is Martin Mills, and this would seem to be his first Australian novel. I suppose it would only be fair to call it an Anglo-Australian novel, since it is preoccupied all through with the tastes and reactions of people who, from an English home (to which parts of the family sometimes return), settle in Melbourne and make the best of it – or thereabouts, for some of them do not make much of it. Well, here is a book with a theme that would justify something in four volumes; and by some method of fastidious simplicity of phrase it has got this Montfort family between one pair of covers. You have the perspectives and groupings as of a great canvas brought together on this small one. The book, as published by Constable, has an extremely clever design on the jacket. A literal family 'tree', bushy and conventional with groups of Montforts in its branches, all drawn in an almost faceless style and brightly coloured like those 'hand-coloured' drawings in broadsheet ballads. On the crest of the tree are conventional figures in khaki and a modern youth and maiden who seem likely to take enough interest in each other to carry on the family name. The motley colouring and the literal yet fantastic design of the jacket manage somehow to convey the nature of the book, which is lightly satirical, shrewdly sympathetic, and, in its great sweep, a considerable work of art.

A Straight Story

To begin with, I absolutely refuse to read *The Montforts* as anything but a straight, objective story. There is, perhaps, a temptation to take it as a 'roman à clef', discovering in the Montfort family, which includes a Victorian Chief Justice, a University professor, and a Premier or two, some veiled description of the well-known Blank family whose branches and twigs are in Melbourne to this day. But no: the Blanks can take care of themselves. This is a story of the Montforts, and the only thing that hinders us in taking the whole book as simple fiction is that we are not used to seeing Melbourne in a novel. London, New York, or indeed, countless far smaller places – these can all be used as a setting without anybody rushing to point out the originals of the characters. Leave it at that. Melbourne is now adult, and need not be self-conscious when it finds itself discussed. In the course of *The Montforts*, Melbourne has become adult: and if it appears as a pretty vulgar form of adult, is it not shown in the book that most of the vulgarity comes from an uncertainty of aim from that very Montfort divergence of desire? Melbourne cannot decide whether to be Australian or to be an imitation England. The earliest Melbourne Montforts, like the latest, cannot quite be sure that they did well to emigrate.

Form of the Book

The Montforts opens with a family tree. Not the leafy tree on the jacket, but a quite literal family tree of the Montforts of Farleigh-Scudamore, England. The tree begins about 1780 with the marriage of the Rev. Simon Montfort and a dashing, determined Frenchwoman, Madeleine du Baux. Henceforth the most characteristic Montforts are those who show something of that Frenchwoman, as if the new graft on the very ancient family stock had given it fresh reason for existence. We meet the grandchildren of the Rev. Simon and Madeleine grown up and settling adventurously in very early Melbourne and its environs. On its title page the book bears the quotation, 'Increase and multiply': and the Montforts obey this injunction, marrying and intermarrying until the reader is intensely grateful for that family tree in front of the book. Not that any book ought to need such an outside and unliterary convenience. It is like putting a real jewel on a statue: it is like – oh, any shocking, labour-saving device! But a book of this size simply could not carry so many personalities and keep them distinct without that tree, so there is no more to be said about it. And within the space limits, the characters are marvellously clear; and they are not mere static silhouettes, they even develop before the reader's eyes. Inevitably the reader is chiefly interested in those Montforts who, in looks and character, hark back to the famous Madeleine. Of these is Sim, the son of Simon, one of the two brothers settled in early Melbourne. Sim is a restless, vivid type, finding no outlet for his misprised energies. As a youth he is sent to Cambridge, and in vacations he visits the English relatives. Seen through Sim's shrewd, glancing eyes these families are clearly placed. Then he goes to see a family whom he had known in Melbourne, including a daughter, Jane, whom, as a schoolboy he had loved. He is excited to see her again.

> Their correspondence had worn thin after years of separation, and then had died. There was nothing to write about. . .Sim occasionally thought to himself: 'I love Jane Wynch,' but the emotion he experienced was similar to that which a parishioner of a Mayfair church might feel on the Sunday after Ascot, if he said: 'I love God'. . .Sim found it easier to love flesh and blood than a sweet memory.

He marries Jane, and henceforward is divided between his passion for genealogies and his love of freedom.

This means that he loves to settle in the old family manor of Farleigh-Scudamore, but cannot conform to English county society. In Australia, when he returns there, he amuses himself with vaguely radical politics, horses, and his children – going on a critical occasion to meet his uncle at the station with a dogcart 'to which he had harnessed six horses in pyramid, one leading, two following, and three in the last row'. Yet Sim was not all farce and grotesque. His difficulty in finding his own form and purpose seems to leave him free to understand the others, all more firmly rooted in one kind of life or another. His grandson, Raoul, carries on the story to the present day, and is indeed the centre of the last third of the book, which is headed with a quotation about a "really heroic mind at a disadvantage". The disadvantage of Raoul is fully explained and developed. Before Raoul, as a child, there was brought a visionary, lovely place, called England, where the wild flowers were like garden flowers and there was snow; and knights.

> England was a kind of fairyland. From his mother he had intense religious instruction, which convinced him of the necessity of getting to Heaven. From his own observation he was convinced of the necessity of getting to England. England and Heaven were the two ultimate destinations of reasonable man.

Raoul goes to England, the England of 1916. After serving in the war he returns to Melbourne with a crate of Hepplewhite chairs and a habit of writing 'Rupert Brookeish poems derivative to the point of plagiarism'. But that is not the whole of Raoul. He sees the joke of himself and of his changes from 'Colonial' when in England to 'Englishman' when in Melbourne. It is well that the conflict between the two aspects of life comes to its culmination in Raoul, this quiet, articulate young man. He has, at the end of the book, gone on the land with his Madeleine, somewhere near Melbourne. He is so real that one wants to send him a note telling him of just one or two tendencies of Australian culture that he seems, after all, to have missed.

LITERARY CENSORSHIP

The Censorship as a Fact

Most of us who were born some time before the war were successfully convinced of the existence of Progress. Thus we thought that liberty was automatically increasing: hadn't we heard how

> Freedom broadens slowly down
> From precedent to precedent?

In the matter of literary censorship, for instance, we believed that the idea was becoming weaker. The impulses that had banned *Jude the Obscure* and *Mrs Warren's Profession* in the 'nineties seemed outmoded. Windows seemed wider open and human beings were being considered adult enough to read for themselves. Then the war came, accustoming people to every sort of regimentation, without protest. The censorship then was military in origin, though its range was surely wider than that of a war measure. One remembers comical instances of its working. One journal printed an old sonnet by Yeats, and had a line and a half struck out of it, so that you had, as a war precautionary measure, to read a sonnet that was halt and maimed; no sonnet at all. I remember a philosophical poem, a long meditation by an Australian, in which the philosopher finally refuses to continue his quarrel with the world and fixes his mind on peace: there was no mention, or suggestion of the war in the whole poem, but the penultimate line was censored till it read like this –

> And give us all the – we're longing for.

The missing word was 'peace', peace of mind. Nobody minded very much at the time, feeling that such discrepancies were part of the war. Everyone expected, though, that a deep sense of release would follow the end of the war: we all expected to be free as never before.

Postwar censorship

What has happened since? The sheer war censorship is over, of course, and 'peace' is allowed to be spelt out straight on a page. *Jude the Obscure* and *Mrs Warren's Profession* have become respectable through the effluxion of time, and the average modern novel is nothing if not outspoken and is not suppressed. Is there full liberty, then? Is it now the case that an adult, studious reader can get the books he needs without feeling that his literature has first been rationed for him by some Peace Precautions body? Well, there is no one to stop 'Flaming Youth' or the books of Elinor Glyn and their congeners, books that are disseminated in cheap reprints and read solely for their emotional appeal. There exists a censorship, however, sometimes exercised by a government department, sometimes, again, by booksellers' unions. These bodies must set their teeth into something, so what they ban is any book that, while possibly 'improper' from their point of view, is also literary in quality. Such a book is not likely to attract the many-headed multitude: the multitude will not cry out at its suppression. James Joyce's *Ulysses*, published in Paris, contains the most remarkable literary experimentation in English, and no student of writing as a sheer craft could fail to be impressed by his skill. Joyce is master of English from the style of Beowulf to the style of a very modern colloquial play, and he amuses himself by treating whatever comes up in whatever kind of prose attracts his virtuosity at the time. If one does not take joy in his themes, probably Joyce did not either. He has a considerable hatred for the world as he sees it, but a prodigious skill in literary exercises upon it. Yet it is such a book, and not the luscious raptures of some illiterate, that is chosen for banning from the few students who might wish to use its plentiful powers of idiom and wit. Here, as very often, the censorship defeated its own alleged aims. *Ulysses* has been handled by thousands to whom such a serious work would have been a mere negligible bore if they had met with it in the ordinary way. In Galsworthy's *Silver Spoon* there is that hateful trial scene in which a girl is being pilloried for whatever can possibly be raked up against her. One of the chief charges made in order to damage her is that she had at one time read *Ulysses* (the book is not named, but the circumstances of its publication abroad make it more or less clear). The point was that she, as a fashionable person, would never have read it if the book had not been made fashionable by the censor's attentions. A further point is, perhaps, that her enemy, Fleur Forsyte, had in all probability read the book too, since, as Galsworthy remarks, 'she was one of the first dozen in London to be shingled and would be one of the first dozen to give it up'. Such a person, believing it better to be dead than be out of the fashion, would read a censored book so as to say she had done so. It is such passion that the censorship feeds! The latest book to be noisily censored is Radclyffe Hall's *The Well of Loneliness*. The chief thing to be said about this is that Radclyffe Hall is a writer whose previous novels gave her distinct status as a literary artist, and that the present book was both helped and hindered by Havelock Ellis's approving preface. A preface by a man who is rather scientific than literary in his interests was apt to distract attention from the purely literary value of such a book: it asked for trouble. Yet Havelock Ellis deserved to sponsor some such work. It is perhaps thirty years since a scientific work of his own, on Radclyffe Hall's topic, was contumeliously banned – and boomed. Havelock Ellis's response, one of the noblest of Quixotic gestures, was to withdraw absolutely the whole remaining issue of the book, so as not to profit by the unsolicited advertisement given to it by the censor. He then, collaborating with Kraft-Ebbing, continued to work on deeper research into the same theme, publishing his results many years later. His gesture, renouncing the profits of the censorship, cannot be too highly praised, and it would be unfortunate if it were to be forgotten. The censorship has never been so clearly and practically rebuked.

An Inarticulate Commission

There may be a case for the present censorship as exercised here and there in our national life, by the customs, by the police, by booksellers and otherwise. The fact is that that case is never stated, and the very list of banned books is never revealed, nor are reasons given for the public banning of any particular book. If the censors would speak out! But such forces are like the forces that destroy forests by axe and fire, without saying why. There are articles, convincing and clear, published in favour of conserving our forests: no one openly demurs, but the axe and the match do their work every season as before. In the same way no one openly supports the clumsy, inconsistent, unenlightened working of the censorship in London, Boston, or Sydney: but it goes on. This is another protest, another query: but the answer is always silence and darkness, what they call, I believe, obscurantism. Is one to suppose that censors are chosen in the first place for being dumb?

AUSTRALIAN LITERARY JOURNALS

The other day someone was good enough to send me the first issue of a new literary monthly, *All About Books*, published in Melbourne. It has a particularly modest scope and ambition, and a businesslike way of pursuing it. It is impossible to be sure that it will actually succeed in helping us to see the wood for the trees; the first impression it makes is that, even with its condensed reviews to help us, readers will still be drowned in the monthly tide of books. Yet if here one reader, and there another, finds a guidepost to something they need, such a journal has done an active service. The need has repeatedly been felt in Australia for literary journals, and has repeatedly, though temporarily, been met. No, I cannot go through the catalogues of all the ghostly, departed journals. Some day, perhaps, with the Mitchell Library to help me! In the meantime, I should like to do homage to a few of these brave spirits.

'Leaders of Revolutions'

The most fervent, reasoned, and explicit manifesto that I have ever read on the necessity of feeding Australians on Australian-made mental food was written in a well published book – about 1860! It reads as 'advanced' even today. The writer was G. B. Barton, who published one book dealing with New South Wales's mental commissariat, and showing that more home-grown food, especially reviews, would be wholesome and another, *Poets and Prose Writers of New South Wales*, naming writers like Deniehy and Harpur, and giving specimens of their work. It is the first book that holds us still. I hope its rousing chapters will be reprinted soon. After Barton's book, every Australian review, whether light or solid, would be regarded as a form of rebellion against the tyranny that would feed us entirely on imported notions. Sometimes, indeed, the weight of inertia seems likely to conquer in the end. One even thinks of Browning's *Soul's*

Tragedy, in which the pursy diplomat chats affably with the leader of the rebels, not being at all shocked: 'Yes, yes, my dear sir. I have known three-and-twenty leaders of revolutions.' Very sympathetic, you see; but at the end of the play, having settled the rebellion and its leader, he remarks: 'I have known four-and-twenty leaders of revolutions.' Well, if I name some of our literary revolutions, and if they are all in the past, that is not to say that they have done nothing, both while they existed and now in people's memory. Here, then are some of the 'revolutionary' publications. I am happening to deal only with some that appeared within living memory; and I am not mentioning journals in which (as in the *Illustrated Tasmanian Mail*) the first purpose of the publication was news, literary matter being the affair of some section only. The publications whose memories I am here evoking all set up to be, more or less strictly, literary 'reviews'.

The Bookfellow

From 1899 to the present day the very Australian review known as the *Bookfellow* has been an intermittent phenomenon in our sky. Its only begetter is A. G. Stephens, known variously as the Bookfellow himself, as the 'Red Pagan', and as the writer of several books – criticism, verse, and stories. Anyone who is lucky enough to have kept some of the earliest *Bookfellow* issues will go back to them with delight. I have seen a few of them. The format was unusual – square and very tiny, about four inches I fancy. The editor and printer were in close collaboration all through the *Bookfellow's* best years. For instance, when the editor believed that a certain poem was of particular merit, he would not use it as a fill-up on a page of prose; he would give it a page to itself, setting it squarely in the centre with some firm utterance of regard. I remember seeing in an issue of 1907 or thereabouts Hubert Church's well-known sea poem, called simply 'Ode', printed in this way, with the blunt statement that 'this is the finest poem that has come out of New Zealand'. There were interviews, vivid, humorous, revealing, set out in something the same way. There were reviews – appreciations and depreciations – all strongly marked by the editorial taste. In order to have a significance, a review needs to have a unity in its policy, and that unity can perhaps be most thoroughly achieved (if with loss of other valuable qualities) when the work is all the expression of one person's outlook. If the *Bookfellow* had been about to continue steadily for the last thirty years as a weekly, a monthly or even a quarterly, it would have put on record at least a transverse section of Australian life and letters: a one-dimensional stream, perhaps, the dimension being fixed by the definite eye-range of the editor. But the *Bookfellow* lapsed out of existence many times. There were years, even many years, when it did not appear at all. Gratitude, none the less, for its appearances and its courageous fresh starts! One remembers from one of the tiny early issues (of the Ming period, so to speak) this kind of conclusion to an unflattering review:

> The author of this book is daring or nothing; and he is not daring.

Again, from a *Bookfellow* dated about 1922 stands out a wonderful account of Dame Nellie Melba at one of her recitals being confronted from the audience by the horrified ghosts of her two Scottish grandmothers with 'Nellie, pull down your skirts!' and similar injunctions. A. G. Stephens has always been able to think in Scots, and one of his steady services has been to keep green the memory of the pioneer Scottish-Australian, John Dumore Lang.

Some Melbourne Reviews

The name 'review' is awkward, being used to describe a journal of a certain scope, as well as a kind of literary writing about a given book. Perhaps we can get over it by spelling the journal with a capital – Review. I have no idea whether the Oxford dictionary would approve. One passes, then, to certain Melbourne 'Reviews'. The *Book Lover*, which ran for perhaps twenty years, was midway between a critical 'forum' and a booksellers' catalogue. It mentioned too many books for it ever to be really constructive. Still, its editor, the distinguished Englishman, H. H. Champion, gathered round him a few Melbourne writers who held genuine opinions on literature, and gave them a place where they could express themselves. A quarterly contrasting with the *Book Lover* in every way, both by its shortness of life and its formidable absence of any business aims, was *The Heart of the Rose*, a quarterly that ran for four issues. It published original poems, sketches, criticism, all conceived and chosen with a certain intensity of purpose, and with Verlaine's 'Art Poétique' translated as a manifesto for the first issue. There were some really significant names among the contributors: Louis Esson, Elinor Mordaunt, Bernard O'Dowd, Archibald T. Strong. O'Dowd's contributions were significant for being in a prose more decorative and ebullient than at that date he ever allowed his sterner poems to be; he called them his 'flights into prose'. *The Heart of the Rose* died like all traditional roses, but its fragrance remains with a few. Almost contemporary with it – about 1909 – was *The Trident*, which, beginning as a University monthly in three modern languages, developed into a review in English, and so ran for a year or so. It published a good deal that might otherwise not have been so much as written – some reminiscences by H. H. Champion, for instance, many critical articles, and some really significant poems. I should like to see a file of it today.

And now comes *All About Books* with its bluntly utilitarian aims:

> We intend to give information rather than criticism. We lay no claim to literary distinction. We do not even desire to be original.

A sort of sutler to the literary army's advance. All power, then, to the camp cook's elbow!

THE NEED FOR AUSTRALIAN LITERATURE

Literature in Australia

Every now and then it becomes necessary to confront certain monotonous and clamant scorners who say, 'But why do we want an Australian literature at all? Surely there are enough good books written in English overseas, more than we'll ever have time to read! Isn't the best good enough for us? Why should we want books written about a crude, new country like this? We want something to take our minds away from it . . .' And so on, and so on, every sentence a kind of quarter-truth. The issue has to be fought out all over again.

And that was but an armistice,
A breathing-space 'twixt strife and strife,
Which we had deemed a peace for life.

Literature Absolute and Relative

Grant certain of these scorners' assumptions. It is true that we do need the best literature of the world; we do need overseas literature, and we can never hope to find time, individually, for all of it. Grant, again, that Australian life is crude and new, in a way that European life once was, and American life much more recently. Then what is the situation?

We want literature that is 'best' in two senses. Literature being an interpretation of life, we cannot do without it. Milton calls to his muse, 'That which is dark, illume.'

And we see light dawn on chaos. Bunyan reveals the city of Mansoul. Conrad in our own day has made us 'perceive men's lives in their natural relation to the seen universe around them'. Such are some of the achievements of great literature, literature whose value is absolute, equal for all readers, whatever their own environment or way of life. All great literature has this absolute value, whether it has what I would call a relative value or not.

And what is this relative value? By relative value I would mean the sheer usefulness of a literary work in interpreting a given environment to the people in it and to its observers. A region or a way of life does not begin to exist until it has been interpreted by one artist after another. As Edward Garnett writes:

> Each generation, because it lives on surfaces and is so dull in its imagination, so harassed by work, so desperate or so contented in its environment, has always baffled feeling that of itself life would be illuminated. And always the generation looks round for the men who are articulate, and. . .recognises that in so far as the past generations are illumined for us it is through the work of the artists.
>
> Whenever the artists are absent – in enormous tracts of life, that is – human nature appears to the imagination absolutely uncanny and ghost-like.

Our Tract of Life

To illumine whole tracts of life, that is then the relative achievement of the artist, the absolute achievement being the illumination of life as a whole. And without this illumination of our own tract of life, the human nature in Australia must 'appear to the imagination absolutely uncanny and ghost-like', or merely uninteresting, unfit to be made into literature! The truth is that every tract of life is unfit for literature unless or until the artists make it into something understandable, into literature, in fact. Looking upon our Australian landscape, D. H. Lawrence exclaimed that it was a region across which no word had yet been written; seeing its beauty, he neverthless drew back from it in a kind of horror. 'This place has not yet been loved!' And it is only the artists who can show us the features and meaning of what we are perhaps beginning to love. A tract of life that already belongs to the past and has never been revealed to us by the artists as 'worthy to be loved', will have nothing for our imagination but these ghost-like human beings; a tract of life that is part of the present time can never seem anything more than chaos, until it has been shown by some artist to have shape and harmony and interest. We in Australia inhabit a tract of life that needs a very great deal of this special illumination. How much has it received from its few struggling artists? And to what extent have their efforts been made barren by the ingratitude and even hostility with which they have been met at the outset?

Light on the Scene

As Edward Garnett has said, whole tracts of human life are doomed to remain unlit, unexplained. Unfortunate are those who live their lives out in such illuminated regions, drawing only on books and pictures from abroad, believing always that the loveliness and meaning of the world exists anywhere but near at hand! Here in Australia, slowly, slowly, our life begins to be illumined; the present generation begins to be faintly aware of living in a world of significant beauty, human and physical. The early colonists, as well as many native-born Australians in more recent times, hated every stone and tree of the country, trying to disguise or transform it in countless ways. They hacked down all native trees, replacing them by imported 'ornamental trees', and making gardens that screened them from all sight of Australian contours. For a long time, too, they hated one another, as people on a steamer suspect all other new arrivals. Unwilling to admit this hostility to other human beings, as being derogatory to any of God's creatures, they were apt to concentrate their expressed hatred on the landscape and its features. Instead of saying 'I hate this indiscriminate crowd of humanity with which as a colonial I am forced to rub shoulders', they would say, with a degree of truth 'I hate this haggard continent!' pointing to the heat, the flies, the droughts and floods.

Then came some interpreters. Lawson took the wavering stream of nomadic life in the bush, and discovered in it that marvellous, characteristic jewel which he called 'mateship'. In story after story, book after book, he showed this quality until it ceased to be something elusive and fantastic. The human beings who possessed it became more and more real, never 'ghost-like and uncanny'. Men who before had hardly admitted the existence of some such happiness in comradeship became aware that it was a common and recognisable mood, a mood definitely Australian, born of the life and hardships and vicissitudes peculiar to Australia. To be Australian, after that, was no condemnation, no misfortune, no negation; it meant something positive and alive.

In something the same spirit came Joseph Furphy, using his pen-name, 'Tom Collins', and putting his slowly-garnered philosophy and observation into *Such Is Life* and in a smaller degree, into his deceptively-named *Rigby's Romance*. The peculiar kind of democracy that is native to Australia shows all through his books. The paradox of human equality becomes clear. And in both Furphy and Lawson there is something to be called Australian humour. Australians are becoming less and less uncanny and ghost-like; ghosts could not display a national, recognisable humour, however quiet and pervasive it might be. Once Australians were reconciled with one another by mateship, fraternity, a common sense of humour, they would no longer find the need of hating their surroundings as a mask of their hatred of one another. They were ready to listen to someone who would help them to see beauty in the very features of the country they had despised. Katharine Prichard, with her dazzling impressionism, has made the bush radiant as never before. The forests of jarrah in her pages flash with beauty; the inland has its own magic, now stark, now lowered and gentle.

Enough, the poet, the Answerer, has come to us in many guises, gradually. He is still considered superfluous in many quarters, and receives rather blame than praise for any creative discovering powers that he may use. ('Why must he write about our untidy wild bush when there are lovely English meadows in the world!') Hardly any of his audience comes to meet him with a cheer. Yet if it is an achievement to make two blades of grass grow where one grew before, surely it is another achievement to make a world appear where none was before. Gradually our Australian writers are revealing the scene on which our life can become coherent and harmonious.

LAWSON'S STORIES

It was when we were looking into a new book, *Selections from the Prose Works of Henry Lawson*, edited by G. Mackaness, that someone said the other day, 'Well, if Lawson is a touchstone for Australian writing, then the most constant quality in our books is that of intimacy. All Lawson's characters meet you on an intimate basis. You don't approve of them, you don't blame them. You know them like your own brothers or cousins, so that you doubt if they are literature at all. Which, of course, means that they have been presented with great literary skill.' We turned to the book again. Is it possible to discover this pervading quality of intimacy? And is this quality characteristic of the best Australian work?

A Selection of Stories

Here is the small book, containing only a dozen stories. The stories are preceded by an 'Appreciation' by Professor J. le Gay Brereton, a matter of a few pages only, obviously first delivered as a memorial oration. To a reader of this 'Appreciation', the most interesting page is where Professor Brereton discusses the fact and the reason of Lawson's being known always as a 'poet', although his best work was in prose.

> Other Australian authors have more often and more completely succeeded in capturing the essentials of poetry than he: but. . .in the present stage of our history the poet Lawson may well stand alone as the typical figure of Australian literature; for his voice is the voice of a

> great democracy. . .What he has to convey in this kind is made more immediately telling, more memorable to men and women of all sorts and conditions, by the mnemonics of rhyme and the emphasis of simple swinging metres.

Perhaps, then, Lawson was the last of the balladists, in the popular sense. There have been times in the world's history, and those times have predominated, in which verse was more popular than prose; a hundred years ago, it was recommended that a story should be turned into verse to make it attractive! And perhaps, Lawson has attracted people in greater numbers by his recited ballads than by his read tales. Nonetheless, it is his tales that will remain and gather strength. It is easier to call a man a poet, that is all. 'The Poet Lawson' is easier to say than 'Lawson, the short-story writer'. If he had written novels, it might have turned out differently; we would have heard of 'Lawson, the author'.

Intimacy

But this intimacy in Lawson is worth examining. If Lawson had been a more sophisticated writer we would probably have discovered it as a sheer literary device long ago. It would perhaps have been called 'modernism', and Lawson would have been raked in by T.S. Eliot and other tendentious writers for 'The New Criterion'. But Lawson's work was done unconsciously, moving like a natural force. He wrote and corrected carefully, but it was not done to satisfy any theory. It was sheer good fortune and natural taste that made him able to handle men and things in his direct way. Take the opening sentences of some stories in the very characteristic dozen gathered in his book. This is the way 'The Loaded Dog' opens:

> Dave Regan, Jim Bently, and Andy Page were sinking a shaft at Stony Creek in search of a rich gold quartz reef which was supposed to exist in the vicinity. There is always a rich reef supposed to exist in the vicinity; the only questions are whether it is ten feet or hundreds beneath the surface, and in which direction.

There you have it, then – humorous, dry and quiet, with

perfectly real individuals, not marionettes with grotesque names. The names, one knows, will appear again in other Lawson stories, each story adding something clear in the mind like figures in some well-rounded novel.

Here is the beginning of another story, 'Black Joe'. It looks a very long sentence, but it is not a heavy 'period' really: Lawson is merely trying to get in as many preliminary memories as possible:

> They called him Black Joe and me White Joe, by way of distinction and for the convenience of his boss (my uncle), and my aunt, and mother: so, when we heard the cry of 'Bla-a-ack Joe!' (the adjective drawn out until it became a screech after several repetitions, and the 'Joe' short and sharp) coming across the flat in a woman's voice, Joe knew that the missus wanted him at the house, to get wood or water, or mind the baby, and he kept carefully out of sight.

So there are the two boys, mates, yoke-brothers against oppressors! After that we are not surprised that at one period White Joe seriously plans to go bush with Black Joe for ever.

> Joe and I had discussed existence at a waterhole down the creek next afternoon, over a billy of crawfish which we had boiled and a piece of gritty damper, and decided to retire beyond the settled districts — some five hundred miles or so — to a place that Joe said he knew of, where there were lagoons and billabongs ten miles wide; alive with ducks and fish, and black cockatoos and kangaroos and wombats, that only waited to be knocked over with a stick.

Needless to say, the boys never sought that paradise, gleaming before their imaginations like the good season celebrated in some lines of Bernard O'Dowd's *Alma Venus* where emu was plentiful, and witchetty grub. If the boys had gone bush, Lawson would not have found pen and paper to tell of it. Hard enough it was for him to do his writing as it was; the hardness of it all is told with extraordinary simplicity in the pages of a brief, partial autobiography published as an introduction to this book. Intimacy again; but never any morbid self-display.

Our Sense of Brotherhood

In a fumbling way, Australian life has discovered brotherhood.

Lawson called it mateship, when it was a powerful and positive thing. In less definite ways, though, there is this brotherhood, something like equality between man and man. (Curious how the three ideas of liberty, equality, and fraternity sometimes seem merely identical.) And it is this quality, whatever its name, that haunts our literature. In *The Fortunes of Richard Mahony* it is ever-present. Richard himself detested it, when he recognised it clearly; resented the sense of having 'every manjack of them' rubbing shoulders with him as an equal. Yet when Richard and his wife went to England, which Richard himself regarded as his spiritual home, and tried practice after practice there, Richard resented the sense of class and discrimination. His relation with the flow of life in Australia was, after all, 'Amo et excrucior'. And it is this relation that Richard's author keeps with her chief characters, making the reader entirely intimate with Richard and Mary and Cuffy by turns, intimate enough to be angry with them, as if they were facts in life. The subject of intimacy in our writing cannot be followed further here, except to suggest it as a link between the vital commentary of Dowell O'Reilly, the satirical, subtle line of Will Dyson, the chants democratic of Bernard O'Dowd, and the 'unconditioned songs' of Furnley Maurice. The word 'intimacy' is not adequate as a link, but one may perhaps use it as a temporary counter, suggesting that such a link actually exists.

BARBARA BAYNTON

It was somewhere about 1904 that the second of Barbara Baynton's two books was published, and nothing appeared after that. Yet when their author died a few weeks ago the books were mentioned as, in a sense, contemporary works. It is a difficult matter, since they are practically unobtainable now. I myself had two copies of her first book of short stories, *Bush Studies*, but took the risk some time ago of giving one away and leaving myself with only one – a frail thread. Then I had a copy of the second book, *Human Toll*, which was lent with fatal consequences. And

I have never been able to see or hear of a copy of *Human Toll* since then. Everyone else who ever read or owned copies of those books would have a similar tale to tell. They were published rather casually and not built for a long life. *Bush Studies* came out in a very interesting series published by Duckworth early in this century, the 'Greenback Library'. The books were all distinguished and brief. Here are a few from the first half-dozen:

Twenty-six Men and a Girl, by Maxim Gorky
El Ombu, by W. H. Hudson
Success, by R. B. Cunninghame Graham.

All those books have survived and been re-published in various other forms, not depending on the Greenback's permanence. Barbara Baynton's *Bush Studies*, also, was actually re-published during the war, under the surprising title of *Cobbers*, with the still more surprising embellishment of a preface by Sir George Reid. So far as I know, though, it had only paper covers and was not well preserved. *Human Toll*, the novel, was published like any other novel; the copy I had was in stiff paper cover, possibly a colonial edition. I hope there are some solid copies preserved somewhere.

Short Sketches

So much about the externals of these books, which I mention through anxiety for their continued existence. What of their contents? Remarkable, courageous, truthful — these words spring to the mind. *Bush Studies* contains six short stories only, all of them being set in some part of the bush that is unlovely and harsh. It is the bush as Paul Wenz sees it, externally; but the characters are always individuals, never types or diagrams. Perhaps I cannot do better than quote from a writer in the London *Book Monthly* in 1914, who selected Lawson, Bernard O'Dowd, and Barbara Baynton as our three writers who most profoundly suggest the Australian character and social atmosphere. Of Barbara Baynton the writer said:

> It is a cold and clear objectivity that distinguishes Barbara Baynton.

> There is certainly no woman writing the English language at present who has it in the same degree. All her characters – shearers, station-folk, bush-women – move about in a hard white light like the noon-day sunlight of the bush, and her attitude towards them is quite dispassionate, unaffected either by hostility or sympathy.
> . . .The democratic note, referred to in Lawson, is noticeable in Barbara Baynton, although perhaps it is not so obvious. . .when I say that Barbara Baynton is democratic, I mean that she individualises her workmen as keenly and subtly as her rich people, and is conscious of the differences that separate the lonely souls of men rather than of the social differences of class and culture.

And how is all this borne out by the book now (alas!) alone on the table, *Bush Studies*? Take the opening few lines of some of these sketches. This is from the first, 'A Dreamer':

> A swirl of wet leaves from the night-hidden trees decorating the little station beat against the closed doors of the carriages. The porter hurried along holding his blear-eyed lantern to the different windows, and calling the name of the township in language peculiar to porters. There was only one ticket to collect.

That 'one ticket' was handed up by a pregnant woman returning to her home outside the township. All the story tells is her struggle through the rain and across a flooded creek, to reach her mother, who has not written to say she expects her. After physical effort and night-fears she reaches the home, dazed and confused, finding only kind strangers in it until

> When she rose one of the women lighted a candle. She noticed how, if the blazing wood cracked, the women started nervously, how the disturbed child pointed to her bruised face, how she who lighted the candle did not strike the match, but held it to the fire, and how the lightbearer led the way so noiselessly.
>
> She reached her mother's room. Aloft the woman held the candle and turned away her head.
>
> The daughter parted the curtains and the light fell on the face of the sleeper who would dream no dreams that night.

In that sketch there are no words spoken. The writing is all in the author's own idiom of thought. So it is with the last sketch in the book, 'The Chosen Vessel', but not with the four others, which are full of extraordinary close records of bush slang and twists of words, all with individuality and character. The second story is called 'Squeaker's Mate', and opens:

> The woman carried the bag with the axe and maul and wedges; the man had the billy and clean tucker bags; the cross-cut saw linked them. She was taller than the man, and the equability of her body contrasting with his indolent slouch accentuated the difference. 'Squeaker's Mate', the men called her, and they agreed that she was the best long-haired mate that ever stepped in petticoats. . .
>
> Nine prospective posts and maybe sixteen rails – she calculated this yellow gum would yield. 'Come on,' she encouraged the man, 'let's tackle it.'
>
> From the bag she took the axe and ringbarked a preliminary circle.

So the stage is set for a climax, for a tragic climax which is no less poignant, in Barbara Baynton's words and thoughts, than the day-to-day situation.

The next story, 'Scrammy 'And', has a good many aspects that are as typical of well-salted bush yarns as stories of the Chinaman's Ghost near any township. 'Scrammy 'And' is the story of an old man who dramatises his whole existence to an audience of one, his dog; but no, 'audience' is hardly the word, for the dog is in himself a congregation, making the correct responses always. On the evening of the story, the old man, a shepherd in a lonely hut, is feeling restless and uneasy for two reasons; one is that a bad character with one hand missing, known as 'Scrammy 'And', seems to be hanging about and may be after the old man's bit of money; the other is the prolonged absence in the township of the man and wife, his only neighbours. He speaks to the dog:

> 'See's there any signs er them comin' back!' 'On'y mist, no dust?' he asked, when his messenger returned. 'No fear,' he growled, ''e won't come back no more; stay down there an' nuss the babby. It'll be a gal too, sure to be! Women are orlways 'avin' gals.'
>
> He looked sternly at the unagreeing dog. 'Yer don't think so! Course yer don't. You on 'er side? Yer are, Loo!'
>
> The dog's name was Warderloo (Waterloo), and had three abbreviations. 'Now then War!' meant mutual understanding and perfect friendship. 'What's that, Warder?' meant serious business. But 'Loo' was ever sorrowfully reminiscent.

The whole scene is subtle, penetrating, full of character and life. That is what the critic meant by Barbara Baynton's 'democratic' attitude to her characters; each one's peculiarities are respected and rendered, whereas to most writers an old miser of a shepherd would be simply an old miser of a shepherd with nothing more than a touch of quaintness to make him even faintly distinctive. This old man, who is never so much as given a name, stands out with as complex a character as any old general in Henry James: complex because his feelings of pity for a hungry lamb are counterbalanced by his proud resolve not to give himself away in front of his dog, and because his feelings of affection for the kindly woman neighbour are crossed by a determined contempt for women in general. The story with all its horror in the climax is a sympathetic one. Barbara Baynton has been able to do what in ordinary life we who are not creative artists fail to do; she has shown a quaint character from within. Most of us have seen such characters and registered their quaintness, from outside only, with perhaps a dull smile.

Kanga Creek

Lately I was re-reading Havelock Ellis's little remembered *Kanga Creek: an Australian Idyll.* Years ago somebody had persuaded me, from the existence of this book, that Havelock Ellis was an Australian; but not so. The book, in so far as it is autobiographical, shows the years Havelock Ellis spent, as a very young man, teaching school in the New South Wales bush. A different bush from that of Barbara Baynton, physically at least! It is a place of many folded hills, with gullies and creeks and ferns. His human beings, in so far as they move and speak, are as crude as hers, externally; and he bestows on them none of her interior vision. All such books, though, honestly written, help to interpret and widen and build up our Australian scene. *Kanga Creek* is almost unobtainable now. We can only hope that something will soon happen to make Barbara Baynton's two books accessible to all interested readers.

A HOUSE IS BUILT

For some time we have all been expecting this novel of Old Sydney, *A House is Built*, by Flora Eldershaw and Marjorie Barnard, and now that it appears, the collaborators' names have been judiciously telescoped into M. Barnard Eldershaw. At once it must be stated that M. Barnard Eldershaw has written a book of rare quality and power. Even if the theme had been something readymade, the treatment and character-drawing would have made the book important; but in this book the theme has had to be made out of what was before non-existent. M. Barnard Eldershaw has made Old Sydney live, solidly, clearly, through consecutive decades from 1840 to 1880. Other books can be built on these bases; the bases will not need to be relaid. The importance of such an achievement, and its difficulty can hardly be exaggerated. Old Sydney has been made a place to 'turn round in'. Its physical life is clear to us, the relation of its parts, 'the shapes of things, their colours, lights and shades'; and its social and mental problems are made alive for us, made typical and general by the history of James Hyde after he left the sea and opened a store abutting on Sydney Harbour in 1839. In the opening chapter James Hyde, a navy quartermaster, strolling through Sydney, is deciding to leave the sea and bring his family to this new country. He speaks to his friend:

> 'I don't know what I'll do yet, Jacob, but it will have to be something to do with ships and supplies, because those are the things I understand. I haven't haggled in every port of the Empire and fought with weevils on the high seas for nothing. . .I don't want to buy into a thing that's made already. I want to make it.'

James Hyde did make it. A house is built. Through the old quartermaster's store the rising colony was fed and furnished, first as an agricultural settlement, then as a gold colony, then again, after the fifties, as a place of sober growth. The activities of James Hyde extended even to Victoria, especially in the peak years of the gold rush there, and the tough humour and vigorous brain of the ageing man seem to appear like a moving flag planted on one distant hillside after another. Meanwhile, his home and family in Sydney are growing, growing and sharing in the growth and significance of Sydney itself.

Externals

This book is pleasantly long, which was necessary for the theme. It is not immense; one had expected something like a three-decker, but it is simply solid and adequate, longer than the publisher's minimum. (For you knew there was a more or less recognised minimum length for the novel published in England today? Somewhere round 80,000 words is required, or the publisher will be afraid of giving light weight to his customers. It is a pity, for some stories are born to be expressed in, say, 40,000 words or less. French publishers and critics recognise this, and will publish and even award prizes to brief masterpieces like Rene Maran's *Batonala*. But this is distinctly a disgression.) *A House Is Built*, then, is moderately long, as was required by its wide and crowded canvas; at the same time every page gives an impression of terseness, economy of words, vigorous pruning. There is much description, handled well and kept subordinate to incident and character. Here for instance is the interior of James Hyde's store in its earliest days:

> Coming out of the brilliant sunshine it seemed immense to the dazzled eyes, and to anyone standing in its rich twilight either doorway framed a brilliant but somehow remote and unreal picture of another world. The merchanise covered the floor and banked up almost to the ceiling in an epic confusion – barrels of tar, kegs of rum and of negro-head tobacco, great tubs of salted meat, sacks of rice and of flour from Van Diemen's Land, dark-coloured custard sugar in bamboo baskets, great coils of clean, blond Manila rope, festoons of nets, whalers' outfits, sawn timber and unsawn logs, cables and chains sluggish and full of strength, blankets of the quality issued to sailors, brine and tallow hides and oil – everywhere homely strong, adventurous things in sufficient quantities to be imposing.

We may not know what custard sugar is, but we are quite sure M. Barnard Eldershaw knows, as she knows that new rope is blond and that cables lying unused are 'sluggish and full of strength'. We see and feel the 'epic confusion'. There is some such quality in the book itself, but no, the confusion is rather an ordered profusion; the goods, the scenes, the events, all radiate in varied perspectives easily caught by the eye.

Psychology

The fact that this book was praised by Arnold Bennett recently may have led people to expect a predominance of these external matters. No matter how frequently Arnold Bennett declares his passion for writers like Dostoyevsky and Tolstoy (and he even suggested recently that probably the twelve best novels in the world were by Russians), he remains in the public mind as an apostle of externals, from bath-taps to bargain-sales. People remember his Grand Babylon Hotel and his Five Towns interiors. I have not seen his remarks on *A House Is Built* in their complete form, but it will be astonishing if he has not, after all, praised this book as much for its psychological sureness as for its vivid externals. There is space here to mention only one, but a very important one, of the psychological relations in it. It is that of the two grandsons of James Hyde, James and Lionel, with their mother, Adela, and with each other. Adela, coming to Australia after five years betrothal to join her fiance William Hyde and marry him, finds him drier, more formal, more unreal than she could ever have guessed or feared. Their first son, James, 'inherited the quartermaster's exceptional ability, William's reserve, and Fanny's pride'. (Fanny is the quartermaster's eldest daughter, a character binding the book together.) The mother, Adela, expends her motherly feelings not on James, the heir, who is hardly her own, but on the second son, Lionel, frailer, less valued by the others, entirely hers. Both the boys love their mother, James uneasily, Lionel confidently; their mutual jealousy is shown to be inevitable and profound, a keynote to tragedy later on. 'An Oedipus complex?' did I hear someone say? Well, if you like; but I prefer the presentation in character to the summing up in such a phrase.

Which reminds me that the other day I heard two writers discussing – not for the first nor last time – the books of Henry Handel Richardson, and A said, 'Marvellous psychological certainty, especially in *Ultima Thule*. It's obvious that she has read all the modern psychologists through and through.' Then B broke in with, 'But where would the psychologists get their data except from the profound intuitions of a few such novelists? Henry Handel Richardson's subconscious certainties could teach them all they know. It might amuse her now and then to verify her intuitions by comparing them with the psychologists' statements.' This was hardly such a fruitless speculation as that of the priority of the hen or the egg. The novel that is written consciously as an illustration of some psychological theory or discovery bears the marks of its origin all through. In the present book the characters of James and Lionel were undoubtedly conceived first as characters, however clearly they may happen to illustrate the theory of the Oedipus complex.

Women

But for many readers the chief interest in this book will be its women. The restless, powerful woman, Fanny Hyde, chafing under the restraints that made it impossible for her to work, for more than a few, snatched years, at the books in her father's store; the shy, bewildered Adela, with all her mistakes;. . .a whole gallery of women, a whole series of problems, interacting and overlapping. The problems are dressed now in muslin, now in tulle, now in *merveilleux* or taffeta; but this is never for a page a mere costume or period book. The house that is built has a living soul, troubled, restless, full of growth.

COONARDOO

The accent is on the first and third syllables, not the second as we might expect. The name means 'the well in the shadow'. The name is that of Katharine Susannah Prichard's new novel, and of its heroine. Exquisitely chosen, with its symbolic grace and power, the name is typical of the book's quality. We had expected much from *Coonardoo*, this book of the North-West, but now when we see it in book form it is shown to me not merely full of vitality and courage, but also shaped and firm. It has form, as a lyric must have it; its movement throughout is indeed lyrical, not epical. Such a form is simple – an arch, rising and falling; a crescent; a boomerang, perhaps. The book stays as a whole in the mind, its few characters keeping their places in an atmosphere to which they all belong.

'No Romance'?

As I read the book I remembered something a man said to me a few months ago. He had read it in serial form, and failed to grasp its intentions and qualities. 'You see,' he said, 'I could have told her beforehand that there was no romance to be made out of the blacks.' Beforehand? Yes, but suppose the author of *Coonardoo* has achieved something that was not there beforehand? The man's contention was simply an admission that our artists, in words or line, had not yet treated the blacks with any consideration or attention. A few, a very few, scientists had set down facts about them, but these facts had not begun to reach the general public. The scientists, like the late Sir Baldwin Spencer, had even set down some facts with an almost literary vividness, but no creation of character had yet appeared, except for the slight sketch of Mrs Gunn's *Little Black Princess*. The recent exhibition of Aboriginal art in Melbourne showed that the tide of interest was beginning to flow, at last. Apart from this, there were some few anecdotes, some black-and-white drawings, dealing with the blacks now as comical, now as pitiable; never anything deeper. Yet all the time there was this undiscovered race of men, undiscovered because uninterpreted, living and moving in regions like the North-West. When a writer interprets it for the first time, as Katharine

Prichard has done, readers are apt to be amazed by the extent of her knowledge and to ignore the aesthetic quality of the work. Let it be said, then, that a general knowledge of the blacks and their ways was necessary for the production of a book like *Coonardoo*, but it was only one of the necessary ingredients. The blacks in *Coonardoo* are seen as individual characters, not as diagrammatic forms. We realise, for instance, the general force of the tradition that causes an Aboriginal to die when an enemy magician or 'moppin' has pointed a bone at him. We realise it is a fact because the scientists have expounded it; but in *Coonardoo* the fact comes alive in the case of the splendid, the powerful, the human Warieda, friend of Hughie and husband of Coonardoo. The centuries of disparity close up so that it is possible for Warieda to belong to the most ancient days as well as to our own. Assuredly to our own, or Hughie would never have missed him so; assuredly to the old, or the man would never have had that mystery about him:

> But there was no moving Warieda's mind. He had been willed to die by rite and magic; believed it inevitable that he should die, and die he did, within a few weeks of the moppin's movement against him.
>
> When the uloo wailed at dawn, there was no one who, in his own soul, wailed more than Hugh. Boy and man, Warieda had stood by him. He had been his right-hand man. . .Warieda, who made songs which Coonardoo said the jinkie told him: Warieda who understood and talked like a white man – Hugh was going to miss him as much as anybody.

Quiet, understating words and phrases, they give the colour of a man's steadier and more permanent thoughts; not Warieda alone, but Hugh himself lives in those few lines.

Bush Idiom

As in *Working Bullocks*, but perhaps more consistently still, Katharine Prichard has interwoven bush phrases, place-names, descriptions of landscape and people, reports of the characters' thoughts, all into one tapestry of language in this book. That is her intentional method and her achievement. Take as contrast a book like Rolf Boldrewood's *A Colonial Reformer*, where the author uses for his own purposes, only the starchiest of unexpressive English. For one chapter in that book, though, there is a blessed relief; this is when the author nominally lays down his pen and lets a bullock-drover talk. Boldrewood had a rare power of rendering such talk, and the chapter is a really literary piece of work. At its close the starch sets in again like a killing frost. Boldrewood should have known better than to separate his methods in that way. The strength of his *Robbery Under Arms* came from his handling it over to the simple idiom of Dick Marsden, the narrator. In *Coonardoo* Katharine Prichard has no special starch in which to turn from her characters to address the gentle reader. The words that her character use, the observation at their command, these are her tools for describing a landscape or explaining a scene. Here begins a landscape:

> Trees stretched out from the foot of the hills, acacia, thorn-bush, and mulga; gidya, round, dark green and glossy-leafed, the water-tree, from whose roots, if you were bushed, you could get water. . .A flock of kangaroos, gingery-red as the earth they hopped over, forty perhaps, young things, does and an old boomer or two, scattered away through the trees or over the plains.

That is meant to be seen more or less through the eyes of Phyllis, Hugh Watt's eldest daughter, returned to the station after many years in town. But here is something seen through the wistful, devoted Coonardoo's mind when only the blacks have been left on the station for a long season:

> How many moons was it since Youie had gone? Coonardoo had seen the slim kylie of a new moon in the sky, wane silverly, belly and wither ten times. She scarred the bark of a creek gum with a sharp stone for each new moon, and watched every dusty wind that puffed and swirled, beside the creek, where the track dipped to the crossing and was hidden among trees, grey-misted against pale blue sky.
>
> Her eyes were birds which had a nest there, so they hovered and whirled round the place.

One word is necessary: the book, charmingly and solidly produced by Jonathan Cape, is not free from misprints, especially of punctuation. This is a pity, because colloquialisms depend on smooth, unquestioned movement. There has been too much haste somewhere. That new moon, surely, should not 'wane, belly and wither'; it should 'wax' first. More serious, though, is a recurring misprint: Cattle are disposed of at £10 or even £8 the 'mob' when it should be the 'nob' or the head. A 'mob' going at £10 would be the end of everything; yet the correct spelling breaks in only once.

It seems necessary to admit these matters because there is all the difference betwen a fundamental mistake and a printer's error. The book is 'true', as far as accuracy goes; more yet, it has high, tragic beauty and a strong current of life.

THE ARTS IN AUSTRALIA

A lecture given by Mr Will Dyson, in Melbourne recently, on 'The Arts in Australia', proved to be an event of major literary importance. The lecturer's concern, for that evening, was primarily with literature rather than with the plastic arts or with music, and he showed clearly why. His reasons were two: first, that literature was more neglected than the other arts; second, that literature – in the widest sense – was the basis, the soil of the arts. As for the first reason, he said:

> In some respects the plastic artist is comparatively the spoilt child of Australia. He has public repute and civic honour. He has scholarships and public bequests are made on his behalf. There is a fashion for buying pictures, not adequate but at least in existence. So if art does not thrive it is not the fault of Australia, who is conscious of her artists. Of her musicians it may be said that they are at least in the public eye, and around them beats the wash of acrimonious debate. Orchestras are talked of and made the basis of organised public activities or private vendettas, but it is when we turn to Australian literature and science and things of pure mentality that we find hope dying – hope stretched to the point of despair.

Will Dyson

Will Dyson, who after a dozen years in Europe, where his reputation as a satirist, in black-and-white was international, and that of his poetry – his quite few poems – profound, returning to Melbourne some years ago found an intellectual desert. He did not find intellectual starvation: you can import food into a desert. What he found was an absence of intellectual expression. Another Australian artist who recently revisited Australia remarked wryly, 'If Australians are doing any thinking it must be the national modesty that makes them conceal it so successfully.' It was Dyson's astonishment at our dumbness, and his certainty that we needed utterance, that made the theme of the lecture on 'The Arts in Australia'. Closely reasoned and simply stated, with a brilliance of phrasing subdued to its theme, the lecture will have deep effect, even though at the time some of its most solid and self-evident and disquieting statements were regarded by self-comforting listeners as mere witty paradoxes. The reverberations will outlast such misunderstandings.

The Denunciation

That the arts are nationally important was the basic axiom of the lecture; and that a country in which the arts and sciences are non-existent is a despised country. Artistic and mental merits are the most permanent of all merits so that 'what the tomb of Tutankhamen glorifies is less that dead potentate than the anonymous artists of Egypt'. Similarly it is Shakespeare that proves England a nation. Well, the lecturer asks, do we as Australians effectively believe in the importance of the arts? He said, 'Australia needs denunciation today, not because of its failing by the standards of England, or any other place, but because of its failure by standards that Australia should set itself.' By failing to provide its writers and thinkers with the means of expression in book form, that is, by failing to establish publishing houses, Australia lacks the attributes of an adult nation. Until we have an active publishing trade we must remain 'colonial, provincial, and outside'. It is the publishing houses of Germany that have made it possible for Germany to be put back on 'the map of human kinship' with books like that of Remarque and of Arnold Zweig; so with Russia soon, and so with America, whose few more vigorous writers find their books poured fourth from the publishing houses, by which the world's harsh and envious verdict on America is tempered. Are we doing anything to cause the world to regard us with sympathy?

It is not intelligence that we lack; it is not even writers (as witness the few that have crept through all the enormous obstacles to expression). What we lack is a centre; in every modern state the publishing house is the centre of the community mind. The lecturer showed how in a population of seven million literate persons as in Australia, the publication of books is by no means an unfinancial proposition, except for certain legal disabilities in our copyright arrangements; and these could be adjusted once our hearts – or our intellects – were in the right place. What we suffer from is a false and dull conviction of consuming as compared with producing.

Are We Pioneers?

Here the lecturer paused as if to listen to a familiar voice, which was rather like that of a parrot. It said something about Australians not expecting to produce literature yet, since they are still in the pioneer stage, developing our great empty spaces. . .We have all heard that voice trail drearily on. It sounds a little comic in the brick-lined streets of 'Marvellous Melbourne', with its million inhabitants and its bookshops booming the latest best-sellers in London. Will Dyson was ready for that parrot-cry:

> It is a little late in the day. We are no more pioneers than the ratepayers of Birmingham, of Dresden, of Munich, of Paris. Less perhaps, for they are pioneering in thought, while we are neglecting the exploration of our great open spaces of the Australian mentality.

Pointing out that with modern transport of news the old isolation had ceased in many ways, the lecturer insisted that we must grow in association with the rest of mankind, and this can only be by creating culture as well as by enjoying it. It is better, he simply observed, to be a good footballer than a good watcher of football.

Creation

In these few paragraphs it has only been possible to give a few crumbs of the lecture, and to suggest its range. Its fundamental proposition was that for a literate nation we are startlingly inarticulate, and that in order to become articulate, at our present stage, we need our attention turned rather to publishing than to writing. The statement was simple, emphatic, and well-documented. It has met with opposition from persons whose minds on the subject were ignorant, apathetic, and encumbered by complex prejudices. There is in semi-cultured minds an instructive hostility to what is creative, and Will Dyson's whole speech was instinct with a leaping flame of creation and of faith in creative possibilities all about us. His opponents have said, first, that in his propositions about publishing he is too idealistic, and second, that he is too exact and practical! That is, he knows too much for booksellers to feel comfortable and undisturbed. The creation of sound publishing houses here would ultimately give the booksellers plenty to do (as in America) but in the first place their methods of distribution would have to be reformed. If editions of our novels, as well as much from abroad, were published in Australia you would have booksellers actually wanting you to ask for *Coonardoo* and *A House Is Built*. As things are, *Coonardoo* (of which Gerald Gould wrote, 'if this is one of the prize-winners in Australia last year, I should like to see the novel that could beat it', and so on without stint or remorse) is offered in some of the shop windows for a week and then vanishes, subject to the booksellers' bored canon of 'never re-order from abroad'. As for *A House Is Built* (of which Arnold Bennett wrote lately, 'I cannot fault this book') it is almost unseen in the capitals. Meanwhile, with tentacles reaching out over all the suburban stationers, the booksellers 'put over' whatever books they have allowed overseas publishers to recommend them to handle in vast quantities. Some of these books are good; some not; but their easy ubiquity emphasises our status as consumers and not as producers.

As Will Dyson suggested, Australia may some day, like Germany, Russia, or America, need the sympathy of the world; and such sympathy is not given to a country that has remained intellectually suburban, derivative and unresponsive.

LITERARY STANDARDS

About three times a week, from one direction or another, the question comes up. 'But are there any standards in books? Isn't one book as good as another if you like it?' That is the roar that comes from, let us say, the right hand. At the same time, with a snapping sound from the left hand comes some dogmatic and unsupported assertion like, 'Well, *Pink Slippers* is the best book ever written in Australia.' On examination, you find that the voices on both hands are those of people who really would not care whether good books were ever written here or anywhere else. Those on the right are only afraid of letting anyone advise them to read what is good for them, while those on the left had never read any Australian book right through before they read *Pink Slippers*, so for them it is the best book ever written in Australia. *For them*, yes, but in giving their judgement they never mention that it is only their own reaction; they speak in absolute terms. Lately someone, very intelligent, was asking me about this novel that I have here called *Pink Slippers*. 'Is it any good?' she said. 'I simply couldn't take it seriously, couldn't finish it.' I said it was not worth taking seriously, though pleasant enough in its way. 'Well, now,' she said indignantly, 'it was quite a brilliant lawyer who told me it was the best book ever written in Australia! I'll never believe him again.' I hope she won't be so drastic; that lawyer will probably remain as sound as ever on the subject of Torts. I doubt, though, if he has studied literature as profoundly as law, and I doubt even more whether he could pass an elementary examination on the books that actually have been written in Australia. Somehow he liked to use the phrase, 'the best book yet written in Australia'; it sounded omniscient. Some people go further; they begin an article like this, 'In all literature, I know of no sentence so charming as this. . .' Most of us do not know 'all literature'. Some few of us have a working acquaintance with the literature of a single country, Ireland, perhaps, or Holland or Australia. The factors that have so far prevented a large literature from growing up in Australia have at least made it possible for students to keep in mind what has appeared. Those of us who have followed it with some care feel chary of using phrases like 'the best book yet written in Australia'. My friend's lawyer had no such hesitation, though I should like to see his face if I, an outsider, buttonholed him and told him that So-and-So was the best lawyer ever known in Australia. One reason why I hesitate to seize on one book or author as 'the best' is that we need a great variety and number of books, so that each may come to be accepted for its own contribution to Australian letters instead of being examined feverishly for its qualifications as 'the Great Australian Novel' – that most futile phrase.

The Bushwhackers

In his recent famous lecture on 'The Arts in Australia', Will Dyson said at one point, 'It is part of the credo of every artist that nothing exists until it has been written down or drawn.' Australia, in this secondary yet all-important sense, is now beginning to exist, whereas a few years ago D. H. Lawrence could say that her landscape had no word written across it. A small but vigorous contribution to this artistic existence of Australia is a book just written in London by P. R. Stephensen, *The Bushwhackers: Sketches of Life in the Australian Outback*. Published in a compact and striking series by the Mandrake Press, this book is grouped with a satirical sketch, *A Tourist's Guide to Ireland*, by Liam

O'Flaherty, and with *A Bed of Feathers*, a story of the Welsh coalfields, by Rhys Davies. In some ways Mr Stephensen has gained by writing these sketches while still abroad (he went to Oxford as a Rhodes scholar about six years ago). His distant view of Australia has led him to a stylisation of the scene, effective enough – no, but rather too 'effective'. If the book has a fault it is this conventionalism, this dealing with stock characters of a bush township, this making of general statements. But it has quite important qualities, and I would like to name some of them.

The Land

The Bushwhackers by its very title shows an awareness of the land and of the way it has been treated by settlers. The first sketch, the most 'colonial' in the book, is about two young fellows from Devonshire who came to Australia and found 'land waiting for them, land lying in wait for them'. So they felled trees for their needs of house and fencing, and then ploughed the soil; 'and they began to prosper, for the earth was astonished at such attentions, and yielded, as a virgin yields, in pained innocence'.

Then the Darleys put cattle on the land, overstocked the clearings, and blamed the land when the grass thinned out. So they cut down more trees.

> Happy days! When the bushwhackers were whacking the land – before the bush started whacking the bushwhackers. . . .When the trees died, the green grass grew all around, like the old song. What the trees had taken from the old earth, the grass now took, and the cattle ate the grass, and men ate the cattle, and the Darleys made Money, which was the idea.

It is a pleasure to write down the sardonic, swinging paragraphs of Stephensen's colloquial, yet well-packed prose. This whole sketch, as it stands, the whacking of the bush leading to a succession of droughts and floods, would serve as excellent propaganda for the various afforestation societies; but it is more than that, for the writer is as sensitive as if he were a tree, or a parcel of ground that had suffered this unthinking denudation. In another sketch he speaks of all the Europeans who colonised Australia, 'hard-adventuring men, who opened the Continent like a bully-beef tin and gobbled the contents'. Contrasting such gobbling with the intensive agrarian technique used by the Chinese settlers of last century, the author is on safer ground than when he assumes that everywhere in Australia it was usual for personal indignity to be put upon the Chinese. When he says that White Australia, as an idea, began in an anti-Chinese drinking-song bellowed in pubs on goldfields, and in townships, we can only protest; there is not space here for refutation.

Besides, the book is not one of propaganda. It is a series of vivid sketches – the snake beside the baby on the verandah; the prospector coming in with nuggets from no-man's-land, and dying in a blind drunk before he will tell where he made his strike; the man with the strength of ten who lifted a ton weight and broke with it; a bush dance; a boy alone in the bush, rounding up wild horses, this last with a lyrical flow:

> As his thoughts raced he dug spurs into Bluey and leaned low along the horse's neck, anticipating the brilliant manoeuvres by which he should round 'em in.
>
> At the Long Paddock gate was thc stockyard. He dropped the slip-rails through which he was going to steer the outlaws, and light-heartedly cantered off towards the swamp to find them. Ibis and plovers were feeding among the waterlilies, and wild duck rose with flickering wings as he cracked his stockwhip, but the brumbies were not there. So he turned up the gully where the wattle blossomed, golden dancers pirouetting lovely in the sun's spotlight, but there was no sign of the six, even on the top of the stony ridge at the head of the gully. As he pushed on along the top of the ridge, amongst grey iron-bark trees now, he startled some bouncing kangaroos, and pursued them with yells, over two ridges full gallop, till they were lost, bouncing, among tall saplings; and there, luckily enough, were the six horses, feeding together on the tender grasses of the uplands.

We can stop there for a breather. It was a good ride, full of actuality. We need not worry about the future of Australian letters, while such a book, slight but sound, is helping to guarantee the succession.

THE TRUTH ABOUT AUSTRALIAN POETRY

A recent overseas critic of our literature – and there have not been many – wrote with some penetration when he insisted that in Australia far too much store was set by our achievements in verse. Our poetry, he insisted, was on the whole negligible: yet when you spoke to an Australian about his literature he would almost invariably think you were referring to verse, and when societies, small or large, met together for the consideration of literature, it was nearly always on poetry that they fastened for one session after another. It is well to be pulled up, now and then, and to be forced to take stock of our possessions. Circumstances of the baser and pecuniary sort have made it easier, so far, for verse than prose to appear in Australia. That is, it has been less impossible for a writer to publish, at his own expense, a small book of verse than to publish, at his own or anyone else's expense, a full-length novel. In the same way, there have been from time to time small literary magazines making possible the publication of verse, and at the time of writing a new one is announced. This is simply called *Verse*, and is to be published every two months in Melbourne, edited by Louis Lavater. It is some years since its forerunner, *Birth*, ended its seven years' career, and another venturer, *The Spinner*, died, I think, the year before last. Horrid obituary lists like this always accompany such ventures! Still, every magazine of the kind has produced a few poems that were worth publishing, and in some cases these might not even have been written if it were not for such a vehicle of expression. On the whole, then, it may be said that verse writing in Australia has had a moderately smooth existence. What has been done? Is the result negligible?

The Verdict of Anthologies

The number of anthologies of Australian verse has been large. For practical purposes, as well as for critical standards, we had better confine ourselves to those made during the present century. What do we gather from turning over their pages? There is the Oxford Book, compiled by Professor Walter Murdoch. Before it there was the Golden Treasury, the work of the late Bertram Stevens. Quite recently appeared *An Australasian Anthology*, edited by Percival Serle: and at this moment comes *The High Road of Australian Verse, an Anthology for Australian Schools*, selected by Professor J. J. Stable. It is not enough, of course, to judge any books by glancing moodily over their pages: but of books whose contents are familiar to us in other settings, we can perhaps feel the aura or essence best by, so to speak, a sort of general inhalation. On making this general inhalation from one of these books after another, then, we are forced to an admission that the odour is not fragrant enough, not characteristic enough. We feel ourselves in touch with something that is less vivid, generous and invigorating than the life we know in Australia. Poetry should be the quintessence of life, should never be weaker than the life it expresses. What has happened? Two things have happened. The anthologists have usually preferred the safe to the vigorous in making their selections; and the poets, in taking up the pen, have more or less unconsciously accepted the same view. Too little honour has been paid, in Australia, to the rough but powerful elements of poetry: too much to the conventional and imitative. If only it were true of all our poets' work, as the poet Frederick Macartney has declared of his own poems, that like the wood smoke sweetening a gully through,

> Thus pervadingly accrue
> The pungent native meanings that my diligent rhymes pursue!

Contrast with America

Reading through a large and satisfying anthology of American poetry compiled by Louis Untermeyer, one feels there the authority and emphasis of the more earthy and crude poets who take their stand along with the more tenuous and unflawed. Vachel Lindsay with his drumming rhythm is there beside the frail exquisite fragments of 'H. D.'. In something the same way, I look forward to an Australian anthology that will really find what power there was, here and there in our careless balladists, and will put their work side by side with lyrics from Chris Brennan and Shaw Neilson. More than this, I hope our poets themselves will be led to widen the scope of their poetry and to take risks with rhythms, to enclose new paddocks in the sphere of poetry, to express more sides of life than before. The only excuse, indeed, for writing any poem is simply to utter

> Things unattempted yet in prose or rhyme.

To have made agreeable verse that would not be challenged if put forth as the work of some minor and cautious poet of England is no particular achievement for an Australian unless perhaps, as an exercise. To have struck an authentic note, one not merely derivative but expressive of new life is to contribute something to the world's store of thought and beauty. Such poems in recent times are, in Russian, those of Alexander Blok, 'The Scythians' and 'The Twelve'. Such in Ireland were those of Yeats, who already in the nineties had, as Newbolt freely says, done more than a century of orators to interpret Ireland to the world. The critic of whom I spoke has discussed our literary scene, and decided that Bernard O'Dowd in his poems has handled the same subject-matter as Lawson and Tom Collins in prose. By this subject-matter he means not only the bush, but also its ways, its philosophy, which is something as nearly egalitarian as is ever likely to exist on earth:

> That man is God, however low,
> Is man, however high.

He finds that O'Dowd has the highest significance for us, and next to him places Shaw Neilson and Furnley Maurice, as promising for the future still.

Need for Reprints

Supposing those three to be the poets to whom we most gladly turn, how do we come into their presence? We can still, by diligent search and demand, get O'Dowd's most important book *The Bush*, in the firm little volume with a stanza on each page. But Furnley Maurice? It was only last week that I found from the publisher his most well-filled volume, *Eyes of Vigilance*, was quite out of print. The same is true of Shaw Neilson's books, which need to be republished in a collected volume. Meanwhile anthologists either here or abroad go on making anthologies from previous anthologies instead of referring to the poets' volumes themselves. Certain poems become reprinted *ad nauseam* and without judgment or re-valuation. If our more significant poets would reprint their finest work in convenient volumes, then an anthologist with a conscience about ten years hence might be expected to compile a large, adequate book of Australian poetry that would be less haunted and paralysed by timidity than any of its predecessors. It will contain. . .it will contain: but who shall prophesy? I hope, for one thing, that it will contain a satisfying quantity of the racy, vigorous, homely work of C. H. Souter, his idiomatic 'Emily' lyrics, his quiet happiness over his 'Mallee Fire'.

AUSTRALIA LEAKS IN

An Ugly Cinderella

It is rather gloomy fun to watch Australia as it appears, sidelong, cornerways, momentarily, in one overseas book or another. So far as I can remember, it always appears unfavourably; it is just a matter of degree. Australia is the ill-favoured one; no, not even the Cinderella, for Cinderella, whatever treatment she received, was admitted to be lovely. Australia appears as a Cinderella who is as ugly as the ugly sisters. She has all the rawness and newness that make any non-European country dubious in a European's eyes; and then she is not represented as beautiful, according to any accepted or conceivable standards. Those of us who have found in Australia some form and comeliness, and have been able to smile at any searching blasts, may have subconsciously memorised some of these attacks. My own list is not at all complete; I have forgotten much that has met my eye; but it is at least uniform in tone. Some overseas writers hate Australia more, some less, but all hate it, keeping it in mind as a handy place to use their hate on. Yes, I know about D. H. Lawrence and his delight in our landscape, but he makes no real exception, since *Kangaroo* and *The Boy in the Bush* were practically written on the spot. For the time, with that chameleon knack of his, he became, as regards our sheer landscape, more Australian than the Australians. Suppose we look at some of the others, those who have written of us from overseas.

Lamb's Essay

The first, of course, is Charles Lamb, with his essay on Distant Correspondents, which was, of course, a kind of open letter to his friend in Australia, Barron Field. We all remember his rather clumsy jests (clumsy for Lamb) about the population of convicts. It is not for his comments on Australian life – of which he knew nothing – that the essay is preserved, but we remember it as an essay in shying sticks at Aunt Sally in her obscurity. It set the tone in which overseas writers might see fit to address us, and since that time they have not come short in their abusiveness.

Big and Little Writers

If Australians have rejoiced to inhabit the

> Last sea thing, dredged by Sailor Time from space,

others from outside have called Australia the 'last place on earth' in quite a different sense. The sticks have been shied by writers of all kinds and qualities, by W. J. Locke and by G. K. Chesterton, by Storm Jamieson and by Thomas Hardy. Conrad has thrown no sticks; neither has he clasped Australia to him with hasps of steel. A place to make a landfall – that was Sydney Harbour, or

Adelaide; a sailor's port in the 'Mirror of the Sea'. But the other writers, without being here, are more explicit. There is the character in W. J. Locke's *Amos*, who shares with the man in Storm Jamieson's *Three Kingdoms* the knack of being no good, just because he was Australian. Storm Jamieson goes the further of the two. In her book there is an Australian who intrudes on a London office scene for only a page or two but the intrusion is like that of a cuttle fish into a radiant pool. Erebus and horror! The man is evil and loathesome, without any explanation being given beyond that of his nationality, which the author assumes to be sufficient in itself. One dear old lady whom I know, seeing quotations from the book about this Australian character, believing she ought to read it, and not flinch. But she was like the man who bought *Hamlet* so as to enjoy an evening with Yorick the fool, and had only a dozen lines to nourish him. The quotations about the Australian arose out of nothing; when Storm Jamieson says that the Australian had better go back to the slime 'whence he came', she gives no data for her picture of Australia. In a realistic novel with regard for details of office furniture and procedure, this ebullition of raging contempt is quite romantic and fantastic, as if a dragon from Borneo should walk down Cheapside; but she means it, means it hard. It seems a waste of good hate.

Thomas Hardy did not hate us. He deplored us; he deplored us in *Jude the Obscure*. His tone towards us was that shown in one of Will Dyson's literary cartoons in the form of an etching. Some of us have seen that cartoon in exhibitions or reproduced in *Art in Australia*. There you have Hardy in tweed suit and cap, standing up to his knees in celestial clouds as in Wessex loam, and drooping his head in the presence of some haloed individual who listens to him with a degree of misgiving. Underneath is written:

> Mr Thos. Hardy tactlessly and not without a gloomy satisfaction, pointing out evidence of canker at the roots in the fields of Asphodel.

'Not without a gloomy satisfaction!' It was with the same type of satisfaction that Hardy settled us. The deed was done in this way, you may remember: a small boy, whose mother had arrived in Australia just before his birth, spends some of his earliest years here, returning to England when he is eight or so. The damage has been done, the mischief is diffused through his being. A few, a very few, years later, his inborn and ingrained melancholy, due to passing some of his impressionable years in a new, crude country, is powerful enough to make him commit murder and suicide. The cause and effect are stated almost in so many words. It is possible to guess what it all meant to Hardy. He himself, though in England, and though in 'Wessex', surrounded by the architecture and the landscapes and the human figures that he loved and understood, did not find life one grand sweet song. How must it be, then, he would argue, for a child exposed to none of the gracious influences that mitigated the horror of existence for him! Australia was to him simply a void, a new crudeness, a mistake; it would never cross his mind that some merely new country might have an alternate loveliness of its own, being virgin and forward-looking.

As for the obiter dicta of Belloc and Chesterton on Australia, you find them here and there, like a dingy thread running through a bright material. It is not only Belloc's parent who mouths with rage at his idiotic son,

> My patience fails –
> Go out and govern New South Wales.

It is not only Chesterton's account of a dreary band somewhere playing 'Australia Will be There', so that it sets his pugging tooth on edge. It is a recurrent note of horror and disdain. Such polemical writers need something to hate; they can hate 'Semitic persons' with one type of the emotion, an active, almost creative type; for Australia they can use their sodden, dreary type of hatred, simply excluding from the thought of us all things bright and beautiful. Some day I shall do what I had meant to do before – go through the essays and stories of the Chesterbelloc, and note down their pained, disgusted references to Australia. It would make a fine little anthology of 'faugh!' There are some references in Chesterton's 'What's Wrong With the World?' We could begin on these, but the gleaming, up and down their works, will be fairly large. Father Brown himself, I imagine, has little of his charity to spare for us. We are among the people he calls 'wrong'.

None of this matters a bit. We are bad enough, we have every sort of guilt by turns, but none of these vague attacks come anywhere near the mark. It is by our own critics that we have to be revealed, or by people from overseas who have known us well. To these let us lean our ear.

AN OUTLINE OF OUR LITERATURE

In mentioning lately the signs of health in our literary development at present, I felt bound to include, and emphatically, the appearance of a new book, *An Outline of Australian Literature*. This book of three hundred pages is no casual outline, but a much-pondered study by a man who has been willing to take it as his task for years; it is to be followed by a complete history, beside which this outline will be – a mere outline. The writer is Mr H. M. Green, of the Fisher Library, Sydney University. It is only a few months since his own second book of verse appeared, *A Book of Beauty*. The present book shows that he is interested in the development of prose as well as verse, and his own prose, when he settles down to exposition, is adequate and clear. Before examining the scope of the book, it might be well to glance at a stretch of Mr Green's own prose in the book, that in which he describes the early, typical *Bulletin* short story and accounts for it:

> The *Bulletin* inculcated, explicitly or implicitly, certain requirements, and since it afforded by far the most important market for Australian writers of the time, those requirements were usually met. They were inculcated directly in the instructions which were then given on the *Bulletin's* leader page; by example, in that they were observed in most of the stories published by the *Bulletin*, especially in its Christmas

> numbers; by the nature of the remarks made to unsuccessful contributors to its correspondence column; and also by the emendations made by its editorial staff. In the main they concerned form. At the head of them stood brevity; the *Bulletin* short story was on the average the shortest of all short stories.

Then follows an analysis of the characteristic stories and their themes, shown with sympathy, but with limitations to that sympathy: 'Many fine stories,' says Mr Green, 'many fine methods of telling a story, would have conflicted with the *Bulletin* canon.' (While admitting Mr Green's capacity and clearness in this analysis, we may question his use of the phrase, to 'inculcate'; it blunders about like a blind bear.) But what matters here is that Mr Green goes on to show what stories actually arose in the '*Bulletin* school' and, further, what stories broke bounds and surpassed its hopes. He shows how the highest point was reached in Lawson's work, and shows why Lawson is the most Australian of our writers, in his unexaggerated humour, tragedy, and courage.

To look at the book as a whole is to pass from the days of Governor Phillip's printing press in Sydney Cove, first used in 1795 for government orders, to the present day, when the book can close on a note about Paul Wenz's Australian tales written in French and published in Paris. Nobody who has carefully read this 'Outline' can ever enjoy cheerful windy ignorance again – the kind of ignorance that so often in the past has had its say in University Literary Societies, beginning with expressions like, 'When, in a century or two, Australia begins to have a literature.' Those of us who, from time to time, have asked such orators whether they really found O'Dowd's poems or Tom Collins's prose quite negligible, have drawn nothing but a blank stare: we might as well have asked for their opinion on some corroboree themes in the Arunta dialect. But now – here is a book that they must face before expressing their bored generalisations. The writer of this 'Outline' has admitted that many of the books he mentions are, for most people, inaccessible:

> Many of the best Australian books are out of print and obtainable only with difficulty in second-hand bookshops or in a few great collections.

Many of those books need to be resuscitated in new editions which can only be called forth by the curiosity and pertinacity of those whose interest is stirred by a book like this. Again, there are other books that can even now be obtained in our bookshops if we ask hard enough. The ordinary circumstances of publishing and bookselling, though, are so hostile to the kind of books that have a quiet, steady sale, that such books are continually submerged by floods of flaring best-sellers and obese gift-books. It is for us to ask that no copy of Louis Stone's two important novels be left unnoticed and unsold in the back or basement of some shop: and that Louis Esson's plays be more widely known and read and produced. Then Mr Green's outline suggests many books for which the materials need only to be assembled. Norman Lindsay's remarkable stories of small boys in a bush township have stayed in the minds of all who came across them many years ago: but they have never been collected. Perhaps when Norman Lindsay's new book, *Red Heap*, appears, set as it is in some such environment, a book of collected small boy stories, may follow.

* * * *

This 'Outline' is prickling with suggestions and will surely lead to discussion not only among those who have always felt an interest in at least some of his themes, but also among those to whom it is all a new country. In his capacity as a librarian, to whom books are naturally sent, and in his quality as an enthusiast, Mr Green has dug out more varied and more important work than we could have hoped to see. He could easily have made his book more imposing by spending undeserved space on writers who, while well enough known, have no permanent importance. As it is, when he has written at length about a writer, we feel that he has done so with intent. In a few instances I disagree with him emphatically, but as he himself remarks in this book, 'the defects of a work of art are of far less importance than its merits'. Taking this outline as a work of value, anything that one of us may believe to be false is less important than what we eagerly welcome as true.

Some day, perhaps, when the book is already accepted as a matter of course in the study of our literary history, I may publish a list of complaints – this novelist taken too seriously, that poet joined to a school when he was really isolated – but not yet. I know one effect the book has had on me, which is to make me determined to get hold of every book mentioned in it. Some short stories of Harley Matthews, for instance, were published during 1918 in a book I had never heard of, though I met with some of his stories in the magazines since then. Or there is another demand we shall make: the novels and poems of Ada Cambridge, which must be reprinted. And, of course, Henry Handel Richardson's one remaining book, her school story, *The Getting of Wisdom*, must be made accessible. All her other books have recently been republished both in England and America. Katharine Prichard's second novel, *Black Opal*, on which Mr Green lays such needed stress, was never properly circulated. Having had my own copy permanently 'borrowed', I managed to get another, but no more after that, from a bookseller last year, after strenuous advertising. A new edition is needed.

* * * *

There has not been space here to suggest Mr Green's treatment of poetry in Australia, but on the whole our gratitude must follow him here too. He has put down what our poets have done, and has made it possible for us to seek out their work. Finally, in quoting from them he has done what newspaper reviewers hardly ever do – he has quoted accurately! The book as a whole is admirably proof-read. The few exceptions I shall keep for my postponed complaints, though others may point them out before that. The index is useful; though in the larger edition we may hope for a list of works as well as of writers.

BUILDING JERUSALEM

Anyone who is a doctor, and who does not dissociate his own career from an ideal of public health and well-being, must have a dream of a perfect hospital, or of a chain of perfect hospitals, enriching his green and pleasant land. Again a painter must, if he is a Melbourne man especially, wish for a perfect picture-gallery with smallish well-lit rooms, each room containing a few pictures significantly grouped. If he is in other cities less beautifully endowed with funds for the purchase of pictures, his first wish will be for pictures in themselves – a Raeburn, perhaps, or a Corot. Those of us who are primarily interested in literature are anxious for its penetration of the life about us, and from time to time we have our dreams of how that might be done. Lately I have been watching a few of such dreams coming true, if only in part, and it seems worth while to record them. It is as if one had stood hopeless in a prison with smooth walls, and as if gradually a series of little doors had opened in those walls. Quite little doors, you understand: inconspicuous *Tapetentürc* for the most part, not grandiose portals. They open on inner passages that may only after a long time lead to the open air. . .Enough of metaphors! Here are some of the dreams and schemes that have been coming true.

The Term

Reading a version of Lawson's brief *Autobiography* some years ago, some writers were struck by these lines:

> We read *For the Term of His Natural Life* (as Marcus Clarke wrote it) in the *Australian Journal* . . . The sight of it in book form, with its mutilated chapters and melodramatic 'Prologue', exasperates me even now.

Talking it over, those writers all came to the same conclusion, that the original author's version of *The Term* ought to be dug out of the *Australian Journal* and published in book form. It seemed a project for the remote future. But other groups also must have been struck by that remark of Lawson's, or had arrived at his idea for themselves. Whatever the genesis of the move has been, here today is an edition of *The Term* as Marcus Clarke wrote it in 1870 or so for the *Australian Journal* in Melbourne. The other edition was altered for and by the English publishers: this new book, which is published by Angus and Robertson with a brief life of Clarke by Hilary Lofting, will fill out what has long been a vacuum in all our minds. It is a matter for fuller discussion later on. This is a bare announcement of something that we could hardly have expected to happen.

For years many of us who have admired and praised the short stories of Henry Lawson felt that they were scattered through too many books in too many odd editions. They needed bringing together, reissuing in a uniform edition; but perhaps the first step, we thought, should be the publication of a Lawson prose anthology. This idea we kept in mind as a possibility, but saw no means of its realisation. Then, suddenly as it seemed, there appeared last year a modest book, primarily for use in schools, being some prose work of Henry Lawson. The book, which was edited by Mr C. Mackaness, had a preface by Professor Le Gay Brereton, and took Lawson's stories as a serious achievement. The book contained only about a dozen stories of varying lengths, thus corresponding to a small room in a gallery, and almost every story was from among his very best. The book was like another door opened. I hope it has been widely circulated since its appearance last year.

Everyone interested in our literature, whether as writer, teacher or reader, has been sure of one thing, that it needed a historian. It needed someone to gather up what has been written and state it in plain terms for better or worse. There is no country in the world where so little is known of its own literary work in past and present; no country in which ignorance in such matters is so heartily condoned and even admired!

A book that has just been published ought to put an end to all that. *An Outline of Australian Literature*, by H. M. Green, published by Whitcombe and Tombs, is a much more solid piece of work than an outline could be expected to provide, and offers a challenge to all who have habitually swept Australian work aside unread. Beginning more or less with Wentworth and closing with Paul Wenz, the book is a competent handling of a most complex and broken theme. On a first reading, its most valuable quality seems to be its perspective: George Gordon McCrae being easily kept in sight while we read about *The Montforts*, for instance; and Furnley Maurice living in the same universe as the author of *Such Is Life*. It is not possible for every reader to know as much as Mr Green, who with great patience has used his powers of access to the most valuable libraries in Australia. He himself remarks that even for him many of the books mentioned were difficult to find. What his outline does make possible, though, is that everyone may follow at least the few most characteristic of our successive books and take them as a basis. Mr Green has written primarily as a librarian, one who knows the questions people ask librarians, and who thinks of the other questions that they ought to be induced to put; and he answers many of these questions. His task has been a heavy one, perhaps a thankless one, since those who disagree with his findings on some small point will forget that it is his doing that the point is brought up (with all its brothers) for discussion at all. He needs thanks for opening an important door, and his book as a whole needs careful attention.

One point that Mr Green raises caught my eye because it names a door that as yet remains shut: 'We really need an Australian ballad anthology.' Last week, in a group of literary friends who were discussing and exemplifying the bush ballad, some with original examples, some with quotations, the same phrase was used, 'We need a ballad anthology.' What one man is writing in Sydney (Mr Green is Fisher Librarian there) and what a group is saying in Melbourne, is probably what someone else is saying in Perth or Darwin: the ideas are converging. It may well be anticipated that before long both a compiler and a publisher for a ballad anthology may be found. On the other hand, some of us believe that the best and deepest of our ballads ought to have found a place in the anthologies that already exist, giving those collections a body and power that has been lacking. Perhaps, after the ballad anthology has appeared, there will be another anthology compiled from both arms of the service – lyrics and ballads. Another door to open!

A year ago, when *Ultima Thule* first appeared, most of its readers were baffled by lacking its predecessors in the trilogy. Since then, amazing as it seems, after all that went before, the two predecessors have appeared, in large and frequent printings, both in England and America. Later still, an omnibus volume has just been announced by the English publishers. This will probably attract some people who have been bewildered by the crab-like progress of the trilogy in its approach to the public eye – volume three coming apparently first. Whether the American publishers will issue an omnibus volume or not, remains to be seen; their production of the three-separate volumes has been both excellent and enthusiastic, and they have also published *Coonardoo* with a similar zest.

SOME FOREIGN RELATIONS OF AUSTRALIAN LITERATURE

A friend of mine, an Australian, who stayed for some time in Java, surprised Dutch residents by the soundness of her French. The Dutch, extraordinary linguists themselves, said that their impression had been that Australians spoke only one language – and that very badly. Without going into this final thrust, we may as well admit that on the whole Australians are not linguists. Our geographical isolation is our excuse, whether a good or a bad one. We rarely speak foreign languages, rarely even read them, and we do not consider our literary work as capable of enjoying a second existence in translation. We do not picture Czechoslovaks pondering over *While the Billy Boils* or Greeks reading *The Fortunes of Richard Mahony*. Yet such pictures are not merely fantastic. There is an intellectual association between different parts of the world, and sometimes it can be detected with the naked eye. Some of our authors are known in Europe, either in the English language or in translations. I cannot pretend to know all the relations that have arisen. Some I know only by hearsay. For instance, I have been told of a German treatise on Lawson's work, but not whether any translation has been included in it. Again Furnley Maurice's distinguished war poem, 'To God, From the Warring Nations', was included in an international library established, I believe, somewhere in Switzerland; so far as I know, it has never been translated, though it may well be recommended as a not impossible task. These are both matters of fact but not of what I may call accessible fact. It has not been possible to read the Lawson thesis nor to see a list of the other volumes in that international library. What some of us have seen and read, though, is a story of Lawson's in French. It was published in that charming little series, 'Les Milles Nouvelles Nouvelles', little red paper-covered periodicals containing in each issue twelve short stories from all over the world translated into French. Lawson's story was 'Camarade de Son Père' – 'His Father's Mate', of course.

But here is something more definite and detailed, something of which a good many copies have reached Australia. A few years ago a young French girl student of Toulouse wrote for her thesis a study on the works of Mrs Aeneas Gunn. She died in 1925, but her thesis was later issued as a solid pamphlet, not indeed without its misprints and sometimes a diverting naivete of interpretation, but showing a wide sweep of observation and a great deal of diligence and interest. In dealing with *We of the Never Never* and *The Little Black Princess*, this student let a great many other topics leak in, citing verses of Lawson, Paterson, Ogilvie; critical opinions from newspaper articles and from a book by the present writer: anthropological observations very often by Spencer and Gillen and (from a forgotten *Nineteenth Century* article of 1906 or so) by Vance Palmer: and naturally alluding, once at least, to an Australian story by the Frenchman, Paul Wenz. Nothing but this last mentioned was ready to her hand. One can only wonder what library supplied her with the other books and references – in Toulouse! After that, anything seems possible in the way of international study. It is cheering to see that the French girl arrives at 'Le culte de la camaraderie' as the dominant characteristic of bush ways. What is this indeed but the quality for which Lawson used the word 'mateship'?

Some day I hope to see a series of French reviews of Paul Wenz's various books. It is to be noted that when Mlle Hauriou mentions a book of his, *The Sundowner* (L'Homme du Soleil Couchant) she refers to it as a story in the *Revue de Paris*, 1915. It was later issued in book form, but will have become known to French readers in both forms. His books, extending over twenty-five years at least, must certainly have made Australia known as a place where people live and move.

But our most wide-reaching and long-standing association with continental Europe has been through the works of Henry Handel Richardson. English and American critics, generally speaking, did not awake to their importance until the publication of *Ultima Thule*. Years before that, critics and literary encyclopedists in Holland, Denmark and Germany had written not only about *Maurice Guest* – the European theme and setting of which would naturally interest them – but about the first and then the second volume of the Australian trilogy. *Maurice Guest* itself was translated into German and published in a two-volume edition in 1912 by Fischer's (Berlin). That was to be expected. As for the trilogy, it has been recently abridged by the author for a one-volume edition in Danish, but the whole work will probably appear in several European languages before long. Meanwhile it is interesting to read what a Danish critic said half a dozen years ago. The criticism opened with an account of *Maurice Guest* and then of *The Fortunes of Richard Mahony* and of *The Way Home*, concluding:

The wind of a new misfortune drives Richard back ruined to Australia.

> What the third volume will bring, it is impossible to tell, from these foregoing pictures so rich in vicissitudes.
>
> An interval of more than fifteen years elapsed between *Maurice Guest* and *The Way Home*, and in this time Richardson to all appearance published only two books. This points to reflection and self-criticism. One sees that the artist is now able to face her work more independently and mould and fashion it with greater freedom. . .Thus the concentration on a few single human fates, as in the first novel, has been succeeded by a wider field of vision, in which the individual is shown in the framework of his time. This is the development of a genuine creative artist. That the glow of *Maurice Guest* has not become less, is shown by the gripping, breathless chapter of John's death in *The Way Home*. This is a piece of intensive poetry set in the midst of a great poetic achievement.

Well, such words are easy to read now, since it has become a normal thing to praise Henry Handel Richardson. *The Way Home* has just reached America (being the last volume of the trilogy to be published there), and the critics have praised it with entire and discriminating seriousness, saying things like this:

> Even her style, which at first one cannot help condemning as oldfashioned, is seen at length to be part of her purpose; and as we read on in a second and third volume, it perfectly sustains a mood and persuades us that we are reading about our contemporaries.

Our foreign relations, as regards America, have been solidly assured by the unhesitating recognition of this great work.

CREATIVE WRITING IN AUSTRALIA

In spite of difficulties and misrepresentations, past all obstacles such as the depression, creative writing in Australia is slowly increasing and now needs examination. Are our present writers of any value for us? Have they any relation to their predecessors? Have they any clear intentions? Are those intentions being carried out?

Our writers might be of immediate or of permanent value for us. Some of them will prove to have been both, but the immediate value is all that concerns us in the first place. Literature that helps contemporaries to understand the problems of their own time and place, helps them to live as contemporaries and not as anachronisms, has been called the literature of *direction* or of *adjustment*, and for the appearance of such work among us we can be grateful. The other kind of literature, which may include the first, is a literature of permanence. As a critic recently remarked:

> It should be the business of the contemporary critic to deal with direction and intention and sensibility, with the life of literature in the making, and leave to posterity the pronouncement of judgements, the assessment of values, the measuring of greatness, the writing of obituaries and the chiselling of tombstones.

So I here propose to chisel no tombstones, even in naming the writers of a previous generation. These too, to name Lawson, Tom Collins and O'Dowd, have for us still a contemporary value. They are part of our literature of adjustment, of direction. It is still too early for us to discuss their survival value, and we have by no means exhausted their immediate value. They were among the first to enrich the scene about us by giving it, as an American critic has put it in some similar analysis, the qualities of myth and value. When D. H. Lawrence looked on our landscape and found it lovely, he remarked in the same breath that it was empty, with 'no word written across it yet'. It was the writers I have named and a very few others like them who began, in the last generation, to frame the letters of that 'word' which was to give myth and value to our social and natural scene. America, like Australia, though now in lesser degree, labours under newness, rawness, and a subtle self-contempt that can only be eradicated by its artists:

> All good literary work (wrote an American critic lately) has a thesis that life is larger than life. Sometimes we try to reinterpret our lives in the light of the artist's vision. The new values. . .when projected into our own experience, make it more poetic, more dramatic, more significant, in a word, more human.
>
> But. . .art has the function of humanising nature itself. Before man can feel at ease in any milieu, whether that of forest, plain or city, he must transform the natural shapes about him by transfusing them with myth. This creation of myth, by whatever name we call it, has con-

> tinued since the earliest times. It is a sort of digestive process, one that transforms the inanimate world about us into food without which the imagination would starve.

The critic goes on to say that this double humanising function of literature, this creation of value and of myth, cannot be wholly performed by the masterpieces of the past. Nor, he implies, by the the masterpieces of remote places. He names a dozen modern American writers who 'have each succeeded in humanising some district, landscape, year or city'.

Coming back to Australia, then, what do we find? Tom Collins has 'humanised' the Riverina and the 'eighties: in doing this, he has shown himself to be the philosopher of the common man. '*Such Is Life*', said Hartley Grattan, 'portrays the types found in Lawson, but seen through a tremendously complex mind.' This mind endowed every scene with myth and value, and *Such Is Life*, with its slighter companion volume, *Rigby's Romance*, ought to be on every Australian bookshelf instead of being unobtainable today.

What Lawson did in the same direction was obvious. He almost created the word and idea of 'mateship', and showed how it was possible for an author to spend his best energies on materials close at hand. It was a French professor, Emile Saillens, writing twenty years ago, who gave what is probably the best appreciation of Lawson's 'unexcited stories' about the bushmen he knew:

> The very tones of their voice are reproduced with an accuracy and a sort of negligent surety of touch which reveals something beside and beyond the most careful study of fact.

That 'negligent surety of touch' is no accident. It is a stylistic necessity in the portrayal of our types, and now that we come at last to our contemporary writers it is important to notice their explicit intentions in the direction of unexcited and almost casual writing. Fortunately several of them have paused for a moment and made their purposes clear. Here, for instance, is a paragraph from a letter by Brent of Bin Bin:

> I find myself capturing a technique to retail the subtleties of Australian life and landscape. It seems to me that a story to be truer than reality

> should follow natural contours and rhythms. An easy, unrazored pipe-smoking, almost casual method is needed.

So much for the method. As for the theme, Brent has made some wide districts of NSW his own, so that people, even quickly driving through, seem to see the landscape and the people with significance for the first time: Brent's country!

H. H. Richardson's trilogy, if for the world at large it is a masterpiece, has for us the additional boon of adding value and myth to our lives. 'Myth', you will perhaps grant, but *value*, when she has shown Australian as a repellant place in which Richard Mahony was tortured for decades. Yes, *value*: for you do not put value on a place merely by praising it, but rather by giving it significance as a place where it was possible to feel intensely. We get in this trilogy an Australia according to Mahony, and Mahony was simply an extreme case of a type not wholly unknown to most of us. The early mining days on Ballarat have left their mark on that city's outline, and today the perspective of the past looks less like a diagram and more like human life, since Mahony's figure moves through it.

But in the beginning of this inquiry we wondered whether our modern writers, whatever their importance had any consciousness of their predecessors or of their contemporaries. Writing in loneliness and often without hope of publication, to say nothing of payment, our serious writers have recently begun to acknowledge a certain cohesion after all. Brent of Bin Bin has uttered a deep and long-standing devotion to Tom Collins. Katharine Prichard, for all her newness and variety of material and her experiments in method, has steeped herself in Lawson and kept eagerly in touch with other creative writers in Australia. O'Dowd with his inspiring visions has been above all a writers' writer, and the writers have not been slow to admit this. When one sees a new sound novelist bringing an unexpected book, like Louis Kaye this year with his *Tybal Men*, one feels that he is in the succession, that he accepts the common task. And what is that task? I seem to have seen its nature stated, not of our own writers but of other literatures of recent growth, those in the modern and separated Scandinavian countries. Professor J. G. Robertson wrote of those recently:

> The Scandinavian writers of today who inspire our respect neither stoop to flatter the multitude by giving them sentimental or sensational books nor the highbrow who demands the attenuated fare he calls 'clever'. They write out of their own hearts; they seek to reflect faithfully, and to recreate physically, the people and the land they know; to be national writers in the old noble sense. Their best literature is soil of the soil, and that is the best that any literature can be.

It is not fantastic surely, but almost obvious, to re-read that passage with the present development of this country's literature in mind.

THE AUSTRALIAN SCENE TODAY

Someone said to me the other day: 'I've got a novel finished, you know, but I'm not going to send it to a publisher. There's simply no demand for Australian books today while Australia's name's mud.' Would she have hoped for a better reception a year ago, I wonder, when Australia was simply unnoticed and unknown? I thought of a letter that came lately from a friend living in Kent: 'I wish so-and-so's novel hadn't appeared last year,' he said; 'if it had appeared now it would have been far more widely known. People are all asking questions about Australian life today.'

What are these questions they are asking here and abroad? What are they reading in reply to them? Yesterday I saw a copy of a Milan weekly, 'The Twentieth Century' (*Il Secolo XX*), with a conspicuous illustrated article on Tasmania by Gino Nibbi. Tasmania, presented as the most idyllic of islands, was described rapidly but clearly, the writer being struck also by human characteristics such as that a peasant woman would be seen to read a book by Galsworthy. Then in German papers of varying types there have been articles, usually unsigned, analysing Australia's present economic situation – analysing and denouncing it, as a rule. One feels, though, that in the European press generally there may at the present time be found more or less sympathetic and eager accounts of our nature and our hopes.

Writing in a New York review lately, Hartley Grattan named the Australian books that would be needed as a basis by anyone who hoped to get a grip of what Australians had written. He named chiefly books that were established, like Lawson's, or, indeed, out of print, like Tom Collins's *Such is Life*. Among the moderns he laid stress on Katharine Prichard, whose books, right down to her last, *Fay's Circus* (called *Haxby's Circus* in England), are to be had in American editions. She is certainly being read abroad, her confident and devout interpretations of our developing and changing life being a part of modern literature in the English language. It is books like hers that help to answer the haughty doubts of a very insular English critic in a recent review: 'It is difficult to understand,' he wrote, 'why the tedious exploitation of our half-settled dependencies should be regarded as material for literature.' 'Our half-settled dependencies' would include, in that commentator's mind, any place, from where the remote Bermudas ride to Hong Kong, and their 'tedious exploitation' would cover pineapple farming in Queensland or Ghandist demonstrations in India – all the same tremendous bore. It is a point of view, and one seldom hears it stated so blandly and unmistakably. It makes a curious contrast to what J. M. Synge once said to one of our writers who had told him about the lives of lonely settlers in our Bush: 'How deeply interesting their lives must be!' Or again, to the advice given by W. B. Yeats many years later to the same writer, who was a playwright: 'Keep within your borders' – that is, remember that the tedious exploitation of that half-settled dependency called Australia may contain material for literature. That is the other point of view, and it is passionately shared by Katharine Prichard.

People abroad are reading about Australia at last. This is a statement that needs to be heavily qualified. Most people abroad read, at most, certain startling headlines about Australian politics which are forced upon their notice. But it is true, up to a point, that some serious reading of books and articles about Australia is going on as never before. It is fortunate that at such a time there should be some new sound books for them to read. As for novels, these readers may come upon Louis Kaye's strongly-built novel of West Australian life, *Tybal Men*. This is a novel where the interest is about equally divided between the characters and their environment. One or two of the characters have a reality beyond that of the rest, which are sound enough. The finest characters in the book are the two superfluous brothers on Tybal station, not the owner; these brothers are Vivian, who was broken in the war, and who half knows that he is dying ten years later, Vivian, to whose eyes Tybal looks miraculously beautiful at the last; and young Don Mac, born to be a boxer, and exercising his talent on anything he sees. Then there is the environment, Tybal itself, the old sheep station settled under such enormous dangers and hardship by the grandfather of the present owner, who will not be persuaded to cut it up into paying but machine-ridden wheat farms. The problem of 'tedious exploitation' presents itself in this dependency as one of great human interest. All over the world today there must be similar problems; shall a man adhere to the good old ways; shall he keep his station a sheep station or shall he go right against the grain of his grandfather's intentions and his own desires and turn his casual station into something as rational as a factory? To Louis Kaye the problem is very clear and real, every yard of ground on Tybal being visible as we approach it. Some of the variety of Australia's economic problems today with the developing Australian character could be understood, I think, by readers of this book anywhere in Europe. An analogous problem – not the same but analogous – was one of the themes of *The Passage*. In that book one question was whether a fishing village should develop its natural resources of fish and sea transport or whether it should be handed over to a sub-divisional expert for exploitation as 'sites'. When the curtain was rung down, the industries so far were victorious. In Australia today, though, more than elsewhere, 'there is no Being but Becoming'. The map is dotted with small towns that once seemed likely to be great ones, but the gold gave out, or some other miracle ceased to operate.

On the other hand, there are stories everywhere of dying townships being revived, usually on another basis. Gympie from being a gold town becomes the centre of a pastoral district. Again, a man may, often must, take up some occupation totally unlike what he had intended his life-work to be. A farmer of Gippsland may find himself acting as carpenter at Cairns, and perhaps in Parliament to boot. Such possibilities, even probabilities, are what overseas readers about the Australian scene are beginning to grasp.

As for French readers of Australian work, I have no means of knowing whether they exist. There may be occasional shocked headlines about us in French newspapers, though newspapers in France are less heavyweight affairs than ours. There may be, indeed there are, certain Frenchmen who still read Henry Lawson's short stories and rejoice in them. Again, there are those in France who read the short stories and novels of that Frenchman in Australia, Paul Wenz. The preface to his new book, *L'Echarde* ('The Splinter') shows clearly that its writer, a publisher, has not so much as heard that any writer in Australia, except Paul Wenz, exists. This preface must have been written quite against the wish of M. Wenz himself, since he knows many of our books quite well. The fact is, though, that to a Frenchman in Paris, like that publisher, no book can be said to exist unless it is in French. One could almost imagine hearing such a man say that there is no American literature except the stories of Julien Green – who writes in French – and the works of Edgar Allan Poe, who was brought as a whole into French literature by Baudelaire. We shall be well known all over the rest of Europe sooner than in France, self-contained and complete as it is. There is no hurry for us to be known. It is important for us to grow and live. If we are under observation, however, it is good to realise that some of the work representing us, like W. K. Hancock's *Australia*, is sound.

MARY GILMORE'S NEW POEMS

Reading Mary Gilmore's new book of poems, *The Rue Tree*, which is her second garnering within a year, I was struck first by certain poems. These seemed profounder, richer, more subtle in their rhythms and words than all the rest. Why? Then I remembered the ways of an editor and reviewer of a certain literary journal. Whenever a book of poems was published in Australia, this man would, whether praising it or blaming it, include a remark such as this: 'but the best poem in the book', or 'the one good poem in the book – is So-and-So'. It would afterwards become clear, to the curious, that the poem called So-and-So had previously been published in that editor's journal. Was this prejudice on his part? Nothing quite so simple! The fact was that, through the circumstance of publishing the poem and then reading it over and over in the type familiar to him, he had been induced to abandon his mind to it as to none of the others. A true poem, like any other work of art, will not yield up its real qualities at first glance.

What then of these poems that stand out from others in *The Rue Tree*? I myself have hardly ever been an editor; I certainly have not published these poems in my journal. But those of us who read a good deal are always mentally editing some forever unpublished anthology. Having read these poems in various places years ago, I added them spontaneously to an anthology in my mind, and they have had to maintain their position there ever since, along with, perhaps, certain lyrics of Bridges, Hardy, Yeats, Alice Meynell, Eileen Duggan. They have stuck it out. I had even felt aggrieved when last year Mary Gilmore's other volume appeared, *The Wild Swan*, and did not include these remembered poems. Yet she was right. They belonged rather to the present collection which is meditative, introspective, religious in its tone and theme. If in reading this new book I lay chief stress on the poems I have known so long, this is to say that perhaps there are others in the book that will actually stand beside them:

only the 'editor' that has been at work in me cannot be brought to admit that straight away. One of these poems was a sonnet, which it is necessary to quote in full:

GUNDARY PLAIN

I have seen distance and have drunk of it.
Quenching a soul's thirst in unmeasured space;
Seen on the pampas' edge great stars enlace
Courses eternal on the darkness lit;
Seen the still snows whose messages time writ
On Andean peaks, where the blue glacier's trace
Shrinks to a line upon a distant face:
On whose far heights the waiting condors sit.
And I have come once more to mine own land,
And stayed my wanderer's heart to her again.
Ah, with what joy unabated now to stand,
Here, in this little town where I was born,
To watch the shadows cross Gundary Plain,
And see the sun dance up on Easter Morn!

That sestet might well stand as a motto, or as the 'argument', for this whole book. For Mary Gilmore is especially a regional poet, drawing nourishment from the world of her own childhood, the roots of her experience:

So was it when my life began
So be it when I shall grow old,
  Or let me die!

She does not 'die'; her work shows increasing vitality and warmth, with increased care, too, in the actual phrasing and rhythm. Looking at 'Gundary Plain' again, one is faintly disturbed by the hiatus in the line –

Ah, with what joy unabated now to stand.

Is the extra syllable intended? If so, we can get it in and read the line to suit it. But is it by any chance a misprint? Such a hesitation is the merest crumpled rose-leaf. On the whole, I am inclined to accept the line as it stands: the book as a whole seems devoid of misprints, the poems well-placed on the page, the footnotes in discreetly small type. There was a characteristic footnote to the last line of Gundary Plain; here it is:

> When we were very little children our parents used to wake us on Easter Morn to see the sun dance, rejoicing in the Resurrection. And as he danced like a great golden dish of light we were taught to turn to our parents, and to one another and say, 'The Lord is risen! Christ is risen today!'

Now in her maturity Mary Gilmore uses Goulburn as her Pisgah, dwelling with delight on its actualities in tree and flower and bird. She is joyfully aware of many trees that are not the rue.

Another poem in this book that, reprinted after I had transcribed it years ago, stands out in my editorial memory is one that comes rather from a vision of some wild open place like Gundary Plain than from the idyllic charm of Goulburn gardens. As printed here, it has for title, 'In the Cry of the Spirit'. It is far too long to quote, but a stanza or two will show its curious, powerful rhythm with the hidden, inner rhythm:

> . . .Up through the trees I lift my searching eyes
> Towards those strange seas where heavenly lanterns rise,
> And watch star-ships pass out beyond our hail,
> Launched from their slips in farthest space to sail.
>
> Changeless they change upon the curve of might,
> Mutating range on tides that mock the sight,
> Yet through what deep, what course the compass shows,
> Onward a-sweep, in certainty each goes!

If that poem has been able to stay in the mind for years, it is above all because of the metre, the echoes of which resound even when the words are gone, being truer than many of the words which are, indeed, here and there redundant. It is a metre almost unknown in English, and one that Mary Gilmore herself would probably use once only, as the expression of an isolated mood. For the most part, her metres are plain and almost trim – the ballad stanza (that fourteener) or something in eights like the words of a quiet hymn:

Being his friend she did not mind
The foolish world that dwelt unkind;
But turning from it went her way,
Finding in friendship strength and stay.

Being his friend she did not ask
Too much his love to overtask;
The dumb she stood, O many a day,
Lest to his hurt she bid him stay!

'The dumb she stood': what is the origin of such a satisfying turn of speech? The strength of Mary Gilmore's work often lies in her acquaintance with certain homely, racy idioms, and in her confident use of them.

The title of the book, though, is, after all, *The Rue Tree*. It is a book of religious poems, and dedicated, by its foreword, to the members of certain religious congregations in Goulburn, NSW.

It is a book of faith, or even of the faith. There is one lyric with this refrain, as if overheard:

Mary Gilmore she died in the faith.

Its themes are haunted by 'ancient, lovely lore', such as that the robin's breast was reddened by a thorn of Christ's crown, or again that legend named with such wistful half-belief by Hardy – 'hoping it might be so' – the oxen kneeling on Christmas Eve. Mary Gilmore muses:

AND YET THE MYSTERIES REMAIN

No longer now by brake and byre
  The cattle kneel on Christmas Eve,
No longer now, a Christmas choir,
  Bees hum their credo and believe;
The robin's breast is red, but none
Comes telling how the red was won.

. . .And so we go sense-held, till all
Old wonders, like leaves falling, fall.
  And yet the mysteries remain. . .

'And yet the mysteries remain.' Mary Gilmore has not the easy, over-informed optimism of Browning, who could write so rapidly

> I have lived, seen God's hand through a life-time, and all was for best.

What she retains from her life-time is something both less and more than such a certainty: it is a sense of inexhaustible mystery.

> Feed the mind and feed the heart,
> Fill thy life with wonder!
> Wonder birds and, though all part,
> Naught there is can sunder.
> Wonder is the word of God,
> Spoken in the soul;
> He, who walketh wonder shod
> Walketh not in dole.

A poem rather pot-bound by its rhyming all through three stanzas on the key-word, 'wonder', this is nonetheless a vigorous utterance of the poet's most zealous impulse. Some of the poems may seem conventional and generalised in theme, but wonder is never absent from them. The child who used to watch Gundary plain

> And see the sun dance up on Easter Morn

is she who has now written this book for us.

TEN YEARS AGO: 'DARK AGES' IN AUSTRALIAN WRITING

In connection with the Australian English Association, some months ago Miss Flora Eldershaw delivered an address, 'Contemporary Australian Women Writers'. Coming from the collaborator in that composite known as M. Barnard Eldershaw, this address, which has been published in a pamphlet, was extremely welcome. It would have been welcome even if it had been less brilliant and expressive than it is. The writers whom Miss Eldershaw discusses are Henry Handel Richardson and Katharine Susannah Prichard. She says:

> In the last few years not only has the volume of Australian literature increased, and its quality improved, but there is an increasing will to

> foster it and ability to appreciate it. These two women, whose work goes back to the 'dark ages' of a few years ago, have done much, the one in vindicating Australian fiction overseas, the other in creating a style essentially Australian, to give impetus to this new forward movement.
>
> It seems to me that they stand at the portals of our new fiction and that their geniuses, divergent as they are, are the foundation-stones of a new era.

It would be interesting here to quote what would amount to several columns of Miss Eldershaw's forthright yet ingenious analysis of these two 'stones'; but that is impossible, and it only remains for the ideas in her pamphlet to penetrate, subtly and gradually, the minds of those for whom they will have most significance. Her careful, witty statements should be in themselves foundation-stones for future students' investigations. Moreover, they will send people back to the books themselves.

Gleams Amidst Gloom

For the moment I want to fasten on to that phrase of hers about the 'dark ages' of Australian writing. We can take a date ten years back and then look round us in the fog. Dark it is indeed, but there are many gleams in the fog, and it is these gleams, or some of them, that I wish to name. To begin with, Miss Eldershaw has said that already in those 'dark ages' her two contemporary women writers were active. They were indeed, active darkling. In 1921 Henry Handel Richardson's first book, *Maurice Guest*, was a dozen years old, and *The Getting of Wisdom* only a year younger. Moreover, the first volume of her trilogy, *The Fortunes of Richard Mahony*, had appeared in 1917; appeared in a dead silence, broken by the sound of the Great War. The book had received almost no reviews in Australia. One prominent reviewer said that it was so well documented in its detail of the period that it seemed to be written by a grocer. Nobody seemed to guess that it was written by an Australian. The fact that Richard leaves for England at the end of the book made readers suppose that the remaining parts of the trilogy would not be set in Australia. The author was taken to be some visiting Englishman with a most thorough piece of investigation to his credit; but very few people in Australia had read the book at all, and its successor, *The Way Home*, was not to appear until 1925. *Maurice Guest* had some constant readers, but was hardly known as the work of an Australian. Indeed even the most eager and hopeful of us had at that time no clue to Henry Handel Richardson's work.

Katharine Prichard's Emergence

In 1921 Katharine Prichard was known as the author of an early novel, *The Pioneers*, which had won a large prize as the best Australian novel in a Hodder and Stoughton competition for overseas fiction. Six years later, in 1921, appeared her second important book, *Black Opal*, a book to which Miss Eldershaw devotes some very interesting passages. *Black Opal* appeared at a time when reviewing in Australia was less alert than usual. . .The book had a 'dark age' all to itself. The only satisfactory thing is that such a neglect has perhaps helped to arouse the interest of critics recently so that both Miss Eldershaw and, in his *Outline of Australian Literature*, Mr H. M. Green have given serious and sympathetic attention to this remarkable book of the isolated opal fields, their characters and problems. *Black Opal* has been out of print so long that we may hope soon for a re-print as of something quaint, a survival; but it will mean far more than that.

Other Lights

But while these 'silent workings of the dawn were busiest', what other lights were pricking through the fog of those dark ages? There was little in the way of fiction, and it is fiction that (sometimes) sells in its thousands and gives the impression of fecundity and activity. The books that were appearing in or from Australia about 1921 were mostly poetry; a few plays; an odd, struggling little magazine of verse; one or two books of essays. Nearly all this work was published at the author's expense and was not expected to pay. It was money in the author's pocket not to write at all.

Padlocks on Pens

Yet – the writers wrote; why not? Why should Australians, alone of civilised people, have padlocks on their pens? In spite of all difficulties writers were aware of something to say, something they alone could say. Hence came Furnley Maurice's two large books of poems collected up to that date. *Eyes of Vigilance*, described as 'Divine and Moral Songs'; and a more secular or less tendencious collection, *Arrows of Longing*. It is probable that both books are extremely difficult to find anywhere now. The anthologies since then have drawn upon them, but it is time that Furnley Maurice's best works, including much in his recent book, *The Gully*, were made into one volume. It is time for his rarest, most daring touches of imagination to become our common property. It was round 1921 that Shaw Neilson's poems first appeared in book form, in the volume *Heart of Spring*. This publication was the achievement of A. G. Stephens, the 'Bookfellow', and he was to follow it up with other volumes of this poet who had known how to say:

> Let your song be delicate.

Procession of Prose

And there was Le Gay Brereton's book, *The Burning Marl*.

But prose in 1921? There had been small books of essays – *Annotations*, by F. Sinclaire, being perhaps the smallest, and certainly the most pungent. A novel by 'Tom Collins', mysteriously extracted many years before from the too vast corpus of *Such Is Life*, was published in an unfortunately curtailed form. This was that most unromantic of books, *Rigby's Romance*, its title being a masterpiece of misleading! Then Dowell O'Reilly's book of most personal short stories, *Fivecorners*, came out quietly, how quietly, and was noticed only by those who somehow, against all odds, were daring to say that the next ten years would see a strangely great development of creative writing in Australia. The person who said this most emphatically just then was Louis Esson, looking at Australia as through a telescope after some years in London. His own book of sincere and moving short plays, *Dead Timber*, was published in London, but he had hopes of following up its success not in England, but in its natural home, Australia. Returning to Australia, he next year set going the movement known for some time as the Pioneer Players. This produced some fifteen original plays, short and long, over a term of two or three years, by many different authors.

Still, there was a 'darkness' over the land, hiding such ventures. It is this thick darkness that has made it possible for Brent of Bin Bin, in the recent book *Back to Bool Bool*, set in Australia of 1928 or so, to say that there is, unfortunately, no national drama in Australia. A visiting actress, in the book, is made to say, over and over again, that if any such plays existed she would add them to her repertoire. Can Brent perhaps send this actress's address to some of the Pioneer Players, actors or playwrights?

Links with Lawson

In 1921 Henry Lawson was still alive and writing an occasional characteristic sketch or piece of reminiscence. Bernard O'Dowd, who had not then wholly deserted the lyre for the law, produced his remarkable book of poems, *Alma Venus!*, the first since *The Bush*. Such were some of the prickings of light through the fog. What we could not have expected, and what Louis Esson only in a moment of enlightenment foretold, was, chiefly, the strange efflorescence in fiction of serious quality during the next few years. It is only necessary to name, in addition to Flora Eldershaw's two 'stones', the books by Brent of Bin Bin, Vance Palmer, Louis Kaye, Martin Mills, Roy Bridges, M. Barnard Eldershaw (and not then be finished) to make us realise the change.

The Way of Hardness

These books have come from no single movement or impetus; they are the work of writers working alone and wholly without encouragement. Indeed for all Miss Eldershaw's remarks, about 'the will to foster it and the ability to appreciate it', one can only say that Australian work still meets with large and regular doses of discouragement. A book appears and its author is bustled out of sight with a rap on the head and a '*That'll* learn ye!' on the part of booksellers and public. Hardy, hardy will be those who survive. Hardy already have been those who worked steadily through the darkness of the past.

THE 'OLIVE SCHREINER' OF AUSTRALIAN LITERATURE

Someone said in conversation the other day that South Africa was very fortunate in having an Olive Schreiner for its first striking creative writer – an Olive Schreiner, with her girlish, yet powerful book, *The Story of an African Farm*, and

> Dowered with the hate of hate, the scorn of scorn,
> The love of love,

instead of, perhaps, a Gene Stratton Porter. Such a book may well have set the tone for what was to follow. Not that writers would copy her – not that Olive Schreiner herself was able to write another *African Farm*. No, but the *African Farm*, with its relentless clarity and strong outlines, has made it seem natural for South African writers to put forth their whole strength in the delineation of character and setting, never being intimidated by suggestions that what they were writing might not be exactly a good advertisement for South Africa! They knew that after all a writer of Olive Schreiner's power, exercising the fulness of her talent, did more to give South Africa literary recognition than any number of conventionally pretty and, apparently, attractive pictures of that country with its characteristic austerity.

Following the Pioneer of Realism

'Pretty books' have, indeed, been written about South African life; but the true creative success has been from Olive Schreiner to such writers of today as Pauline Smith, author of *The Little Karoo* and *The Beadle*, and Sarah Gertrude Millin, who has recently published a powerful novel of a decaying diamond field, *The Sons of Mrs Aab*, perhaps the most uncompromising of all the books she has written during the last fifteen years. It is not too much to say that Sarah Gertrude Millin's work would have been, if not impossible, then at least improbable, if Olive Schreiner very many years before had not made it seem natural for sincere books to appear. Re-read *The Story of an African Farm*. Smile if you like at some girlish crudities of writing or imaginative bombast. Yet you will marvel at the spirited girl who looking at the self-complacent and overweight Boer woman, Tant Sannie, drew her as clearly as Jane Austen drew her Lady Catherine – as relentlessly, but with far more open indignation. The mere Tant Sannies of this world were to make way in Olive Schreiner's dreams for women of mysteriously finer spirit like Lyndall, who is a kind of abstract summary of all the virtues ascribed by an eager feminist of the nineteenth century to the woman of the future. Living in the nineteenth century, Lyndall dies in her young beauty, dies almost of her virtues, if her pride is one of them. The bare, significant South African landscape, with its few human figures, remains fixed in the mind by such a book, which was written with all Olive Schreiner's young powers and without a hint of apologetic colonialism. This was, then the frontispiece of South African fiction.

Australia's Inferiority Complex

On the other hand, as a writer in an English review remarked a year or two ago, 'inferiority complex was bequeathed to Australian fiction by those eminent Victorians, Rolf Boldrewood and Marcus Clarke'. In spite of the great value of their best works, these two writers were, in fact, 'Victorians', in some of the more narrowing senses of the term; they were, that is, not Australian but colonial in their chosen attitude. Sometimes, it may be granted, their attitude broke down, to the betterment of their delineation of Australian life and character; but colonial they preferred to be, and it has taken a long time for our novelists to break through to the firmer ground that has been both discovered and won in recent years.

Miles Franklin – Past and Present

One of the most emphatic moves in the direction of confidence as opposed to colonisation was made, over 30 years ago, by Miles Franklin, who resembles Olive Schreiner, at any rate, in this, that her book was written in girlhood, and with passion. *My Brilliant Career* she called it. It has long been out of print, but has never been forgotten. Now that a successor has been at last announced – for a book written in America, *Some Commonplace People and Dawn*, hardly seems to have been a successor – the reading public of Australia will ransack old libraries for *My Brilliant Career*. What will they find? A bush girl's indignant semi-autobiography, up to the age of, perhaps, 20. If Olive Schreiner's heroine were not exactly autobiographical – for she died within the span of the book – neither is Miles Franklin's; but every scene in *My Brilliant Career* is based on some sort of personal experience or perception, often hot with anger or numbed with the swift, intolerable grief of youth, youth thwarted, youth misunderstood and unpraised. The frightful, slovenly family of the McSwats, to whom the heroine in her misfortune goes as governess, what are they but some incarnation of the Baleful Beast pursuing Spenser's heavenly heroines? Then there are young men, healthy, handsome, brave, perhaps, but not brave enough to understand and support the colossal aspirations of a little bush girl, who asks for freedom to be, let us say, Melba and Shakespeare at once! So the heroine's career is broken off short; she is seen beating her wings against her cage – the cage that Miles Franklin was to break for herself by the very writing of this straightforward book of bush life on station and selection. It was published by Blackwood, with a quietly welcoming preface by Lawson, whose stories in *Joe Wilson and His Mates* Blackwood was publishing at that time.

Old Blastus of Bandicoot

Miles Franklin, as is well known went abroad soon afterwards to America, and specifically to Chicago, where, with that famous Australian, Miss Alice Henry, she worked for many years on tasks that were anything but literary. One book did, indeed, arise from that work. This was *The Trade Union Woman* by Alice Henry, a book summarising and analysing many years of struggle and development in America. From Miles Franklin no word came of those years. The book now announced, *Old Blastus of Bandicoot*, suggests a return to the region of the McSwats. Whether the ink with which Old Blastus is described is dipped in the gall of bitter indignation that was used to show us the McSwats, we are not told. All I know so far is that a very important Australian author, who had seen the book either in manuscript or in an advance copy, wrote to me about it with great respect. If it is, indeed, as she asserts, and we must believe, a book of genuine character and feeling, then one of the forerunners that chiefly made its existence possible was undoubtedly its own author's first book, with its girlish fling at the truth, *My Brilliant Career*. We have heard *Old Blastus of Bandicoot* announced since before Christmas. The 'chorus of indolent reviewers' will have had time to dig out copies of *My Brilliant Career*, and to find out where they stand.

The Literary Essayist

EDITOR'S NOTE

Talking it Over was published by Angus & Robertson Ltd, Sydney in 1932. It contained twenty-eight essays on a variety of subjects, from 'The Art of Conversation' to 'On Surfing', which had originally appeared in the *Courier* (Brisbane), *Illustrated Tasmanian Mail* (Hobart), *Sunday Mail* (Brisbane), *Argus* (Melbourne) and *Telegraph* (Brisbane), the main outlets for Nettie Palmer's occasional journalism in the 1920s and early 1930s. Most of the essays were lightly revised for publication in book form. Those selected here illustrate some of her main concerns: natural observation, questions of style, Australian English and the status of Australian writing and culture.

Essays from Talking it Over

THE RIGHT TO ORIOLES

Reading a charming article on bird-watching in an English paper I was pulled up with a jerk by a word that seemed to crash like a flung stone through some sensitive place of still dawns and leafy lanes. The writer was quietly ruminating on why the Latin peoples, in spite of all their lively cultural interests, had been indifferent to the charm of birds, their looks, their ways, their song. The English, for their part, had always been nature-lovers: they had drawn spiritual comfort from the natural world – their own loved countryside. Even abroad, in a landscape unfamiliar to them! For, as he remarked, during the war, 'the golden oriole and icterine had solaced many a British officer'.

Many a British officer! What can have been in the writer's mind that such a distinction should slip to the surface so inevitably? One paddles about rather wildly in an attempt to find his current. We may suggest a few imperfect alternatives, but the truth is clearly beyond us. Let us suggest, as part of his meaning, that in war, as in peace, it is only people of a certain class who are sensitive enough to be in need of solace; and that people of this class always hold commissioned rank. Or that a knowledge of birds, and an interest in them, implies the kind of culture picked up only at the schools from which officers come. Or that. . .

But it is idle to speculate. One thinks of that young Irish soldier, Francis Ledwidge, who, because he had once done some manual work, was gruesomely labelled the 'scavenger poet': was he, by virtue of his famous little lyric on the blackbird, or some other of his bird-poems, promptly given a commission? I fancy not. Perhaps our reviewer had never heard of him or of his many comrades in the ranks who had sung or written of birds. His underlying conviction seems, after all, to be that people born to man trenches are born also without the senses that would enable them to see and hear golden orioles.

But what is the truth of the matter? Who are the people among us that use their minds and senses to surprise the half-hidden secrets of Nature? Who can say:

> Hearkeneth the blissful briddes how they singe,
> Ful is myn herte of revel and solas!

Certainly they are not people of any privileged or leisured class. Look at the papers that publish a regular column of 'Nature Notes' (this, in Australia, includes almost every paper of standing); and you will detect a surprising variety in the correspondents who have something to say about the ways of birds and animals they have seen. A schoolboy in Gippsland gives a little description of watching lyrebirds on their dancing-mound; a farmer in the Wimmera contradicts something that has been previously written about the habits of the mallee hen; someone else has been observing the harmonious thrush and has found that it can sing more than a bar or two. One often has the impression of a whole countryside listening and watching with a prick-eared intentness. An illusion, perhaps! The capacity for such self-surrender is not universal, and there must be many people in the country who never look at a bird except with more or less vague hostility. Still the truth is that to many people, all over Australia, birds, distinct and familiar, are a steady source of delight and interest.

And this delight, this interest, have not been brought into being by what is usually called 'education', which often means a closing of the mind to everything but what can be learnt from books. One of the letters I prize most came from an old farmer, hardly literate and quite unknown to me, who had seen a few scanty bird-notes of mine in some journal and wrote to supplement them. Coming from an old man, who obviously wrote seldom, these recollections and impressions of birds seemed deep and rich. There had been the skylarks he remembered as a child, singing above the daisy: there were the magpies with their morning song daily around his country home: then there was that night, when he was driving home late through the bush, and in passing a paddock of ripe wheat had heard some mysterious bird singing, above everything for beauty — he had had to pull up and listen to it in the cold for half an hour.

'Poetry', says Arthur Symons, 'has nothing to do with woman as a lady.'

Nature, one may transpose it, has nothing to do with man as an Old Etonian, a Rotarian, or even an officer in the Guards. People, however subversive it may be to admit it, are born with all sorts of qualities and capacities that cut across the distinctions of class. Usually this fact is covered up a little by the way formal and certified culture is distributed. One man, with no aesthetic instinct at all, is admitted by his education into a world where it is customary to have opinions on music, architecture and the plastic arts: a slight familiarity with the language and accent of this realm enables him to talk of Mozart and Cézanne as if each meant something to him personally. He may even come in time to hold ideas that are more or less his own. Another man, naturally more sensitive and responsive, finds himself, by the accidents of birth and education, shut out from this accepted world of opinions. He has to gain access to it, if at all, by an effort that often cripples his best qualities, and makes him seem blundering, heavy-footed, or even, cruellest of all, insincere.

But there is no standardised way of becoming sensitive to wonder and beauty in the natural world. A navvy is just as likely as a company-promoter to feel the wings of a rainbow-bird brush his heart in its dazzling flight through the air: more likely, indeed, since the nature of his work leaves him open to such impressions. It is the chance of first-hand observation that makes unlettered men, particular those whose work lies out of doors, so often interesting in their talk. They have at least seen a few things with their own eyes and thought about them. Their minds are not so likely to be cluttered with ready-made phrases about the beauties of Nature, nor with other people's scientific opinions, half understood. Some of them, indeed, through their close contact with the world they see, and their imaginative interest in it, have attained a rare culture that is as valid as any other. A culture not dependent on measurable information, but rich with delicate observation and fine feeling.

No, it is not dreamy, literary officers, as such, who retreat from the noises of common life towards leafy places where they can listen darkling. The people who do so have often little resemblance to one another in the circumstances of their external lives; certainly they cannot be found in any one social group; they are like one another only in their temperament and their obedience to its commands. Yet they are alike, too, in a certain abandon and impersonality. While we are reading a great book, says E. M. Forster somewhere, we forget both its author's name and our own — especially our own, surely. In the same way these different people, while they are watching birds and listening to them, will forget whether they are plumber or clerk. The part of them that listens to the bird, their immortal soul if you will call it so, is not their visible personality, labelled with its status, but something shared with all mankind. Every poet has known this, and none better, perhaps, than that daring, broken woman, Emily Dickinson. One of her lyrics, probably uncorrected, has this for its second verse of two:

> The sun went up
> No man looked on,
> The Earth and I and One,
> A nameless bird, a stranger,
> Were witness for the Crown.

So we have come back to the orioles. Notice how Emily Dickinson's bird was a 'stranger'. You had the sun, known to all men; the earth, mother of us all; the bird — to whom the writer had not been introduced. Was it different, then, with those orioles in France? Were they, unlike any other birds on earth, determined to bring the solace of their songs only to those who had the signs of rank on their shoulders? Or was the writer of that charming article merely betraying his bondage to a rather vulgar illusion?

COLONIAL WARES

In Berlin there used to be – probably still are – shops announcing their contents as 'Kolonialwaren' and 'Sudfruchte'. The colonial wares were, I imagine, coconuts or spices from whatever places in the sun had been won by Germany overseas, and there was an exotic aroma about the word. Kolonialwaren! It used to seem puzzling and suggestive. What did it mean to the stolid Berliners who gazed at the wares through the glass? Had a colony a fixed nature? Was every colony peopled by the same sort of beings, cultivating the same fruits, having the same habits of life, bringing forth the same ideas?

Again, in France during the early days of the war, there was a sudden enthusiasm for things 'colonial', particularly colonial troops. When the reserves of men were being so quickly depleted, there was comfort in the thought of the teeming masses of the French Empire overseas. In every paper little paragraphs lauded the bravery of the zouaves, the Turcos, the Senegalese. Even our Australian troops came in for some share of this enthusiasm for helpers from afar. Were they not 'colonials' too, hardy, brave, savage, unlikely to burden themselves with prisoners, or to be hampered by compunctions that, perhaps, marred the effectiveness of less primitive fighting men?

Colonial? Does the word bring up the same images in all languages? Does it connote any common qualities? If so, are they qualities of which a civilised person could feel proud?

These questions are no mere rhetorical flourishes. They have arisen after reading a strange paragraph by J. C. Squire, who, in recent years, used to take his Sunday morning walks through the London *Observer*, allowing the public in the guise of a small and not very intelligent dog to accompany him. One morning Mr Squire's walk took him through some of the literature of 'the Colonies'. Where the remote Bermudas ride, perhaps, or to the quaint polyglot Seychelles? No; on this occasion it was New Zealand and it was South Africa, the twain 'looking equal in one snow', like

Little Billee's land that was

> Jerusalem and Madagascar
> And North and South Amer-i-kee.

That is, instead of considering the individual quality of the writers under review, or how truly they had represented the character and social life of their widely-different countries, Mr Squire preferred to group them as colonials:

I do not apologise for using the word 'colonial'. It is a very euphonious word: it has a Roman tradition behind it: it conveys the notion of a swarming overseas. Some years ago the *Times* invited its readers to suggest alternatives, certain inhabitants of the colonies having, apparently, a dislike of a word which, to them, suggested domination by the Colonial Office. . .

One pauses there for breath in a long sentence, but there is another sentence that is more breath-taking still:

'No poet, at any rate,' says Mr Squire, 'will object to being called colonial.'

No poet? It seems that Mr Squire, in his advocacy of the journalistically-useful word, has stretched his net too far. What kind of poet does one usually associate with such an adjective? Could anyone, indeed, be a poet and a colonial at the same time?

This brings us to the heart of the subject, for if a word is impossible to use in connection with the poet, the creator, there must be something derogatory or superficial about it. Poetry, surely, has nothing to do with political arrangements, but with the relation of man to the universe and the natural world about him. W. B. Yeats's country, the Irish Free State, has the status of a dominion at present, but who would call him a 'dominion poet'! Or Rabindranath Tagore an imperial sage!

And yet there really is a type, an attitude of mind, a relation, to which one can apply the word in a generic way. What is this colonialism? One recognises it most easily in an unfamiliar *milieu* – on a French boat, for instance, one returning from Noumea or French Indo-China. The people on board are French, and yet not French. They have imbibed some of the atmosphere of the strange places in which they have spent the best years of their lives, but these have never been 'home' to them. They are always 'from', never 'of', Indo-China or Noumea, and any books they produced about these places would be those of exiles, written from outside for outsiders. They talk of going 'home' regularly, but it is hardly possible to believe that they would be perfectly happy again in the France they romanticise, for, unknown to themselves, certain filaments of thought and habit bind them to Indo-China or Noumea. That is the pathetic, sometimes the tragic, thing about them. Henceforth they will always be colonials.

Even in our own country, though only a small percentage of its present population was born outside its borders, we are well enough acquainted with something that can only be called the 'colonial' attitude in political and social life. It is marked by a certain rawness of judgement, a timidity of thought, as of people not fully adult or confident of their power and authority to act as complete human beings. Three or four generations have not been enough to allow us to get thoroughly rooted in the soil. Waves of uncertainty sweep over us. Is this continent really our home, or are we just migrants from another civilisation, growing wool and piercing the ground for metals, doomed to be dependent for our intellectual and aesthetic nourishment – our books, interpretations of art, theories of the social order – on what is brought to us by every mail from overseas?

There are colonials among us (often powerfully-placed and vociferous) who would accept such a situation without qualms and make the most of its material possibilities, but they are not to be found among the poets or creative writers. The facts, in spite of Mr Squire, are quite otherwise. All our vital writing has been done by people who have taken their status as complete human beings for granted and found a spiritual home in their environment. Their task has been to interpret life as they see it, where they see it. The name of Australia rarely appears in their work, since they are not inventing generalisations about their own country for exhibition to another: the word 'colonial', except in some historical political sense, cannot enter their minds. They have become creative writers, indeed, by virtue of having exorcised the feelings and relations it connotes, or by never having known them.

Mr Squire, himself, seems to have some vague sense of this.

'The truth is,' he concludes, 'that the colonies, as yet, have produced very little good literature by the native-born, but that, in time, they are likely to come to maturity, as America is. It is all a matter of getting the pioneering stages over.'

At this we may expect any colonial dog that may be listening to wag its tail (still at the pioneering stage) and to look hopefully toward the future.

But what is 'getting the pioneering stages over' if it is not developing out of colonialism into some more mature and dignified state? We are probably, in literary matters, where America stood a century ago; but whatever strength America was gaining at the time was not due to a spirit of colonialism; that was dying a lingering death. America was still making its colonial mistakes, a hangover from the attitude of earlier times. How strange it is, for instance, to read that when Fenimore Cooper, that robust backwoods-man, first contemplated writing novels, about 1830, he decided it was necessary to go to London society for his matter! Red Indians, at the time, indeed the whole landscape and life about him, were too vulgar and local to be the subject of literary art. A hundred years ago, too, America still exposed her offspring. What porridge had Edgar Allan Poe? What was done with Herman Melville's genius except to stifle it? How timidly and evasively Whitman was received! It is hardly with pleasure that we accept the status of America in last century, but, learning from her, we may reasonably hope to better the instruction.

Meanwhile there will be a European market (not so good as in former times) for our colonial wares – our 'frozen meat and Philistinism', our novels of the more flamboyant and naive kind, the after-dinner sentiments of our politicians. In several such departments we may expect to continue the supply of quite recognisable 'lines' during more decades than one cares to imagine.

ON MISPRINTS

What the authorised function of a printer's devil is, we are not clearly informed. To wait about in a hopeful and yet unhelpful way, to drip with ink – these are some of his habits. It may be humbly suggested though, that his chief power is to cause misprints. How he does so it is not for an outsider to know; whether by clouding the printer's mind or by jerking the machine, who can say? The fact is that misprints, some of them blatant, ugly, and obvious, others insidious and specious, do appear in the most surprising places. Who could be responsible for them if not the printer's own devil?

The obvious kind of misprint, in which the type is somehow pied and the reader is suddenly confronted with a word like pxvtkr, is harmless enough. One simply passes by on the other side. There is one standard and unpronounceable group of letters that is apt to appear at the end of a paragraph. Printers can tell you about it. It is caused by the printer's devil having all his own way on the linotype for a few seconds; it is probably his swear word, and our failure to pronounce it is fortunate. There are other misprints of the same kind, ugly enough, but so quickly recognised that they also are harmless. Books published soon after the war were subject to them. Some French books published before the stabilisation of the franc were faulty enough to make the reader's reason totter at the end of every line, where the printer – or his devil – repeatedly printed words from the close of line two in the line before, and vice versa. No serious harm was done, though, for the reader was at least aware that something was the matter, and he could, in addition to the pleasure of reading the complex sentences of Marcel Proust, enjoy a little mental pleasure over the transposition of those words. Hardly fair to the aesthetic quality of Proust, you will say, but considered as a deed of a printer's devil, this disturbance was so slight that one can almost praise it. Only the crudest and most innocent devil will let you see that he is misleading you.

It is the disguised misprint that is dangerous. When the trail of a serpent is over all a landscape we know where we are; but when a printer's devil has made a visitation upon a paragraph and left it, apparently, a smiling Eden still, we are his prey. It is rarely that the inspired enemy does anything so crude as to insert a negative or to omit one; but his alterations often have that effect, while leaving the sentence to flow as naturally as if it had been so conceived by the writer. In a notebook I have collected a few of these particularly devastating specimens of the misprinter's subtle art: they have none of the racy charm possessed by the howler or the spoonerism; they are not amusing; they are simply deplorable.

Here is one of the very simplest. The writer of an article was regretting the limitations of the modern neat-and-complete flat, from which all the impedimenta of living seemed to be excluded, its inhabitants 'apparently preferring this balder kind of existence'. The printer's devil called it a 'bolder' kind of existence wiping out the whole argument by a single letter. Again, in a recent novel, came an innocent-looking sentence in a passage that went towards building a certain character: the sentence dealt with 'Boyd's enforced friendliness', not such a bad phrase for a certain type of human association, except that it was totally opposed to the rest of the analysis. Thinking it over – though for a reader to think it over is against the printer's devil's rules – you could only feel sure that what the author had written was 'unforced friendliness'. That was a misprint of great wiliness.

To bring about either of those effects the operator had to alter a letter, but he can manage by the alteration of something less, a mere comma, or dash, or point. It is not enough for his purpose to leave the mark of punctuation right out, for the reader's eye instinctively points one in – yes, even into a lawyer's document if it be at all intelligible. It is necessary for the imp to insert a false stop in some vital place. Even if he fails to bring about an entire collapse of the passage, he may at least hope for an effect of confusion that will be ascribed wholly to the author. There is a famous passage in *Ultima Thule* in which a comma does all the misprinting it could hope to accomplish with its modest powers. The German baron, a naturalist and musician, who has come on a visit to Richard Mahony, in a bush township, is talking to the little son whom he has stirred by his playing of Schumann's music. Cuffy jumps about crying, 'I will say music, too, when I am big,' but his friend answers:

'*Ja Ja*, but so easy is it not to shake the music out of the sleeve!. . .Here is lying' – and the Baron waved his arm all round him – 'a great, new music hid. He who makes it, he will put into it the thousand feelings awoken in him by this emptiness and space, this desolation; with always the serene blue heaven above, and these pale, sad, so grotesque trees that weep and rave. He puts the golden wattle in it, when it blooms and reeks, and this melancholy bush, oh, so old, so old and this silence as of death that nothing stirs. No, birdleins will sing in *his Musik*.'

Well, there is the intrusive comma, between 'No' and 'birdleins'. The whole passage is controversial in theme, and when its argument is complicated by the presence of a misprint, you have all the material for a knotty passage that will engage the *apparatus criticus* of scholars with variorum editions in generations to come. You see, the question is that of the silence of our bush. The baron meant that there would be 'no birdleins', that is, he believed in the silence of the bush – may our harmonious thrush and all her ravishing cousins forgive him for his unattuned ear! The false punctuation in the book, the fatal comma, seems to make him say that it will be the musician's part to make the birds sing 'in his music', to provide a conventional bird-music to fill the silence. The former is clearly the true reading, though the comma has been wrongly inserted in both the English edition and the reset American edition. So it becomes clear that printer's devils are not hampered in their movements: *peregrinantur*, they can cross the Atlantic, they are as mobile as Puck.

There is again another kind of printer's devilry, very hard to endure: this is the self-righteous type. The alterations made by this evil genius exhibit zeal for someone's welfare or reputation. Thus a poet who uses the word 'mystery', intending it for a dissyllable with a tremolo, will find it printed 'myst'ry'; the printer's devil would assure him that it was thus rendered more 'poetical'. At times certain authors have had fixed ideas of spelling which have been at variance with the convictions of this all-too-learned, all-too-hidebound variety of hypercritical imp. All through Meredith's novels the 'e' is retained in words like judgement: he liked it so, and he succeeded in bringing it off. But then Meredith was a publisher's reader, and he would know how to lord it over whole legions of printer's devils when necessary. Other authors are less successful. In a recent essay, Hilaire Belloc complains that it is almost impossible for an author to follow his own notions of spelling: 'If you do, you are in for a lifelong war with the printers. For forty years have I now attempted most firmly to fix and root the right phrase 'an historian' into the noblest pages of English, but the bastard 'a historian' is still fighting for his miserable life, and may yet survive'.

He may indeed: so may many another word against which the mere writer battles in vain. For still, at the peak point, in the best strategic position, stands, illiterate but cunning, the printer's devil.

THE SONG OF BIRDS

The recipe for the smooth, firm lawns of England is simple and well known: 'You mows them and mows them for hundreds of years.' It is the same with the general countryside of Europe. It has been gazed upon with love for centuries. Henry James speaks – for once as a foreigner – of the 'rich, humanised landscape' in England. Every bird and flower there has not only its scientific nomenclature, but also its homely name that can be used by any writer. All the bird-songs have been marked, as in the old springtime refrain:

> Cuckoo, jug-jug, pu-wee, ta-witta-woo!

Hundreds of years this has taken, and the theme is not exhausted yet. In recent years it was possible for Robert Bridges to reinterpret, in a new poetry, the English countryside, showing it like something rich with old associations, yet seen now for the first time. There were its flowers:

> Lily-of-the-vale, Violet, Verbena, Mignonette,
> Hyacinth, Heliotrope, Sweet-briar, Pinks and Peas,
> Lilac and Wallflower, or such white and purple blooms that sleep i' the sun.

There were again its birds:

> Lov'st thou in the blithe hour
> of April dawns — nay marvelest thou not — to hear
> the ravishing music that the small birdës make
> in garden or woodland, rapturously heralding
> the break of day; when the first lark on high hath warn'd
> the vigilant robin already of the sun's approach,
> and he on slender pipe calleth the nesting tribes
> to awake and thrill and fill their myriad-warbling throats.

It is difficult with the many-branched and flourished passages of Bridges to stop quoting, but these lines at least will have shown two things: that Bridges, almost like Blake, comes with childlike freshness to his marvellous theme, and that at the same time he is aware that his feet can tread only in the footmarks of older poets. He uses thus the 'birdës' of Chaucer, the 'slender pipe' of Virgil as if indicating his thanks and acknowledging the succession.

Here in Australia, with its new birds, new seasons, new 'values', there are no beaten tracks for the poets to follow. None? Well, perhaps that is untrue, since certain old-world birds, being brought here, have made themselves marvellously at home. The bulbul, from Persia, storied, musical, and, I believe, predatory, is well known in Sydney gardens, and sometimes it is heard in those of Melbourne. The skylark is everywhere over level fields and paddocks round Melbourne, especially near the open sea. Nobody could walk even a few minutes away from trains and noise without coming to a region where, as in the line of one of our poets, 'the bubbling larks climbed clear'. Perhaps with the disappearance of much native timber the native birds have left those parts, and the larks have seized their chance. Nowhere in Europe have I heard more lark-songs, closer together or more continuous. Then there are blackbirds and thrushes, both European, both settled in our gardens. The thrush's song is by far the fuller, with its elaborate trills and glides and general bravuras. The blackbird, though, with its few clear notes, a modest run, a pause, a little call, has something that pulls fiercely at the heart-strings.

Someone writing in England has remarked that the blackbird's tune varies from county to county. Probably, but its tone is the same, its voice, its summary challenge to dull souls. It goes everywhere, and, wherever it may be, the blackbird sings. I have heard one at evening in the pauses of traffic in a square by Potsdamer Platz, in the centre of Berlin, and others in London, in the French countryside, and in our own Dandenong Range. For the blackbird, unlike its European comrade, the thrush, has wandered far beyond suburban gardens and made many a home in the bush. To those for whom its pure, haunting notes are a reminder of complex, urban, and ancient places, it is astounding to hear them on some tangled track by a bush creek. It is as if we called in at a bush hut for a drink of water and were answered in old French. The bulbul, the skylark, the thrush, the blackbird – those are perhaps our best-known invaders. For these, for their songs, poets through the centuries have found words. Many who had never heard or seen these old-world birds could probably compile an anthology about each of them. But what of our own birds? Do we know them?

When Bridges describes the birds of his English dawn – the lark on high, the vigilant robin, then all the nesting tribes – we can think as a contrast only of our own dawn chorus as we hear it in the ranges. Its ways vary, of course, and if I try to describe it here, there will be many to say that the case is otherwise. I can put down only what I heard as I remember it.

On a night then, somewhere between the seasons, there had been mopokes calling, on and on, beneath a late-rising moon. 'The moon's voice!' I once heard a child say, when he heard the sweet, blunted notes of the mopoke, which, like the cuckoo, says its own name over. There was, so far, no dawn light in the sky; yet the stars had a bewildered look. What was it – 'dawn's left hand', piccaninny daylight? The mopoke ceased utterly. We heard another bird of two notes, this time the same note repeated as if someone twice plucked it on a stringed instrument.

It was the eopsaltria, the harper of the dawn, and this was his dawn note in the darkness of the tall timber. (All day in the sunlight he will sing a little run, ending with a single harp note.) The sound came from all directions. The harper's name is legion. It was followed by the kookaburra, the long gloug-gloug up the scale followed by the macabre old laugh, which after all, could not drown the sweet jargoning that now arose. For by this time it was a real chorus, even an orchestra, so that we needed two separate kinds of ear, being drawn sometimes to listen to individual songs, sometimes to the whole complex world of sound. We began by hearing the individuals as they seemed to waken and become aware of themselves.

There was the small golden whistler's most recognisable song, a chain of clear sound for which all the phrases like 'linkèd sweetness long drawn out' have been made. There was the fresh poignancy of the mountain thrush, that grey bird, Gould's harmonica, its notes always seeming to be quickened as if by dew or by rain. Lovelier in song than any bird I have ever known, this inconspicuous grey shrike-thrush has the liquid note of its cousin the magpie – that piping crow! – and the haunting pathos of its other cousin, the butcherbird, together with a contemplative, continuous richness of its own. The harmonious thrushes, then, in this deep dawn that was still quite dark, sang on and on. Between their gravely beautiful notes came the tinkling songs of the blue wren, almost ironically named the superb warbler, his tiny throat making such a limited little musical-box.

It had now become more difficult to disentangle the singers, unless one determined to follow only one all through. The chorus lasted perhaps twenty minutes. Then, almost suddenly, one was aware of deep silence – a silence that lasted perhaps an hour. At the end of that hour, real dawn had come. The birds now frankly awoke and were busy. On a leafless tree, catching the first flicker of a sunbeam, two magpies yodelled marvellously; higher still a butcherbird repeated his strangely beautiful high treble call. The harper of the dawn, now revealed as that friendly little fellow the robust yellow robin, shook out his stream of daytime notes. But that earlier, full chorus: had we only imagined it? Or had the birds really uttered it?

Yes, it had been objective reality. Many sons of men have heard it: perhaps it was what one of them meant by 'the morning stars sang together'.

But how many hundreds of years will it take, how many human minds will have to be mown and mown again, before that dawn chorus can be translated into works of art and so become part of our general consciousness?

AUSTRAL ENGLISH

Every now and then, in reading or in writing of our own country, we are stuck for want of an authority. We meet with words and phrases that belong to our life and landscape, but we are not sure sometimes of their spelling, sometimes of their exact meaning and usage. Constantly we find that the words have different meanings in different parts of the country; and this applies not only to native words, with their peculiar accidents of transmission from the Leeuwin to Cape York, but to slang and idiom of our own.

We need a searching dictionary with illustrations from all types of speech and writing. It would be work for someone's lifetime – with this proviso, that when 'twere done 'twas not done, for the subject-matter would be changing in the course of that lifetime, and new usages would have to be recorded. In this it would be like the game of croquet in *Alice in Wonderland* with the living hoops and balls that kept moving away at pleasure. Our eager dictionary would seek out the origin and meanings of the singular word *hatter*: of *swag*, and its derived words, *swagger, swaggie, swagsman*, and *swagman* – the last being generally familiar today: of *ropeable* – does it perhaps mean *unropeable*? – and of *borak*, which, about 1880, turned into *barrack*, and is still a hard saying.

Those are a few nuts to crack, and their kernels will have very interesting and delicate flavours. We need a book about them, but the latest book about them, already thirty years old, was incomplete, and achieved rather a gleaning than a harvest.

While putting on record our gratitude to Professor Morris for his *Austral English* (1898) we can express at the same time our amazement that the book has had no successor. 'Austral English, a Dictionary of Australasian Words, Phrases, and Usages, with those Aboriginal-Australian and Maori Words which have become incorporated in the Language and the Commoner Scientific Words that have had their Origin in Australasia'; such was the wording on the title page. Like most books that go pioneering in a subject, the dictionary attempted to cover too much ground. The Maori words obviously needed a separate volume, a separate study. In a few 'colonial' phrases, Australian and New Zealand settlers coincided; but the words of natives in the two countries had of course no relation at all. Again, *Austral English* was not by any means complete as a book of slang and idiom, and the scientific words would have been better kept apart, except when they made a useful commentary on some colloquial name, such as *she-oak*, *tea-tree*, *tree-fern* (or *fern-tree*). The book is chiefly valuable in so far as it shows the origin and development of colloquialism, such racy phrases as give continuity and character to the English language used in Australia.

Professor Morris, who held the chair of Modern Languages in Melbourne for many years, was unlike the majority of academic men in his zest for doing some creative and original work. Lecturing on English to his students, he found that they knew nothing of the language that was growing round about them. It was important, he realised, for every Australian to know, for instance, what a *duffer* means, or meant, and a *sundowner* and a *jumbuck*. So *Austral English* was written, with these words in the preface:

> English has certainly a richer vocabulary, a finer variety of words to express delicate distinctions of meaning, than any language that is or that ever was spoken: and this is because it has always been hospitable in the reception of new words. It is too late a day to close the doors

against new words. This *Austral English Dictionary* merely catalogues and records those which at certain doors have already come in.

The motive and intention of the work were admirable. Its basic reason for existence was the revelation of words concerned with natural objects and orders of things that were Australian and new. The genuine Aboriginal words in the dictionary are themselves of very great importance, but may mostly be looked for in other compilations. Together with them are some of the Anglicised corruptions of those words written down according to the fantastic law of Hobson-Jobson, which is sometimes delightful enough to watch in its operations. Such a corruption is *paddy-melon*, the name not of a fruit but of a quaint little marsupial living in sandy country. There was some lost and rather long Aboriginal word with halves that were made into two existing but absurdly unrelated English words, *paddy* and *melon*. By the same omnipresent philological 'law', there arose names like *pudding-ball* for the fish in Moreton Bay called by the natives *puddenba*. Such distortions are comparable to the Australian-French of the war years: 'The way to ask for bread in French is just to say Japan.'

When there was no Aboriginal word for an object or for a state of affairs new to the settler, new words arose naturally enough: *billy*, *free-selector*, *boundary-rider*, *dummyism*, *stockman*, *sundowner*. Take the last, which our French-Australian, Paul Wenz, has made into the title of a novel, *L'Homme du Soleil Couchant*. Professor Morris, following his fine system of illustrating the gradual acceptance of every word by dated quotations, here cites for *sundowner* a half-true remark by one who was perhaps our most brilliant visitor:

> 1891, Francis Adams:
> Swagsmen: genuine, or only 'sundowners' – men who loaf about till sunset, and then come in with a demand for the unrefusable 'rations.'

Loaf about – if by loafing about you mean tramping the miles between one station and the next, which you are lucky to reach by sundown! Paul Wenz, with an ironic twist, puts it better than that in his book.

Most of such words, though, are supported in the dictionary by quotations dated a great deal farther back than the nineties, some few of them attaining, as Professor Morris could say even in 1898, the respectable age of a century. The word *billy* supersedes *camp-kettle* somewhere in the fifties, but its derivation will always be as uncertain as what song the sirens sang. Some say it is short for an arbitrary name, *William*, as we say *Long Tom* or *Spinning Jenny* or as facetious persons may call their typewriter *Marmaduke*. Others derive it from the French *bouilli*, as billies were often made from tins that had contained *boeuf bouilli*. A third explanation gives the Aboriginal word, *billa*, water or a river (as in billabong, a dead river, a lake left by a river-flood). Take your choice. The billy, as distinguished from a kettle or a jackshay, is described, though the name is not used, in 1835.

The word *bush*, though originally Dutch, has perhaps more Australian aroma about it than any other. Here are some quotations given in *Austral English* (though Professor Morris missed the voluble bewilderment of Mrs Nickleby, whose emigrant ex-suitor, she declared, went out after some sheep that were 'lost in a bush: I don't know how they got there').

1837, Dunmore Lang:
His house was well enough for the bush.

1857, W. Westgarth:
The gloomy antithesis of good bushranging and bad bush-roads.

1896, The *Argus*:
The Ministry did not assume its duty of leading the House, and Mr Higgins graphically described the position of affairs by stating that the House was 'bushed'.

There you have the word as noun, adjective, and verb. There is no mention of what, perhaps, is more recently grown, the word *bushie*, meaning you or me when we live in the bush: and we need instances of the word *bushwhacker* (as in the title of P. R. Stephensen's striking little book of Queensland stories) used before 1899. It was used several times in the Melbourne *Tocsin* of that date, without any fuss, so one gathers that its general use goes much farther back.

Such is part of the tribe of new words that 'at certain doors have already come in'. Professor Hancock, in his book *Australia* has made a little mound of them in a crowded paragraph or so for our inspection. The subject is indeed wide open to research by specialists and to discussion by all of us. This presence in English of new words and phrases that are rapidly melting into the old rhythms is of the strangest importance. How much of the English-speaking world's awareness of South Africa's character and landscape is due to our familiarity with words like *veldt* and *kopje*? In Australia such words as *creek* and *gully*, having come to stay, will gather their own magic. Other special words of ours, though, with great richness and colour, may disappear through our own unimaginative lethargy. Experimental writers like Katharine Prichard show how idiom and slang can be used to create an atmosphere. Colloquial words? Why should we resist or deprecate them if they are alive? The first time two of our Aryan forefathers grunted a similar syllable and then looked at one another in a mild surmise that it might mean something, they were being colloquial in the extreme. Yet it is their old 'new' noises that we now solemnly accept as pre-classical roots. Some colloquial words prove spurious and superfluous, others are vital. That is why we need a full book of our words, sifting the quick from the dead in our Austral English.

ROMANTIC AUSTRALIA?

Lately I was rereading two letters, trying to reconcile their contradictions, or at least to see where the truth in both of them lay. Both were written in sincerity: both dealt with our life as a subject for novels. The first writer found it entirely nourishing, the only difficulty lying in the expression of it with enough simplicity, and without strain or over-emphasis. The second writer – well, perhaps I had better translate some of his clear and admirable letter at once. He is a foreign writer who has published many books of stories set in Australia. He is sympathetic with American books and ways, having translated at least one American novel into his own language. As it will appear, for all his very long acquaintance with us, he is not sympathetic with this country, at any rate as material for art.

He writes about a novel:

> I believe that the very sincerity of the descriptions expresses only too well the monotony of the Australian bush. Australians themselves refuse to accept this monotony; they say it does not exist; they cannot judge by comparison, therefore they cannot judge at all. Every work on the Australian bush suffers in the same way; even *Coonardoo*, which I admire greatly.

Then he warms to his theme:

> In this country the picturesque is lacking; there is no terror, no mystery; the people themselves are not picturesque. A Mexican, an Argentine gaucho, an Arab, each takes a little pride in his saddle or bridle, or in his clothes. Here, the man on his old saddle has nothing photogenic – his trousers pulled half-way up his legs, his socks (if he has any) falling down over his half-laced shoes, never giving him the look of a real horseman.
>
> One could make a comparison between the American authors and the Australians who have described the same life of the plains, the bush and the gold-mines. In America the settings are more grandiose, their mountains, forests, rivers; their Redskins are replaced here by a race that, having no history, is interesting from the ethnographic point of view alone. We have not so much as the rifle and the revolver, which for them make by no means negligible accessories.
>
> To come back to my first point: what I miss in Australian authors is a pathos, an emotion, something to make the heart beat a little faster, 'something exciting'.

The last words were written in English, as if in a kind of despair.

All this indictment seemed extraordinarily interesting to me in its frankness. The writer deplored, in one breath, our life and our expression of it: our life was uninteresting, and our books, unfortunately, were sincere enough to express it as it was. If only our life were romantic, or, failing that, if only our novelists were able and willing to apply some cosmetics to its sallow face!

I turned back to the first letter. It had come from a novelist whose books, which must have been long pondered, have come before us in quick succession recently, making a chronicle of country life through our few generations. Here is a statement of the intention of these books: its very breathlessness is exciting:

> The attempt to make others see and feel as I do the atmosphere and unique qualities of the landscape which are spiritual breath to me, is half ecstacy – in almost capturing it – half torment in feeling that it is an impossible feat and that I am so feeble for it . . . . It seems to me that a story, to be truer than reality (that mirage effected by grouping and selection), should follow natural contours and rhythms. A pulse artificially accelerated, or extraneous outlines because of spurious conventions as to what is really 'action', must be eschewed. The desultory style of pioneer settlements themselves should be suggested, growing up unpretentiously as they did to meet immediate need. An easy, unrazored, pipe-smoking, almost casual method is needed. The old pioneer yarns, 'yarned' by the old bush granddads (with as like as not a grandma contemptuous of their inconsequences and deviations from original versions) rubbing their tobacco in their palms, and holding up the climax (there mustn't be too much climax) to light and draw, have a charm as characteristic as their environment.

A charm in the yarns as characteristic as their environment – this when the other letter-writer denied both charm and character! Where and what is truth? Is it entirely subjective? And is an interest in art dependent on interest in the kind of life that is its matter?

What emerges from the second letter is this, if one may make a general statement: that so far from seeking to emphasise high lights and to heighten climaxes, Australian writers are so deeply aware of passionate currents and high adventures that their effort is rather to *damp down* their accounts of them. Right or wrong, that is their intention both in literature and life. Take it or leave it, an Australian will give you, on the whole, under-statements of splendour: he will speak of wonderful moments, but casually, with a wary avoidance of anything like rhetoric. In spite of appearances, many a bushman is proud of his horse, his saddle, his light, well-fitting boots, his leather leggings, and the work these all mean: but he will not, like the Mexican, the Argentine gaucho, the Arab, draw attention to these by fringes and colour; more probably he will divert attention from them by some carelessness in detail. An American buckjump-show goes by some large, ambiguous, and glorious name such as 'Rodeo', every point in the manoeuvres being emphasised by skilled 'salesmanship'. The Australian buckjump-show has no such knacks of emphasis and display, the most dangerous and difficult moments being passed over with a kind of pride in ignoring them. When this technique is habitual in the novel or the short story, those who enjoy it will say that it is our own native flavour: others will say that all the opportunities have simply been missed.

Missed? For my part I accept this quietism as our method, as our character. It reminds me of a most striking passage – striking because of its very lack of emphasis – in Conrad's great book, *Nostromo*. Conrad, in one brief paragraph, causes the hero to ride an immense number of miles over the mountains at night, narrowly escaping a hundred deaths – and then allows the psychological actualities of the book to proceed. Another author would have extended that paragraph to a series of breath-taking chapters, though that would be to distort the framework of the book. Its framework? Not merely that, but its inner meaning.

For all its dissatisfaction with our life and our literature, that letter finding fault with our literature *because* it succeeded, up to a point, in expressing our life, seemed to me a basis of satisfaction, and not the reverse. Everything points the same way, to the assurance that our best way of writing is the quiet, the unemphatic, the simple and sincere. Take Lawson's stories, like 'Telling Mrs Baker', with the possible melodramatic twist quite evaded. Or Henry Handel Richardson's version of the Eureka Stockade in the first chapter of her trilogy. Obedient to the demands of her story and the outlook of her chief character, she shows the affair not full-face, but sidelong, not in its direction, but in its confusion, not in its leaders, but in its subordinates. Then a phrase comes to mind from Professor Gregory's small, pregnant book on Australia, where he said (speaking actually of our politics) that Australians were idealist rather than romantic: 'The average

American seems to me essentially a romanticist, for he is interested in the unusual because it is unusual.' We cannot compete with the American on this ground: our strength, whatever it is, lies elsewhere.

Take us or leave us (and probably it would be best for us to be left for a while) our 'inconspicuous' landscape will need treatment that is rather subtle than emphatic. Our character will be best rendered by understatement. When Louis Esson's drover, in a brief, memorable play, is left to die alone on the waterless plain, all that his mates can say as they ride off faithfully with the mob of thirsty cattle is: 'So long! We'll tell the boys about it at Brunette!' No attitude is struck; everything depends on the conviction that the deepest emotions, being present, are deliberately dammed back. The heart, indeed, beats faster, it races as we read: hence the reticence, the evasion, the lack of emphasised 'romance'.

ON STOPS

In a book the other day I came across a lady who always used the word 'table napkin', and when she wished to divide humanity into two classes she thought of those who said 'table napkin' and those who said 'serviette'. Well, I have heard of more foolish methods of division, from Lilliput onwards! Sometimes I have found myself dividing humanity into two classes, those who like using stops, and those who do not. As for those who do not, I shall not discuss them here. They are at liberty to enjoy themselves in any other way that occurs to them. I turn from them to those who think of punctuation as an important part of writing and speaking — in fact, as a mode of human intercourse.

These interested people, so far as I have met them, may be of all ages. I have met one, aged five, and have received entrancing letters from another aged ninety-four. The person aged five was just beginning to read, and, what was more, to write: and better than all her words she liked the little marks she learnt to put beside them. She liked the question mark you could make out of a pothook, with a little ball underneath it, when you wrote down important questions out of games like, 'O say, what is she weeping for?' There was another mark, though, more interesting still. It was just a stick balanced upright in the air, with a little ball underneath it, and you called it a wonder-mark. It came in when some grown-up might say, 'She's got her shoes muddy.' The person aged five liked putting the wonder-mark directly against the most surprising word, even if it made a bumpy-looking sentence. This way: 'We climbed that hill in ten! minutes.' I think she was right to experiment. My correspondent aged ninety-four was perhaps less revolutionary, but his punctuation was elastic and expressive enough. With him a comma was a comma, never a mere casual concession to habit. He used no promiscuous pepper-castor to distribute his full-points. His colons and semi-colons, sparingly used, had their separate purposes. He could even use a dash, and he did, saving it up for that kind of epistolary crisis when nothing but a dash will serve.

The other half of humanity, to return to it for a moment, knows no form of punctuation but a blurred dash. Every sentence, every half-sentence, ends with one: but what happens when they really need an expressive dash? Nothing happens. On the whole, that correspondent of mine in his nineties was liberal with stops, though never a spendthrift or a pedantic vulgarian. He knew his purposes in framing sentences like well-laid streets, whose lamps, perhaps, were those little points called stops. Feeling unhampered, he seldom broke a rule. For there are rules of punctuation, though it is considered almost improper to mention them nowadays. Those who do know them, having been initiated into their arcana during the Dark (or Victorian) age, find an interest in keeping them, and a considerable interest in deliberately breaking them now and then.

One way of using stops is, of course, to omit them with discretion. I am not speaking here of lawyers' documents, which are, by intention, unreadable and a verbal catacomb. What I have in mind is a kind of literary work produced by an artist in words who is dissatisfied with the limitations caused by the ordinary use of stops. Not being able to invent new symbols for slighter pauses than ordinary commas suggest, the writer decides to omit his commas. He considers that his punctuation is, to use Henry James's sleek phrase, 'beautified by its omissions', so he writes like this:

> Entering the room Alec saw that it was full of bamboos weapons boomerangs and knives.

What does that mean to you? I think, without being sure, that the writer hoped to present the room's contents to you simultaneously, or with equal force, coming at you from all sides at once. The use of commas would suggest that bamboos caught your eye first, and knives four stages later. But, even without commas, the words had to be put in some order. There is no way to make them simultaneous except by painting a picture, and even then the arrangement gives priorities. In music the impressions have to follow one another: time is of its essence. In writing, too, there is no such thing as the present time, for the duration of more than one word. Every word is either dropping into the past or else appearing from the future, whether commas delay them or not.

But other writers have omitted their stops on different grounds. George Moore, within the last few years, has written whole books with only the minimum of full stops, and no commas at all – even inverted ones. In his *Heloise and Abelard*, for instance, he writes on like this:

> What a lovely day Heloise thought and the clouds reflected themselves in the lake.

This is certainly done on purpose, and, of course, the sentence would not really stop before a page or two more. The object is to make the whole book seem an excursion of the author's own mind, which, to be frank, every book is. The characters approach, speak, depart, without affecting the flow of George Moore's narrative thoughts. It is one way of writing. As for other authors' omissions in various kinds, they are innumerable. We may not like them: they may seem ineffectual to us: but we know they meant something to the writer, made for him the written word approach more nearly to the rhythm in his mind. It is John Galsworthy's practice to print what is uttered aloud between doubly-inverted commas: "Come here" said Jon: while what is only thought by his characters is whispered only between singles 'like this.' An ingenious device, but for the eye, not the ear. Other writers think chiefly of the ear, so that, sometimes, if we read a page aloud, we find that the chaotic-looking, stopless page is, after all, well-balanced and clear. This is especially true of poetry, where no mistake is worse than over-punctuation, too many stops. With such danger in mind, T. S. Eliot in his most recent small book of meditative poems, *Ash Wednesday*, leaves the lines themselves, with their faint rest at the end, to express any pauses.

Punctuation is too often looked upon as a mere delight for the eye and a detail of grammar. It should have the more important function of marking genuine breath-pauses in time: I am grateful to it for that, and I am not the first person to feel grateful. When I was a child, my grandmother used to tell me about a grandmother of her own, who was 'the most beautiful reader I ever heard, in enunciation, pronunciation, and punctuation'. That punctuation used to puzzle me greatly; in my mind I used to see grandmother's grandmother making little commas, semi-colons, and colons in the air with her fingers, and counting one, two, three, whenever she paused. That was because I had been told that punctuation consisted of those little marks we made on pages! (Do you remember how Lewis Carroll's little Bruno drew a first bracket in the air before a confidential remark, and drew the second, closing bracket, when he had finished?) But what my grandmother really meant, of course, was that a perfect reader was never hurried, never out of breath, yet never dawdling and purposeless.

Stops, it seems to me, are as useful in writing as pauses in music or dancing. If T. S. Eliot in poetry, and George Moore in prose, omit them today it is only after consideration and for some special purpose: they are not acting in ignorance, nor as the Gentiles do. In many modern schools children are not taught about stops till they are nine or ten, that is, until they have been writing somehow without stops for years. It is my belief that they should be allowed to play with stops quite early, as they play with beads. They may then grow up to use them, or even omit them, with understanding and purpose.

THE GNAT PROPOSES

Do people read Lewis Carroll now? The centenary celebrations, with the discovery and revival of obscure Carrolliana, hardly count. Is he read as a general thing? One reason why, for all the charm of his books, children take his *Alice* books with a rather sober and modified joy is, I fancy, that they guess there is more in them than they can quite understand. They feel that they are being got at in some way. It is as if they found that in eating 'hundreds and thousands' on a birthday cake they had mysteriously been caused to solve a problem in decimals.

They are right in their suspicions, as children often are. What Lewis Carroll gives them, with their hundreds and thousands, over and above the straight story, which is always exciting and memorable, is not merely an intellectual addition: it is more still. The whole of *Alice Through the Looking Glass* is a game of chess where Alice becomes a queen at the close, but, apart from such ingenuities, odd aspects of the human mind are shown by situation and phrasing all through. The two *Alice* books are both extraordinarily good representations of a child's dream, deep, continuous, accepting everything as natural up to the last moment, when it melts into the common day. The dreaming in *Sylvie and Bruno* is just as well done, but it is different in kind: here is no child's sound sleep, but the cat-naps of an elderly man, who wakes up on a railway carriage to see the pretty girl opposite giggling at him behind her handkerchief. What has been done or said? It seems he woke up saying indignantly, 'Ug-gug, indeed!' The pretty girl thinks that had no meaning, does she? Well, we'll just show her: we'll just drop off to sleep again and continue our dream, in which the undesirable Prince Ug-gug is being proposed as successor to the throne.

'Is there not,' says a recent critic, 'something a little too tight, too constrained by logic, in Lewis Carroll, for the perfect freedom craved by the nonsense-loving mind?'

Undoubtedly there is. There is precious little nonsense in the *Alice* books, and some of their motifs that may seem like nonsense at first glance are really psychological truths, vividly personified. Take, for instance, the gnat in *Alice Through the Looking-Glass*.

The characters, including, I think, the sheep, are seated in a stationary railway-carriage, with some talk going on, and suddenly Alice notices a very thin little voice that cuts through what is said. Its words are printed in the smallest type, and its suggestions are all of the same kind. Hearing some remark made, it says, 'You might make a joke out of that, you know,' and dragging two words into juxtaposition makes them almost suggest a pun. This the tiny, undiscoverable voice does repeatedly: it is maddening. Alice is relieved to find it is only a gnat. But what else could so well represent the maddening persistence of a trivial thought that is less than a thought! The joke was nearly made, but perceiving its inadequacy in time, we preferred to smother it with a cough. That time they were talking about a judge, who might have had a better salary abroad, and you begin to mumble, 'His Honour had no profit in his own country' – and then the words wilted on your lips, not seeming worth saying! Other times there were, too, countless times, when you saw two words looking at you as if they were going to cross and make a spark: what energy you wasted in trying to coax them together as they jigged in the air! 'You might make a joke about that.' On the whole, though, it was your despair at your own incompetence rather than any righteous abhorrence of mere punning that made you subscribe to Carroll's own solemn lines in his own version of 'The Two Voices':

> The good and great should ever shun
> The wicked and abandoned one
> Who stoops to perpetrate a pun.

We then decided to be good and great, but rather ruefully, remembering some of the marvellous squibs that have been brought off from time to time by persons with both erudition and presence of mind, people not unmindful of the gnat's proposals. How do they manage to be on the spot at the one moment since the creation of the world when the particular quotation would fit in? We can understand it, to some extent, in the written word: the writer sets his stage and thereupon deliberately stumbles over his own intentional joke. Chesterton is always doing this, like a boy walking through a doorway that he has himself loaded with a bucket of water to fall on his head at the right moment. But in a speech, or in an impromptu, it seems a miracle: the gnat's advice would come too slowly for any help. We can only admire in amaze.

There is, for instance, that well-known couplet about the moon that

> Nightly, to the listening earth
> Repeats the story of her birth.

What do you think some wag was lucky enough to do with that? He noticed a man who was very proud of his ancestry, and who bragged about it without remorse or mitigation. Obviously the couplet was ready for this braggart; but stay, his name was Knightly:

> And Knightly, to the listening earth
> Repeats the story of his birth.

Could anyone have hoped for such luck? The only Knightly at hand might have been a man of modesty; or the only proud person might have been named Jones, or – more frankly – Mussolini. But to find a Knightly, and to find him in character, and to remember the couplet – all these things together were enough to make ten thousand gnats clap their wings with microscopic huzzas.

Then there is the story of Dean Swift and the Virgilian line, a story that makes it for ever clear why the man was called Swift. It came from that cry of Virgil's shepherd, lamenting that his beloved town, Mantua, was too dangerously near the distraught Cremona with its fighting. Swift, being in company, where a lady whisking her long train, swept down a fine fiddle and broke it, cried out:

> Mantua vae miserae nimium vicina Cremonae!

If that 'fine fiddle' was not a Cremona it was as near as made no difference, and if a long train, in the seventeenth century, was not a mantua, what was it? Swift had done a wonderful bit of fielding.

It is not so marvellous, as we have found, when lucky finds are made by the writer of a book. Still in the preparation of his pages there must have been a very happy moment when the new notion swam up to his pen. Do you know the French word 'gosse?' Rather colloquial; a 'kid', a 'brat': you would use it readily of your own children, but hardly risk it for those of someone else. (Has it anything to do with the Irish 'gosson?' Nobody has ever told me.) Well, there was that French word, 'gosse', and there was the elderly English critic who wrote an excellent book about his relations with his own father, a striking, difficult character, Philip Gosse. The book was called *Father and Son*, but can't we all feel a little of the comfortable glow that pervaded a critic who discussed the book and its theme under the heading *Père et Gosse*?

It is a cold-blooded thing to explain such delicate word-play: it is like unpinning a bomb at the wrong time and so preventing it from hitting its objective. But there is a zest in watching anyone who has not failed, as we have done – how often! – to act promptly in obedience to the high and shrill commands of the omnipresent gnat.

A CHILD'S THEATRE

It is notorious that children can make a toy out of anything at all, calling a stick a doll, and a billet of wood a car. But if it is wonderful to see a child able to make a dream-castle out of some bits of bark and pebbles of his own, I think it is even more wonderful when he can make a story-book world out of things that he cannot possess, things made by grown-ups for the unimportant world they call the real one.

For instance, I once knew a tiny boy, who lived in a London flat. His only outings were along the shopping streets, where he had to behave and keep up with his mother, and over the road to a demure little park, where his greatest liberty was in trotting a little on the neatly-gravelled paths. But what a wonderful story-book place that little park was for him! It was the flowers, you suggest, or perhaps butterflies and birds? Hardly: for flowers were there at one season only, and the same (only more so) with butterflies and birds. Even the trees were not constant, but shed their leaves and changed so continually that you would hardly remember them. The tiny boy wanted something steadier, more enduring to be the heroes of his dream-spun fairy-tale. His heroes were the garden taps! One tap with a very big mouth he called Tom Tiger; another, much smaller, was Tiny Tim. He could not do anything to the taps except visit them, and they were always in the same spots, which might have seemed a little dull on their part. But no; he found them endlessly interesting. When he was in bed at night, he used to remember them standing out in the rain, Tom Tiger, Tiny Tim, and all the others in between. This romance, found in such commonplace plumber's work, always seemed to me rather pathetic. What would such a child make out of a few months spent in the country, with wood to whittle and trees to climb and all kinds of pleasant beasts to watch and understand and know!

It was while I was watching another tiny boy the other day that I remembered the little tap boy in London. The boy here seemed to me not merely more fortunate in his life, but actually happier. His playthings in his playworld were not luxurious or complicated. The most important of them were not even his own, except that he could use them as a spectacle, nobody else having paid for seats. He had, as his own, some sticks and boughs to make a sort of humpy, which was nearly all opening: he sat in it for one purpose only, which was to look out from it. It was like a box in the theatre, and he had the show all to himself.

The show? It was provided, day by day, continuous sessions,

dawn to dark, by his grandmother's fowls. A round dozen of them! He could watch whenever he liked; when he was bored, he could switch his attention off with the nonchalance shown by a radio-listener. The fowls were never offended by his leaving the theatre, any more than a great *prima donna* stamps with rage when Mr X, of some outer suburb, remembers, in the middle of her aria, that he has left the bath-tap running. In any case he has no need to apologise to the performer. So the little boy does not apologise to the chooks, whose drama goes on with the same vigour as before – eleven hens and one rooster, building up a comedy together in the most natural and convincing style.

So far the performance has been all comedy, though there are indeed tragedies in the life-story of fowls. Much of the present drama depends on the activities of the solitary rooster, a perfect Chaplin of comedians, named, for some reason, Pompey. He is pompous and self-satisfied, to outward looks, but every now and then his pomp and vainglory collapse, and he is a mere little figure of disappointment, making one think of that old stock picture of a rooster on a wet day, muttering: 'One damned thing after another: today we're eggs and tomorrow we're blooming feather-dusters!' But his humiliations are rare.

The little boy was enjoying himself a good deal this morning. The rooster, who for some reason has been given the name of a general, might be expected to look dark and dashing, but he is actually, like most of his wives, of a spotless white, with the whiteness of well-starched shirt-fronts. This adds to his conventional assurance. He spends a great deal of his time and ingenuity safeguarding this pomposity – in vain, for even if his wives fail to see through him, his audience is not so dull. What happened today was that the little boy banged rather gently on an old tin plate. The rooster turned to his wives: 'You careless, unobservant women, can't you hear that a meal is ready? Follow me at once!' He trotted forward, they followed. At once he was aware that it was a false alarm; he had to cover his tracks. Falling back behind his wives, he began pecking the grass for some imaginary grain, seeming to mutter to himself: 'Stupid women! What are they running after? Making me run like that when the merest chicken could see that there was nothing there!'

The little boy found it was possible to have this whole performance repeated several times, at discreet intervals. The rooster forgot that it had happened before, or perhaps he always thought that the previous performances were only rehearsals. At least he managed to bear the white plume and the red comb of dignity through all these episodes.

But there was that half-hour yesterday when the dignity did seem in danger of breaking down. For some reason, while most of the fowls were out, the rooster with two hens was still shut in the wired yard. They wanted to get out: and he felt that his dignity required him to find the exit for the party of three. He could not, or would not, believe that the outlet, which sometimes existed, was this time missing. Fussily, he trotted up and down, inside the fence and the gate, eyes very bright, elbows spread out a little. He had a white hen on each side of him, and whenever he turned about, they turned about, too, with utter faith in his capacity to find a way out. Up and down they went, ten times a minute, for at least half an hour. Never once did the rooster fail to say, almost in words: 'Now don't get flustered, you women! Leave it all to me. The gate's just here, and I'll find it in a moment, as I always do.' In the end someone, a mere human being, did open the gate, when the rooster strutted out, followed by his two adoring, admiring, grateful wives, who had 'left it to him'. The audience in his leafy 'box' did not fail to see the point.

Indeed the audience sees more comedies in that theatre than it can ever describe. Happy little audience of one! Never since Chaucer made a whole long Canterbury Tale about Dame Pertelote and Chauntecler did chooks give more unsullied amusement. But the necessary competence of the little audience came from his being given large periods of fertile solitude.

ON LITERARY FASHIONS

Fashions, even in books, might have their uses and qualities if they moved forward and out of sight with some degree of slowness, if their existence had some dimensions, if they gave us time for a long look at them. In this speed age, however, they trot past us like talkie-shorts, gone before we have really seen them. Take the present Victorian revival in which books have shared as well as side-whiskers, macassaroil and the accompanying antimacassars — the 'present' revival, did I say? It is already past, or at least exhausted. In reviewing Barnard Eldershaw's novel, *Green Memory*, which was set in Sydney of the sixties, an English critic seriously remarked that really we had heard by this time all that could be said about the Victorian period and its problems. So soon! Barnard Eldershaw's previous novel, *A House is Built*, was not yet two years old, yet it was, if anything, too early to get the benefit of this quickened interest in what is Victorian. It was among the forerunners, and its successor was condemned as belated. Less than two years! I think literary fashions used to last a little longer.

The history of literary fashions is of course quite different from the history of literary development. Many writers become the fashion, for some obscure reason, long after they are dead. Others happen to catch the tone demanded by their contemporaries: with others again it is no happening but a matter of intention. Meanwhile the true currents of literature go on underneath, out of sight. For the moment we may glance at some fashions of the past. So far as I can find, they were more durable than those of today; the horse age was more leisurely than the age of aircraft.

About a hundred years ago, Scott's novels were, as we all know, very popular, and also very powerful. You have the aged Goethe, in his conversations with Eckermann on a kind of Pisgah-height, seriously discussing Scott's latest, analysing the psychological truths in *The Fair Maid of Perth*, and wondering what the Wizard of the North will give us next. What the Wizard did not write, of course, his legion of imitators did. The world of English books swarmed with bards, heather, clouds, and delirium, and by the late twenties not only Scott's novels but every work of fiction that had the slightest success in England was at once translated into French, and read on the Continent generally. This was due not to a love of English books, but to the themes and methods made familiar by Scott. Ten years before this, young Frenchmen had been producing vague 'Ossianic' novels with some success, but it had needed Scott to show them how a novel could be at the same time romantic and robust. The novels read by Lydia Languish had been lacking in the 'crowded hour of glorious life' which, with his footnotes and appendices, Scott presented to his hungry readers. But Scott, for all his energy and his really tragic speed of production, could not satiate the circulating library readers. It was his followers who tried to do this, being aware of the fashion. French novelists attempted to be among his followers, but the Gallic *clarté* could not evoke the Caledonian mists, and it had to be acknowledged that the English novels – that is, the Scottish and the pseudo-Scottish – had it all their own way. It was in honour of Scott that the *Times* and *Morning Chronicle* were widely read in Paris, and that young Frenchmen, instead of going to Switzerland, made pilgrimages to Scotland. Byron's *Don Juan*, of which a prose translation had just come out – but one breaks off there to consider the phenomenon of *Don Juan* in prose! As well boil ice and drink it tepid! *Don Juan* without rhyme and metre:

> Strange that the mind, that very fiery particle
> Should let itself be crushed out by an article.

Could you put that into French prose? Indeed one might add as a footnote:

> Strange that the French, so very strong in sanity
> Should take *Don Juan* as a prose inanity.

What should they have done, do you ask? Translated it into rhyme, a long, difficult, dangerous task? No, hardly: but they should have learnt enough English to understand the original.

Barbarous suggestion, of course: French people will never see fit to abandon their mind to languages inferior to their own; that is, to the acquisition of anything but their mother-tongue.

To return to Scott, we can probably say that the fashion for Scott – apart from the genuine appreciation of Scott, which is another matter – lasted more than a decade. As late as 1836 a French review gave a recipe for concocting historical novels, which is like a formula used by Scott's imitators.

> To make an historical novel, you rummage in the archives of some town; you unearth the usages and customs of the time, the names of the sheriffs, the prerogatives of the corporations, the scandalous chronicles of the time: add to this a hopeless love, four or five orgies, duels, seduction, two adulteries, and a more or less threadbare denouement, and you have a historico-dramatic or quasi-historico-dramatic novel.

But the publication of this formula shows that the recipe had been too freely used: the vogue was nearly over. Now came the novels of Stendhal with their deliberate understatements – his presentation of Waterloo, and even of Napoleon, as matters that a dazed young man at the back of the army might see, and yet not know that he was seeing. The romantic and decorative historical novel was to make place for Stendhal's uncompromising psychological intensity. He was little read at the time: his renown has been a matter of recent years. But his books were heralds of a great change and made paths for the movements of realism, naturalism, and their variants, which were arriving first as a revolt – then, in their turn, as a fashion.

There are those who like being in the fashion with what they read, and those who do not. Personally, I find it difficult to read a book when everyone is talking about it, but I am not going to quarrel with people who like reading what their friends are enjoying at the same time. All my demurrer is this: that the existence and reputation of a book should not depend on merely accidental and fashionable success. Scott's novels are what they are, whether in or out of favour: so are those of his imitators. Homer is great, whether he happens to have 'come back' in the columns of some

English review or not. Fashions can be refreshing, curious, or amusing; but those whose whole zest as readers consists in an excited following of them are likely to have no breath for anything else.

COBBERS

It came as a shock to see in a law report not so long ago that, when the accused said he would call two of his cobbers to give evidence in his favour, the magistrate rebuked him. 'We don't want to hear 'cobbers' here,' he said, 'cut out the slang.'

What is slang? 'Cut it out' is surely a specimen of moderately vigorous slang, but 'cobbers', no matter how the word is used today, has at least an older origin to boast. Why this hostility to a word that, in Australia, is now surrounded with meaning and glow? Was it perhaps because the accused, being accused, was not to enjoy himself with the use of such a warm and comfortable word? Or was it the magistrate's opinion that slang, as opposed to 'grammar', was demoralising in all circumstances? But then why did he say, 'Cut it out?' We are to suppose that he, like most of us, could not tell where the border ran between slang and current usage. Unlike most of us, though, he was seated on a magistrate's bench, which gave him the habit of speaking with authority.

Words, in their contraction and expansion, their strange development upward or outward or downward, are simply mesmeric in their fascination. Human minds have caused them to change, have made them work hard, or have left them to obsolescence. Cobber, I believe, was an old, sound dialect word from the north of England, and it has somehow become adopted by Australians. The late Barbara Baynton, when republishing her early book, *Bush Studies*, renamed it *Cobbers*, the word that by 1918 or so had become known to everyone. 'Cobbers' will probably persist a long time, side by side with 'mates', both familiar to Australians. In England the corresponding words, each slightly different, are 'chums' and 'pals'. But which of these words is slang, and which is not? The Oxford Dictionary says that 'chum' dates from 1684, but its etymology is dubious. No suggestion of slang. As for 'pal', it is frankly labelled slang, but its etymology is not dubious; it is English gipsy. 'Mate', of course, has its origin in 'one of a pair, especially of birds'; but its chief use is given as '(In working-classes) companion, fellow-worker (also as general form of address)'. This use is commoner, surely, in Australia than abroad. Professor Walter Murdoch, for instance, in a recent book of essays, says he felt instantly at home when, on his landing at Fremantle after travel, someone said to him, 'Got a match, mate?' One more word in this group, 'bloke', is described not as slang, but as a colloquialism. So where exactly are we, and where is our dogmatic magistrate?

At all times it has been difficult to write down the words and phrases of human beings as they naturally use them, and to suggest their rhythm. Most reporters evade the difficulty by standardising language and summarising ideas. A *Hansard* report, set down in malice, verbatim, and without any doctoring from beginning to end, has, indeed, been heard of with some delight, but it ran only for a short stretch. On the other hand, reporters in different periods have been given space and verge enough to produce a facsimile of a witness's garrulity and idiom. Some of the law reports round about 1726 were so full and vivacious, reproducing even the Liverpudlian accent of a north of Englander with a cold in the head, that the poet Gay could use them as a basis for much of the speech in *The Beggar's Opera*. While we cannot expect such vivacious reproductions as a common thing, our sense of humour may protest against the other extreme. In a newspaper report, some years ago, there was an account of shooting in the lively suburb of Fitzroy. It was dark, every house in the lane was suspect: one window shot up: a woman's voice said: 'Whom do you want?' Would any policeman 'want' anybody after such a flawless, unexceptional use of the objective case in an emotional crisis! But do you suppose that this phrase from the child's grammar-book really shot out through the startled night? That final 'm', I dare swear, was put on in the office.

On the whole, it is easier to write safe 'grammar' than to write idiom; that is, to write stiffly and formally instead of racily and with atmosphere. It has often been a usage of the past for writers to divide their characters into gentlemen and workmen. So long as a gentleman, or the author himself, is holding the floor, the speech is uniform buckram. Immediately a member of the lower orders enters, the page is spattered with apostrophes, denoting dropped 'gs', dropped 'hs', irregularities in pronunciation and general disturbance. It is usual in such pages to meet with words like 'pritty', but when one asks how otherwise the recognised gentlemen would speak the word there is no reply. 'Pretty women': how does anyone speaking English today spell those words except as 'pritty wimmen?' Indeed, if all our talk were written down in accurate phonetic script, instead of in the comically false conventions of ordinary spelling, it could easily be shown that while irregularities and clippings and variations are more or less usual among all types of speakers, no one, no one at all, pronounces English as it is spelt.

We may as well give up the attempt, then, to write down just what we say as we say it, except now and then in a phonetic script for students. How do you pronounce 'castle', for instance? Whatever you reply, you will add, 'of course'. Is it 'cassel', or 'cahsel', or something in between? No matter. We shall hardly trouble to indicate it if we put you into a novel. What we may hope to do, though, is to entrap some of your characteristic words, some of the metaphors that come naturally to you, your colloquialism, your rhythm of speech, your slang. Modern novelists of the sincerer sort, including some in Australia, have been aiming at just this kind of idiomatic rendering of their characters' speech and thoughts. Their task is to discover what Beethoven called 'unbuttoned rhythms' for them, and to suggest them in appropriate words.

To return to cobbers. The word is not in the *Oxford Dictionary* yet, at any rate in its concise edition, but it undoubtedly will be. That dictionary is always putting out its tentacles for new words:

the fine octopus, with its splendid appetite, issues S O S lists requesting the whole world's collaboration. On one recent list we were invited, as usual, to give an instance of the use of several Australian words: could anyone quote an instance of the word 'eucalyptian' earlier than 1870? Of the word 'eucalyptus-green' before 1923? Well, can anyone do this? And does the Oxford Dictionary know that one of our poets, H. M. Green, has used the word 'eucalyptive' instead of 'eucalyptian'? Even if it does, the dictionary would not express preference: it would obediently record. The final word in the list is not introduced to please the magistrate. It is 'fair' (– absolute Australian). Do you know that word, in a 'fair scorcher'? Not at all the same word, you see, as in a 'fair bit'. Perhaps the clearest use of 'fair' is in this emotional comment, of which, unfortunately, I cannot give the date: 'Australia is the only country where you can call a dark horse a fair cow, and be understood.' I would suggest that to 'cut out' such slang would be a sin, except to cut it six inches by four (the size of the slips recommended by the dictionary) for preservation between those hospitable covers.

Who then are the custodians of our speech? Is a man who evicts 'cobbers' likely to care for vitality? It was good to see Ben Jonson, after one of his classical tragedies, rendering and preserving with delight the accents and phrases of *Bartholomew Fair*. But that magisterial mind with its perfunctory evictions – what kind of words are likely to find room on its little shelves? Clotted and unexamined phrases, most likely: Pet Aversions with Brazen Defiance, a Recourse to Violence being met by Commendable Restraint, or (perhaps if Cobbers occur) by Vitriolic Abuse. From such fatigued catenations, with their insidious habitual authority, may all good cobbers rush in to save us!

OLD MELBOURNE

There are older cities than Melbourne. Take Troy, for instance, or

Ur: but when you take Troy or Ur you take them not only horizontally, but vertically, till you find Troy under Troy, Ur upon Ur, each new-built city having lost all count of its predecessor on the same site. In Melbourne's soil no such secrets are buried. 'This would be a good place for a village,' remarked John Batman not a hundred years ago, and soon the village grew up. It grew through the decades, and now it is possible, across its simple, single extent, to read the story of those hundred years – a century in stones.

Many of the earliest houses were of wood. Wood can be built to endure even for centuries, but usually it is temporary. We cannot hope to find early Melbourne in its wooden houses. A hint here and there, perhaps, in some squat little house with a bare face like a poley cow: but usually when you go up to such a house you find that, after all, it is not wood, but painted stone or plastered brick. It is, perhaps, a late-comer; but the survivors of very early days were nearly all built of blue stone. Or is it 'bluestone' in one word? The stone is not very blue, after all – blackish, with a hint of slaty grey, and cut with a rough surface so that you never forget its identity with the stones for roadmaking – an unforgettable solidity about it. For bluestone made a cathedral, a jail, impregnable warehouses, and some dwellings which their delighted owners must have felt were more durable than even their own Dundreary whiskers. Bluestone was Dundreary period, but it must have continued to be used during many decades.

Going up and down Melbourne with a child or so – and the right way to see anything is with a child, who not knowing an insurance agency from a stockbroker's office, will look at things as they are – we can sometimes thread the whole city as if on a chain of bluestone. There is – there was – the jail. (It is important to spell it that way instead of 'gaol', which word, through sinister accidents of print or script, awaits, alas, the inevitable 'goal'.) Not far away are certain square bluestone warehouses and factories with longstanding names printed right across their fronts. Keeping away from the rebuilt centre of the city, we come, in the northern end of Queen Street, to a carefully imposing row of bluestone houses with a clock-tower in the centre. It is obvious that the Prince Consort was not long dead when this terrace was composed, as the name shows, in honour of Victoria. Whatever may have happened indoors since then, the exterior is unchanged and – short of violent demolition – unchangeable: one has startling glimpses of crinolines cruising along the pavement or warping in at the doorways. Farther on, through lanes and offings, come huge bluestone warehouses, some of them with stone courtyards entered by tunnelled archways. Fine stamping-grounds for big horses with heavy lorries these are. The darkness of the over-arching stone makes any shaft of sunlight come as a dramatic moment. 'This seems to me,' said a tiny girl gravely, 'very like the cities of Rome.' *Fumum et opes strepitumque Romae?* It was easy to guess what she felt about it.

In some of the wide, windy streets farther on there are big bluestone buildings which seem today as dead and unaccountable as Stonehenge. Flush with the street, their doors are shut, rusted, cobwebbed: their many, four-paned windows seem immovable, too, like eyes not so much closed as blinded. By day these buildings are desolate enough: in twilight they seem fit only for treasons, stratagems, and spoils. It will take centuries to wear them out, but they would seem already to have outlived their functions, except to serve as monuments of a bygone age. What has followed them? Brick, of course, sometimes visible, sometimes covered with stucco, and stone, and today all the variants of steel-and-concrete. What would Melbourne have been if Parliament House, the Public Library, the Law Courts, had all been made of bluestone? Yes, and the Treasury Building, too, and even Government House. As it is, these are all in the whitish-grey that we have come to associate with public works. They might have been worse than they are. An early drawing of Parliament House, for instance, shows it with embellishments, most of which were never actually added. Along the top of the roof, as a kind of upright frill, were urns and urns, and balanced at the corners stood life-size human figures in groups of two and three. 'Portraits of statesmen about to throw themselves down from the roof in despair,' would seem to have been the intention. In the midst rose a tower, variously ornate in the wax-flower style, requiring only a glass case and a position on a marble mantelpiece. This we were spared, probably through a lack of public funds. Yet people say that poverty is not a boon.

Drawings of the same period show the Public Library as it actually was, except that an enormous level lawn seemed to overflow Swanston Street and beyond, giving fine play to promenading crinolines, and to shrubs, sundials, and fountains. There was no hint of the unforetellable domed roof of the new library, rising in the centre today like a vast bulb. Such a dome was perhaps beyond this whitey-grey period. It would certainly have been impossible earlier, in the crouched restriction of bluestone. The whitey-grey expansive period dated roughly with the mutton-chop whisker and the revived bustle. Sometimes its achievements were superb.

Whatever the dates of the Law Courts as a whole may have been, the effect is something permanently beautiful, something that does not merely 'date'. The simple pillars of the dome, casting their clear, slanting shadows across one another, are like some round sundial. Law in its majesty is here made to 'count the sunny hours'. Then beneath the dome is the spreading library, its great window-panes slightly curved in conformity with the general design. That was surely a building made in the unstinting days of Marvellous Melbourne, before booms had burst and set us all puzzling about the zigzag nature of the march of progress. Just beside the Law Courts one comes on something that at once reveals their distance from us. It is a single-storied, practical, very modern building, in red brick simply finished with stone, its entrances marked with little trees in tubs. It is labelled, to the astonishment of a child versed in fabulous and magnificent titles, nothing less than 'The High Court of Australia'. Much history lies in that. You have the State Courts made striking with their high, symbolic dome, while the Federal Courts operate in a *pied-à-terre* adequate but modest. Is our lapse from the grand manner a new modesty, or mere disillusionment?

The mind returns to Government House, dated, mannered, visible in its park, and symbolic of the eighties or so. Like other great houses appearing in the suburbs at the same period, it had an air, a tower, a late-Victorian challenge. Consider the haughty though possibly attractive lady standing with averted face in the gilded drawing-room of Orchardson's picture, *The First Cloud*: it is conveniently at hand in the National Gallery. Keeping her in mind, look again at the tower of Government House or its contemporaries in Hawthorn and Toorak. Is the connection not clear? High-necked, soaring, self-confident, both the lady and the houses depend, for the greater part of their dated dignity, upon the existence of something like a bustle.

The force of period could no farther go. As for the really modern buildings in Melbourne, with the ferro-concrete masses and the lace-work tops, these are growing too fast to be recorded by anyone whose eyes are on the past. The old bluestone buildings may be supposed to utter the remark written in golden letters on one of the newest towers, 'Apa?' Apa means, in Malayan, simply 'What?'

ON SUBURBIA

If people may be grouped according to their likes and dislikes, a good touchstone is that of suburbia. Some people really like suburbia. They cannot conceive of a life without it; they would never live in a city, and they dread the country. Suburbia is to them the only natural place for a home. All that matters, for them, is to choose a suburb with every good point and none of the bad ones. No need to mention that such a place cannot exist! Their ideal suburb must be near town and near the country; full of fresh gardens, yet supplied with good shops and the right schools; devoid of loud-speakers – except one's own – and with streets that are remarkably quiet, yet perfect for cars. These are only a few of the minimum requirements, but they are hopefully propounded by people who are determined, whether these demands are satisfied or not, to spend their lives somewhere in the suburbs. Where else, they ask, would anyone live? In the city, like an office mouse? Or in the country, like fat or lean kine?

Their opponents, or opposites, are those who resent the sheer existence of suburbs. They point to compactly planned cities, like the modern Stockholm, with fields beginning just outside the city streets. They praise Munich, where it is – or was – usual to walk home at night after the theatre or concert. They have probably grown up with the not unnatural notion that a suburb, being something under-urban, is by nature inferior to what is urban, a suburb being a sub-city, something left over, negligible, deplorable. In their minds the syllable *sub* means *below*, not merely in the matter of position but in essential quality of living. Their conviction is today borne out by sinister facts, but this is just an instance of 'nature creeping up' to match someone's wayward idea.

It was in a really old German town, that of Marburg, in Hesse, that I first really grasped the original meaning of suburb as something on the flats below the city. There was the city itself, centuries old, wound tightly round and round its hill, with the castle as culmination; and below it, stretching in fairly modern streets along by the river, was the suburb, containing chiefly pensions for the students attending its famous university. The old town, you felt, was a fortress. Like ants before rain, people from outlying districts would climb up into it when war or danger threatened. All the precious things were kept in the castle: all the memorials of St Elizabeth of Hungary, who had sojourned in the place. It was definitely the core of the city's life.

There must be countless other European cities like Marburg, in which the compact, original city is still visible, though its function as fortress is long obsolete, and its ducal castle has – since 1866 or some other sinister date – somewhat the status of a de-licensed hotel. The inevitable modern suburb in such circumstances was not horrible: its streets were graceful enough, planted with rows of trees whose avenues melted out soon into the unfenced patchwork fields of the villages round about. This is not to say that Marburg will always be so beautiful. Multiply the university students by three, for instance, and it may become overcrowded without new arrangement or design. A European town, though, is relatively static. Salamanca, for instance, can today have a population of only thirty thousand and still be famous. Such towns are not so likely as ours to be disturbed by the discovery of a silver-lead field, or abandoned because mines or industries have been closed in despair. No: one can perhaps still believe in the existence of Marburg as a quiet, thoughtful little city. Indeed, someone showed me lately an advertisement of a Marburg University holiday-course for students of all nations, which makes it seem likely that those suburban streets planted with roundish laburnums and tall lindens will still have room for a few of us without needing to board us far out among the farming villages in the neighbourhood.

For that is what some cities do; they spread outward until you have not only the core, the city itself, and not only the immediately surrounding suburb, but outlying hamlets also included in the greater-city scheme. Such is the case of Berlin, that modern city. A letter from a suburb called Wilmersdorf reminds me that Berlin is surrounded by suburbs ending in 'dorf' (thorp or village). The large, flat city has stretched its tentacles like a land-crab, and has included innocent villages that were miles away, linking them up with modern garden suburbs made on purpose. You can soon see the difference between the modern-made suburb and the suburb that began originally as a village. There was Zehlendorf, for instance. At first you noticed its modern groups of well-planned flats, its new town hall, and its large, brick churches; but still there was something else. That ornamental sheet of water near the town hall; that neat, oldish chapel near the gate of the cemetery: surely they meant something! It seemed clear enough; were they anything other than the original village pond and the village church? One was confronted then, with the symbolism of Carlyle's modest village, Entepfuhl, Duckpond, which no amount of later town-planning could wholly obliterate.

Zehlendorf was linked by train and road with the suburbs that Berlin has deliberately made for itself, yet it will never be quite like the others; it will always be one of the villages lying on the road between Berlin and Potsdam.

A suburb in Paris can be the most self-contained little area. One hears a great deal of over-centralisation in France, but, really, if remote provincial towns were half as inward-looking as, say, Bourg-la-Reine, which is probably no farther from the city than Camberwell is from Melbourne, Paris would not be regarded as a menace. (Has any Frenchman felt the need to name Paris, as Cobbett named the London of his day, simply 'The Wen'?) The little suburb, with its narrow, white, stony street and small, unambitious shops, seemed, in those pre-war days, to be full of old homes, having their paved courtyards in front and their flower and fruit gardens at the back, the whole kept very private by high stone and stucco walls. There were avenues of limes in little side-roads; there were brooks in a small way; there was even 'scenery'. But I cannot answer for Parisian suburbs as a whole. Bourg-la-Reine may have been an oasis of mellow age in a modern world. It hardly fits into the French world of Sacha Guitry's more ebullient plays, where the young heroes make their spectacular fortunes by using the exhaust gas of motor-cars.

Suburbia in Australia is a variegated monster presenting you now with brick-bats, now with bouquets. His motives on the whole are sinister. He lures people out and out, away from the centre, without assuring them of any positive advantages such as might accrue to little communities with parks, theatres, and concert-halls of their own. He does not so much as guarantee greenness and a view. In the phrase of a character in one of Furnley Maurice's plays, 'the bush has moved fifteen miles further out'; so one gains little by spending hours travelling to and from town every day. There are exceptions; parts of outer suburbs with haunting glimpses of far hills, places built near Sydney's craggy gorges, or on river-side slopes near Brisbane or Perth.

Yet these rare and beautiful notes in the cacophony of suburbia may all be happy accidents. One would like to ascribe to accident their opposites – a frightful majority of suburban areas that shall here be nameless. If we are to believe that modern suburbia, taken as a whole, expresses the modern mind, what, we ask with trembling, can the nature of that mind be?

RUSKIN TODAY

The trouble with Ruskin was that he was usually so beautifully published. You saw his complete works, perhaps in wine-coloured morocco, perhaps in scarlet kid, on drawing-room bookshelves: there they sat and sat like wallflowers at a dance. On the fly-leaves the owner's name was written. It was often feminine, a complete Ruskin having been given her when she was twenty-one, and had begun to 'take up' painting. Perhaps the owner had read, say, one volume out of thirty-six. Even that volume she had used only in some small literary society, working over it chapter by chapter, writing little papers on it and listening to others. Ever afterwards that one volume sits on the shelf looking like a white blackbird. In contrast with all its fellows, it has a worn, weathered, yet active look: the rest are sleeping partners. It is some years, though, since I saw a complete Ruskin on anyone's shelf. Shelves are fewer, homes less settled, complete sets of all writers are becoming unwelcome, even to confirmed readers.

Ruskin's complete editions have not merely gone the way of well-thumbed editions of Dickens and Scott. They have been unthumbed. Or, if we omit novelists, I would suggest that Ruskin has been more heartily forgotten than Carlyle. Why is this? And what, on the other hand, were the few volumes of Ruskin that did succeed in getting nobly worn by a little use?

The best known and most read of Ruskin's books has unfortunately been *Sesame and Lilies*, remembered by its exhortations to young women to make the most of their lives for the common good. I say unfortunately, because it is a book with passages that innocently lay themselves open to derision, and it is not only the post-war young woman that has protested. Ruskin's suggestion that woman's real task is to buckle on her knight's armour and send him forth to 'do things', while she stays at home, feeding the poor and improving her mind by reading books like Ruskin's, is in tone rather too near the humiliated poet's advice to the haughty, trivial Lady Clara Vere de Vere:

> Go teach the orphan boy to read,
> Go teach the orphan girl to sew.

Women, in an England that had not imagined the War or even the Suffragette Movement, were heard to demur as they struggled for a little wider freedom. What, they asked, is a woman to do if she has no knight? And is the problem of education to be solved by a little unselfishness and voluntary homespun? They felt that Ruskin's solution of economic and private problems was a mere sweetish fairy-tale. Even when attracted by his call to an archaic simplicity of living, they resented his ignoring of their very real difficulties in a swiftly changing world. These changes, he declared, were for the worse: let them be ignored! They refused to be ignored. Ruskin's condemnations of what he believed to be a smear of mechanisation over modern life were savagely and often wittily documented, but what had he to offer a bewildered girl in the seventies?

The story of Ruskin's conflict with the forces known as progress, and of his more or less harmonious association with workers and visionaries like William Morris, is a very long one. It can best be found, if we are to depend on that long row of books in the drawing-room, from the four volumes called *Fors Clavigera*. It was like Ruskin to give a heavy Latin title of uncertain symbolic interpretation to a series of chapters designed as open letters to working men. Yet it must be said that there is a great deal of common sense and a kind of robust charm in *Fors Clavigera* absent from much of Ruskin's other work. Ruskin's life, purposeful and active, made him actually better at ease with men who were overworked than with those who were underworked. In these letters, with their special circumstances of publication and subscription, he extends himself, when he feels it appropriate, in the direction of healthy invective. His attacks on the tyrannies of vested interests are comparable, in their frank scorn, with those of Cobbett in his *Rural Rides*, some decades earlier. Where is such invective today? Some say that the law of libel, replacing the right of duelling, has made public truth impossible: but Ruskin did not regard himself as a duellist, merely as a 'plain blunt man that love my friend'.

And who was his friend? All his powers are exerted to show that he understands the working man's point of view, even to the extent of sneering, for a moment, at his own enthusiasm and preoccupations. He describes himself, for instance, as going through some quiet north-country town with a group of ladies to whom he had been expounding the beauties of a neighbouring abbey. Suddenly they find themselves jostled by a crowd of dusty working men: the charm is broken: they feel that such men could never appreciate the beauty of what they have been seeing. Ruskin suddenly turns round and looks at himself and his companions, asking by what right they spend their tranquil days 'admiring abbeys' while others have no leisure or energy for such an occupation.

Admiring abbeys! He makes it sound almost vicious. His mood is in tune with a drawing somewhere in the *Fors* volumes, the one caricature of his that I can at all remember. What he has drawn is a mid-Victorian miss, all sugar and spice, but with no grace nor power, a 'niminy piminy chit'. It is as if he had heard people describing the type of young lady he seemed to outline in *Sesame and Lilies* and had wanted to show that he had been entirely misunderstood. What Ruskin wanted a girl to be was something that has never yet appeared on earth – a combination of all the incompatible qualities; and yet – and yet – most of the vital and charming people we know are precisely a combination of impossible and opposite qualities. If Ruskin wishes a girl to be as wise as Socrates, and yet 'to keep that hid', to be as brave as Flora Macdonald and patient as Griselda – perhaps we shall meet his Blessed Damozel some day, after all. Christina Rossetti, with her other-worldly angelic air, going on errands of mercy in hateful, thick boots and coming home to write *Goblin Market* might do: but no, he bitterly deplored the unorthodox forms of *Goblin Market*. I think, perhaps, he had a glimpse of his ideal in Kate Greenaway, whose drawings he loved as he trusted herself. It is good to remember, when faced with his lonely tragedy, that she could invite him to come to her in some very shy, gentle verses ending:

> And be not long in coming, for to her
> You – song and flowers and Heaven's all things are.

We used to be told to read Ruskin for his exquisite English: then we were told not to. Which advice was right? It all depends on what you want from the English you read. If you can stand purple patches, if you enjoy getting half-drunk on a description of a sunset or a mountain glade, then Ruskin, especially in the volumes of *Modern Painters* will give you what you want. If, however, you feel that these rhapsodies are the affair not of a prose-writer and critic, but of a poet, and that the poet should write in recognised poetical form, then Ruskin will be hidden behind Swift and Defoe on your shelf, and will stay there. Sometimes, indeed, Ruskin commits one of the worst literary crimes of all – he introduces a line or more of verse inadvertently into his prose. Demosthenes would hound him out, Cicero would call on the Roman gods for help, to see a phrase like this, in which Ruskin is describing the famous hostile shores of the Black Sea: 'Every sob of wreck-fed breaker round these Pontic precipices.' That is magnificent, if you like, but it is not prose. Ruskin himself would probably admit that it was falsely ornate – yet I think he would hug it to his heart, recognising in it the efflorescence of a youthful passion for verbal beauty.

For that was Ruskin's persistent quality – youthfulness. Hence came his purple patches, good or bad; hence his indignant humanitarianism and his frank hostility toward the world cynical or commercial-minded adults had made. Hence also his tireless energy in research and in exposition of the beautiful, causing a modern Frenchman like Marcel Proust to applaud and translate his commentary on Amiens Cathedral. Ruskin's books (in spite of the wine-coloured morocco) are mines of precious metals, immensely varied and unusual. He felt his responsibility as a miner in the depths of his own experiences, somewhat as Proust did when his life was closing; but with this difference, that Ruskin was primarily a reformer and a man of action, while Proust as a devout artist rejected every call to propaganda as a temptation of the devil. Ruskin's aesthetic expositions of Giotto's symbolism or Turner's landscapes usually have a string to them, an explicit moral which we can bravely ignore. In his perennial youthfulness, the qualities that so recently had significance for Proust remain an inspiration today. He need no longer be kept, periodically dusted but unopened, on drawing-room shelves, those chill oubliettes: he can be taken out, opened, aired and actually read.

Home and Abroad

EDITOR'S NOTE

Notes kept by field naturalists, as well as diaries of observation, natural history and travel books form an important strand in Australian writing. Equally important is the slim volume of local history that traces the growth and development of a particular place or area. Some of Nettie Palmer's freelance journalism consisted of paragraphs of nature notes submitted to the *Bulletin* and the *Australian Woman's Mirror*. Two of her more extended pieces in this vein were included in the previous section, The Literary Essayist. These pieces, 'The Right to Orioles' and 'The Song of Birds' appeared in *Talking it Over*. Her powers of observation may be seen at their most attractive in the Green Island section of *Fourteen Years* and in some of her letters.

In 1934, Nettie Palmer published the following articles on the growth of an area in the Melbourne *Argus* under the general title *The Meaning of the Dandenongs:* 'Breaking the Hills', 19 May; 'In the Fifties', 26 May; 'A Little Settlement', 2 June; 'The Monbulk District', 9 June, and 'Landscape and Labour', 16 June. They formed the basis of *The Dandenongs*, a book published by the National Press, Melbourne, 1952 in a limited edition, with a small second impression. The volume was illustrated with linocuts by Ronald G. Edwards.

Spanish Days consists of three articles based on Nettie Palmer's short stay in Spain in 1936. 'In the Sun' was published in the *Argus*, 8 August; 'Rain' in the *Argus*, 13 August; and 'Civil War' in the *Sydney Morning Herald*, 14 August. These articles form an important supplement to the Barcelona section of *Fourteen Years*.

'Life on a Coral Island' appeared in *The Listener* (London) on 5 February 1936 and refers to the Palmers' life on Green Island.

The Dandenongs

PREFACE

When I was a child the remote wavy blue wall of the Dandenongs used to fascinate me, looking eastward from a Melbourne suburb over the intervening stretch of flat country that was green in winter, tawny-grey in summer. It was far enough away to contain all the inhabitants of that other world, more vivid than the one I knew, of which picture books were the reflection. Dragons and leprechauns? Well, perhaps; but chiefly the more kindly and elvish creatures; only when dark storm-clouds hung over the wall could there be any thought of dragons.

Later, when I had gone to live there, the idea of the Dandenongs being a separate world – a green oasis cut off the great burning spaces of the continent – still persisted, a legacy of childhood, or maybe the need of a young mother to build up a secure imaginative retreat from the war then raging, a war that seemed oppressively near in London and during the long ship-journey home with dowsed lights. Here was a four-square little cottage, well away from main road and railway, twenty hilly acres, some in forest and some in grass, a landscape almost as idyllic as that of Brittany or southern England. With its intimate fern-gullies, grassed hillsides and patches of forest, it was country to love and explore. You could easily imagine yourself taking root there, developing a local patriotism, bringing up children to know its history and become attached to its soil.

The cottage itself, for all its sketchy structure, had an atmosphere. Partly through the Tennysonian name of 'Rose Charman's Cottage', by which it was locally known, partly through memories of Louis and Hilda Esson, who had made it their home for some years just before us. Afterwards, when we were away for a while, it was bought by Katharine Prichard, who finished her *Black Opal* there. She proved a generous landlord, holding on to the twenty acres for our benefit when it would have been more profitable to sell to the entrepreneurs, who, under the stimulus of a post-war boom, were buying the untilled green hillsides and cutting them up for building allotments.

And so for some quiet years the place became our home, and there arose an impulse to probe into the past of this little area of hilly country, learn why our neighbours (or their fathers) had come there in the beginning, and how they had established their footing. They were mainly orchardists, or tradesmen like the two busy blacksmiths, or workers in the great nursery that took up the whole of one hillside; but the place held enough eccentrics to give it variety – the old prospector camped among the tree-ferns and holding on to his miner's right with passionate pride, the broken-down 'Oxford' man, and the ancient hatter whom the schoolchildren believed to be Dan Kelly.

There were few holidaymakers at the time; very little accommodation existed for them; but visitors from town, mostly writers, came to us at the weekend, with their gifts of wine and fruit and their news of what was happening down below. Poetry was in the air then, and a good many of the visitors were poets: one remembers Furnley Maurice, Frederick Macartney, Henry Tate, R. H. Long, P. I. O'Leary, Dora Wilcox, and Gerald Byrne. The bathroom door, a tablet of clean white pine at the end of the veranda, tempted them to record their impromptu verses in pencil – verses that seemed pointed and enduring at the time but that have faded from the mind now, except for one fragment, in his characteristic free verse, by Frederick Macartney.

To make a poem out fire
was my desire,
to have the lightning shine
in every line;
but lacking flint and wanting steel
I feel
that it is good
to make a poem out of wood.

But the poet of the hills was R. H. Long. This gentle, witty, highly original character knew them from one end to the other, and there was hardly a cleared space near any of the running creeks that he had not camped in at one time or another. A carpenter by trade, he would work for a while to secure enough for his simple needs and then make for freedom with his light, skilfully-built swag – a swag that contained all he needed for sleeping out, its ballast being a copy of perhaps *Walden*, *Lavengro*, or *Moby Dick*. To many people living in the Dandenongs this loveable recluse (half-satirist, half-saint) was a familiar figure. How often at the close of day have I heard the excited crescendo of childish voices as he came across the paddock:

'It's not a swaggie. It's not. . .It's Dick – Dick Long!'

He took them for long rambles. He brought gifts he had made – kites that would really fly, pairs of stilts to match each child, wooden gymnasts on wires. And there was the day he appeared with the most wonderful gift of all – a donkey that had come from some circus or other, and that could be held on very long loan. For a year or so, Mitty proved a continual delight, especially on picnic journeys, though one had to hide her carefully in the bushes beside the road when a farmer's cart appeared. Her long ears and mousey coat could fill the sleepiest horse with sudden incredulity and terror.

Satirical, Long's cheerfully-whittled rhymes often were, for he enjoyed poking fun at the conventions and hypocrisies of the world around, but the poet in him was really shown by the way he could take the names of places he loved – names as raw as Mooroolbark or Begley's Bridge – and steep them in haunted water. He had a strong local sense; indeed, it was intense enough to amount to a passion. For him every crest of the hills, every spring, every settled clearing, had a special character.

And so it is his name that comes to my mind when I think about the Dandenongs. We are always being told that we don't know our country well enough, and this usually means that we have not let our minds wander over the endless spaces enclosed by its outline. But there are other points of view. There is a good deal to be said for letting the mind rest in one spot, small enough to hold the affections and, perhaps, to be understood.

1 BREAKING THE HILLS

There is a phrase of Kipling's about penetrating the curtain that hides the past, especially the past of hill-country. Only by complying with certain conditions could you make a successful journey of discovery. It had to be a midsummer morning and you had to meet Puck and go barefoot in the dew; other compulsions just as arbitrary were laid upon you. Then, if you were the right sort of person, you might count on 'breaking the hills'.

That is, you might see and feel the hills as they used to be. On Pook's Hill you might meet and talk with such ancientries as Wayland Smith, or a Roman soldier, or Queen Elizabeth. You might, in fact, hear the story of that part of England from the lips of the people who had shaped it, or at least given it its legend.

What, then, about breaking our own hills, the Dandenongs, and visiting their past? It is not a distant past, at least not in the European sense; only a little more than a century lies between us and that period when they were an unknown part of the great Dutigalla estate which stretched away into the infinite from Batman's village. Yet travelling back to our beginnings is not easy, for there is no magic formula. All we can do is to peer through certain mists and broken lights, reporting whatever seems at all clear, in the hope that the fragmentary glimpse may make a picture. There are no Pucks or Roman soldiers to listen to; only a few old men whose human memories have become dimmed by time and who, even so, have to rely mainly on what has been told them by their fathers.

At first sight it would seem that the Dandenongs were well known today as never before. They have been opened up in many directions, made accessible by excellent roads and visible by clearings; their most tangled gullies have been threaded by tourist tracks.

'It's a fine afternoon; why not come for a run?' says the Melbourne host to his guest. 'I'll show you the Dandenongs; it'll only take a couple of hours.'

And off they spin to that low blue wall in the east. Yet to run through the hills in this way is not to learn what they are all about or even to get a flickering sense of their history. There are few memorials there to call up the past, hardly a landmark to show the slow stages by which they have been won.

This range that lies like a banked cumulus cloud across Melbourne's eastern sky has a special character that is likely to be blotted out by the city's increasing sprawl. From end to end it is already looped to the metropolis by a bitumen road. The circuit from town, out and back, is a small matter, and thousands of people make it. What is more significant, the foothills are beginning to take on the aspect of outlying suburbs. A novel by John Morrison, *The Creeping City*, shows how the productive little holdings are being gradually absorbed.

Indeed, in some ways, the Dandenongs have been adopted as a place where Nature can be easily improved to meet suburban taste. Those houses lining the road in the high places have a smugness about them, an air of imposing their own pattern of life upon the hills. Many of them make no effort to fit in with their natural background; each seems determined to assert its difference from the others, in style and colouring, as well as its detachment from the native growths around.

'Look at me,' it seems to be saying. 'I have a scenic window at the back opening out over wide expanses, yet I can boast of every modern gadget, and these orderly beds of annuals in front prove that my owner is thoroughly urban and civilised.'

The road, too, with its signboard advertisements for oil and paint, has something assertive and triumphant about it. Every car driver could run off the names of stopping-places and significant points, or guarantee to stop at a spot where the lyrebird can be heard 'thieving the ballads from his neighbours' throats', as Dick

Long put it. And yet it remains an attractive, even a quiet road except on holidays. The rise from the plain beginning at Ferntree Gully passes through Tremont, up through Ferny Creek, Sherbrooke, Sassafras, Olinda, on to Mount Dandenong, Kalorama, and so downwinding again to Montrose, Kilsyth, Croydon, on the plain for home.

The car driver could almost drive blindfold to the spots on the road with the most striking south-westerly views to the two bays – broad Port Phillip, with the intended You Yangs showing across it, or little Westernport with its two islands. He can pause at the right corners, too, for those views toward the impressive ranges to the east, above Warburton and Healesville. He will know the ways of the road itself, and how a car can wind through Mount Dandenong and Kalorama without the use of power, the very gradual downslope being so definite.

Being hills linked with further great inland ranges, the Dandenongs can sometimes have their slight brief share of snow, its strange weight splitting a leafy loquat tree so that you wake with the sound rather than with any sight. The car driver will know that if the snow does come it will be thickest on Olinda, and this not only because of height, but through some accident of its situation, away from winds. He will be able to answer most of the questions a casual visitor would ask as he winds down his prescribed route, and so home; but in the very ease and swiftness of his going he will himself have been prevented from asking the questions that might have broken the hills for him.

How long is it since a settlement was made on these hills? What kind of people came here, and with what hopes? Are there any records of those early days of pioneering?

There are, it must be said, very few written records. It is only by burrowing into people's memories, exploring old sites, sifting various kinds of rubble, that some hint of the beginnings may be found.

As for the roads, it is the old dim, abandoned tracks that count. They are mainly overgrown now, but here and there on stony cliff-faces you can trace the path of the early invaders who came pushing up from the plains below, threading the forest of the hillsides. They were invaders, not settlers, these first explorers, and it was the tall mountain ash that attracted them, for timber was poor on the flat country, and little could be found fit for building. The white gleaming boles of the mountain-ash could be seen from miles away.

Is it true that they caught the eye of Flinders – Matthews Flinders, RN – when, in 1802, he was seeking a mast for his little ship? No; unfortunately it is only a legend. Flinders did not set foot in the Dandenongs; his furthest point away from this coast was seven or eight miles north from Arthur's Seat. But two or three years after Melbourne was settled, a few people with their flocks and herds began to straggle out over the park-like plains to the north and east, and among those were the first timber-seekers to explore the Dandenongs.

2 DANDENONG

Today when you mean to address a letter to someone at Mt Dandenong and forget to write 'Mount', it goes to a thriving market-town, the Gateway of Gippsland, away on the plains toward the sea, and you wonder why so many places are called by the same name. There is a London in Canada, and one I believe, in England. There may be others; it sometimes seems as if the power of inventing names had become exhausted.

In the matter of the two Dandenongs, though, there is no coincidence; it is a connection. In the eighteen-thirties the land around the Dandenong creek, beginning in the range and winding through the plain, was all one – all Dandenong. There was a little trouble about the spelling of the name at first. Captain Lonsdale (who, in 1838, took over the land from an even earlier settler and built a hut where the market-town now stands), called it Dan-y-nong: a few years later a surveyor wrote it down as Tangenong, both versions, probably, being attempts to put down the difficult

Aboriginal sounds in an English notation. But the name soon wore itself smooth.

Already, with the town only three or four years old – it was merely a muddy hamlet, with a dozen or more weatherboard houses and turf hovels – a few settlers were percolating out to the great park-like plains at the foot of the hills and finding pasture for their cattle. The first man to cross the Dandenong creek from Melbourne was John Highett, who seems to have gone on a foraging expedition over the flat country with a few head of stock, but John Hawdon, two years later, was actually the first man to settle there. He did not stay long. Almost immediately he sold his cattle to Captain Lonsdale and departed; and the hut built by Lonsdale for his overseer was the nucleus for the present township of Dandenong.

The same year another settler appeared – the Rev. James Clow, a clergyman from India – and he took up a station a little further on. Clow was an extraordinary man, restless, public-spirited, with some of the qualities of his fellow countryman and co-religionist, John Dunmore Lang. The son of a poor family in Scotland, he had held the sympathies of his relatives because of a deformed arm; they combined to give him an education and he was sent out to India as chaplain in the employment of the East India Company. There he married a wife who brought him a little money and, his health being uncertain, he sought a more congenial climate.

Arriving in Melbourne in 1837, Clow soon began to gather a congregation of Presbyterians together. The difficulty was to find a place of worship. There was only one church, an Anglican one, and some sharp bargaining was necessary before he could secure the use of it on Sunday afternoons from two till four. He was relieved in a month's time by the Rev. James Forbes, and within a year of landing in the new country had become a pastoralist and the holder of some potentially-rich allotments in the city.

Soon the land at the base of the hills was taken up with holdings, and the pioneers did not all come from the port of Melbourne. In 1838, for instance, the Ryrie brothers – William,

Donald and James – overlanded from the Monaro district of New South Wales, bringing with them their cattle and household belongings – an enterprising trek that won the admiration of Rolf Boldrewood. They settled at Yering, and a significant part of their baggage was a number of vine-cuttings that were to lay the base of a future wine industry.

For a while living on these tree-studded plains was difficult. There was timber all around, but little suitable for building yards and houses. When Batman's village was first settled it was decided to import all building timber, ready cut, from Tasmania, and this was done; some even came from England; but transport was easier by sea than by the unmade roads. The straggling little station homes had to be as self-contained as possible. An essential part of the plant was a small mill, something like an old-fashioned chaffcutter, and a patch of land was turned up round the homestead for grain. The crop was cut with a sickle, threshed with a flail, and the wheat ground down and sieved off till fine enough for bread-making. Often grain standing unreaped one morning was eaten as damper next day.

But rough roads were gradually made and means of transport established. Over the grassy plains station-drays plodded down to Melbourne for stores; splitters pushed up into the hills for fence-posts and railings. Roadside shanties began to appear, as Strzelecki noticed when he came back from his first exploring journey into Gippsland – shanties with queer names, like 'No Good Damper' and 'Camp Here Johnny'.

Later, there were the beginnings of agriculture, and curiously enough the grape was the pioneer. When the Ryrie brothers brought their cuttings down from Monaro, it was probably with the idea that a small vineyard would be a pleasant adjunct to a station home. They planted out an acre of grapes, and an old Swiss, Dardel, put them in the way of making their own wine and keeping their own cellar.

Even when the Ryries' property was purchased, in 1850, by Paul de Castella, another Swiss, it was with no thought of viticulture. Castella came from a part of Switzerland where vines were not grown; he meant to carry on Yering as a cattle station. But one evening when he was entertaining some friends from a French ship, the supply of imported wine ran out and there was great consternation till a supply of the local product was unearthed in the cellar and brought to the table in a wash-jug. It was sampled, pronounced by one of the French guests to be 'better than Pommard', and the idea of experimenting with viticulture was put into the new owner's head.

Castella went about the business in a thorough, Swiss way. In 1854, he imported a consignment of vinecuttings from Chateau Lafitte in France, and a good many struck. It was found that a red wine like Burgundy and a white like Sauterne could be produced, and the prospects for the new industry seemed favourable. Soon three great vineyards were flourishing near Yering – one owned by Paul de Castella, another by his brother Hubert, the third by Baron Guillaume de Pury. None of these men was a trained vine-dresser, but they found experienced Swiss immigrants to help them, and by the end of the sixties there were 367 acres of the country north of Lilydale under vines. A small brick village, called Little Neuchatel, had been built for the Swiss experts; the country beneath the hills had taken on a settled look.

But the hills above – the Dandenongs proper – remained as yet virtually untouched. There was an outlying cattle run or two, a camp of prospectors, and a few huts occupied by casual timber-splitters. To trace the settlement it is necessary to go back a little and look at the Dandenongs through the eyes of the first pastoralists who were chiefly interested in what they could provide in the way of timber for their building and openings for their cattle.

3 BACK IN THE FIFTIES

The Rev. James Clow called his cattle run after the mountain at the head of the creek on which it was placed, Mount Corhanwarrabul. This is still one name on the maps for Mount Observatory, or its twin sister-peak, Burke's or Barnes's Lookout. Corhanwarrabul is written in various ways by different recorders, but it is easier to say than appears at first sight and stands out as one of the blacks' names that might well be remembered and preserved; indeed it has been in the title of one of Henry Tate's vivid nocturnes.

Looking up from Melbourne toward the Dandenongs, it is those two softly-curved mounds that strike the eye. To the north of them, and appearing far lower, is the gap or razorback of Kalorama, once known as Mount Dandenong North. To the south there is the deep inward sweep of the gorge below Olinda and Sassafras; farther south again the forward ridge of Sherbrooke, Ferny Creek and Ferntree Gully.

During the forties and fifties, a few pastoralists pressed tentatively into the timbered country. Further in from the holding at Corhanwarrabul, some miles to the east, there was created a sheep station called Monbolloc; small and scrubby, wrote Mr Clow in 1853; it had passed through many hands since its foundation. Then on the south-east of Monbolloc there was a sketchy cattle station, Will-Will-Rook, held for a long time by a family named Varcoe.

All these early names – Corhanwarrabul, Will-Will-Rook, Monbolloc – were Aboriginal, and this was natural, since the settlers were constantly in touch with the blacks. Members of the two tribes came about the Dandenongs – the Yarra Yarras from the north and the Westernports from the south – and apparently they were friendly people. Joseph Furphy, who was born on Ryrie's cattle run at the foot of the range, and must have seen much of them in his youth, speaks of their gentleness and generosity; and one of his most moving stories traces the development of a friendship between a black youth and a white that ended in a tragic way.

But there was no future for these wandering people in a country that was being quickly settled. The best that could be hoped was that they should be spared the cruelties that were inflicted on them in wilder parts and that an atmosphere of goodwill should be created toward those that remained. This depended on the growth among the settlers of some understanding of their character and culture. About 1850, Mr Thomas, Assistant Protector of Aborigines, established a station for them at Narre Warren, and inquired closely into the tribal customs, ideas, and languages of those still living in the old ways.

Thomas seems to have been a kindly, imaginative man and, in addition to his humanist activities, did something toward standardising the Aboriginal words and names. In the early days every sort of contradictory spelling is to be found, and it is sometimes difficult to be grateful to the privileged pioneers who made their separate researches and reports, but never seem to have compared notes. It was natural enough to write Monbolloc sometimes as Monbulk and both forms were clear, but how could two such different spellings as *ngare* and *yarra* be given for the word meaning hair? The divergence was so great that they ceased to be associated. *Yarra* (flowing) was ascribed to the river and the tribe near it. *Ngare* – beginning, of course, with the sound in singer, not in finger – was taken to be used for the hair of the head (again flowing), or eyebrow; and so for the she-oak, the casuarina, that hair-tree.

As for the place, Monbolloc or Monbulk, I have heard (and I think the statement came from Mrs Aeneas Gunn, who has delved into the history of the place) that the place meant something like sanctuary, or meeting-place of the tribes. From Monbulk's position at the core of the Dandenongs it might well be a good place for seasonal assemblies. There were such places in the Blackall Ranges of Queensland, where the different tribes met for the annual feast on bunya-nuts; corroborees were exchanged, competitions held, and all feuds, for the time being, forgotten.

Then, as now, there were at least two ways of regarding the blacks, even in friendliness, and these ways opposed and incompatible. Either you were anthropological in bent, valuing each small detail of tribal custom and lore, desiring to alter nothing but rather to preserve every vestige of a strange pattern of culture; or else you were missionary in outlook, intent on changing the Aboriginal's ideas and way of life, perhaps absorbing him into the white mass. But in those days the anthropologists were few and the blacks of the Dandenongs neither numerous nor tenacious of their tribal habits. They seemed to disappear like mist.

Thomas, an eager and exact observer, could look at them with sympathetic eyes, and his slight but tentative account of the corroboreeing at Monbulk has hardly been bettered:

> Dances: They have various kinds, day and night. Although a stranger, after seeing one, may think the whole alike and merely a monotony of sounds and motion, such is not the case: the song and words are to the motion of the body like our country dances and reels. One ignorant of dancing would look upon the movements as monotonous; there is as much sense in one as in the other. If the blacks' orchestra is inferior, their time and motion are better.

Thomas also has some interesting notes on the bear (koala) which, being sacred, was not to be skinned, and this in a district where skins were necessary for warmth and where 'possum skins were the stable form of dowry.

> The bear (he writes) is a privileged animal, and is often consulted in very great undertakings. I was out with a celebrated Westernport black, tracking five other blacks. The tracks had been lost for some days at a part of the country where we expected they must pass. We ran down a creek; after going some miles, a bear made a noise as we passed. The black stopped and a parley commenced. I stood gazing alternately at the black and the bear. At length my black came to me and said: 'The big one stupid: bear tell me you no go that way.' We immediately crossed the creek and took a different way. Strange as it may appear, we had not altered our course above a mile and a half before we came upon the tracks and never lost them after.

What are we to gather from this rather naive account? That Mr Thomas was over-eager in his curiosity about the mysteries of an ancient people, and that some of the shrewdest of them had begun to play on his curiosity? Perhaps so. Yet there seems no doubt that the bear was not only protected, but revered, and it is easy to sympathise with a race that could take to its heart an animal that, in its comic innocence and grotesque decorative quality, is such a choice gift to humankind.

It was the blacks, then, who chiefly peopled the lyre-bird gullies and forested hillsides of the Dandenongs in the fifties. Except for the two or three small cattle runs on the western face there was no trace of settlement. Those were the days when gold was being mined at Ballarat and Bendigo, and floods of eager adventurers were pouring into Port Phillip. The early pastoral age was coming to a close; the quiet port of Melbourne had taken on a new face; men occupied on stations or in the various trades were joining the new immigrants in a rush to the fields. Soon the alluvial gold would have petered out and there would be disappointed miners wandering over the country, prospecting every flat and creek, but for the time being all interest was in the known places.

The Dandenongs, in spite of their nearness to the city, remained comparatively unexplored. Looking back, it is not easy to describe them except with a list of negatives. The tangled fern-gullies were not touched, save perhaps by a side-spurt of Black Thursday's holocaust. The only tracks were a few bridle-paths and occasional waggon-tracks made by the timber-getters. There were no group settlements, hardly a roof except on the huts of the straggling cattle runs.

What tracks there were ran inwards, that is, eastwards, from the front to Monbulk. There was hardly a cognisance of the range running north and south as its motor-road does today. As for the landscape, there was no series of idyllic green and cultivated ledges to gleam through belts of timber. There were no squared plantations of raspberry canes or apple-trees or gladioli. For good or bad, no erratic tangles of blackberries; nor blackbirds to spread them. No sawmills yet. No shaven hills covered with the moth-brown nonentity of bracken, showing that they had once been cleared by fire, only for disuse. There were no rabbits bobbing through the bracken at the edge of cleared paddocks; no foxes sneaking after them through the undergrowth. All these were to come in the next decades.

4 THE BERRY-GROWERS

Towards the end of 1867, John Hardy, assistant-surveyor in the Lands Department, was instructed to make a topographical survey of the Dandenongs and report on the magnificent forest that was known to cover it. This forest was supposed to hold some of the world's tallest trees – the giant mountain-ash rising from four to five hundred feet. There was a belief, too, that the hills might hold land suitable for agriculture.

By that time the flat country below was fairly well settled. At the spot where Captain Lonsdale's overseer had built his hut there was now a flourishing little market-town of three hundred inhabitants. Practically all the land around had been taken up for pasturage or crops. Lilydale had sprung into being. At Yering, where the Ryries had halted on their long journey from Monaro, there were three large vineyards – Yering, St Hubert's, and Yeringberg – and their wines were becoming widely known. David Mitchell, the father of Melba, had also planted sixty acres of grapes on his place at Coldstream, nearby.

But John Hardy, working his way along the forested hills, found little sign of human activity. A few settlers were making clearings on the slopes to the north, in anticipation of future settlement. At Emerald, in the interior, there was a little camp of fossickers and splitters, about fifty people in all. Some gold had been found in what was later to be called Menzies Creek, but not more than would provide a handful of miners with a living. A few paling-splitters were at work, and their drays had made tracks on the southern and western sides of the mountain.

Hardy made a plan of the area, with hatched ridges and spurs, recommending a large part of the Olinda and Monbulk districts for permanent reservation because of their scenic beauty. Olinda he called after the wife of his chief, Clement Hodgkinson: Sherbrooke and the upper part of the Monbulk he left unnamed, though the latter stream, famous for its lyrebirds, was afterwards called after him, Hardy's Creek.

The clearings being made in the north were due to some inaccessible and heavily-wooded slopes, facing the Lilydale plain, being thrown open for homesteads. The first aim was cattle-raising; the settlers had looked for land along the Yarra flat towards Healesville, but large landowners outbid them. So the first real attack on the timbered country began, four families from Melbourne pegging out land together, narrow strips of about a hundred acres each that rose from a rich valley to the ridge of what is now called Kalorama. The old plans show the settlers' names along the ribbon strips – Child, Jeeves, Richardson, Hand – three of the names being present in the same place still.

If the land, with its sections of a hundred acres (to which the different families gradually added another fifty, and another) had to be regarded as possible pasture, it was a disappointment. The new settlers had to make their livelihood as best they could. The procedure was for the men to do a little clearing, then go back to work at some trade while the timber dried – returning later to burn off; a dangerous matter with standing forest all about. A bark hut was built, a few cows and fowls brought in, and a footing secured.

Next – this was the case with the Child family, father and son being trained carpenters – they split timber and built a home of two rooms; so their family life in the district began. Together with the other families they made a rough road of seven miles, going through South Wandin (now Silvan) to Lilydale, which had become a significant centre for a huge district. With Lilydale as market, they kept dairy cattle for butter, poultry for eggs, and grew potatoes to barter for groceries, the daughter of the family riding in with the produce.

During the first years the only word for their way of living was struggle. The needs of the place were always in excess of its return. What surplus cash they had was spent on tea, sugar and white flour – luxuries used seldom except for visitors. For themselves the large family grew wheat, which they ground for bread; or they ate it boiled (*frumenty*, as the Scots have it). There were potatoes; for meat they snared wallaby.

The other families developed their resources in different ways. The natural gravitation of the Jeeveses was toward timber, for they belonged to a notable pioneer family in the Huon Valley that thrived by turning the mountain ash of the heavily-wooded slopes into timber for Hobart. The original Tasmanian pioneers were two brothers, one an ex-clergyman, and today they have over a thousand descendants and a flourishing port on the Huon named after them, Geeveston.

There was plenty of work for the pitsaw the Victorian Jeeves set up in the valley. All building was in the valley at first; clearing, or thinning, the forest could only go on slowly. But before long there was a special reason for getting clearings in it established as fast as possible. A profitable crop had been discovered.

Someone – it is not certain who – had begun to exploit the possibilities of berry-growing in this Mooroolbark area. Perhaps it was one of the Swiss vine-dressers who had been so successful with the grape. Soon there were cleared pockets of land, facing the east and screened by tall timber, where strawberry plants, but still more raspberry canes, were flourishing and bearing as never on the plains.

After that, the starvation days were over. The district seemed to live for those seven weeks of summer when, on the longest of days, picking went on from magpie to mopoke. The soil was new and rich; there were no pests and the shade was right. After all, in European countries the berries grew inside forests, so these mountain glades could be expected to be at their best for the fruit while the timber was still tall and copious.

In those early days of berry-growing there seems to have been little difficulty about markets for the large, well-paying crops. The journey to town would have been an undertaking, but the speed of today was unnecessary. No attempt was then made to sell fruit fresh and unbroken in little open punnets. Instead, it was put into casks and delivered at a specified jam-factory, from fifteen hundredweight to a ton at a time. There was a union of growers, and through it the whole crop from Mooroolbark to Wandin, about four hundred tons each year, was sold to three Melbourne factories.

Later, the experiment of a factory at Wandin was made, but that is another story. Up to 1890, the casks of fruit were carted to town in a covered waggon, drawn by two horses; down one day and up the next. Then the railway came as far as Lilydale, and the long drive was not needed.

Meanwhile a more direct road had been built to Lilydale. One of the four settlers – Thomas Hand, senior – had been made first shire engineer of Lilydale and rode up and down to the shire offices. After living at first on the valley end of his strip he set up a new homestead at the top, on what is now known as Cherry Farm Hill, and made at his own expense the Inverness Road which still exists, winding down the extreme northern face of the range.

As for other roads to connect this upland Mooroolbark region with what we call Olinda and Sassafras, there was none. The Mooroolbarkers looked mostly north, and when they left their fastness it was to go down on to the northern plain. The Hands, indeed, by another track of their own might drive down more in the direction of Montrose; but there was still no traversing the range from end to end, north to south.

The little settlement knew its own works and ways very well, and that was enough for the time. There was, it is true, a track up Mount Observatory, which looked out on a wider world, but the top, now public property, was occupied by a private house belonging to Robert Singleton, who used to amuse his family by making heliograph signals from it to his home facing the east in Malvern.

5 EMERALD

In the late sixties, when John Hardy was making his topographical survey of the Dandenongs, he had found a little camp of miners at Emerald, sinking shafts in the pockets along

Menzies Creek and timbering them roughly with the boles of tree-ferns. They were a tiny section of the great army of prospectors that was spraying out all over the countryside now that gold could only be found on Bendigo, Ballarat and other fields at deep levels. A good deal of the real exploration of the mountainous districts was accomplished by these fossickers who, laden only with their mining-tools and a little food, went ahead of even the timber-getters.

At some points along Menzies Creek the frames of their wooden sluices can still be seen in the water nearly a century after their passing, but the blackberry-vines cover up most of their abandoned shafts. Further east, over barer ridges looking towards Warburton, there was another tiny mining-camp at Macclesfield, and it is said that Henry Kingsley, author of *Geoffry Hamlyn*, once swung an exploring pick there.

But the reddish soil of the Emerald slopes was too rich to be left long untouched by a generation looking hungrily for cultivable land near the city. It caught the experienced eye of a robust young Swede who was working at a nursery in town and spending his weekends searching for a suitable place to make a home.

Carl Axel Nobelius had been born in Sweden in 1850, one of a peasant family settled in Skane, the flat, fertile southernmost edge of Scandinavia. The name Nobelius had been taken from Nobbelov, a village in that part of the country, but when one of the family enlisted in the Army he had to drop his last three letters, Latin names having then upper-class connotations and being frowned upon in the ranks. This was Immanuel Nobel, father of Alfred, the explosives king and founder of the Nobel Prize. At the time young Carl arrived in Australia, there was a disaster in Sydney that had to do indirectly with his famous cousin. This was the explosion, in 1866, of two cases of nitro-glycerine in a Sydney warehouse – an explosion that completely obliterated the building as well as many adjacent dwellings and caused an undetermined number of deaths.

It was literally a shot heard round the world, for there had been widespread rumours about this marvellous new explosive that was going to displace gunpowder and perhaps prove terrible enough in its destructive power to put an end to war. The Sydney explosion was soon followed by others in different countries; a general panic led to restrictions being placed on the transport of this dangerous substance. But the story of nitro-glycerine's transformation into dynamite and gelignite has more to do with Alfred Nobel than with his green-thumbed relative.

For the young immigrant's gift was making things grow. As a lad he had been trained as a nurseryman, and when he reached Melbourne in the late sixties he soon found employment in the nurseries of South Yarra and Toorak. There he made friends with other young men who were to play a great part in the agriculture and horticulture of Victoria – men like Cheeseman, George Rimington and the Brunnings – all day-labourers then, but all ambitious to have places of their own.

Nobelius found that the red soil of the Dandenongs were specially suited for making good rooting-systems in fruit-trees. After some experiment he took up a large area of land in Emerald, on the northern slope facing Warburton. It was heavily-timbered, but he set to work clearing it, patch by patch.

No real settlement at Emerald yet existed; there were no roads, only rough bush-tracks, and no direct link with Melbourne. For some time Nobelius continued his work in the city nurseries, taking the train to Narre Warren late on Friday. It was a sixteen-mile tramp over the flats and up the uncleared hills to his new holding, but he was young, vigorous, and of indomitable will. Gradually the hillsides were cleared and burned off, and by 1880 he could make his home there and open up a nursery.

At first it was a matter of rearing seedling fruit-trees for known customers, but he was led into experimenting with European trees that gave good shade in summer. Part of his place was turned into an acclimatisation garden, a sort of laboratory. In the hot little townships growing up in the north, there was need for trees of leafy foliage that would absorb the dust. To the shire councils of such places came circulars from the nursery at Emerald, telling what could be supplied in the way of 'ornamental' trees that would give shade in summer, let the sun through in winter.

The nursery, started with such difficulty, became a great organisation, the finest of its kind in the continent. By the end of the century, Nobelius could advertise that he had a million trees for sale. His name was known overseas; he had built up a trade with India and Brazil. A settlement had grown up around his place; it was fed by a narrow-gauge line that wound on past Emerald, through his tilled slopes to Gembrook.

But this is to skip lightly over twenty years of arduous and difficult development, both in the Nobelius nursery and the country around. Towards Gembrook there were some miles of country, heavily-timbered and uneven in the quality of its soil. In 1871, Arthur Backhouse, a teacher with a school of his own at Brighton, selected nearly a thousand acres of this country, afterwards selling out portions of it as settlers percolated into the district. They came gradually, as conditions were difficult and there was no certainty about the kind of crops the district could profitably produce, for what throve in one part was a failure a few miles away. In 1884, Andrew Carmody, an Irishman, selected some of the Gembrook land, clearing twenty acres and putting them in potatoes. This proved a success, and he was followed by another Irishman, Joseph Casey. A sawmill was also established to make use of the good timber, that was often wastefully burned when new land was cleared.

Not all such clearing was well-directed, as is proved by the numerous patches still producing nothing but bracken, a growth not native to these hills, some say, but blown over from Tasmania on an unlucky wind. Even some enterprises that promised well in the beginning came to a shabby end. At Emerald, for instance, a vineyard, Chateau D'Yes, was established in the eighties by a Swiss named de Bavay, who had been inspired by the success of the growers around Lilydale. It flourished for some years, producing wines that recalled the French Medoc, but it had to be abandoned in the end.

Even the viticulture that had once thrived so well in the original areas below was languishing. The frosts seemed to come earlier now that the timber had gone down and a succession of severe ones played havoc with the vines. Many of the old owners were getting out, and the new ones had little taste for an industry that called for such care and patience. Besides, it was difficult to find a firm market for their wines, in spite of the foreign awards they had won. The people who drank wine with their meals preferred something with a French brand. Not that they were all capable of distinguishing the differences in bouquets and vintage-years, but wine is a commodity that lends itself to snobbery, and a generation and class that was essentially colonial in its outlook had, paradoxically, a shrinking from any article to which the humiliating word could be applied. As for the wine-bars, they had little use for the fine dry wines it had been the pride of the early growers to produce; they wanted a thick, sweet wine that could be drunk between meals.

But all these difficulties were surmounted by the growers in the north and west of Victoria, in spite of the phylloxera that devasted their vineyards. Probably the chief reason for the abandonment of viticulture in the areas around Melbourne was that, now the city was growing at such a rate, these areas had become very profitable for dairying. It is another instance of how in new countries there can be nothing stable in the use of the soil; there must be continual change and adjustment.

6 THE MONBULK DISTRICT

The story of pioneering in any district must be one of repetition. It may be 'opened up' several times, the first tentative clearings abandoned, for one reason or another, or quite a new growth superimposed on the first.

There are such palimpsests in the Dandenongs, many of them centering in the name, though not always in the present district, of Monbulk. That name, now restricted in its use, once spread itself 'overthwart and endalong a wide forest', the forest that today is broken up into many entities – Olinda, Sassafras, Sherbrooke and the rest.

The first settlement at Monbulk had been made by the Varcoes, who grazed cattle there, and by the owners of Monbolluc, who ran sheep. But the area was too heavily-timbered to allow much pasturage for stock, and as yet it held little lure for agriculturists since it was difficult of access.

The second settlement, with very different purposes, began in 1877. A Melbourne veterinary surgeon named Dodd, travelling on his tasks, often heard the Monbulk district praised and made up his mind to visit it. It attracted him greatly, and he took up land – it was then part of the Berwick shire – on the southern slopes, not far in from Ferntree Gully. Bringing his family there, he built a homestead; first, just from palings with a shingle roof; later they got weatherboards, pitsawn.

There was no thought of the kind of building a member of the Dodd family would one day introduce to the hills – comfortable houses of round logs, with a pugging of the special clay found in the district and a chimney of local stone.

The homestead ready, the father continued on his six weeks' round of veterinary work and left the growing boys to carry on the farm, or whatever the holding proved to be. But clearing in those forested gullies was extremely slow, and it gradually occurred to the Dodd family, and some others who settled near, that the timber might be more an asset than a handicap. The gullies and ridges began to be explored and rifled. Crowding all the gorges with a southerly aspect were giant blackbutt or mountain ash, rising out of sassafras, blackwood, silver wattle, musk and fern. On the sunny ridges opposite, exposed to the north, was more open forest country, with stringy bark and messmate. All these might be more profitable than crops.

Much potentially valuable timber had already been destroyed in the hills. The Dodds now set to work to see how it could be used to best advantage. Blackwood and wattle were cut into staves for tallow casks. In those early days, with no refrigeration in sight, the sheep on Mornington Peninsula had to be rendered down for tallow whenever a dry spell struck the country. Another small timber-industry from the gullies worked by the Dodds and their fellow settlers seems a strange one; the bulbous roots of the musk-tree were sawn into slabs and sent to Germany for veneer purposes. The possibilities of mountain ash had hardly begun to be understood; today it is largely used for cabinet work and fine flooring.

For a long while the labour of timber-getting was enormous, the logs being hauled by bullocks up the steep sides of Holden's range, outside what is now Olinda township. When roads existed at all, they were twin ruts of mud or dust, according to the weather. It was many years before they were metalled, even in short sections.

But some permanent settlement was being made. In the early eighties pockets of red soil were being planted with berries, as at Mooroolbark and Wandin, though Monbulk had no connection with those places. The Mooroolbark settlers, being at the northern end of the range, sent their fruit down by way of Lilydale, or, later, to a factory at Wandin. The Monbulk growers were forced to carry theirs down to a waggon at the foot of the range. There was no metalled road before Ringwood, but the waggon jogged its way over the swampy plain, making a fresh track wherever the old became impassable.

Except at the fruit season's end or the times when they had timber to send away, the settlers themselves seldom thought of going to town. If they had made the journey, it was a matter of walking down the gullies to the plain and then northward across that until they struck the famous White Horse Road. Near Ringwood, or perhaps nearer Croydon, they could catch one of Cobb & Co.'s coaches, running from Lilydale to Melbourne. As for any stores they needed, these were all taken up the range by packhorse.

Such connections as existed between the little settlements were not roads but creeks. The Dandenong Creek, of course, rose away from the ranges, westward and southward, ending in Port Phillip;

but there were others that rose in the hills. The Woori-yallock creek, starting at Sassafras, wound east and north behind the hills; but first it was joined by the Emerald and Menzies creeks. The pioneers of these tracks were, first, miners, then timber-getters, then prospective settlers looking for land.

In spite of the clearings round the few settlers' homes and the invasion of the forest for the logs snigged out by bullock-drivers ('to spoil and havoc more than they can eat'), the ranges up to the nineties were, on the whole, virgin. A continual cause of anxiety to the settlers was the danger of bushfires. There were, indeed, some bad fires, a typical one, in 1880, destroying the east side of what is now generally called Burke's Lookout. The Dodd homestead had to be protected by the burning of a huge break around it, for a north wind swept the open messmate country and it seemed as if the flames would carry everything before them; but the dewy slopes of mountain ash were finally left undamaged. Dodd senior was a careful man and was accustomed to take precautions against outbreaks.

'If you have a lot of little fires,' he would say, 'you'll never be destroyed by a big one.'

He made a practice of burning off every tree as it fell, of letting no piles of rubbish lie, and there were no bushfires of his starting.

As the years went on, more and more naturalists came to the ranges and there was talk of declaring a great sanctuary around Olinda. John Hardy, indeed, had marked out special places for reserves in his original plan, but little notice had been taken of his recommendations. Now with the land boom at its height and every open space around the city being carved up into allotments, there was more concern with preserving what virgin country lay near at hand. A noted bird-lover, A. J. Campbell, campaigned vigorously for the idea, demanding that at least a thousand acres should be set aside. He called attention to the unspoilt beauties of what he named Lyrebird Gully, taking photographs of its lyre-birds and making lantern slides that are still cherished as unique. The Government itself toyed with the idea of creating a great National Park in the Dandenongs.

But this movement toward a national park began too late. Precisely in the early nineties arose an opposite impulse toward closer settlement of the ranges. It was the bursting of the boom, followed by widespread unemployment, that led the then Minister for Lands to turn toward the Dandenongs and open up several new parts with schemes for berry-growing.

This settlement scheme fell into two parts – one for people with a little capital, the other for assisted village settlers. The latter were helped with a subsidy of ten shillings a week, a reasonable sum in those days, and were encouraged to eke out the grant by working on a new and very necessary road. This Clare's Hill road ran, or rather climbed, from Bayswater to Sassafras. It would help the Monbulk growers, as well as the new arrivals, to get their berries more easily to market.

To long-established onlookers this new settlement of out-of-work townspeople seemed amateurish and haphazard. It is said that selectors were told, in April, 1893, to choose their blocks of ten acres, and these would be surveyed as soon as possible. But the newcomers had no idea of size, and, indeed, on such tangled slopes it would be difficult for anyone to visualise an exact ten acres. When the surveyors finally began their work, they often found two families on the one block; others had too ambitious ideas of their property's extent; there were exasperating changes and expropriations.

Many other difficulties lay before the new Monbulk settlements, but the greatest was that of roads, which were mainly sectional, not continuous. Berry-growing, without facilities for rapid transport, can never succeed on a large scale, and this is what was now being attempted. An experiment was made, in 1897, to solve the problem of distance. The growers opened a jam-factory at Ferntree Gully, but it seems to have been doomed from the beginning. There was an unsatisfactory manager, and after a few seasons a fire, in which even the books were burnt, left the place in ruins; so that was that.

Fresh efforts were to be made later on, when roads were entirely changed in scope and kind, and a little narrow-gauged railway was beginning to thread the hills.

7 LANDSCAPE AND LABOUR

We know, both in ourselves and through endless repetition from outside, that we are a young country. The bones of the continent are old, but everything created by the hands of man has an unweathered look; it has not had time to merge inconspicuously into its background. Solid though it may be, it has the aspect of something unsettled and fugitive.

Yet there are places that give the illusion of an earth long tamed and humanised. Agriculture in the Dandenongs is a comparatively new experiment. There are men still living who knew the ranges when comparatively few acres of their soil had been upturned. But when our eyes rest upon the terraces of certain cultivated valleys as they glimmer between the boles of a tall forest, it is hard to believe that such a complex pattern was made in a short time. Every spreading tree – pear, apple, great walnut, Spanish chestnut, Lombardy poplar going up like smoke – has already a mellowness. Fully-grown and at home, they do not seem like strangers as they gently slope down into the red-soiled valleys.

This idyllic landscape as a whole, contrasting its planned acres with the neighbouring combe of secondgrowth mountain ash and ferny undergrowth, has nothing fugitive or temporary about its look. Some of the rich acres of the Patch might have been tilled for quiet centuries. It is as if their problems had all been solved, each field bearing its set fruit in due season.

Such tranquillity is, of course, an illusion. Even in a European landscape, with actual age behind it, every season brings its own problems and changes. Here in the Dandenongs the changes have been unceasing and many problems remain to be solved. Quick growth covers up mistakes of the past. You may be impressed by a towering row of pines around an old homestead, pines with a look of ancient peace about them; but you will be told that there is a more impressive and larger row further back, planted twenty years earlier, and guarding nothing but a burnt-out chimney. The first home had been built in the wrong place.

The *pinus insignis* is an immigrant, and a quick grower now that it has been acclimatised, but in quickness it is eclipsed by the mountain ash. Many hillsides cleared of this fine timber in the early days have now a second growth almost as robust as the original one, though looking more domesticated and subdued. It is this that gives a pastoral look to the ranges now, the bush itself harmonising with the tilled country.

But let us go back to the end of last century when, apart from a few enterprises like the Nobelius nursery, there existed only those separate settlements of berry-growers and timber-getters in different parts of the ranges – Mooroolbark on the north, Monbulk in the centre, Ferntree Gully to the south, running down to the plain. The land boom affected these districts as it affected other parts of Victoria, and land at the Mooroolbark end began to sell at thirty pounds an acre. A heavy price in those days! Only while the price of berries remained fairly high could growing be made to pay.

The new village-settlers sent up by a bewildered Government when the boom burst created a fresh problem. They did not entrench on the original holdings of the old settlers – those 100-acre ribbons running up from the creek to Kalorama ridge and belonging to Jeeves, Hand, Child and Richardson; the new closer settlement, in ten-acre blocks, stretched upward and south toward the township now known as Mt Dandenong. This meant, among other things, opening a road, the Ridge Road toward Olinda; the gradual turning of the mountain into a single chain instead of a series of pockets.

But soon the difficulty was not one of land or of roads; it was one of markets. The raspberry market gradually became flooded. The early growers had made a fine art of adapting their output to the market, combining – they were few – to send their fruit in barrels to the factories at a fixed and satisfactory price. There was complete co-ordination between supply and demand; it was a tight little well-adjusted system.

In 1890, the output of Mooroolbark growers was about 400 tons, and not a berry was wasted. When the new growers on the

Mt Dandenong slopes got into their stride there were, perhaps, another 400 tons; and there were also the growers in several parts of Monbulk. Such heavy supplies meant a slump; the price of raspberries fell to a penny-farthing a pound; it hardly paid to pick them. As yet there was little demand for fruit on the part of the urban population, and retailers did not like handling such a perishable product as berries; they were only regarded as fit for jam.

The old settlers' response to the situation took two forms. One was to pull up most of their raspberry canes. The eastern slopes of Cherry Farm Hill had held nothing but raspberries; they were now replaced by cherries, strawberries, and potatoes. A few orchards were planted with apples and stone-fruits.

The other form of response was to look for new markets. One of the old originals, Ellis Jeeves, formed the Wandin District Pulp Extract Society, for sending tinned raspberry pulp to Great Britain. Its works were in South Wandin, or what is now Silvan, and the site was that of the present Silvan dam.

But the particular scheme ended in catastrophe through a bad flaw in distribution at the English end, and the hopeful growers lost heavily. Yet there is something about a special industry that exacts its own loyalty. Some of the old berry-growing families have stuck to the crop with which they pioneered the ranges, and the young members – they claim that they were weaned on raspberry juice – have organised ways of distributing their product direct.

This has become more feasible through rapidity of transport, either by train or with motor-lorries on good roads. With efficient packing and a little dry ice in the bucket, fruit can be sent great distances; it used to be a matter of disaster if more than twenty-four hours passed between the time of leaving the canes and of reaching the consumer. And housewives in town, or even in the interior, now expect raspberries to arrive fresh and recognisable, not as mere pulp.

This is going forward much too fast, though. At the beginning of the century things in the berry-growing settlements were still difficult. The journey to town was slow and rough; the roads down the mountain were still sketchy, steep, and full of hairpin bends. They were narrow; there are tales of one road so narrow that a rule for one-way traffic had to be solemnly observed, even to the blowing of a horn that echoed out through the hills when a coach or dray set out, upward or downward.

Away from the known tracks and roads there were secret hideouts, though not used by bushrangers. It is hard to get at the truth about the number of illicit stills that used to be worked in the ranges. Who owned them, and what sort of potheen did they brew? Why was one of them built near the crest of Mount Observatory, with no water at hand?

A whisky-flavoured legend still hangs about one old garden where the rise begins, just above Montrose. They say it belonged to a Frenchman with a delight in goldfish. He built a series of linked fish-ponds, one below the other, of brick or concrete; but the bottom pond had no fish in it at all, and very little water. Ultimately the place became too public, even for goldfish.

Some of the village settlers did fairly well with their berry-holdings – well enough, anyhow, to flood their market, yet seldom well enough for them to hold their land for long. Few of them were trained agriculturists with their hearts in the soil. Many of the blocks reverted to the Government and were thrown open to selectors who used the land in various ways, seldom for intensive berry-growing. They tried mixed farming, sometimes market gardening; growing turnips, for instance, and taking them downhill overnight in their springcarts, then over the plain in the morning to the White Horse Road, and so to the Victoria Market, twice a week:

> The roads come in, roads dark and long,
> To the knock of hubs and a sleepy song.
> Heidelberg, Point Nepean, White Horse,
> Flemington, Keilor, Dandenong,
> Into the centre from the source.

It was hard work for little gain. Meanwhile, as one old man said recently:

'On my holding, when I'd cleared it from big timber I thought

I'd finished. But no fear! The little saplings came popping up, crowding out my turnips. I used to knock'em over like walking-sticks. Yet, come to think of it, if I'd let 'em grow where they wanted to, I might have done better. Reared a stand of mountain ash that'd've paid me better than all the turnips I've raised in forty years. And done it by simply looking on, without slaving out in all weathers.'

An overwhelming thought, with one small catch in it; there would have been little to eat while the mountain ash was coming to maturity. There exists, though, a genuine irony in the management and mismanagement of our timbers, and it takes a shrewd old man's comment to bring it out. Mountain ash is now used for everything, from flooring-boards to cabinet-work, for everything, that is, except what goes into the ground like posts. It has been used for paper-pulp. Only a very rich agriculture could make up for what has been destroyed and the labour of destroying it.

This idyllic landscape, then, with its tranquil exterior, has been nothing less than a battleground, with certain heights won and others lost. The settler has had to contend not merely with the variation of the seasons and the lessening richness of the soil, but with pests of increasing number and virulence. Some of the pests any onlooker would recognise as such: certain new weeds, insects like thrips, new Australians like the rabbit and the fox. Others are more surprising; we may be used to hearing hard things said about the blackberry, but what about the blackbird? Is there any reason for farmers to go purple when they spy its yellow bill and its neat dark figure?

There is. The blackbird, unlike most native bush birds, eats berries and not insects or pests. As one who has rejoiced in the blackbird's haunting note wherever heard in the old world or new, I feel it a very painful duty to repeat in clear terms the strong, the unbreakable case against the blackbird in the berry-growing bush.

8 SOME LANDMARKS

There is the pastoral aspect of the Dandenongs, and there is the wild, natural one. Seen from a peak in the quietly-drenching light of a summer afternoon, they can still appear almost untouched, their surface only varied by the thickness or the thinness of the forest – which, indeed, in a few places is almost burnt away. There are as yet many miles of what appears virgin country, fold after fold of messmate-covered ridge and fern-filled gully, and from many an outlook the different cleared settlements with their rich detail are visible.

It takes a long time for the natural contours to be altered in any large way, a long time for people to create any lasting memorials. Builders in the Dandenongs have made surprisingly little use of the local stone. For a century now almost every house has been built of wood, and not often of the strongest construction, either. By fire or by decay one house after another has disappeared, and some districts could tell of a whole vanished series of homesteads. How many such have been on the very crest of Mount Observatory!

This is not to ask how many slab huts with shingled roofs have been abandoned at different times all over the range, sinking into the ground like some fungus till the very memory has been forgotten. The pathetic thing is that so few of the homes that sheltered several generations have lasted. At times the district seems to have contained only the temporary homes of nomads who expected their shelters to go up in flames when they moved away. The house on a rise is least likely to endure. In one district three such houses – each on its hill-top – were burned down in a couple of summers, leaving those who escaped to wonder whether their own was next in order of succession. Sunk without trace? Not quite. There are forsaken scorched chimneys marking many a deserted orchard until they, too, crumble away.

In one place the scenic effect of these standing brick chimneys is dramatic, not to say melodramatic. Look down the open gorge flanking the main road into Olinda from Mount Dandenong and you see, at the beginning of the rise from the Bayswater basin, a spot that has been persistently ravaged by fire. Walk a little way along the red road that winds just beneath the main one and you can see, in that old danger-spot, a remnant that might almost have been designed as a ruin.

(Designed? Yes, they make artifical ruins overseas. Not only ghostly ruined castles on the Rhine, dated 1850 or so. Much earlier, Frederick the Great, for instance, had a little Greek ruined-temple built just across a valley from his *Sans Souci* palace at Potsdam. You are meant to meditate, 'Sic transit', as you look towards it.)

This ruin below Burke's Lookout is comparatively recent. From the distance it looks like huge Egyptian columns set in some kind of order in a space between dark trees. High brick chimney, probably double-storied, an elaborate gateway; at the rear of a few nondescript outhouses. Nothing else remains of the very solid homestead, Dongala.

It had itself replaced a much earlier building of the same type. Known originally as Fern Glen, the old homestead was owned, first, by George Bruce, and then by Sir Mathew Davies; it was burnt down in 1892. In each case a bush fire was the cause, not a fire from within. There seems to be, at that spot, something like a funnel for hot-weather winds, but this was not recognised when Dongala was built. After standing for nearly forty years, it, too, was burnt down in 1932, the fire coming on it so quickly that it was a heap of smoking ruins before the neighbours knew it was in danger.

To an extent such widespread fires are a thing of the past in the Dandenongs. In the early days they were partly a product of panic. At the first sign of smoke on a neighbouring hill the settlers rushed to burn a break around their own homes; many little fires became a big one. And there was a fatalistic acceptance of the bush fire as part of the hazards of country life, especially in the driest months.

(Y' always have bush fires in February or March. Lucky if they happen to come without a hot wind behind 'em.)

Such acceptance of the inevitable is no longer general. There are organised bands of fire-fighters; also there are penalties for those who start the trouble by burning off heaps of rubbish in the dry autumn months. Perhaps for such people the Dongala chimneys might be preserved as an awful warning, as the unspeakable Mr Fairchild showed his little Henry the man hanging in gibbet-chains.

The landmarks of the Dandenongs, then, are not many:

A cairn of stones to mark the top of Mount Observatory, and to give a raised platform for the astonishing view over a wide stretch of country from Donna Buang to Arthur's Seat; heights never seen so clearly, as on some autumn morning when they rise out of an unbroken floor of white cloud, which is over Lilydale and Oakleigh and Melbourne!

A curious castle in bluestone at Olinda, indestructible enough but not likely to prove that bluestone is always a comfortable building material.

The tilled slopes of Emerald that Nobelius of Sweden shore of timber to found his great orchards and nursery. These are hardly more than pleasure-grounds now, for they fell on evil days during the First War. In those years they could not get the supplies of super-phosphate needed; the shipment of seedlings overseas was checked; the shrewd, experienced founder died. Part of it is now devoted to a Country Club, with swimming-pool and golf-course; part is an ornamental lake.

But what is perhaps the most significant landmark in the Dandenongs is so modest and unpretentious that it might easily pass unnoticed. It stands a little above the turn at Five Ways, Kalorama – one rough granite boulder set upon another. A plaque with a design approximating to the Rising Sun of the AIF badges contains the words, 'In Memory of the Peace, 1919', and underneath are the names of the local fallen.

The idea came from Percy Kernot, architect and artist, a long-time resident of the district; and the work was carried out by Douglas Richardson, the sculptor.

Compared with the usual ugly memorials in country towns – the stiffly-accoutred Boer War soldier set up on his pedestal by some monumental mason to stare everlastingly at the public-house across the way – this small arrangement in stone is a miracle of grace and feeling. It gathers into it the spirit of place; it evokes memories of obscure lives carrying out a chosen task with courage and dignity. In its simplicity it reminds one of similar memorials in the fields of Brittany, where one granite boulder, standing out only a little from the rest, will be stamped with the bronze image of a poet of the region, and perhaps a line of his verse.

9 THE FUTURE

What is the future of the Dandenongs likely to be? At present they still retain something of their old character. There are the forested hills with the close growths of mountain ash, the secret gullies with their suggestions of Lawrence's fern-world, and always the song-birds, whistlers, whip-birds and the rest. Then the prominent bluffs where you can stand on frosty winter mornings and watch the sun bouncing from the floor of cloud that covers the flats below and the far city.

Their agriculture connects them with the past. The families of some of the first berry-growers remain, and in the tilled holdings of Emerald and Monbulk you can trace that long struggle to get a foothold on the treed slopes. Each small settlement has its special reminders of the way it has grown up, apart from the others.

There are even links with the oldest settlers of all. Somewhere in the northern gullies is an underground cave that was the home of a large community when first discovered eighty years ago or more. It still shelters a few wombats, much to the distaste of neighbouring farmers, who are revolted by their habit of digging under every stretch of wire-netting fence and making a free passage for the rabbits. But the wambling night-wandering wombat is harmless in its activities compared with the recent immigrants and his survival is, on the whole, a happy thing.

It is not merely sentiment that prompts the desire to preserve some of the old character of the Dandenongs. With their variety, their natural beauty, their mixture of the idyllic and the wild, they are a fortunate gift to a city that lies stretched on a flat and featureless plain. Melbourne, in recent years, has been swift in its absorption of the rural areas around it. It has cut up many pleasant little apple-orchards, swallowed market-gardens by the score, rooted out natural growths and planted deciduous trees that have an alien look, covered a wide area with brick and bitumen. Its surrounding villages have been swamped by suburbs that have separate names, but almost nothing else to differentiate them in their monotony of stucco picture palace, trim dwelling and shaven plot.

This is almost inevitable with a city that is expanding and has decided against doing it by small, self-contained flats in multi-storeyed buildings, with open spaces between. But it would be a pity to let the suburban tide flow over these further hills and blot out whatever is individual and characteristic about them. They have, as has been shown, an interesting past. Their intimate beauty has endeared them to three generations; their name has already been celebrated by a line of poets, from R. H. Long to Victor Daley.

'O City, look the eastward way,' wrote one.

A city is lucky when its look is rewarded by a line of hills so near, and when the name of those hills that are the home of singing-birds rhymes with song.

Spanish Days

1 IN THE SUN

These articles were written by Mrs Nettie Palmer before the January Spanish general elections, when the Socialists and Communists were elected to power. She sojourned in Spain with her husband while the country was still calm.

'You're going to find Spain terribly hot, you know,' our friends in London said when we left for this Mediterranean coast north of Barcelona. Before their eyes, dimmed by years of London smoke, Spain's peninsula lay like a large square frying-pan, human beings quivering or bouncing on it with the intense heat. And to have put off our time in Spain until May, when spring was well advanced! Wasn't that asking for trouble?

For several days after we had lightly dug ourselves into a cool concrete house with cool tile floors and a cool white courtyard with hanging white trumpet dahlias against its high walls, the Mediterranean, about 20 yards from our front door, seemed bent on practising its harmless varieties of chilly spring storms. Sometimes it was slate-grey with a wind from the north. Was this France's mistral? After all, the milestone on the beach road in front of our garden says, 'Francia, 146 kilometres', while the other side says, 'Madrid 640 kilometres'; so our weather is rather French than peninsular. Sometimes, again, the Mediterranean glowered and rained darkly with a wind from somewhere south; to this wind I can give no name. After that it cleared, became blue, became all that we understood by Mediterranean, although indeed, its harmless breakers continued their impotent pounding for some time.

When the sunny days came there was nothing about them to

justify the warnings of our English friends; simply good picnic weather, a warm sun, a cool wind, and people knowing how to make the most of both. It was still May, and in this country, as in so many others, there is marked approval of that month. Perhaps the real summer months will be more searching. May!

Indeed this hinterland is inexhaustibly charming in May; or, if you had exhausted if, you would suddenly be relieved by coming to a fine little town, with avenues of plane trees leading to it, and thick laburnums shading the chief street. In many of the gardens there are very fine eucalypts throwing shadows on the smooth plaster walls of the wide houses. But the trees of Spain – or of Catalonia – are a discovery in themselves.

Back on the beach we see how the Catalonians can enjoy their May weather. Go across for a dip as early as you like at the weekend, and long before seven o'clock you will see picnic parties from Barcelona, 14 kilometres away, settling in for the day with a family beach tent and several large family picnic baskets. It is not only for young people, this festival. As the day goes on there are groups of elderly men and women seated around folding tables for long meals and longer talks.

Catalan is more difficult to learn than Spanish. It looks charming enough on the page or on a poster; a little like old French, a language for comedy – Rabelais or Montaigne. It looks like part of a robust life, when a poster assures you that some product is 'El Millor licor del mon,' and you can make it out easily enough in some Catalonian newspaper when the news is about Starhemberg or Mussolini or Baldwin; you have your clues and can take your time. To the unlearned ear, however, Catalan is noisy and obscure, only illuminated every now and then by an immensely trilled r-r-r that seems to hang almost visibly in the air after the sentence has ended. 'El Millorrr licorrr del mon.'

The young people sea bathe or sun bathe, taking their first summer tan perhaps more easily than even an inured Sydneysider. Physically they look sound but not very powerful. I have seen no figures like those fairly usual among our life-saving club members. The standard of personal beauty here in Catalonia is very high indeed. People hold themselves well, face the sun easily (often hatless), dress carefully without fuss or stiffness, and keep expressive faces.

At first I was apprehensive for the decay of all their radiance and good looks. If this is your minimum, how do you feel when old age begins to steal the beauty, distort the outline? There is a way out, though. You become a 'Catalan type', with a face wrinkled like a tattooed Maori, showing you are a character.

As for Catalonian women, in youth they are entrancing, actively as well as passively, if you understand. Well-made dresses, international in design, are worn with an air by the busiest factory girl. She has even-bleached hair and a complexion, out of many bottles, loading the air with scents that only the freshness of the air makes tolerable. This young woman can be described as a deliberate knockout. Married, or thirty-ish, or both, she abandons all elaborations and becomes a comfortable, amiable, vigorous woman, usually to be seen with her market basket full of hard-bargained greens. Give her a few decades more, though, and she is a very interesting figure of an old woman; not so consciously a type, perhaps, as the man, but assured and dignified.

People sit much in the sun in Catalonia, or walk in it. I am waiting to see them go into the shade, which they delay in doing. So far the sun by this sea is quite unfrightening, but perhaps June will give us something to remember. The Catalonian admires his May month, as I have said. An obviously sentimental house near here, all shiny tiles and superfluous turrets, and with a poem in heavily rhymed Catalonian hung like a medallion on its ample bosom, has for its name, 'Sempre Maig'.

2 RAIN

This is the second article by Mrs Nettie Palmer, who, with her husband, Mr Vance Palmer, was spending a holiday in Spain before the outbreak of civil war. Mrs Palmer here writes of life in Catalonia, on the eastern coast.

In London last month a really wet day meant a period of withdrawal and inwardness. You probably decided not to go out at all, and if it grew properly dark you drew the curtains, turned on the light and wrote, staring into the fire. The world outside might have been part of New York or Melbourne or Nowhere; it had no existence for you. Here in Spain, after a week of more or less steady sunshine, a frankly wet day seemed welcome enough. It would surely be a time for shutting things out, taking stock, remembering the crowded impressions of the last week. What makes better for concentration than the drumming of rain on the roof, quenching all other noises?

It was rather daunting in the first place to notice that the rain was one of the few things in this part of Spain to act in silence. The high, thick tiled roofs cannot resound with it, and the gravelly earth of the little street receives it gently. So opportunity was left, after all, for the usual noises to come in. The next discovery was that in Spain on a wet day the only place to sit is by the window. There is no concentrating in the dark middle of a room; you simply carry your writing table – it is flimsy enough – across to the one place with light: but where is your day of living inwardly?

If Spanish houses have little furniture their windows are all the more complex. This one is on the ground floor, and is obviously the most important part of the room. It opens on to the narrow paved footpath beside the tiny road that today is so muddy. Sitting at the window you look through its wrought-iron grille, the upright bars, six inches apart, being spiral and painted a soft green. Inside the grille is a window-sill, quite two feet deep, sloping downward, in glazed cornflower-blue tiles. There is a solid summer blind with green laths, tightly drawn up today. Then come the two casements of the window itself, and, attached to each by a hinge, two thick wooden shutters. A pretty complete outfit to keep out burglars, cold, stares, heat; or to let in warmth, coolness, and, in general, life, or perhaps Life; but surely not on a day of steady rain?

Sounds come in, but most of them are remote or at least impersonal; they can be ignored. Not a hundred yards away, just beyond the little front gardens belonging to this irregular row of houses, the Mediterranean pounds hard. Today, at the edge it mixes the sand with the surf rather repulsively just as Virgil used to say it did whenever his sailors were shipwrecked on its shores. Sometimes, though, a wave sounds like a serious climax, louder, louder; but that will be a motor-lorry on the beach road just below, speeding with its incredibly high pile of baskets containing greens or round bottles of sulphur or wine or live fowls. A census of the baskets, soft or hard, used in this country would be revealing. So would a census of noise. For that lorry piled with baskets, like the private car following it and the bus that comes next, has never heard of proposals for the abatement of noise. Every car on the road seems to rejoice in the demonstration of speed by means of a noisy engine; and to augment this comparatively natural noise by the continual use of versatile horns and hooters. The strange thing is that these noises are not exactly horrible here, as they would be in London, for instance, where they are simply forbidden today. Perhaps the open sea carries half of them off, or perhaps as you perforce listen in a morbid fascination you are conscious of a Catalonian exultation behind them.

On this wet day, the covered carts returning slowly from the city market and drawn by a horse, a mule, or even a small donkey, seem like something exposed to continual insults or threats from the modern vehicles that shoot past or near them. Fast asleep, one hopes, the driver lets his half-asleep animal pick its way home after a long night. There are little bells in a row on the head harness with its polished brass studs, or on the scarlet net collar hung below the creature's neck, and those bells with their innocent chime, centuries older than the also outmoded horns and hooters, utter a gentle, ineffectual protest against the triviality of mere noise. The appearance of the Spanish cart, as you consider it in the rain, agrees with its sound. The tarpaulin cover is fastened to a frame of withies usually painted a bright green, while the wheels, their spokes on some traditional pattern, curving outwards to the rim, which is level with the axle tip, will be a deep orange.

Those sounds from the beach road were mine only if I chose to listen to them. There are others in our own little lane, more insistent. Quite early a man draws up his covered cart in front of one door after another, its driver masterfully uttering that sound between a hiccough and a yodel that for some reason is taken to mean 'Milk' in every part of the world. 'Ho-la-a!' he remarks to me, when I appear with my jug and pennies, and 'Adi-os', as he leaves. Perhaps it is fortunate that in no language accessible to us both is it possible to crack old jokes about the rain getting into the milk. A while later comes the daily dustman, and if you don't recognise the blunt sound of his horse's bell it will be your fault; he never knocks, but he will always stop if you have the presence of mind to hail him earnestly. You tip your little rubbish bucket into a limp basket of his. Having filled this basket from three or four houses, he lovingly carries it to his open cart, tips it in, driving slowly off in the rain. Altogether an unpretentious little performance, but it has the great virtue of frequency. The baker, an hour or two later, is a more serious person, as he draws up shouting 'Pan', with a very long 'a.' I wish I knew his politics. Stern and unremitting, I am sure, whether turned in the direction of Fascism or perhaps toward the plans of the leader with the superb name of Largo Caballero. As for his bread, it is good enough to overcome all the confused attacks of the slimmers. Take your choice — a longish flute of snapping white, or a large round bun of brown, 'integral' brown, philosophical in its wholemealness.

Now all these visits, with one that was to follow, occurred in a household where, for the sake of quiet, tradesmen are not encouraged to call. Once a day, with doubtful exercise of acumen, we do our own marketing, except for milk and bread. So this wet day, in addition to its seclusion offered by the rain, was as quiet as devising could make it; but quiet it was not. Even in the rain there are voices in the little street, people calling along from balcony to balcony, then the ancient sound of feet clop-clopping in the wooden sabots drawn on over canvas shoes. These noises again are not our affair; but one listens to it all, becoming aware of a tune in the way of living, the rhythm of Catalonia; surely less difficult to detect than the tune and rhythm of most countries. One more visitor. The postman, with mail sent on weekly. Inquiries: 'Isn't it very quiet in your village?' Alternate inquiry: 'Isn't everything very exciting and dangerous near Barcelona?' There are no answers. Perhaps I could ask the milkman tomorrow morning if he often puts dynamite in the milk.

CIVIL WAR EXPERIENCES – AUSTRALIAN WRITER'S ACCOUNT

By Nettie Palmer, the Australian writer, who was at Barcelona when the revolution began.

My first news of the insurrection in Barcelona came from the village milkman, who drove round as usual early in the morning. I heard him talking in a low, anxious voice to the woman next door, who said, 'There's a revolution. Don't you hear the guns?'

I ran down to the beach, where my husband was bathing. We could see the Barcelona skyline round the curve of the bay, and could hear the cannons and then the rattle of machine guns.

Our personal concern was for our daughter who, for once, had stayed in Barcelona overnight. She was interpreting for the bureau that was to entertain the foreign athletes arriving for the People's Olympiad, and we knew she would be kept late. We were to meet her in town in the afternoon to go to the opening of the Olympiad together. There had not been the faintest anticipation of trouble in our minds. Hundreds of foreigners were arriving in Barcelona for the games, and the only difficulties had seemed to vanish – the partial transport strike was ended, and summer weather had set in.

A few evenings before, I had gone to hear La Passionaria (Senora Ibarruri), Spain's great woman orator. She and others were to have addressed a mass meeting in the bull-ring. Everyone was astonished when the meeting was postponed, and the crowds coming away were simply told that a political crisis had kept La Passionaria in Madrid.

But now, on this bright morning, there were signs of a crisis everywhere. No trains ran along the cliff to the town, the telephone was cut off, and soon we heard that the rebels had occupied the great telephone building in the city. Men were pulling up paving stones on the highroad and were making barricades. The Civil Guards and police, whom we knew well by sight, had disappeared, and it was said that they had deserted and joined the soldiery, who were attacking the city.

We tried to walk to the town along the main road, about fourteen kilometres, but, like everyone else, we were stopped at the first barricades. Peasants and other civilians, with shotguns, revolvers, and any old weapons, were pouring into Alcaldia, and were signing on to patrol the roads.

Next morning, before dawn, the firing in Barcelona began again, and, for want of definite news, things seemed worse than before. A village woman, who did our cleaning, came with stories that had leaked through. Barcelona was just a heap of ruins, she said. The hospitals were crowded out with wounded, and dead were lying in all the streets. It could not be worse. She sat crying in the kitchen, wondering how she would ever get news of her parents, who lived in an alley near the centre of the fighting.

There was a sense of dreadful things happening everywhere. The milkman told about a heart-breaking affair not far along the road where two lorries carrying eager militiamen had mistaken one another for enemies in the dark.

During the morning I heard shots, and looked from the balcony. Our next door neighbour, who had been reading under a eucalyptus tree in the lane, was stretched behind a stone seat, protecting his head with a newspaper. Down the main road a couple of well-dressed motorists, one curiously like Trotsky, had been turned out of their car and were standing with their hands up. Lorries and cars full of armed men came racing up from both directions. There was a rattle of questions, and it looked as if there might be a gruesome execution there at the bottom of the garden. But after a long examination, the car was allowed to drive on.

Lying awake that night we determined to get to the city at all costs. We knew that General Goded (the insurgent leader, whose execution was reported yesterday) had been captured, so that the worst of the fighting was over, but the district was full of fugitives and suspected Fascists.

While we were having our breakfast, there was a loud banging on the front door. There had been some firing on a military lorry at the end of our lane, and armed peasants were searching every house for firearms.

No, it was not at all harrowing, just a little unreal, those heavy, tired men doing their duty solemnly and even courteously. The leader was blunt in his refusal to accept our word, and his 'off-sider', a tall, quiet boy, was careful to say, 'We will not bother you long. We have to search the whole street, but if we don't find anything, we will go away immediately'. Downstairs and upstairs they ransacked cupboards, earnestly peering into my harmless diaries and notes on Spanish literature.

Our Spanish neighbours warned us against trying to reach Barcelona, but lorries and vegetables had been going in under armed guards, so we made for the Committee of Safety at Alcaldia – it was full of armed, excited militiamen who had been without sleep. After long explanations, a clerk wrote us a pass. They even found us seats or mattresses in a lorry packed with armed unionists enlisting for Saragossa.

Barcelona still looked a wrecked city. The bodies of men and artillery horses and mules had been removed from the streets, but many buildings had been shattered and churches burned. After some false clues, we found our daughter. She had sent us a letter and a telegram saying that she was safe, and these actually arrived days later. She was kept busy in the Olympic Bureau. She speaks English, German, French, and Spanish, so was useful as a liaison officer in helping visitors to send reassuring cables home, or make plans to leave, mostly by sea, which was what agitated consuls and managers were insisting that they should do.

The courtesy of these anxious newly-armed men was remarkable. The outbreak of the revolt had been unexpected and savage, and they had had to fight it furiously, but already they seemed free from vindictiveness. Retaliation on buildings and institutions, but not on the people, seemed to be the popular instinct.

Life in Barcelona had begun to look normal when we left. Most of the government forces were away on the Saragossa front, where they must be still, but the unionists were policing the city and running the services. It surprised me when I reached London last night, after a few days in Paris, to find my Australian mail awaiting me, carefully readdressed by the kind owner of the fonda at the end of our lane.

Life on a Coral Island

For nearly a year I house-kept without any house; only a tent among trees, on an island so small that you could walk round the beach in twenty minutes. A launch calling once a week would bring our mail and what stores we had remembered to order the week before. There was water on the island, rain-water caught from a shed roof in a single tank. That was nearly all we knew in advance, except that the little island was a coral cay, not a peak in some submerged mountain range. That is, it was a flat knob of coral sand like a button fastened to the middle of a huge, irregular saucer, the encircling coral reef, which itself stood in the midst of indigo-deep sea. The island was in the tropics, sixteen miles from the mainland; and it was halfway along that huge process called the Great Barrier Reef, which runs a thousand miles up the north-east coast of Australia.

Our reasons for going to the island were simple enough. We wanted quiet, to write and read; and we wanted to know something about the mystery of coral reefs, not as scientists but as seekers after the world's wonders. In story books you are always shown coral islands far out in the ocean; no one reaches them except by being neatly wrecked on them. Here, on the other hand, were coral islands to be reached on purpose; and we wanted to take the chance of one, though we expected it to be rather comfortless. It was April, the end of summer, but the rainy season forgot its time was up. It forgot it for most of May, too. It was easy to understand how the huge, varied trees on the island had such luxuriant leaves, fed on soft air and rain. As we neared the island in the launch we saw it peer timidly over the sky-line looking like a flat fern-basket; those ferns were its trees, some eighty feet high. We camped among them, the floor of the camp-clearing being a coral gravel, stamped flat by the very beat of the rain. This porous ground – coral and leaf-mould – let the heavy rain straight through, so that there was never an inch of mud in the camp.

There were queerish moments in those rainy, uncertain weeks. I remember cooking pancakes over an open fire when the rain suddenly descended and hissed and spattered into the pan – yet the pancakes were a success – or sitting down to a sunny breakfast at the rough trestle table out of doors, being overtaken by a shower that made us seize crockery and food and dash into the tent, to be imprisoned perhaps for hours; or being visited by touring friends who had come across with the weekly mail to spend a few hours in this earthly paradise and had to huddle with us in the tent, listening to the drumming of rain on its roof.

When these rainy weeks were over, I settled down to what proved to be the most satisfactory year's housekeeping of my life. It was worthwhile to plan and adapt things a little; this left me free to enjoy the astonishing place; the complex little jungle on the island itself, with all its singing birds and brightly coloured pigeons; and the incredibly rich reef, bared at low tide so that by following it out for a mile or more we could spend perhaps three hours exploring one small segment of the vast circle.

Looking back, I find I can honestly describe this home with all the salesman's pat phrases; desirable summer residence; soft fresh water; good lighting; fine baths; garden! To come down to facts, the tent stood just above the slope of the white beach, under a huge, heavy-leafed tree that drooped down over the beach too. In good weather we used the tent only for dressing after a swim in the daytime and for sleeping at night – with light camp mattresses rolled out on the ground sheet – or for reading on deck chairs in the evening, with a powerful hurricane lantern set on one of the little rough cupboards. Our meals were taken at a big casual trestle table under some trees; we sat on upturned boxes. There was another table fastened against another tree, a sort of carpenter's bench, for washing up and preparing food. A few nails in the tree-trunks held cups and mugs. The open fireplace – two iron rails laid between two rocks from the beach – stood just on the edge of the tiny cliff: we stirred our pots as we looked out over the smooth lagoon to the open sea. There were plenty of dry sticks and light boughs, with coconut fibre for kindling. The wooden boxes in which we had brought over our gear and provisions were made into cupboards; one stood, a tall-boy of three boxes, under the washing-up tree, and held whatever could be kept in tins and jars. Another, a single box with a hessian curtain, hung from a tree. The rope fastened to its four corners was passed through the corked neck of a broken bottle after hanging it from the tree. This was to keep marauding ants from the food.

These ants were very small and inoffensive-looking, and they had no interest in sweet things. We had no need to worry about sugar or jam or cakes. They were meat-ants; whatever we kept in that hanging safe was meat, within the meaning of the ants. Actually we never had meat on the island, except a little in tins: as far as the ants were concerned, though, fish was meat, and so was bacon, and butter and cheese: but the cord through the inverted bottle kept all these things safe – except once, when the ants were not to blame, but a different and more charming tribe. As the weather grew hotter, I kept the butter in a bowl covered with a cloth damped with seawater. Once I went away from camp for an hour or two, having accidentally left the bowl of butter on top of the hanging safe, still well shaded by the great tree. One thing I had forgotten was the flock of about fifty tiny grey-green birds, silver-eyes, that visited our camp hopefully and regularly each day. When I got back, the drum-tight cloth over the butter-bowl was pierced all over with neat little stiletto-holes, the butter inside pitted to match. Those silver-eyes, canary-like creatures, had enjoyed their discovery. After that I kept the butter bowl well inside the safe; if the silver-eyes wanted food, there was usually an opened coconut lying ready for them. The only trouble was that they had to dive into it one at a time, with nothing but a flickering tail to show who was in the tuckshop!

Ants were the only pest on land, unless you count occasional mosquitoes and sandflies at the tail-end of the rainy season and when the camp was all too well protected from the sea breeze. These were never bad enough to interfere with sleep if you spread a scrap of mosquito net over your face. But there were larger pests, not on land but in the water: there were sharks. Sharks are only dangerous in deep water and when you can't see them; but at low tide the lagoon round our little island was nearly empty and so shallow that your bathe was hardly a swim, just a dip. Any sort of shark would have gone out to sea by then. At high tide things were not so safe, but you never went far into the water, and anyhow it was clear.

But there are bigger fish than sharks. From the meat-ant to the shark is a big step: and from the shark to the whale. One very calm day indeed, when there was nothing to mark any difference between the water inside the lagoon and the deep sea, we rowed out through the entrance and anchored, fishing sleepily for whatever happened, and blinking at the sunglare on the water. Suddenly something huge and black appeared, cataracts pouring down its great sides, all dazzling in the still air. We remembered we were trespassers on the whale's acre. The creature was a good way off, but we heard its whistling wheesh as it sank, to come up – where? Under our boat, for instance, tossing us out? And those deep waters were infested with sharks. We knew the whale wouldn't, couldn't, enter a calm lagoon at low tide; we could, we did, rowing furiously. When the whale rose to blow it was a mile out at sea, and we were well inside our shallow saucer. Drawing the boat up on the sand we went back to camp and sat down in the cool shade to count our blessings.

Notes to Fourteen Years

It is not practical to annotate all the names that appear in *Fourteen Years*. The following notes are highly selective and include only the information that is useful to students and general readers approaching *Fourteen Years* for the first time. In the main, Australian names have been chosen, as there are fewer biographical reference books in this area than there are for overseas authors. Where possible, notes have been written about writers with whom Nettie or Vance Palmer had contact, rather than about the authors Nettie Palmer had read.

Adams, Arthur (1872–1936). New Zealand-born poet, novelist and playwright, he was at one time literary editor of the *Bulletin*.

Adams, Francis (1862–93). Adams came to Australia in 1884 and spent nearly six years here. He was a literary journalist, essayist, poet and novelist. *Australian Essays* (1886) was followed by *The Australians* (1893).

Anand, Mulk Raj (1905–). An Indian novelist, writing in English, Anand's best known novels are *Untouchable* (1935) and *Coolie* (1936). He was in London during the 1930s at the same time as the Palmers.

Astley, William (wrote under the name Price Warung) (1855–1911). Born in England, he came to Australia as a child. Journalist on the *Bulletin* in the 1890s, he is best known for *Tales of the Convict System* (1892) and *Tales of the Early Days* (1894).

Aurousseau, Marcel (1891–). Writer and geologist, Aurousseau wrote *Highway into Spain* (1930); his translation of *The Letters of F.W. Ludwig Leichhardt* appeared in 1968.

Ball, William Macmahon (1901–). Friend of the Palmers, he was professor of Political Science at the University of Melbourne 1949–1968.

Barnard, Marjorie (1897–1987). Barnard was a historian, critic and novelist who collaborated with Flora Eldershaw as M. Barnard Eldershaw. Their novels include *A House is Built* (1929), *The Glasshouse* (1931), *Plaque with Laurel* (1937) and *Tomorrow and Tomorrow and Tomorrow* (1947; uncensored edition 1983).

Baylebridge, William (Charles William Blocksidge) (1883–1942). An isolated and neglected poet whose chief work is *Love Redeemed* (1934), a series of love sonnets; Baylebridge also wrote stories and theoretical work.

Baynton, Barbara (1857–1929). Baynton was born at Scone, New South Wales, and brought up on the Liverpool Plains. Married three times, her last years were divided between England and Australia. Her first story was published in the *Bulletin* in 1896. *Bush Studies* appeared in London in 1902, and her short novel *Human Toll* followed in 1907.

Bedford, Randolph (1880–1944). Prolific writer of poetry, short stories and novels, editor and founder of the *Clarion* (1897–1909), Bedford's publications include *True Eyes and the Whirlwind* (1903), *Explorations in Civilisation* (1914) and *Naught to Thirty-Three* (1944).

Billard, Jeanne. The only available information about her life and work is in *Fourteen Years* itself. Nettie Palmer first met her when they were students together in England and they corresponded intermittently throughout their lives. They met again when Nettie was in Paris in 1935.

Birtles, Dora (1904–87). Her publications include *North-West by North: Journal of a Voyage* (1935) (which includes an account of Vance and Nettie Palmer on Green Island) and *The Overlanders* (1946).

Blake, William (real name Blech). Blake was the husband of Christina Stead, and a banker and economist as well as the author of a number of works of fiction.

Boldrewood, Rolf (Thomas Alexander Browne) (1826–1915). A prolific novelist best known for *Robbery Under Arms* (1888) and *A Colonial Reformer* (1890).

Brennan, Christopher (1870–1932). Brennan was born in Sydney, and became a poet, philosopher, classical scholar, and lecturer in French and German at the University of Sydney. In 1920 he was appointed professor of German and comparative literature but was forced to resign in 1925 when his wife sued for separation. Brennan's chief volume *Poems* (1913) appeared in December 1914; his prose in 1962.

Brent of Bin Bin (Miles Franklin) (1879–1954). A prolific novelist who wrote a series of Brent of Bin Bin novels which chronicle the life of several squatting families from the pioneering days. *My Brilliant Career* (1901) and *My Career Goes Bung* (1946) were written under her own name, Miles Franklin.

Broomfield, Frederick John (1860–1941). Journalist, bookman, editor, and a significant figure in Australian literary life, not so much for his own creative writing as for the encouragement and help he gave other writers such as Henry Lawson and Victor Daley.

Burdett, Basil (1897–1942). Burdett was a journalist, art critic and art dealer who travelled widely in Europe in the 1930s. As art critic of the Melbourne *Herald*, he helped to promote the work of Australian modernist artists like Nolan, Boyd and Tucker. He was killed in an air crash in Sourabaya, Java, on 1 February 1942.

Chidley, William James (1860–1916). An early theorist and proponent of sexual and civil liberties; Havelock Ellis included extracts from his autobiography in *Studies of the Psychology of Sex* (1897–1910).

Cobb, Chester (1899–1943). Author of two experimental novels, *Mr Moffatt* (1925) and *Days of Disillusion* (1926).

Eleanor Dark (1901–86). Daughter of the poet Dowell O'Reilly, her best known work is her historical trilogy *The Timeless Land* (1941). *Storm of Time* (1948) and

No Barrier (1953). Other novels include *Prelude to Christopher* (1934), *Return to Coolami* (1936) and *Lantana Lane* (1959).

Davison, Frank Dalby (1893–1970). Novelist, best known for *Man-shy* (1931), *The Wells of Beersheba* (1933) and *Dusty* (1946). Like many writers of his generation he was haunted by the long novel or the trilogy and in 1968 published his massive work *The White Thorntree.*

Dorrington, Albert (1874–1953). Born in London, Dorrington settled in Sydney in 1895. A frequent contributor to the *Bulletin* in the 1890s, he published a book of short stories, *Castro's Last Sacrament and Other Stories* (1900), and collaborated with A.G. Stephens in *The Lady Calphurnia Royal* (1909). He returned to England in 1907.

Duggan, Eileen (1894–1972). New Zealand Catholic poet whose work Nettie Palmer very much admired and with whom she corresponded for a number of years.

Duhig, Dr James Vincent (1889–1963). Medical practitioner and first professor of Pathology at the University of Queensland 1938–1947. A nephew of Brisbane's Archbishop James Duhig, he became president and patron of the Queensland Rationalist Society. One of his plays, *The Ruling Passion*, was included in *The Best One-Act Plays of 1935* (London, 1936). He was associated in the early years (1942–1943) with *Meanjin Papers.*

Dyson, Edward (1865–1931). Balladist, novelist and prolific short story writer, Dyson was best known for his tale of the goldfields, 'A Golden Shanty' (1887).

Dyson, Will (1880–1938). Younger brother of Edward; born in Victoria, Dyson worked as an artist on the Adelaide *Critic* and in 1902 returned to Melbourne to work on the *Bulletin* and Melbourne *Punch*. He married Ruby Lindsay in 1910 and went to London, where he worked on the *Daily Herald*. During World War I he was an Australian war artist and cartoonist. In 1925 he was given a large salary to come back to Australia and work for the Melbourne *Herald* and *Punch*, but in 1930 returned to London, where he spent the rest of his life. Vance Palmer seems to have met Dyson first in London in 1919. He was one of those figures (like A.G. Stephens) whom the Palmers knew but whose influence on them was primarily through the impact of his work and opinions, which they admired and often shared.

Ellis, Havelock (1859–1939). Born in Croyden, Surrey, Ellis spent three years teaching in Australia 1875–1878, the source of his novella *Kanga Creek: An Australian Idyll* (1922). An energetic pioneer in the field of sexology, his major work is *Studies in the Psychology of Sex* (1897–1910). Ellis was also a literary reviewer, translator and editor of the unexpurgated Mermaid Series of Elizabethan Dramatists (1887–1889). His autobiographical *My Life* appeared in 1939.

Esson, Hilda (Dr Hilda Bull). Louis Esson's second wife, a medical practitioner who supported Esson in his theatrical aims and provided the financial upkeep of the family.

Esson, Louis (1879–1943). Born in Edinburgh, Esson was brought to Australia as a child. Poet and freelance journalist, he was much impressed by the Abbey Theatre experiment and hoped to found its equivalent in Australia through the Pioneer Players. His career was blighted by ill health and he did not achieve in his lifetime the recognition he worked for. A number of his short plays like *Dead Timber* and *The Drovers* have found a continuing life in the Australian theatre. *The Time is not Yet Ripe* (1912) has been successfully revived in recent years.

Evatt, Herbert Vere (1894–1965). Appointed justice of the High Court in 1930, he was a leading figure in the Labor party from 1940 to 1960. His books include *Rum Rebellion* (1938) and *Australian Labor Leader* (1940). Friend of the Palmers.

FitzGerald, Robert (1902–87). One of the most important modern Australian poets. His volumes include *The Greater Apollo* (1927), *Moonlight Acre* (1938), *Between Two Tides* (1952) and *This Night's Orbit* (1953).

Fitzpatrick, Brian (1905–65). Writer, freelance journalist, radical socialist historian and editor, his books include *British Imperialism and Australia* (1939) and *The British Empire in Australia: An Economic History 1834–1939* (1941).

Franklin, Miles. *See* Brent of Bin Bin.

Furphy, Joseph (Tom Collins) (1843–1912). One of the most remarkable and admirable figures in the history of Australian literature, Furphy worked as a bullock teamster in the Riverina carting wool and other goods until forced by ill-luck to move to Shepparton in Victoria where he worked at his brother's foundry. His novel *Such is Life* (1903) is now regarded as one of the classics of Australian writing.

Grattan, Hartley (1902–80). American journalist based in New York 1926–1964 and professor of History 1964–1974 at the University of Texas. He first visited Australia in 1927. His booklet *Literature Australia* appeared in 1929 with a foreword by Nettie Palmer. Other publications include *Introducing Australia* (1942) and *Australia* (1947).

Hancock, Sir Keith (1898–). Professor of History at the University of Adelaide, 1926–1933, later professor of Economic History at Oxford. In 1957 he was appointed director and professor of History at the Research School of Social Sciences at the Australian National University. A friend and admirer of the Palmers, his many volumes include *Australia* (1930), *Discovering Monaro* (1972), *Today, Yesterday and Tomorrow* (1973) and two volumes of autobiography, *Country and Calling* (1954) and *Professing History* (1976).

Haskell, Arnold (1903–). Writer, lecturer, journalist, one-time director of the Royal Ballet School, Haskell visited Australia as guest critic of the Melbourne *Herald* and Sydney *Daily Telegraph* in 1936–37, and again in 1938–39. His publications, apart from studies of the ballet, include *Waltzing Matilda: a background to Australia* (1940); *Australia* (1941) and *The Australians* (1943).

Higgins, Bertram (1901–74). Not related to Nettie Palmer. Poet and editor, Higgins wrote important critical articles in Edgell Rickword's *The Calendar of modern* *letters* (1925–27). His selected poems, *The Haunted Rendezvous*, appeared in 1980.

Higgins, Henry Bournes (1851–1929). Nettie Palmer's uncle, Justice Higgins was largely responsible for the establishment of the Federal Arbitration Court. His famous *Harvester* judgment of 1909 led to the concept of the Basic Wage. A figure of considerable importance in Nettie's life, he encouraged her intellectual and literary pursuits from an early age and assisted her financially when she travelled to Europe in 1910 to continue her studies. After his death, she was paid by his widow to write a memoir of his life and work, which she published in 1931.

Hübener, Professor Gustav (1889–1940). German academic; 1922–25 taught at Königsberg; 1930 – professor of English at the University of Bonn; pioneer in the study of Australian and Canadian literature in Germany in the 1930s. Visited Australia 1934; died in Canada. For further details see Volker Wolf, *Die Rezeption australischer Literatur im deutschen Sprachraum von 1845–1979* (1982).

Hughes, Randolph (1890–1956). Expatriate author and academic, editor of Swinburne, his critical essay *C.J. Brennan: An Essay in Values* was published by P.R. Stephensen in 1934.

Kernot, Mary (–1954). Born Mary Robertson, Kernot was at school with Henry Handel Richardson and remained in correspondence with her throughout her life. Her letters to H.H.R. are in the Mitchell Library.

Lancaster, G.B. (Edith Joan Littleton) (1874–1945). Born in Tasmania of a pioneering family, she published thirteen volumes of popular fiction. *Pageant* (1933), a saga of life in Tasmania, won the Australian Literature Society's Gold Medal.

Landolt, Esther (1893–1943). Born in Switzerland, Landolt came with her husband to Australia in 1937. Author of four novels in German, two of which have Australian settings: *Ewige Herde* (1942) and *Namenlos* (1947).

McCrae, Georgiana (1804–90). The mother of George Gordon McCrae and grandmother of Hugh McCrae, she was a talented artist, who migrated to Australia in 1839 and became an important figure in the cultural life of her time. Hugh McCrae edited some of her journals, *Georgiana's Journals* (1934).

McCrae, Hugh (1876–1958). The son of George Gordon McCrae, he was born in Victoria. He studied art and architecture, but decided to support himself by writing verse and satirical sketches in the Melbourne *Punch*, the *Bulletin*, the *Lone Hand* and the New York *Puck*. He was an actor of considerable talent, and appeared in Australia and the United States. He edited the *New Triad* in its last stages. His main achievement, however, was in poetry, and many of his books were illustrated by Norman Lindsay. From 1917 to 1929 he lived in Melbourne, where he was a close neighbour and friend of the Palmers.

Mann, Leonard (1895–1981). Melbourne poet and novelist, his books include *Flesh in Armour* (1932), *Human Drift* (1935), *The Go-Getter* (1942) and *Venus Half-Caste* (1963).

Marshall, Alan (1902–84). One of Australia's most popular and best selling authors, especially noted for his autobiography *I Can Jump Puddles* (1955). The Palmers knew him when he was first starting to make his way as a writer. The reference in *Fourteen Years* is to Marshall's work as an accountant for a struggling shoe company. The novel *How Beautiful Are Thy Feet* appeared in 1949.

Maurice, Furnley. *See* Wilmot, Frank.

Neilson, John Shaw (1872–1942). One of Australia's finest lyrical poets, Neilson had little education and spent most of his life on labouring jobs: roadmaking, quarrying, fruit-picking, fencing. His *Collected Poems*, edited with an introduction by R.H. Croll, were first published in May 1934. Neilson was one of the poets Nettie and Vance Palmer most admired. Vance was a pallbearer at his funeral.

Nibbi, Gino (1896–1969). Born in Fermo, Italy, Nibbi arrived in Australia in 1930 and died in Rome. Writer, critic and bookshop proprietor, and a well known figure in the Melbourne art world of the 1930s, Nibbi visited Australia in 1928 and returned to settle in 1930 to conduct the Melbourne bookshop, which quickly became a focal point of avant-garde and international art and literature.

O'Dowd, Bernard (1866–1953). Born in Victoria, O'Dowd took a degree in arts and law at Melbourne University and became assistant librarian at the Melbourne Supreme Court Library. He was later parliamentary draftsman. A fervent radical, he helped found the weekly *Tocsin*. He also wrote for the *Bulletin* and published six collections of verse, including *The Bush* (1912) and *Alma Venus* (1921), as well as legal textbooks. O'Dowd was an important figure in Nettie's life and development, having a strong influence in her early years on her political ideas and poetry.

Orage, Alfred (1873–1934). Editor of the *New Age* (1906–22) and the *New English Weekly* (1932), Orage encouraged Vance Palmer in his London years and exerted considerable influence on his thought and development.

Palmer, Aileen (1915–). Aileen (A) is the elder daughter of Vance and Nettie Palmer, and was educated at the University of Melbourne. She served with the medical section of the International Brigade in Spain 1936–38 and with the London Auxiliary Ambulance Service, 1939–43. A collection of her poetry, *World Without Strangers?*, appeared in 1964.

Palmer, Helen (1917–79). Helen (H), younger daughter of Vance and Nettie Palmer and sister of Aileen, was educated at the Presbyterian Ladies' College and the University of Melbourne. After World War II, she was a high school teacher and writer. She wrote a number of historical texts for schools in collaboration with Jessie Macleod as well as a number of studies under her own name. She was founder and editor of *Outlook: An Australian Socialist Review*. A commemorative volume, *Helen Palmer's Outlook*, edited by Doreen Bridges, was published in 1982.

Palmer, Vance (1885–1959). The foremost man of letters in the Australia of his day, Vance (V) Palmer's career spanned over fifty years of writing. Novelist, poet, short story writer and dramatist, interpreter of Australian historical and literary development, as well as a stimulating critic and literary journalist (much of his best work in these areas remains uncollected), he made a significant contribution in all the fields in which he worked. No understanding of his time is complete without some knowledge of his life and work.

Penton, Brian (1904–51). Editor, journalist, commentator and an important figure of the Australian thirties and forties, he wrote two novels, *Landtakers* (1934) and *Inheritors* (1936).

Pitter, Ruth (1897–). English poet whose work was greatly admired by Nettie Palmer, to whom she addressed a poem. After World War I when she worked with the War Office, she joined an arts and crafts firm, then in 1930 established with a friend a craft business of her own in Chelsea. Her work appeared in Orage's *The New Age*.

Richardson, Henry Handel (Ethel Robertson, née Richardson) (1870–1946). A famous expatriate Australian novelist, her novels include *Maurice Guest* (1908), *The Getting of Wisdom* (1910) and *The Fortunes of Richard Mahony* (1930). Nettie Palmer, who met her in London in 1935, published the first full-length study of her work in 1950.

Robertson, J.G. (1867–1933). Husband of Henry Handel Richardson, he was the first professor of German in the University of London. A prolific writer of scholarly and academic studies, his well known *History of German Literature* is now in its fifth edition. An account of his life and work is available in Dorothy Green's *Henry Handel Richardson and her Fiction* (1986).

Stead, Christina (1902–83). Stead was born in Sydney but spent most of her life abroad from 1928 until a return visit in 1969. In 1974 she returned to make Australia her home. An abundant and prolific novelist, her works include *Seven Poor Men of Sydney* (1934), *The Man Who Loved Children* (1940) and *For Love Alone* (1944).

Stephens, A.G. (1865–1933). Born in Queensland, he worked as a journalist there. In 1894 he joined the editorial staff of the *Bulletin*, and in 1896 instituted the Red Page, a literary and political section of reviews, poems, articles and short stories that drew upon the best talent of the day. He ran the Red Page for ten years, with a break in 1902 when he went to Europe. In 1904 he produced the *Red Pagan*, a book of essays culled from the pages of the *Bulletin*. He also published the *Bulletin Story Book* (1901) and the *Bulletin Reciter*, popular books which helped to spread the work of contemporary Australian writers. In 1907 he returned to Sydney from New Zealand and took over the running of the *Bookfellow*. Vance Palmer published an important study (and selection) of his life and work in 1941.

Stephensen, P.R. (1901–65). He has an important place in the history of editing and publishing in Australia. In the 1930s he set up the Endeavour Press and other short lasting publishing enterprises. His best known work is the highly influential and vigorous polemical essay *The Foundations of Culture in Australia* (1936). In his later years he became a ghost writer and editor of Frank Clune's books.

Wilmot, Frank (1881–1942). Wilmot wrote under the name Furnley Maurice. He was born and educated in Melbourne, worked for Cole's Book Arcade and eventually managed the firm. He became the manager of the Melbourne University Press in 1932. He was the author of some ten books of poetry and was a close friend of both Nettie and Vance.

Index to Fourteen Years

Select Bibliography

PUBLISHED WORKS OF NETTIE PALMER

Poetry

South Wind. London: J.G. Wilson, 1914.
Shadowy Paths. London: Euston Press, 1915.

Essays, critical studies, translations, miscellaneous

Modern Australian Literature 1900–1923. Melbourne: Lothian, 1924.
Henry Bournes Higgins: A Memoir. London: Harrap & Co., 1931.
Talking it Over. Sydney: Angus & Robertson, 1932.
Spanish Struggle. Melbourne: Spanish Relief Committee, 1936.
Australians in Spain. Sydney: Forward Press Pty Ltd, 1937.
Liesel Asks Why. I. Schnierer, translated by Nettie Palmer. Sydney: Angus & Robertson, 1940.
Fourteen Years: Extracts from a Private Journal 1925–1939. Melbourne: The Meanjin Press, 1948.
Henry Handel Richardson: A Study. Sydney: Angus & Robertson, 1950.
The Dandenongs. Melbourne: National Press, 1952.
Letters of Henry Handel Richardson to Nettie Palmer. Ed. (with commentary) K.J. Rossing. Uppsala, Lundequist: 1953.
Bernard O'Dowd. Victor Kennedy and Nettie Palmer. Melbourne: Melbourne University Press, 1954.
Letters of Vance and Nettie Palmer 1915–1963. Selected and edited by Vivian Smith. Canberra: National Library of Australia, 1977.

Editions, introductions

An Australian Story Book. Selected by Nettie Palmer. Sydney: Angus & Robertson, 1928.

Literature Australia. C. Hartley Grattan. Seattle: University of Washington Book Store, 1929.

Tom Petrie's Reminiscences of Early Queensland. Preface by Nettie Palmer. Sydney: Angus & Robertson (2nd ed.) 1932.

Centenary Gift Book. Ed. F. Fraser and Nettie Palmer. Mel bourne: Robertson & Mullens, 1934.

The Poems of Lesbia Harford. Foreword by Nettie Palmer. Melbourne: Melbourne University Press, 1941.

Memoirs of Alice Henry. Ed. (with a postscript and chronological resumé of Alice Henry's life) Nettie Palmer. Melbourne: multigraphed edition of 100 copies, 1944.

We Went to Spain. A.F. Howells. Foreword by Nettie Palmer. Spanish Relief Committee, n.d. (1947?).

Coast to Coast, Australian Stories. Selected by Nettie Palmer. Sydney: Angus & Robertson, 1950.

SELECTED CRITICISM

Books

Modjeska, Drusilla. *Exiles at Home: Australian Women Writers 1925–1945*. Sydney: Angus & Robertson, 1981.

Smith, Vivian B. *Vance and Nettie Palmer*. Boston: Twayne Publishers, 1975.

Walker, David. *Dream and Disillusionment: A Search for Australian Cultural Identity*. Canberra: Australian National University Press, 1976.

Articles and Entries in Books

Barracchi, Guido. 'Nettie Palmer'. *Overland* 32 (1965): 37–*38*.

Barry, J.V. Introduction to the Palmer Commemorative Edition of *Meanjin* XVIII (1959).

Clark, C.M.H. *A History of Australia VI*. 'The Old Dead Tree and the Young Tree Green'. Melbourne: Melbourne University Press, 1987.

Dark, Eleanor. 'Appreciations'. *Meanjin* XVIII (1959): 247–49.

Docker, John. *Australian Cultural Elites: Intellectual Traditions in Sydney and Melbourne*. Sydney: Angus & Robertson, 1974.

Eldershaw, F. 'Nettie Palmer'. *Overland* 5 (1955): 6.

Fitzpatrick, B. 'The Palmer Pre-eminence'. *Meanjin* XVIII (1959): 211–17.

Green, H.M. *A History of Australian Literature*. 2 vols. Sydney: Angus & Robertson, 1962, passim i & ii.

______. *An Outline of Australian Literature*. Sydney: Whit combe & Tombs, 1930, pp. 171–73, 261, 274.

Heddle, E.M. 'Nettie Palmer'. *Meanjin* XVIII (1959): 227–30.

Hope, A.D. 'The Prose of Nettie Palmer'. *Meanjin* XVIII (1959), 225–27. Reprinted in *Native Companions*. Sydney: Angus & Robertson, 1974.

______. *End of an Age*. Obituary article. *Australian*, 24 October 1964.

Inglis, A. *Australians in the Spanish Civil War*. Sydney: George Allen and Unwin, 1987.

Jordan, Deborah. 'Nettie Palmer as Critic'. In *Gender, Politics and Fiction*, ed. Carole Ferrier. St Lucia: University of Queensland Press, 1985.

______. 'Nettie Palmer: The Writer as Nationalist'. In *Double Time: Women in Victoria – 150 years*, ed. Marilyn Lake and Farley Kelly. Ringwood: Penguin Books, 1985.

______. 'Towards a Biography of Nettie Palmer'. *Hecate* VI, no. 2, 1980; 65–72.

Levy, E. 'Nettie Palmer'. *Meanjin* XVIII (1959): 231–36.

______. 'Yours as Ever. . .N.P.'. *Meanjin* XXIV (1965): 329.

McLeod, J. 'Nettie Palmer: Some Personal Memories'. *Overland* 31 (1965): 20–21.

McQueen, H. *The Black Swan of Trespass*. Sydney: Alternative Publishing Cooperative Ltd, 1979.

May, Bernice, 'Nettie Palmer'. *Australian Woman's Mirror*, 26 February 1929: 11, 47.

Miller, E. Morris. *Australian Literature from its Beginnings to 1935*. 2 vols. Melbourne: Melbourne University Press, 1940.

Miller, E. Morris, and F.T. Macartney. *Australian Literature*. Sydney: Angus & Robertson, 1956, p.369.

Moore, T.I. 'Aid to Writers', *Meanjin* XVIII (1959): 206–10.

Prichard, Katharine Susannah. 'Appreciations'. *Meanjin* XVIII (1959): 243–45.

Rickard, John. *H.B. Higgins, the rebel as judge*. Sydney: George Allen and Unwin, 1984.

Schnierer, I. 'Nettie Palmer'. *Meanjin* XVIII (1959): 236–38.

Serle, Geoffrey. *The Creative Spirit in Australia: A Cultural History*, Richmond: William Heinemann Australia, 1987.

Smith, Vivian. 'Vance and Nettie Palmer: The Literary Journalism'. *Australian Literary Studies* vol. 6, no. 2, October 1973.

______. 'Nettie Palmer: A Checklist of Literary Journalism 1918–1936'. *Australian Literary Studies,* vol. 6, no. 2, October 1973: 190–96.

Stewart, Douglas. 'Conversation Piece'. *The Bulletin*, 3 August 1949.

Tipping, Marjorie. 'Remembrance of Palmers Past'. *Overland* 100, 1985: 10–18.

Walker, David. 'The Palmer Abridgment of *Such is Life*'. *Australian Literary Studies*, vol. 8, no. 4, October 1978: 494–98.

UQP AUSTRALIAN AUTHORS

The Australian Short Story
edited by Laurie Hergenhan
Outstanding contemporary short stories alongside some of the best from the past. This volume encompasses the short story in Australia from its *Bulletin* beginnings in the 1890s to its vigorous revival in the 1970s and 1980s.

Writing of the 1890s
edited by Leon Cantrell
A retrospective collection, bringing together the work of 32 Australian poets, storytellers and essayists. The anthology challenges previous assumptions about this romantic period of galloping ballads and bush yarns, bohemianism and creative giants.

Catherine Helen Spence
edited by Helen Thomson
An important early feminist writer, Catherine Helen Spence was one of the first women in Australia to break through the constraints of gender and class and enter public life. This selection contains her most highly regarded novel, *Clara Morison*, her triumphant autobiography, and much of her political and social reformist writing.

Henry Lawson
edited by Brian Kiernan
A complete profile of Henry Lawson, the finest and most original writer in the bush yarn tradition. This selection includes sketches, letters, autobiography and verse, with outspoken journalism and the best of his comic and tragic stories.

Christopher Brennan
edited by Terry Sturm
Christopher Brennan was a legend in his own time, and his art was an unusual amalgam of Victorian, symbolist and modernist tendencies. This selection draws on the whole range of Brennan's work: poetry, literary criticism and theory, autobiographical writing, and letters.

Robert D. FitzGerald
edited by Julian Croft
FitzGerald's long and distinguished literary career is reflected in this selection of his poetry and prose. There is poetry from the 1920s to the 1980s, samples from his lectures on poetics and essays on family origins and philosophical preoccupations, a short story, and his views on Australian poetry.

Australian Science Fiction
edited by Van Ikin
An exotic blend of exciting recent works with a selection from Australia's long science fiction tradition. Classics by Erle Cox, M. Barnard Eldershaw and others are followed by stories from major contemporary writers Damien Broderick, Frank Bryning, Peter Carey, A. Bertram Chandler, Lee Harding, David J. Lake, Philippa C. Maddern, Dal Stivens, George Turner, Wynne N. Whiteford, Michael Wilding and Jack Wodhams.

Barbara Baynton
edited by Sally Krimmer and Alan Lawson
Bush writing of the 1890s, but very different from Henry Lawson. Baynton's stories are often macabre and horrific, and her bush women express a sense of outrage. The revised text of the brilliant *Bush Studies*, the novel *Human Toll*, poems, articles and an interview, all reveal Baynton's disconcertingly independent viewpoint.

Joseph Furphy
edited by John Barnes
Such is Life is an Australian classic. Written by an ex-bullock driver, half-bushman and half-bookworm, it is an extraordinary achievement. The accompanying selection of novel extracts, stories, verse, *Bulletin* articles and letters illustrates the astounding range of Furphy's talent, and John Barnes's notes reveal the intellectual and linguistic richness of his prose.

James McAuley
edited by Leonie Kramer
James McAuley was a poet, intellectual, and leading critic of his time. This volume represents the whole range of his poetry and prose, including the Ern Malley hoax that caused such a sensation in the 1940s, and

some new prose pieces published for the first time. Leonie Kramer's introduction offers new critical perspectives on his work.

Rolf Boldrewood
edited by Alan Brissenden
Australia's most famous bushranging novel, *Robbery Under Arms*, together with extracts from the original serial version. The best of Boldrewood's essays and short stories are also included; some are autobiographical, most deal with life in the bush.

Marcus Clarke
edited by Michael Wilding
The convict classic *For the Term of His Natural Life*, and a varied selection of short stories, critical essays and journalism. Autobiographical stories provide vivid insights into the life of this prolific and provocative man of letters.